SADLIER-OXFORD

Progress in Mathematics

Workbook

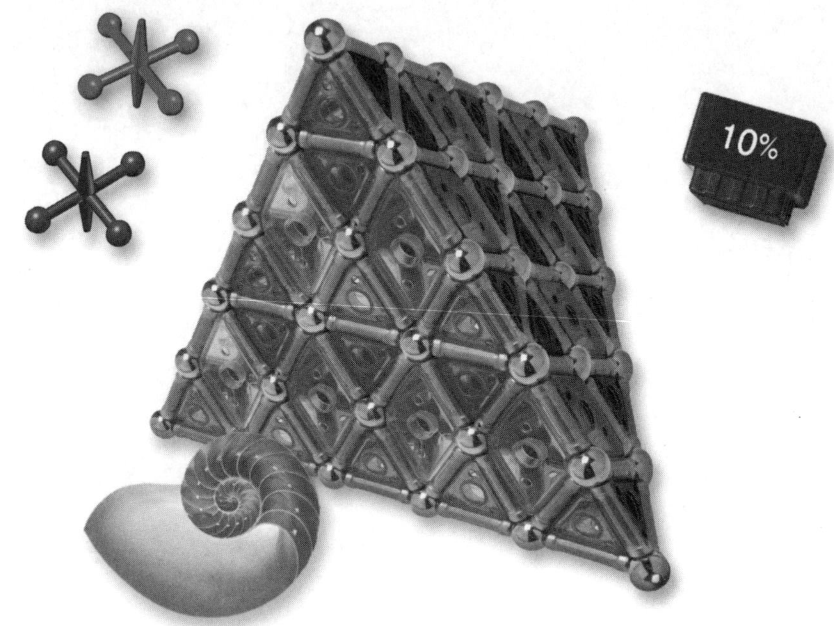

Catherine D. LeTourneau

with

Elinor R. Ford

Sadlier-Oxford
A Division of William H. Sadlier, Inc.
www.sadlier-oxford.com

Dear Student,

This workbook is part of the *Progress in Mathematics Common Core Enriched Edition* program. It has four sections to help you master the work of each chapter:

- Practice of the mathematics taught in the student text lessons.
- Additional Common Core lessons with practice pages.
- Performance Tasks that let you show your understanding of the Common Core mathematics taught in *Progress in Mathematics*.

Before starting a workbook page, read the title. If you need to review the lesson, look at the bottom of the workbook page to find where the lesson is taught.

Most lessons in *Progress in Mathematics* support the Common Core State Standards (CCSS) for Mathematics. A **C** before a lesson title on a Contents page in this workbook means that it is a Common Core lesson.

Contributing Illustrators: Batelman Illustration, Sarah Beise, Mary Bono, Mircea Catusanu, Jackie Stafford, Gregg Valley

Contents

C Denotes Common Core lesson.

iii

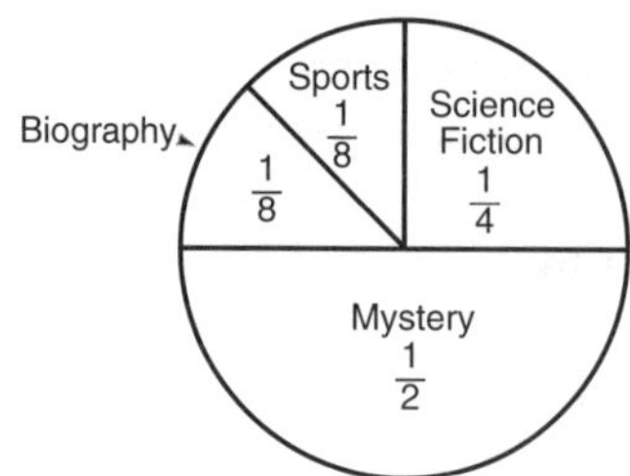

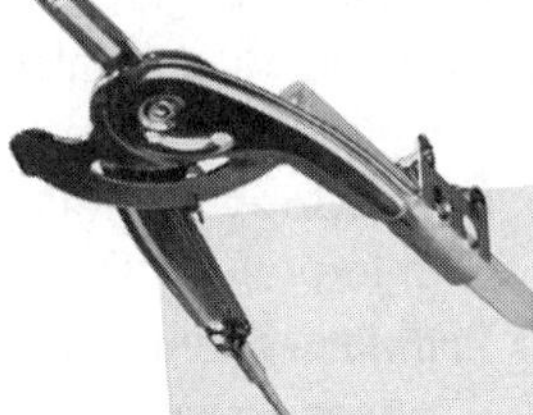

iv

Ⓒ Denotes Common Core lesson.

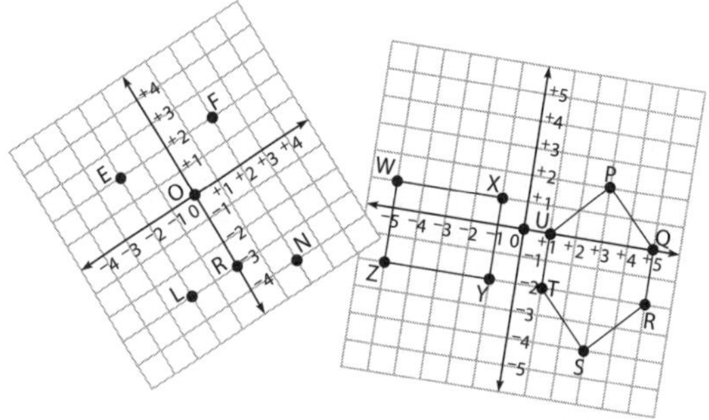

C Denotes Common Core lesson.

v

Additional Common Core Contents

vi

Place Value

Name _______________________

Date _______________________

	Trillions			Billions			Millions			Thousands			Ones				
hundreds	tens	ones	hundreds	tens	ones	hundreds	tens	ones	hundreds	tens	ones	hundreds	tens	ones	tenths	hundredths
	5,	1	9	0,	0	0	5,	2	0	0,	0	0	0.	8	3		

Standard Form: 5,190,005,200,000.83
Word Name: five trillion, one hundred ninety billion, five million, two hundred thousand and eighty-three hundredths
Short Word Name: 5 trillion, 190 billion, 5 million, 200 thousand and 83 hundredths

Write the place of the underlined digit. Then write its value.

1. 818,218,661,306

____

2. 58,802,151

____

3. 192,955.193007

____

4. 3,550,584,990.179301

____

Write the word name for each number.

5. 16,800,009 _______________________

6. 10.00506 _______________________

Write each number in standard form.

7. one billion, fifty-two thousand, six

____

8. 45 million, 70 thousand, two hundred

____

9. 79 hundred thousandths

____

10. one hundred six millionths

____

Problem Solving

11. In 2000, the population of New York City was eight million, eight thousand, two hundred seventy-eight. What is the standard form of this number? _______________________

12. Jordan bought 7.06 meters of rope. What is the word name for this number? _______________________

Use with Lesson 1-1, pages 34–35 in the Student Book.
Then go to Lesson 1-2, pages 36–37 in the Student Book.

Expanded Form

Name _______________________________

Date _______________________________

Standard Form	**Expanded Form**

$326{,}462 = (3 \times 100{,}000) + (2 \times 10{,}000) + (6 \times 1000) + (4 \times 100) + (6 \times 10) + (2 \times 1)$

or

$326{,}462 = 300{,}000 + 20{,}000 + 6000 + 400 + 60 + 2$

Complete each expanded form.

1. $243{,}006 = (\underline{\hspace{2em}} \times 100{,}000) + (\underline{\hspace{2em}} \times 10{,}000) + (\underline{\hspace{2em}} \times 1000) + (\underline{\hspace{2em}} \times 1)$

2. $6{,}003{,}080.05 = (\underline{\hspace{2em}} \times 1{,}000{,}000) + (\underline{\hspace{2em}} \times 1000) + (\underline{\hspace{2em}} \times 10) +$

   $(\underline{\hspace{2em}} \times 0.01)$

3. $40{,}000{,}200{,}000{,}100 = (\underline{\hspace{2em}} \times 10{,}000{,}000{,}000{,}000) + (\underline{\hspace{2em}} \times 100{,}000{,}000) +$

   $(\underline{\hspace{2em}} \times 100)$

Write the expanded form for each in two ways.

4. $23{,}893$ ____

   ____

5. $480{,}216$ ____

   ____

6. 8.201165 ____

   ____

Write each expanded form in standard form.

7. $(3 \times 10{,}000{,}000{,}000) + (4 \times 1{,}000{,}000{,}000) + (7 \times 100{,}000)$ _______________

8. $(5 \times 10{,}000{,}000) + (6 \times 1{,}000{,}000) + (4 \times 100) + (7 \times 1)$ _______________

9. $6000 + 200 + 3 + 0.008 + 0.00004$ _______________

10. $400 + 0.3 + 0.00007 + 0.000004$ _______________

2

Use with Lesson 1-2, pages 36–37 in the Student Book.
Then go to Lesson 1-3, pages 38–39 in the Student Book.

Place Value and Exponents

> An exponent tells how many times to use the base as a factor.
>
> $10^2 = 10 \times 10 \longrightarrow$ read as "ten to the second power"
> $10^0 = 1 \longrightarrow$ read as "ten to the zero power"
> $10^{-2} = 0.01 \longrightarrow$ read as "ten to the negative second power"
>
> **Standard Form**   **Expanded Form**
>
> $523.407 = (5 \times 100) + (2 \times 10) + (3 \times 1) + (4 \times 0.1) + (7 \times 0.001)$
> $= (5 \times 10^2) + (2 \times 10^1) + (3 \times 10^0) + (4 \times 10^{-1}) + (7 \times 10^{-3})$

Write each power of ten in standard form.

1. 10^6 ______________________

2. 10^{-6} ______________________

3. 10^{-5} ______________________

4. 10^9 ______________________

Write each as a power of ten.

5. $10 \times 10 \times 10 \times 10$ ______

6. $10 \times 10 \times 10 \times 10 \times 10 \times 10 \times 10$ ______

7. 0.000001 ______

8. 1 ______

Write each number in expanded form using exponents.

9. 534 ______________________

10. 7025 ______________________

11. 16.53 ______________________

12. 781.003 ______________________

Write each in standard form.

13. $(2 \times 10^5) + (3 \times 10^4) + (6 \times 10^3) + (1 \times 10^2) + (6 \times 10^0)$ ______________________

14. $(5 \times 10^5) + (2 \times 10^4) + (1 \times 10^{-1}) + (4 \times 10^{-2}) + (8 \times 10^{-4})$ ______________________

15. $(7 \times 10^7) + (7 \times 10^2) + (7 \times 10^0) + (7 \times 10^{-3}) + (7 \times 10^{-4})$ ______________________

16. $(8 \times 10^5) + (9 \times 10^{-4})$ ______________________

Compare and Order Decimals

Name _______________

Date _______________

<table>
<tr><td colspan="2">

Compare 1.590 and 1.578.

1.590
1.578   [1 = 1]

1.590
1.578   [5 = 5]

1.590
1.578   [9 > 7]

So 1.590 > 1.578.

</td><td>

Order 0.5214, 0.5380, 0.6000, 0.5372 from greatest to least.
Compare the digits in each place. Start with the greatest place.

6 > 5   So 0.6000 is greatest.

5 = 5, 3 = 3 and 8 > 7   So 0.5380 is next greatest.

2 < 3   So 0.5214 is least.

In order from greatest to least the decimals are:
0.6000, 0.5380, 0.5372, 0.5214

</td></tr>
</table>

Compare. Write <, =, or >.

1. 0.09 _____ 0.0956
2. 8.07 _____ 8.189
3. 6.8 _____ 6.0087
4. 10.06 _____ 10.6715
5. 19.08 _____ 19.462
6. 36.9 _____ 39.6
7. 0.0893 _____ 0.0891
8. 20.6 _____ 20.048
9. 10.39 _____ 10.390
10. 87.642 _____ 87.6405
11. 24.24 _____ 2.42
12. 100.1 _____ 10.1

Write in order from greatest to least.

13. 1.44, 1.28, 1.45, 1.70

14. 0.181, 0.38, 0.139, 0.319

15. 0.74, 0.7, 0.75, 1.07

16. 0.4935, 0.492, 0.4921, 0.4853

Write in order from least to greatest.

17. 3.8049, 1.9942, 3.8490, 2.3756

18. 0.3886, 0.0886, 0.8386, 0.0688

19. 0.3426, 0.34, 0.342, 0.4342

20. 8.3, 8.03, 8.301, 8.3001

Problem Solving

Use the information in the table to answer each question.

21. Which city had the most rainfall? _____________

22. Which city had the least rainfall? _____________

23. Which city had less rainfall than Dead Eye? _____________

24. Write the rainfall for the cities in order from least to greatest. _____________

City	Rainfall in inches
Benson	1.6
Alpha	2.05
Dead Eye	0.92
Calhoun	0.903
Essex	1.06

4

Use with Lesson 1-4, pages 40–41 in the Student Book.
Then go to Lesson 1-5, pages 42–43 in the Student Book.

Round Whole Numbers and Decimals

Name _______________

Date _______________

Round to the:

nearest cent	nearest thousandth	greatest place	greatest place
$23.87<u>2</u>2	23.87<u>5</u>2	<u>2</u>,671,813	0.9<u>7</u>309
↓	↓	↓	↓
$23.87	23.875	3,000,000	1.0

Round to the nearest cent.

1. $2.399 _______
2. $26.472 _______
3. $12.091 _______
4. $.029 _______
5. $.9666 _______
6. $39.995 _______
7. $56.433 _______
8. $1.998 _______
9. $.128 _______

Round each number to the underlined place.

10. <u>0</u>.73 _______
11. 0.<u>2</u>4 _______
12. 0.6<u>1</u>7 _______
13. 25.00<u>6</u>5 _______
14. 4<u>3</u>.382 _______
15. 4.1<u>2</u>27 _______
16. 12.<u>8</u>033 _______
17. 4.66<u>6</u>6 _______
18. 0.49<u>9</u>5 _______
19. <u>8</u>6.2216 _______
20. 400.00<u>9</u>7 _______
21. 55.5<u>5</u>02 _______

Round each number to the greatest nonzero place.

22. 0.64 _______
23. 8.23 _______
24. 0.7008 _______
25. 0.488 _______
26. 0.86345 _______
27. 643.0029 _______
28. 159.45 _______
29. 3205.442 _______
30. 2840.75 _______

Place the decimal point in each numeral so that the sentence seems reasonable. Then round the decimal to the nearest tenth or nearest cent.

31. Kira hiked 3125 miles in one hour. _______

32. Danny bought a new CD for $15987. _______

33. The temperature of the lake water was 58795°F. _______

Problem Solving

34. The measurement of 1 kilometer is equal to 0.62137 miles. Round this decimal to the nearest tenth, hundredth, and thousandth. _______

35. The distance between two cities is 325.65 km. About how far apart are they to the nearest kilometer? _______

Estimate Decimal Sums and Differences

Name _______________________

Date _______________________

0.56 + 0.24 + 0.71 is about ?	38.82 − 13.45 is about ?
Front-end Estimation **Rounding**	**Front-end Estimation** **Rounding**

0.56 + 0.24 + 0.71 is about ?

Front-end Estimation

$$\begin{aligned}0.56 \\ 0.24 \end{aligned}\Big\}\ \text{about } 0.1$$
$$\underline{+\ 0.71}$$
about $1.4 + 0.1 = 1.5$

Rounding

$0.56 \longrightarrow 0.6$
$0.24 \longrightarrow 0.2$
$\underline{+\ 0.71 \longrightarrow 0.7}$
about 1.5

A reasonable estimate of the actual sum is 1.5.

38.82 − 13.45 is about ?

Front-end Estimation

$$\begin{aligned}38.82 \\ \underline{-\ 13.45}\end{aligned}$$
about 20.00

Rounding

$38.82 \longrightarrow 40$
$\underline{-\ 13.45 \longrightarrow 10}$
about 30

Both 20 and 30 are reasonable estimates of the actual difference.

Estimate the sum or difference. Use front-end estimation with adjustments.

1. $\begin{aligned}75.73 \\ \underline{+\ 62.65}\end{aligned}$	2. $\begin{aligned}76.54 \\ \underline{-\ 32.16}\end{aligned}$	3. $\begin{aligned}8.3 \\ \underline{-\ 5.4}\end{aligned}$	4. $\begin{aligned}17.98 \\ \underline{+\ 52.01}\end{aligned}$
5. $\begin{aligned}0.82 \\ \underline{-\ 0.35}\end{aligned}$	6. $\begin{aligned}85.41 \\ \underline{-\ 26.03}\end{aligned}$	7. $\begin{aligned}0.63 \\ 0.9 \\ \underline{+\ 0.35}\end{aligned}$	8. $\begin{aligned}0.5 \\ 0.37 \\ \underline{+\ 0.42}\end{aligned}$

Estimate the sum or difference by rounding.

9. $\begin{aligned}6.4872 \\ \underline{+\ 5.8429}\end{aligned}$	10. $\begin{aligned}4287.4512 \\ \underline{+\ 9503.6745}\end{aligned}$	11. $\begin{aligned}0.46828 \\ \underline{-\ 0.02157}\end{aligned}$	12. $\begin{aligned}521{,}438{,}417 \\ \underline{-\ 314{,}583{,}014}\end{aligned}$
13. $\begin{aligned}58.2065 \\ \underline{-\ 6.8214}\end{aligned}$	14. $\begin{aligned}7{,}453{,}214.7 \\ \underline{-\ 802{,}354.42}\end{aligned}$	15. $\begin{aligned}374.0148 \\ 570.214 \\ \underline{+\ 483.73059}\end{aligned}$	16. $\begin{aligned}4.50581 \\ 12.84 \\ \underline{+\ 0.66267}\end{aligned}$

Estimate by rounding each amount to the nearest dollar.

17. $\begin{aligned}\$24.95 \\ \underline{+\ 32.63}\end{aligned}$	18. $\begin{aligned}\$65.04 \\ \underline{-\ 27.95}\end{aligned}$	19. $\begin{aligned}\$299.87 \\ \underline{-\ 84.15}\end{aligned}$	20. $\begin{aligned}\$825.46 \\ \underline{+\ 70.28}\end{aligned}$

Problem Solving

21. Myra biked 45.28 km, and David biked 33.95 km. About how much farther than David did Myra bike? _______________

22. Jessie bought shirts for $12.95, $10.50, $13.52, $11.48, and $9.89. About how much was the total cost of the shirts? _______________

Use with Lesson 1-6, pages 44–45 in the Student Book.
Then go to Lesson 1-7, pages 46–47 in the Student Book.

Addition of Whole Numbers and Decimals

Name ___________________

Date ___________________

Add: 8.35 + 0.7995 + 15

- Align the decimal points in the addends.
- Write zeros as placeholders as needed.
- Write the decimal point in the sum.

$$\begin{array}{r} {\scriptstyle 1\ 1\ \ 1} \\ 8.3500 \\ 0.7995 \\ +\ 15.0000 \\ \hline 24.1495 \end{array}$$

Estimate using rounding. Then find the sum.

1.	10.47 + 0.78	2.	2.32 + 3.5	3.	$18.96 + 23.08	4.	29.2 + 36.59	5.	16.2 + 8.49

6.	7,651,965 + 2,076,941	7.	341,830,544 + 821,198,337	8.	4,521,684,147 + 90,664,753	9.	421,965 + 95,978

10.	796.868 98.2176 + 232.26179	11.	6.54783 0.432261 + 71.53351	12.	3.55080383 6.36940144 + 9.4567438	13.	61.328854 479.05795 + 92.28214

14.	118,527 390,195 + 307,697	15.	396,118,519 98,339,165 + 89,463,834	16.	2,827,645,282 280,135,170 + 81,131,191	17.	19,335,050 587,285,644 + 34,898,825

18. 0.3104 + 0.24 + 0.437 _________

19. 247,335 + 75,813 + 4921 _________

20. 0.3771 + 9.8 + 0.0686 _________

21. 3,946,032 + 92,913,318 _________

22. 2.6184 + 0.012 + 0.6967 _________

23. 275,949 + 3,558,609 + 84,706,675 _________

Problem Solving

24. The school store earned $625.32 one week, and then $98.36, $145.98, and $304.09 during the next three weeks. How much did the school store earn in the four weeks? _________

25. An African elephant weighs 14,432 pounds. A white rhinoceros weighs 7937 pounds. If an airplane that already has 9205 pounds of cargo transports both animals, what would be the total weight of the cargo? _________

26. Harry, Devin, and Teo ran a 3-man relay race. Harry ran 6721 m, Devin ran 7009 m, and Teo ran 8032 m. How far did they run in all? _________

Use with Lesson 1-7, pages 46–47 in the Student Book.
Then go to Lesson 1-8, pages 48–49 in the Student Book.

Subtraction of Whole Numbers and Decimals

Name _______________

Date _______________

Subtract: 4.7 − 1.8265

- Align the decimal points.
- Write zeros as placeholders as needed.
- Subtract. Regroup if necessary.
- Write the decimal point in the difference.

$$4.7000 - 1.8265 = 2.8735$$

Subtract: 0.667 − 0.485

$$0.667 - 0.485 = 0.182$$

Estimate by rounding. Then find the difference.

1. 0.303 − 0.089	**2.** 7.5321 − 5.4432	**3.** $243,907 + 110,462	**4.** 8,980,329 − 730,464
5. 68,785,018 − 9,127,553	**6.** 32.86149 − 3.94924	**7.** 858,824,587 − 650,898,470	**8.** 177.6637 − 97.18
9. 0.394 − 0.207	**10.** 7.5124 − 2.4639	**11.** $473,403 − 336,941	**12.** 6,339,712 − 239,394
13. 36,137,993 − 1,943,670	**14.** 87.63354 − 4.32705	**15.** 665,920,009 − 638,354,451	**16.** 338.3346 − 66.36

Align and estimate by rounding. Then find the difference.

17. 1.96 − 1.326 = _______

18. 0.7175 − 0.5374 = _______

19. 8 − 4.42996 = _______

20. 3,386,036.57 − 459,465.29 = _______

21. 91,493.417 − 103.297 = _______

22. 7,913,582,141 − 4,217,299,105 = _______

Problem Solving

23. The sum of a number and 532,714 is 789,206. Find the number.

____

24. Jeff drove his race car at a speed of 299.307 kilometers per hour. Rick drove his car at a speed of 283.98 kilometers per hour. How much faster did Jeff drive than Rick?

____

Use with Lesson 1-8, pages 48–49 in the Student Book.
Then go to Lesson 1-9, pages 50–51 in the Student Book.

Addition and Subtraction of Decimals

Name _______________________

Date _______________________

Add: 58.3 + 74.1 + 19.8 = ?

- Align the decimal points.
- Add. Regroup if necessary.
- Write the decimal point in the sum.

$$\begin{array}{r} \overset{2\,1}{58.3} \\ 74.1 \\ +\ 19.8 \\ \hline 152.2 \end{array}$$

Subtract: 0.085 − 0.0094 = ?

- Align the decimal points.
- Subtract. Regroup if necessary.
- Write the decimal point in the difference.

$$\begin{array}{r} \overset{\quad\ \ 14}{\overset{7\ 4 10}{0.08\cancel{5}\cancel{0}}} \\ -\ 0.0094 \\ \hline 0.0756 \end{array}$$

Find the sum.

1. 0.47 0.5 0.78 + 0.29	**2.** 1.68 3.7 6.34 + 9.5	**3.** 12.09 14.04 20.35 + 3.6	**4.** 15.04 3.12 10.02 + 0.46	**5.** $10.36 3.14 8.24 + 2.03

6. 205.319 + 499.161	**7.** 719.274 225.601 + 46.9	**8.** 0.378 0.0957 + 0.0154	**9.** 472.665 996.7 9.13129 + 125.672	**10.** 0.079 4.45562 19.263 + 75.4174

Find the difference.

11. 0.6932 − 0.3481	**12.** 0.5 − 0.3889	**13.** 0.81 − 0.687	**14.** 10.43 − 4.921	**15.** 72.1 − 12.385

16. 36.2 − 24.3295	**17.** $12.00 − 8.32	**18.** 16.537 − 8.7	**19.** $13.00 − 7.94	**20.** 4.013 − 0.0987

Align and add or subtract.

21. 2655.04 + 976.903 + 699.8 = _________

22. 0.57 + 63.6941 + 554.109 = _________

23. 9433.04 − 6002.395 = _________

24. 1.620493 − 0.62717 = _________

Problem Solving

25. Roman buys a sandwich for $3.95. There is also $.32 tax. He gives the cashier a $20 bill. How much change should Roman get? _________

26. Laura wants 5 lb of nuts for her mixture. She buys 0.75 lb peanuts, 2.6 lb cashews, and 1.08 lb walnuts. How many more lb of nuts does she need? _________

Addition and Subtraction Expressions

Name _______________________

Date _______________________

Numerical expressions use only numbers.	Algebraic expressions use variables.	Word phrases use words and numbers.
$45 + 98$ $0.72 - 0.098$	$x + 437.3$ $85 - y$	12 more than 6 a number subtracted from 7

Write each word phrase as a numerical expression.

1. 43 less than 86

2. the sum of 278 and 563

3. 39 added to 2.07

4. 50 decreased by 8

5. 2.91 subtracted from 72.9

6. 21 more than 15

Write each word phrase as an algebraic expression. Use x as your variable.

7. a number added to 33.8

8. 600 minus a number

9. the sum of 3.5 and a number

10. difference of a number and 42

Write each mathematical expression as a word phrase.

11. $\$9.31 + \$9.74$

12. $204 - a$

13. $7.1 + t$

14. $y - 0.23$

Problem Solving

Write a numerical expression or an alegebraic expression to show how you would solve the problem.

15. Mac has a suitcase weighing 47.1 pounds. Dorothy's suitcase weighs 41.4 pounds. How much more does Mac's suitcase weigh than Dorothy's? _______________________

16. Cayden is 4.3 inches taller now than he was last year. Last year he was h inches tall. How tall is Cayden now? _______________________

Use with Lesson 1-10, pages 52–53 in the Student Book.
Then go to Lesson 1-11, pages 54–55 in the Student Book.

Evaluate Addition and Subtraction Expressions

Name _______________

Date _______________

Evaluate $87 - x$, when $x = 14$.	Evaluate $75 + s + t$, when $s = 2$ and $t = 5$.
$87 - x$ ← Replace x with 14. $87 - 14$ ← Subtract. 73 ← value of expression	$75 + s + t$ ← Replace s with 2 and t with 5. $75 + 2 + 5$ ← Add. 82 ← value of expression

Evaluate each expression.

1. $339 + 638$ _______

2. $1801 + 73$ _______

3. $46.8 + 780$ _______

4. $381 - 137$ _______

5. $71,715 - 4813$ _______

6. $930 - 38.7$ _______

7. $6.05 + m$, when $m = 12.68$ _______

8. $h - 146$, when $h = 293$ _______

9. $g + 52,819$, when $g = 975$ _______

10. $17.0302 - k$, when $k = 2.2$ _______

Find the value of each algebraic expression when $p = 2.9$ and $q = 7.05$. Remember to work from left to right.

11. $4 + p + q$ _______

12. $p + q + 3.49$ _______

13. $95 - p - q$ _______

14. $37 - p - q$ _______

15. $p + 191 + q$ _______

16. $q + 7.1 + p$ _______

17. $p + 82.3 - q$ _______

18. $q + 3.57 - p$ _______

Write and evaluate an expression for each situation.

19. Erika has d dollars. She spends \$3.75 for lunch. What expression represents the amount of money Erika has left? Evaluate the expression when $d = \$12$. _______

20. Ian's stamp collection has 606 stamps from the U.S. and s stamps from other countries. What expression represents the number of stamps in Ian's collection? Evaluate the expression when $s = 109$. _______

Problem-Solving Strategy: Write an Equation

Name _______________________

Date _______________________

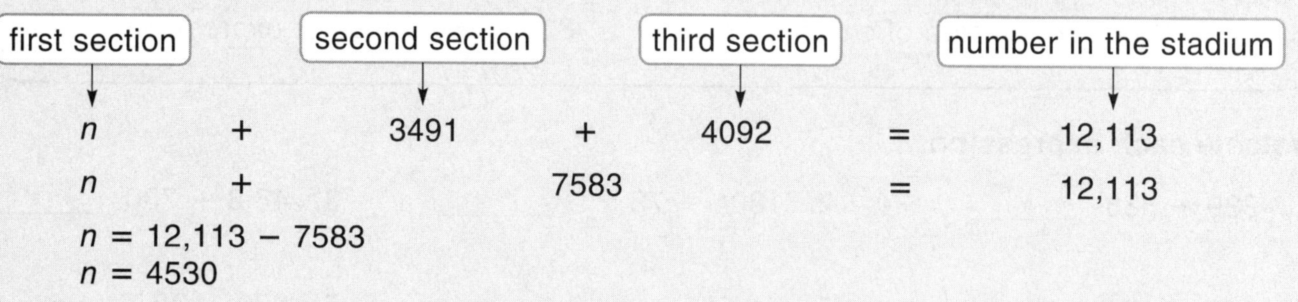

A stadium has 3 sections. There are 3491 people in the second section of the stadium, and 4092 people in the third section. If there are 12,113 people in the stadium, how many people are in the first section?

Use the information to write an equation.

| first section | second section | third section | number in the stadium |

$$n + 3491 + 4092 = 12{,}113$$
$$n + 7583 = 12{,}113$$
$$n = 12{,}113 - 7583$$
$$n = 4530$$

There are 4530 people in the first section.

Write an equation to solve each problem. Do your work on a separate sheet of paper.

1. Alex weighs 5443 grams more than his younger brother. If his brother weighs 32,658 grams, how much does Alex weigh?

2. Maria is 76 millimeters taller than she was this time last year. If she is 1219 millimeters tall now, how tall was Maria this time last year?

3. Antwan's Collectibles has 12,261 more trading cards than George's Memorabilia. If Antwan's has 36,829 trading cards, how many cards does George's have?

4. If Aunt Agatha had $749.63 less in her checking account, she would have $595.95. How much does Aunt Agatha have in her account?

5. Darby House holds 8031 more people than Sycamore Theater. If Darby House holds 13,311 people, how many people does Sycamore Theater hold?

6. The price of a car is $1205 less this week than last week. If the price was $19,299 last week, what is the price this week?

7. There are 4 shows each day in the planetarium. If 745 people can see each show, what is the total number of people who can see the shows each day?

8. Juan bought three computers for $4485.96. If each computer cost the same amount, what was the cost of one computer?

Use with Lesson 1-12, pages 56–57 in the Student Book.
Then go to Lesson 1-13, pages 58–59 in the Student Book.

Problem-Solving Applications: Mixed Review

Name ___________________

Date ___________________

Solve each problem and explain the method you used. If needed, do all your work on a separate sheet of paper.

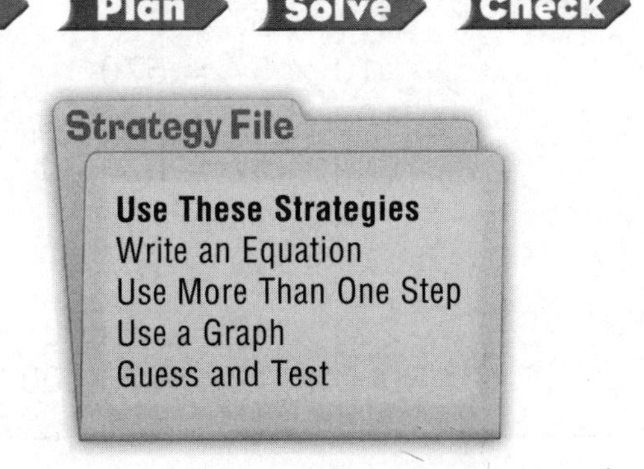

1. Last week, Kari ran 3.4 miles on Monday, 3.9 miles on Thursday, and 6.8 miles on Saturday. Did Kari run more than 15 miles last week?

____

2. The sum of Linda's and Steve's ages is 113. Steve is 11 years older than Linda. How old is Linda and how old is Steve?

____

3. Hunter can walk 1 mile in 21.25 minutes. If he continues this rate of speed, how long will it take him to walk 4 miles?

____

4. Greg buys three bagels for $0.96. Aaron buys three bagels for 27 cents each. Who spends more money? How much more does he spend?

____

5. Jill goes to school for 6 hours each day. The day is divided into 9 periods that are each the same length of time. How long is each period?

____

Use the graph for problems 6–9.

6. About how many students play volleyball?

____

7. About how many more students play soccer than play volleyball?

____

8. The drama club has twice as many members as the track team. About how many students are in the drama club?

____

9. About how many students in all play these sports?

____

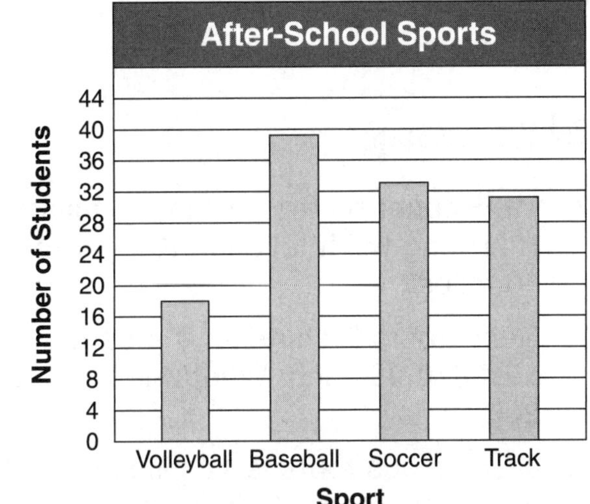

Use with Lesson 1-13, pages 58–59 in the Student Book.

Multiplication Patterns

Name _______________________

Date _______________________

$1 \times 57 = 57$	$10 \times 0.65 = 6.5$
$10 \times 57 = 570$	$100 \times 0.65 = 65$
$100 \times 57 = 5700$	$1000 \times 0.65 = 650$
$1000 \times 57 = 57{,}000$	$10{,}000 \times 0.65 = 6500$
$3 \times 42 = 126$	$10 \times 0.0074 = 0.074$
$30 \times 42 = 1260$	$100 \times 0.0074 = 0.74$
$300 \times 42 = 12{,}600$	$1000 \times 0.0074 = 7.4$
$3000 \times 42 = 126{,}000$	$10{,}000 \times 0.0074 = 74$

Multiply.

1. $10 \times 68 =$ _______ 2. $300 \times 6.6 =$ _______ 3. $4000 \times 36 =$ _______

4. $80 \times 0.048 =$ _______ 5. $50 \times 25 =$ _______ 6. $50 \times 64 =$ _______

7. $300 \times 9.2 =$ _______ 8. $40 \times 0.29 =$ _______ 9. $6000 \times 32 =$ _______

10. $3000 \times 0.075 =$ _______ 11. $900 \times 0.14 =$ _______ 12. $8000 \times 63 =$ _______

Find the products. Then write them in order from least to greatest.

13. **a.** $10 \times 340 =$ _______ **b.** $100 \times 31 =$ _______ **c.** $1000 \times 33 =$ _______

____

14. **a.** $100 \times 0.04 =$ _______ **b.** $10 \times 0.6 =$ _______ **c.** $1000 \times 0.007 =$ _______

____

15. **a.** $1000 \times 0.0059 =$ _______ **b.** $100 \times 0.002 =$ _______ **c.** $10 \times 0.032 =$ _______

____

Find the missing factor.

16. $a \times 18 = 3600$ 17. $c \times 48 = 480$ 18. $300 \times m = 4500$

_______ _______ _______

19. $200 \times n = 2280$ 20. $4000 \times v = 2$ 21. $w \times 17 = 6800$

_______ _______ _______

Problem Solving

22. Mr. Krieger runs 1 mile in 7.6 minutes. How long will it take Mr. Krieger to run 10 miles?

23. Ceci orders T-shirts for the band. Shirts cost \$10.95 each. What will be the cost for 200 shirts?

24. Jason's bus route is 12 miles long. If he drives the route 20 times in a day, how many miles would he drive in 5 days?

Use with Lesson 2-1, pages 66–67 in the Student Book.
Then go to Lesson 2-2, pages 68–69 in the Student Book.

Estimate Products

Name ___________________________

Date ___________________________

Estimate: 572 × 6189

$$6189 \longrightarrow 6000$$
$$\underline{\times\ 572} \longrightarrow \underline{\times\ 600}$$
about 3,600,000

Estimate: 17.63 × 8.91

$$17.63 \longrightarrow 20$$
$$\underline{\times\ 8.91} \longrightarrow \underline{\times\ 9}$$
about 180

- If both factors are rounded up, the actual product *is less than* the estimate.
- If both factors are rounded down, the actual product *is greater than* the estimate.
- If one factor is rounded up and the other is rounded down, the actual product *is close to* the estimate.

Estimate the product.

1. 448 × 713	2. 795 × 284	3. 838 × 567	4. $9.26 × 361
5. 5009 × 735	6. 1781 × 857	7. $595.17 × 258	8. $60.98 × 167

9. 31.5 × 86 _______ **10.** 4.55 × 7.78 _______ **11.** 209 × 6.23 _______

12. 4715 × 2.6 _______ **13.** 8.9 × 2314 _______ **14.** 22.63 × 3.82 _______

15. 32.4 × 9.2 × 31.29 _______ **16.** 29.28 × 17 × 4.6 _______ **17.** 2.37 × 22.71 × 178 _______

Estimate to compare. Write <, =, or >.

18. 654 × 896 _______ 654 × 392

19. 4596 × 749 _______ 4596 × 875

20. 759 × 121 _______ 204 × 725

21. 3012 × 343 _______ 9623 × 565

22. 92 × 617 _______ 349 × 67

23. 6195 × 7319 _______ 7017 × 5843

Problem Solving

24. Last year, Fred's Appliances sold 274 color television sets. The cost of each set, including tax, was $357.44. About how much money was taken in from the sale of all the television sets?

____

Multiply Whole Numbers

Name ___________________

Date ___________________

Multiply: 406 × 372

Long Way	**Short Way**
372	372
× 406	× 406
2 232	2 232
0 000	+ 148 800
+148 800	151,032
151,032	

Use the **Distributive Property** to help find products of larger numbers.

$$708 \times 35{,}147 = (700 + 8) \times 35{,}147$$
$$= (700 \times 35{,}147) + (8 \times 35{,}147)$$
$$= 24{,}602{,}900 + 281{,}176$$
$$= 24{,}884{,}076$$

Estimate by rounding. Then find each product.

1. 124 × 206	**2.** 536 × 410	**3.** 159 × 203	**4.** 203 × 509

1.   124   **2.**   536   **3.**   159   **4.**   203
    × 206   × 410   × 203   × 509

5.   483   **6.**   324   **7.**   1970   **8.**   2790
    × 507   × 440   × 3406   ×   601

9. 404 × 6487 = _______________

10. 530 × 3571 = _______________

11. 670 × 5909 = _______________

12. 907 × 7246 = _______________

13. 5013 × 1221 = _______________

14. 1007 × 4409 = _______________

Use the Distributive Property to compute.

15. 430 × 821 _______

16. 140 × 383 _______

17. 260 × 3401 _______

18. 405 × 6743 _______

19. 603 × 72,468 _______

20. 380 × 189,352 _______

Problem Solving

21. A backhoe lifted 170 tons of dirt per day for 203 days. How many tons did it lift? _______________

22. The Apple Fruit Market received 720 cases of apples. Each case held 107 apples. How many apples did the market receive? _______________

Multiply with Decimals

Name _______________________

Date _______________________

Multiply: 12 × 9.623

Estimate by rounding.	Multiply as with whole numbers.	Write the decimal point in the product.

Estimate by rounding.

12 × 9.623

10 × 10 = 100

Multiply as with whole numbers.

```
    9.623
  ×    12
   19246
 + 96230
  115476
```

Write the decimal point in the product.

```
    9.623
  ×    12
   19246
 + 96230
  115.476
```
3 decimal places

Write the decimal point in each product.

1.
```
  0.617
×     8
  4936
```
____

2.
```
  0.6
× 21
  126
```
____

3.
```
  0.419
×   0.9
  3771
```
____

4.
```
  62.35
×  0.26
 162110
```
____

5.
```
  16.79
×   1.8
 30222
```
____

Multiply. Round to the nearest cent when necessary.

6.
```
   0.5
× 34
```

7.
```
  0.72
× 18
```

8.
```
  0.96
× 43
```

9.
```
 $43.25
×      7
```

10.
```
  0.613
× 5.81
```

11.
```
  0.715
× 0.02
```

12.
```
 $7.02
×  1.6
```

13.
```
  14.5
× 6.8
```

14.
```
 $2.90
×  2.4
```

15.
```
 $60.30
×    5.2
```

16. 0.13 × $85.28 = _______________

17. 2.03 × 1.2 × 0.5 = _______________

18. 0.2 × 0.4 × 0.6 = _______________

19. 0.04 × 0.1 × 0.3 = _______________

Problem Solving

20. Harry bought 4 dozen eggs at $1.09 a dozen. How much did he pay for the eggs? _______________

21. Lacey bought 15 T-shirts for the hiking club. Each shirt cost $12.75. How much did Lacey pay for the shirts? _______________

22. Mary had 0.8 gallon of milk. She gave 0.3 of the milk to Tom. How much milk did Tom get? _______________

23. A square yard of carpeting costs $46.50. What is the cost of 3.8 square yards? _______________

Exponents

> An *exponent* tells how many times to use the *base* as a factor.
>
> 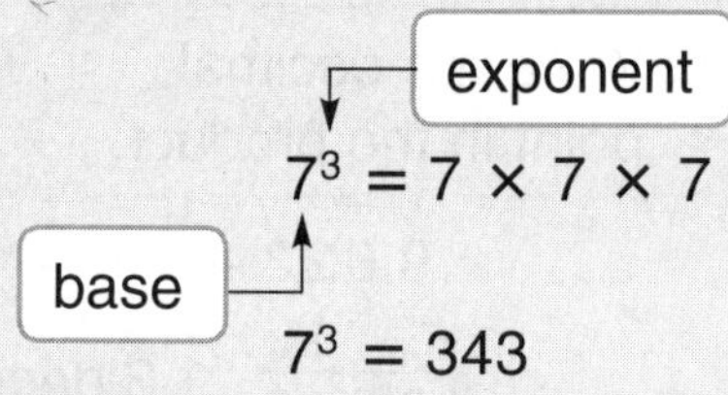
>
> exponent
>
> $7^3 = 7 \times 7 \times 7$
>
> base
>
> $7^3 = 343$
>
> Read 7^3 as:
> "7 cubed,"
> "7 to the third power," or
> "the third power of 7."
>
> 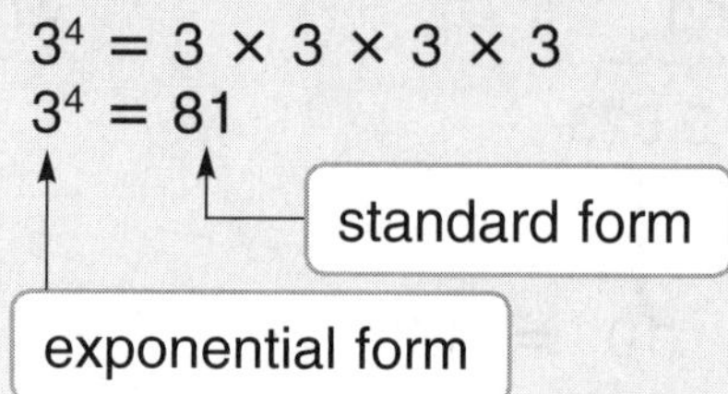
>
> $3^4 = 3 \times 3 \times 3 \times 3$
> $3^4 = 81$
>
> standard form
>
> exponential form

Write each product in exponential form.

1. $5 \times 5 \times 5 \times 5 \times 5 \times 5$ **2.** $21 \times 21 \times 21 \times 21$ **3.** $3 \times 3 \times 3 \times 3 \times 3$

________   ________   ________

4. $7 \times 7 \times 7 \times 7 \times 7 \times 7 \times 7 \times 7 \times 7 \times 7$ **5.** $12 \times 12 \times 12 \times 12 \times 12 \times 12 \times 12 \times 12$

________   ________

Write the standard form for each.

6. 8^4 **7.** 9^2 **8.** 5^3 **9.** 6^0

________   ________   ________   ________

10. 13 cubed   **11.** 9 to the 4th power   **12.** 16 squared   **13.** the 2nd power of 18

________   ________   ________   ________

Write the missing exponents.

14. $8^x = 64$ **15.** $12^y = 1$ **16.** $10^n = 100{,}000$ **17.** $11^a = 1331$

________   ________   ________   ________

Compare. Write <, =, or >.

18. 3^5 _____ 4^3 **19.** 2^4 _____ 4^2 **20.** 5^4 _____ 25^1 **21.** 8^3 _____ 22^2

Problem Solving

22. There are 5^5 students at West High School and 4^6 students at East High School. How many students are at both schools combined?

____

Use with Lesson 2-5, pages 74–75 in the Student Book.
Then go to Lesson 2-6, pages 76–77 in the Student Book.

Scientific Notation

Name _______________________

Date _______________________

> **Write 156,000,000 in scientific notation.**
>
> 1̰.̰5̰6̰,̰0̰0̰0̰,̰0̰0̰0̰. | 1.56 is greater than 1 but less than 10.
>
> 1.56×10^8 | Move the decimal point 8 places to the left. The power of 10 is 10^8.
>
> So $156,000,000 = 1.56 \times 10^8$.

> **Write 4.17×10^5 in standard form.**
>
> $4.17 \times 10^5 = 4.17000$
>
> $= 417,000$
>
> So $4.17 \times 10^5 = 417,000$. | To multiply by 10^5, move the decimal point 5 places to the right.

Write in scientific notation.

1. 120,000 _______   **2.** 485,000 _______   **3.** 25,000 _______

4. 2,750,000 _______   **5.** 714,500 _______   **6.** 47,000,000 _______

7. 143,700,000 _______   **8.** 1,505,000 _______   **9.** 28,000,000 _______

10. 6,202,000 _______   **11.** 300,000,000 _______   **12.** 6500 _______

Write in standard form.

13. 7×10^2 _______   **14.** 8×10^3 _______   **15.** 9×10^5 _______

16. 2.4×10^3 _______   **17.** 1.9×10^4 _______   **18.** 3.75×10^5 _______

19. 2.01×10^5 _______   **20.** 3.436×10^6 _______   **21.** 7.005×10^7 _______

22. 4.3×10^6 _______   **23.** 7×10^8 _______   **24.** 5.286×10^5 _______

25. 9.415×10^8 _______   **26.** 6.012×10^5 _______   **27.** 8.02×10^9 _______

Rename each number in either scientific notation or standard form.

28. Neptune is about 2,800,000,000 miles from the Sun. _______________________

29. Saturn is about 900,000,000 miles from the Sun. _______________________

30. Jupiter is about 4.8×10^8 miles from the Sun. _______________________

Use with Lesson 2-6, pages 76–77 in the Student Book.
Then go to Lesson 2-7, pages 78–79 in the Student Book.

Problem-Solving Strategy: Use Simpler Numbers

Name _______________

Date _______________

Kathy wants to buy a bicycle that costs $149.95. She has saved $54.35 so far. Last week she earned $28.50. This week she earned $22.75. How much more money does she need to buy the bicycle?

- Substitute simpler numbers to help you choose the operation(s).

  $150 - (\$50 + \$30 + \$20) = \$50$

- Now solve the problem using the actual numbers.

  $149.95 - (\$54.35 + \$28.50 + \$22.75) = \$44.35$

Kathy needs $44.35 more.

Solve. Do your work on a separate sheet of paper.

1. At the beginning of the month, Craig had $384.37 in his checking account. During the month, he wrote checks for $29.50, $16.85, $44.90, and $127.38. He made a deposit of $585.50. How much did Craig have in his checking account at the end of the month?

2. Karen and Karim are playing a game with Bob and Betty. Karen scored 24 points during her turn, and Karim scored 18 points during his turn. Bob scored 21 points. How many points must Betty score during her turn if Bob and Betty are to win the game?

3. Elly, Marge, and Bryan babysit to earn money. Last month, Elly earned $27.50. Marge earned $8.25 more than Elly. Bryan earned $12.40 more than Marge. How much did Bryan earn?

4. Paula, Willis, and Ted are training for a marathon. Each day Paula runs 4.75 miles. Willis runs 0.3 mile less than that, and Ted runs 1.55 miles more than Willis. How far does Ted run each day?

5. Shana's balance in her savings account was $278.76 at the beginning of the month. During the month, she withdrew $55.00. She also made deposits of $19.55 and $17.60. If the interest earned for the month was $.90, what was her account balance at the end of the month?

6. Raul and Marta are planning to hike from base camp to Doone, which is 89.7 km away. If they hike 27.5 km the first day, 33.85 km the second day, and 28.35 km the third day, will they reach Doone?

Use with Lesson 2-7, pages 78–79 in the Student Book.
Then go to Lesson 2-8, pages 80–81 in the Student Book.

Problem-Solving Applications: Mixed Review

Name _______________

Date _______________

Solve each problem and explain the method you used. If needed, do all your work on a separate sheet of paper.

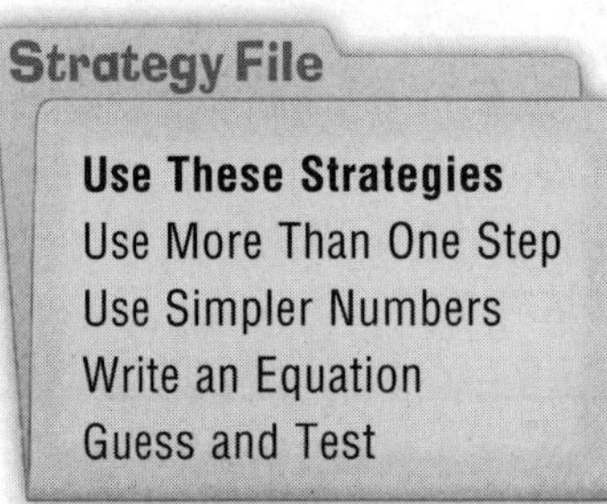

1. Maggie's Market sells a 5-pound bag of coffee for $5.95. Coffee Corral sells the same coffee for $1.15 per pound. Which store has the better buy?

____

2. J.P. bought 7 lemons at $.29 each and 5 limes at $.18 each. He paid with a $10 bill. How much change should J.P. have received?

____

3. Leslie buys an 8-serving package of chicken. There are 3.6 ounces in each serving. How many ounces does the package weigh?

____

4. Carlos can buy a 16-ounce package of trail mix for $9.87, or he can make his own trail mix for 65¢ an ounce. Will Carlos save money if he buys the 16-ounce package? How much?

____

5. Vera spent $42.75 at the grocery store. She spent twice as much on fruits and vegetables as she did on the other groceries. How much did Vera spend on fruits and vegetables?

____

Use the table for problems 6–9.

6. How much does a box of apples cost?

____

7. In one week, the store sold 53 boxes of apples, 37 bunches of bananas, and 38 bunches of grapes. How much was spent on these purchases?

____

Fruit	Amount	Unit Price
Box of apples	15 apples	$0.24 each
Bunch of bananas	3 lb	$0.27/lb
Bunch of grapes	5 lb	$0.43/lb
Bag of pears	10 pears	$0.56 each

8. Cody buys 2 boxes of apples and 3 bunches of grapes. How much does he spend altogether?

____

9. Mica buys one box, bunch, or bag of each fruit. She pays with a $20 bill. How much change should she receive?

____

Use with Lesson 2-8, pages 80–81 in the Student Book.

Short Division

Divide: 1639 ÷ 6

$$6\overline{)16^43^19} = 273 \; R1$$

| **2 × 6 = 12**
16 − 12 = **4** | **7 × 6 = 42**
43 − 42 = **1** | **3 × 6 = 18**
19 − 18 = **1** |

A number is divisible by:
- 2 if it is an even number.
- 3 if the sum of its digits is divisible by 3.
- 5 if its last digit is a 0 or a 5.

Find each quotient by short division. Use R to write remainders.
Check by multiplying the divisor and the quotient and then adding the remainder.

1. $4\overline{)6452}$　　2. $3\overline{)\$8475}$　　3. $5\overline{)2143}$　　4. $7\overline{)5218}$　　5. $9\overline{)7863}$

6. $7\overline{)8485}$　　7. $2\overline{)3579}$　　8. $9\overline{)6089}$　　9. $6\overline{)1379}$　　10. $3\overline{)\$7041}$

11. 7337 ÷ 4　　12. $5130 ÷ 3　　13. 4135 ÷ 6　　14. 15,231 ÷ 7　　15. $7296 ÷ 8

16. 5984 ÷ 5　　17. $43,659 ÷ 7　　18. 16,379 ÷ 6

19. 285,031 ÷ 8　　20. 457,286 ÷ 4　　21. 768,671 ÷ 3

Write the divisor. Use divisibility rules to help you.

22. $\overline{)9741}$ = 3247　　23. $\overline{)29,567}$ = 5913 R2　　24. $\overline{)89,937}$ = 9993　　25. $\overline{)5474}$ = 684 R2　　26. $\overline{)6471}$ = 719

Problem Solving

27. Mrs. Lee bought 6 computers for the library for $8292. Each computer cost the same. How much did each cost? _______________________

28. The bookstore received 22,725 books in 3 equal truck loads. How many books were in each load? _______________________

Use with Lesson 3-1, pages 88–89 in the Student Book.
Then go to Lesson 3-2, pages 90–91 in the Student Book.

Estimate Quotients

Name _______________________

Date _______________________

Estimate the quotient by using compatible numbers: 28,376 ÷ 62

$$28{,}376 \div 62$$

$$30{,}000 \div 60 = 500 \longleftarrow \text{Estimated Quotient}$$

So 28,376 ÷ 62 ≈ 500

Two numbers are compatible numbers when one number divides the other evenly.

Estimate the quotient. Use compatible numbers.

1. 7764 ÷ 38 _______   **2.** 3523 ÷ 39 _______   **3.** 2402 ÷ 54 _______

4. 6138 ÷ 58 _______   **5.** 8943 ÷ 32 _______   **6.** 9402 ÷ 89 _______

7. 22,140 ÷ 189 _______   **8.** 39,521 ÷ 520 _______   **9.** $3697 ÷ 83 _______

10. 629,093 ÷ 632 _______   **11.** 478,812 ÷ 473 _______   **12.** $92,880 ÷ 861 _______

13. 785,229 ÷ 350 _______   **14.** 632,029 ÷ 231 _______   **15.** $123,067 ÷ 529 _______

Circle the letter of the best estimate.

16. 54)‾2935‾ ≈   **a.** 6   **b.** 60   **c.** 600   **d.** 6000

17. 19)‾78,281‾ ≈   **a.** 4   **b.** 40   **c.** 400   **d.** 4000

18. 21)‾13,482‾ ≈   **a.** 5   **b.** 50   **c.** 500   **d.** 5000

19. 57)‾240,584‾ ≈   **a.** 4   **b.** 40   **c.** 400   **d.** 4000

20. 37)‾162,432‾ ≈   **a.** 400   **b.** 4000   **c.** 40   **d.** 40,000

21. 462)‾438,217‾ ≈   **a.** 800   **b.** 80   **c.** 8   **d.** 80,000

22. 641)‾619,473‾ ≈   **a.** 10,000   **b.** 100,000   **c.** 1000   **d.** 100

Problem Solving

23. A small aircraft carried 6217 passengers in 28 days. If about the same number of passengers flew each day, about how many passengers were carried in one day? _______________________

24. The 22 basketball teams in Big City scored a total of 8496 points. On average, about how many points did each team score? _______________________

25. There are 24,842 cassettes to be boxed. Each box holds 485 cassettes. About how many boxes can be filled? _______________________

Use with Lesson 3-2, pages 90–91 in the Student Book.
Then go to Lesson 3-3, pages 92–93 in the Student Book.

Divide Whole Numbers

Name _________________________

Date _________________________

Divide: 282,426 ÷ 47

Estimate.

300,000 ÷ 50 = 6000

Not enough hundreds or tens. Write zeros in the quotient.

Divide.

```
        6 009 R3
47)282,426
   -282
     0 426
     -423
        3
```

Check.

```
    6009
  ×   47
   42063
 +24036
  282423
 +      3
  282426
```

Estimate by using compatible numbers. Then find each quotient.

1. 2392 ÷ 64

2. 9288 ÷ 43

3. 2118 ÷ 72

4. 3581 ÷ 25

5. 58)19,847

6. 212)9598

7. 416)12,896

8. 39)19,773

9. 153)154,071

10. 723)385,622

Find the value of the variable.

11. $x = 29{,}481 \div 93$

12. $10{,}455 \div 17 = b$

13. $581{,}204 \div 26 = z$

14. $y = 725{,}625 \div 125$

15. $687{,}232 \div 208 = c$

16. $d = 601{,}555 \div 31$

Use with Lesson 3-3, pages 92–93 in the Student Book.
Then go to Lesson 3-4, pages 94–95 in the Student Book.

Divide Decimals by 10, 100, and 1000

Name _______________________

Date _______________________

To divide a decimal by 10, 100, or 1000:

- Move the decimal point to the *left* one place in the dividend for each zero in the divisor.
- Write zeros in the quotient as needed.

$5.1 \div 10 = 0.51$

| 1 zero: Move 1 place to the left. |

$007.9 \div 1000 = 0.0079$

| 3 zeros: Move 3 places to the left. Write 2 zeros as placeholders. |

To write a decimal between 0 and 1 in **scientific notation:**

- Place the decimal point to the *right* of the first nonzero digit.

$0.0053 \longrightarrow 5.3$

- The *negative exponent* of the power of 10 is the number of places the decimal point was moved.

$0.005.3 = 5.3 \times 10^{-3}$

Complete each table. Use patterns to help.

	Number	÷ 10	÷ 100	÷ 1000
1.	16.2			
2.	8.9			
3.	165			
4.	0.72			

	Number	÷ 10	÷ 100	÷ 1000
5.	1679			
6.	56.29			
7.	0.286			
8.	126.93			

Divide.

9. $8 \div 10 =$ _______

10. $93 \div 10 =$ _______

11. $0.47 \div 10 =$ _______

12. $2.54 \div 100 =$ _______

13. $0.08 \div 100 =$ _______

14. $3427.1 \div 100 =$ _______

15. $1 \div 1000 =$ _______

16. $3.006 \div 1000 =$ _______

17. $82.45 \div 1000 =$ _______

Find the value of the variable.

18. $0.14 \div a = 0.014$

____

19. $7.6 \div n = 0.076$

____

20. $21 \div b = 0.021$

____

21. $d \div 1000 = 3.175$

____

22. $m \div 100 = 7.253$

____

23. $y \div 100 = 0.32$

____

Write in scientific notation.

24. 0.0000067 _______

25. 0.0000000129 _______

26. 0.00000764 _______

27. 0.00003 _______

28. 0.000845 _______

29. 0.004035 _______

Problem Solving

30. Driving at a speed of 100 km per hour, how long will it take to drive a distance of 475.1 km?

____

Divide Decimals by Whole Numbers

Name _______________________

Date _______________________

Divide: 56.84 ÷ 7

Write the decimal point in the quotient directly above the decimal point in the dividend.

$$7\overline{)56.84}$$

Divide as you would with whole numbers.

```
        8.12
   7)56.84
    -56↓
      08
    -  7↓
       14
     - 14
        0
```

Check.

```
    8.12
  ×    7
  56.84
```

Divide and check.

1. $9\overline{)\$28.35}$
2. $4\overline{)45.12}$
3. $2\overline{)0.286}$
4. $5\overline{)7.20}$

5. $8\overline{)\$9.76}$
6. $7\overline{)19.4691}$
7. $3\overline{)22.008}$
8. $4\overline{)0.852}$

9. $4\overline{)25.72}$
10. $7\overline{)9.513}$
11. $4\overline{)0.924}$
12. $9\overline{)\$346.32}$

13. $12\overline{)4.344}$
14. $23\overline{)9.89}$
15. $38\overline{)\$66.88}$
16. $17\overline{)\$21.76}$

Compare. Write <, =, or >.

17. 0.81 ÷ 3 _______ 8.1 ÷ 3

18. 0.72 ÷ 4 _______ 0.72 ÷ 0.4

19. $9\overline{)0.45}$ _______ $9\overline{)0.045}$

20. $6\overline{)2.4}$ _______ $0.6\overline{)0.24}$

Problem Solving

21. Jamail paid $13.92 for 16 identical pens. How much did each pen cost?

____

22. Nine packages weigh a total of 21.06 kg. Find the weight of 1 package if they all weigh the same.

____

Use with Lesson 3-5, pages 96–97 in the Student Book.
Then go to Lesson 3-6, pages 98–99 in the Student Book.

Patterns with Tenths, Hundredths, Thousandths

Name _______________________

Date _______________________

<table>
<tr><td>

Patterns:

$85 \div 0.1 = 850$
$85 \div 0.01 = 8500$
$85 \div 0.001 = 85{,}000$

$415.6 \div 0.1 = 4156$
$415.6 \div 0.01 = 41{,}560$
$415.6 \div 0.001 = 415{,}600$

</td><td>

Divide:

$5.24 \div 0.1 = 52.4$

1 decimal place in the divisor. Move the decimal point 1 place to the right.

$5.240 \div 0.001 = 5240$

3 decimal places in the divisor. Move the decimal point 3 places to the right. Write 1 zero.

When you divide by 0.1, 0.01, or 0.001, the quotient increases as the divisor decreases.

</td></tr>
</table>

Complete each table. Use patterns to help.

	Number	÷ 0.1	÷ 0.01	÷ 0.001
1.	23			
2.	439			
3.	7.1			
4.	15.3			

	Number	÷ 0.1	÷ 0.01	÷ 0.001
5.	10			
6.	2.78			
7.	24.14			
8.	326.89			

Divide.

9. $47 \div 0.1 =$ _______

10. $52 \div 0.01 =$ _______

11. $78 \div 0.001 =$ _______

12. $589 \div 0.1 =$ _______

13. $423 \div 0.01 =$ _______

14. $932 \div 0.001 =$ _______

15. $0.6 \div 0.1 =$ _______

16. $0.65 \div 0.01 =$ _______

17. $3.4 \div 0.001 =$ _______

18. $253.8 \div 0.01 =$ _______

19. $3.78 \div 0.001 =$ _______

20. $9 \div 0.1 =$ _______

Compare. Write <, =, or >.

21. $17.5 \div 0.01$ _______ $7.5 \div 0.001$

22. $7.1 \div 0.01$ _______ $71 \div 0.1$

23. $96.7 \div 0.01$ _______ $967 \div 0.01$

24. $52 \div 0.01$ _______ $52 \div 0.1$

Find the quotients.

25. $78 \div 0.01 =$ _______

26. $0.7 \div 0.1 =$ _______

27. $3.2 \div 0.001 =$ _______

28. $7.892 \div 0.01 =$ _______

29. $42.5 \div 0.001 =$ _______

30. $1.94 \div 0.1 =$ _______

Problem Solving

31. How many dimes are in $45? _______________________

Use with Lesson 3-6, pages 98–99 in the Student Book.
Then go to Lesson 3-7, pages 100–101 in the Student Book.

Estimate Decimal Quotients

Name _______________

Date _______________

Estimate: 65.4 ÷ 0.83	Estimate: $.41 ÷ 5.8	Estimate: 14.9 ÷ 5.1
Dividend > Divisor: Quotient > 1	**Dividend < Divisor:** Quotient < 1	**Front End:** $10 \div 5 = 2$
65.4 ÷ 0.83	$.41 ÷ 5.8	**Compatible Numbers:** $15 \div 5 = 3$
64 ÷ 0.8 = 80	$.42 ÷ 6 = $.07	**Rounding:** $15 \div 5 = 3$
So 65.4 ÷ 0.83 is about 80.	So $.41 ÷ 5.8 is about $.07.	So 14.9 ÷ 5.1 is about 2 or 3.

Estimate to place the decimal point in the quotient.

1. 45.9 ÷ 7.2 = 6375 _________

2. 14.28 ÷ 3.4 = 42 _________

3. 55.8 ÷ 6 = 93 _________

4. 286.44 ÷ 15.5 = 1848 _________

Estimate each quotient. Use compatible numbers.

5. 31.8 ÷ 4.1 ______

6. 12.4 ÷ 6.5 ______

7. 50.2 ÷ 6.9 ______

8. 27.3 ÷ 8.5 ______

9. 58.3 ÷ 7.9 ______

10. 35.1 ÷ 4.2 ______

11. 62.34 ÷ 8.98 ______

12. $18.3 ÷ 2.75 ______

13. 321.6 ÷ 8.2 ______

14. 146.4 ÷ 6.8 ______

15. 211.3 ÷ 19.5 ______

16. $485.7 ÷ 50.4 ______

17. 590 ÷ 32.4 ______

18. 900.67 ÷ 41.8 ______

19. 241.34 ÷ 23.72 ______

Compare. Write <, =, or >.

20. 5 ÷ 9 ______ 1

21. 11.8 ÷ 3.2 ______ 1

22. 1 ______ 18.3 ÷ 0.496

23. 0.87 ÷ 6.2 ______ 1

24. 3.5 ÷ 47.1 ______ 1

25. 1 ______ 0.2 ÷ 0.4

26. 1.29 ÷ 0.78 ______ 1

27. 1 ______ 1.22 ÷ 0.248

28. 2.79 ÷ 0.4 ______ 1

Estimate each quotient to complete the table.

		Front End	Compatible Numbers	Rounding
29.	44.7 ÷ 5.2			
30.	$32.40 ÷ 6.4			
31.	52 ÷ 4.9			
32.	233.7 ÷ 5.2			
33.	487.9 ÷ 18.1			

Problem Solving

34. Tony paid $48.75 for 7.8 yards of fabric. About how much per yard was the fabric? _________

Use with Lesson 3-7, pages 100–101 in the Student Book.
Then go to Lesson 3-8, pages 102–103 in the Student Book.

Decimal Divisors

Name ___________________

Date ___________________

Divide: 23.04 ÷ 0.6

Move the decimal point in the divisor and in the dividend the *same number* of places.

$$0.6\overline{)23.04}$$

$$6\overline{)230.4}$$

Place the decimal point in the quotient. Divide.

$$6\overline{)23^50^2.4} = 38.4$$

Check.

$$\begin{array}{r} 38.4 \\ \times\ 0.6 \\ \hline 23.04 \end{array}$$

**Move the decimal point in the divisor and in the dividend.
Then write the decimal point in the quotient.**

1. $0.9\overline{)8.1}$ **2.** $0.6\overline{)5.4}$ **3.** $0.8\overline{)3.2}$ **4.** $0.2\overline{)1.4}$ **5.** $0.5\overline{)4.5}$

6. $0.3\overline{)0.21}$ **7.** $0.7\overline{)0.35}$ **8.** $0.4\overline{)3.24}$ **9.** $0.6\overline{)1.26}$ **10.** $0.8\overline{)6.48}$

11. $0.2\overline{)64.4}$ **12.** $0.5\overline{)85.5}$ **13.** $0.8\overline{)3.36}$ **14.** $0.9\overline{)5.166}$ **15.** $0.4\overline{)8.52}$

16. $0.7\overline{)15.12}$ **17.** $0.3\overline{)14.673}$ **18.** $0.6\overline{)12.72}$ **19.** $0.8\overline{)5.272}$ **20.** $0.2\overline{)65.8}$

Divide and check.

21. $0.3\overline{)5.76}$ **22.** $0.9\overline{)7.83}$ **23.** $0.06\overline{)3.042}$ **24.** $0.68\overline{)0.6936}$

25. $86.4 \div 0.2$ **26.** $3.5 \div 0.5$ **27.** $0.92 \div 0.4$ **28.** $367.2 \div 0.6$

Problem Solving

29. The length of a quilt is 2.4 m. Each square patch is 0.2 m a side. How many patches are in a row that runs the length of the quilt?

Zeros in Division

Divide: 21 ÷ 5.25

$$5.25\overline{)21.00} \longrightarrow 525\overline{)2100}$$
$$\begin{array}{r} 4 \\ -2100 \\ \hline 0 \end{array}$$

Write 2 zeros as placeholders *in the dividend.*

Divide: 0.043 ÷ 0.5

Write a zero *in the quotient.*

$$0.5\overline{)0.043} \longrightarrow 5\overline{)0.430}$$
$$\begin{array}{r} 0.086 \\ -40 \\ \hline 30 \\ -30 \\ \hline 0 \end{array}$$

Write a zero.

Divide. When needed, write zeros as placeholders in the dividend.

1. $0.4\overline{)0.6}$ **2.** $0.6\overline{)12}$ **3.** $7.5\overline{)9}$ **4.** $0.64\overline{)0.8}$

5. $0.6 \div 1.2 =$ _____ **6.** $0.06 \div 0.025 =$ _____ **7.** $0.01 \div 0.008 =$ _____

Divide. Write zeros in the quotient as needed.

8. $4\overline{)0.16}$ **9.** $3\overline{)0.21}$ **10.** $7\overline{)0.287}$ **11.** $4.1\overline{)0.123}$

12. $3.6\overline{)0.144}$ **13.** $4\overline{)1.208}$ **14.** $3.4\overline{)0.017}$ **15.** $5\overline{)1.505}$

Problem Solving

16. Samantha can run 1.68 miles in 12 minutes. What is her average distance per minute? _______________________

17. Jack bought 6.5 pounds of grapes for $7.02. What is the cost of one pound of grapes? _______________________

Use with Lesson 3-9, pages 104–105 in the Student Book.
Then go to Lesson 3-10, pages 106–107 in the Student Book.

Multiplication and Division Expressions

Name ___________________________

Date ___________________________

Multiplication Expressions	Division Expressions
Write as: 62×3 $62 \cdot 3$ $62(3)$	Write as: $450 \div d$ $\dfrac{450}{d}$
Read as: 62 times 3 62 multiplied by 3 the product of 62 and 3	Read as: 450 divided by d the quotient of 450 and d the result of dividing 450 by d

Write each word phrase as a numerical expression.

1. fifteen times twenty-one

____

2. the quotient of 39 and 3

____

Write each word phrase as an algebraic expression. Use _x_ as a variable.

3. a number divided by 8

____

4. the product of 21 and a number

____

5. a number multiplied by 127

____

6. 305 divided by a number

____

Write each mathematical expression as a word phrase.

7. $59.1 \div 3$

____

8. $67j$

____

9. $46.7(61)$

____

10. $\dfrac{125}{a}$

____

11. $37 \cdot 7$

____

12. $\dfrac{96}{12}$

____

Problem Solving   **Write an expression for each situation.**

13. The pro shop has 261 tennis balls in cans. Each can contains 3 tennis balls. How many cans of tennis balls are there?

____

14. Krista knits 6 scarves each month. She knits for _m_ months. How many scarves does Krista knit in all?

____

15. Marc buys a package of paper plates for $3.62. There are _p_ plates in the package. What is the unit price per plate?

____

C Use with Lesson 3-10, pages 106–107 in the Student Book.
C Then go to Lesson 3-11, pages 108–109 in the Student Book.

Evaluate Multiplication and Division Expressions

Name _______________

Date _______________

Evaluate $11h$, when $h = 2.5$.

$11h = 11 \cdot 2.5$ ← Substitute 2.5 for h.

$= 27.5$ ← value of the expression

Evaluate $x \div 35$, when $x = 164.5$.

$x \div 35 = 164.5 \div 35$ ← Substitute 164.5 for x.

$= 4.7$ ← value of the expression

Evaluate each expression.

1. $71 \cdot 2808$ _______

2. $0.43 \times 5 \times 20.2$ _______

3. $5.8z$, for $z = 50$ _______

4. $\frac{78.8}{f}$, for $f = 4$ _______

5. $241.4 \div 3.4$ _______

6. $\frac{16.2}{t}$, for $t = 3$ _______

Evaluate each algebraic expression for $c = 0.6$ and $d = 300$.
Remember to work from left to right.

7. $d \div c \times 400$ _______

8. $d \div 50 \times 7$ _______

9. $24 \div c \times d$ _______

10. $15 \times c \times 25$ _______

11. $d \div 15 \times 1000$ _______

12. $d \times 720 \div c$ _______

13. $d \times 20 \times c$ _______

14. $19 \times d \div c$ _______

15. $150c \div d$ _______

16. $\frac{c + d}{75}$ _______

17. $c \cdot 500 - d$ _______

18. $(d - c) \times 400$ _______

Problem Solving Write and evaluate an expression for each situation.

19. A bird flew at a rate of 11 miles per hour. After h hours, the bird reached its nest. If the bird flew for 2.25 hours, how many miles did it fly?

____

20. The McPhersons packed d dishes into 60 boxes. They put an equal number of dishes into each box. If they used 5 boxes, how many dishes did they pack in each box?

____

21. Mrs. Fox buys p pairs of pants at $23 per pair. She pays with a $100 bill. If she buys 3 pairs of pants, how much change should she get back?

____

Use with Lesson 3-11, pages 108–109 in the Student Book.
Then go to Lesson 3-12, pages 110–111 in the Student Book.

Round Quotients

Name _______________________

Date _______________________

$5 \div 6 = ?$ Round to the nearest tenth.	$\$1.50 \div 8 = ?$ Round to the nearest cent.	$0.83 \div 7 = ?$ Round to the nearest thousandth.
$\begin{array}{r} 0.8\mathbf{3} \\ 6\overline{)5.00} \end{array}$ $\boxed{\begin{array}{c}3 < 5\\ \text{Round down.}\end{array}}$	$\begin{array}{r} \$\ .18\mathbf{7} \\ 8\overline{)\$1.500} \end{array}$ $\boxed{\begin{array}{c}7 > 5\\ \text{Round up.}\end{array}}$	$\begin{array}{r} 0.118\mathbf{5} \\ 7\overline{)0.8300} \end{array}$ $\boxed{\begin{array}{c}5 = 5\\ \text{Round up.}\end{array}}$
$5 \div 6 \approx 0.8$	$\$1.50 \div 8 \approx \$.19$	$0.83 \div 7 \approx 0.119$

Divide. Round to the nearest tenth.

1. $6\overline{)0.4}$ **2.** $13\overline{)8}$ **3.** $4.7\overline{)30}$ **4.** $3.2\overline{)12}$

5. $0.6\overline{)1.4}$ **6.** $3.4\overline{)0.6}$ **7.** $4.1\overline{)5.5}$ **8.** $0.7\overline{)0.9}$

Divide. Round to the nearest hundredth or nearest cent.

9. $9\overline{)12}$ **10.** $7\overline{)8}$ **11.** $4\overline{)7.1}$ **12.** $8\overline{)3.9}$

13. $4.2\overline{)6.6}$ **14.** $0.9\overline{)6.2}$ **15.** $3.4\overline{)0.6}$ **16.** $8.1\overline{)2.3}$

17. $0.07\overline{)1.7}$ **18.** $8\overline{)\$4.21}$ **19.** $7\overline{)\$6.33}$ **20.** $3\overline{)\$9.47}$

Divide. Round to the nearest thousandth.

21. $6\overline{)0.7}$ **22.** $8\overline{)4.19}$ **23.** $3\overline{)1.024}$ **24.** $0.7\overline{)4.5}$

25. $12\overline{)0.911}$ **26.** $7.1\overline{)3.117}$ **27.** $0.07\overline{)0.1}$ **28.** $13\overline{)141}$

Use with Lesson 3-12, pages 110–111 in the Student Book.
Then go to Lesson 3-13, pages 112–113 in the Student Book.

Problem-Solving Strategy: Interpret the Remainder

The county fair committee will give a free T-shirt to every 15th person who comes through the ticket gate. If 5525 people attend the fair, how many T-shirts will the committee give out?

Divide: $5525 \div 15$

```
      368 R5
15)5525
   -45
    102
   - 90
    125
   -120
      5
```

Check.

```
    368
  ×  15
   1840
 + 3680
   5520
 +    5
   5525
```

Since T-shirts are given only to every 15th person, they do not need an extra shirt for the remainder.

The committee will give out 368 T-shirts.

Solve. Do your work on a separate sheet of paper.

1. The fair committee wants to decorate each ride with 40 balloons. There are 13 rides. If balloons come 24 to a package, how many packages will be needed?

2. The Ferris wheel has seats for 36 people. If 105 people are waiting to ride the Ferris wheel, how many times will the ride need to operate in order to accommodate all of the people?

3. The fair committee hopes to raise $10,000 for charity. A book of 15 ride tickets costs $12. How many books does the committee need to sell to reach their goal?

4. A vendor plans to sell containers of juice at the fair. She packs 72 containers to a crate. How many crates will be needed if 6000 containers of juice are to be sold?

5. Bleacher seating for a concert on the fairgrounds consists of 6 sections. Each section seats 144 people. If 715 people attend the concert, how many sections will be needed? If 890 people attend, how many extra chairs will be needed?

6. The fair committee has planned a talent show for Saturday night. They have scheduled 2 hours for all the acts, including the awarding of prizes. If 9 minutes are allowed for each act, how many acts can they have? How much time will be left for the awarding of prizes?

Use with Lesson 3-13, pages 112–113 in the Student Book.
Then go to Lesson 3-14, pages 114–115 in the Student Book.

Problem-Solving Applications: Mixed Review

Name _______________

Date _______________

Solve each problem and explain the method you used. If needed, do all your work on a separate sheet of paper.

1. During a 24-hour highway study, 19,104 cars passed by a survey point. If the same number of cars passed by each hour, how many cars passed the survey point each hour?

2. There are 825 sixth- and seventh-grade students at the dance recital. There are twice as many sixth-grade students as seventh-grade students. How many are sixth-grade students?

3. Mr. Lester needs 6811 ceramic tiles to finish a mural for the library. If the tiles are sold in packages of 475, how many packages must he buy?

4. In 1999 Lance Armstrong rode the Tour de France at an average speed of 25.026 miles per hour. In 2000 he rode at an average speed of 24.587 miles per hour. How much faster did Lance ride in 1999 than in 2000?

5. Kellie bought 3 balls of red yarn at $3.59 per ball, 7 balls of tan yarn at $8.39 per ball, and 9 balls of black yarn at $0.99 per ball. How much did Kellie spend altogether?

6. Elena can make one sandwich in 45 seconds. If she made 34 sandwiches for the swim team, how many minutes would it take her?

7. Write and solve a problem modeled on problem 3 above.

Use the bar graph below for problems 8 and 9.

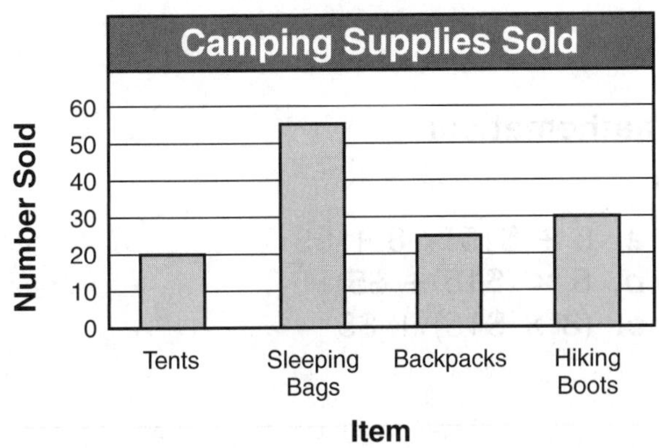

8. What was the total number of items sold?

9. Tents cost $95 each. How much money was spent on tents?

Use with Lesson 3-14, pages 114–115 in the Student Book.

Order of Operations

Name _______________________

Date _______________________

Order of Operations Rules:

- First compute operations within *grouping symbols*.
- Next simplify numbers with *exponents*.
- Then *multiply* or *divide* from left to right.
- Last *add* or *subtract* from left to right.

$(36 \div 3) \times 2 - 16 \div 4 + 10^2$

$12 \quad \times 2 - 16 \div 4 + 10^2$

$12 \quad \times 2 - 16 \div 4 + 100$

$24 \quad - \quad 4 \quad + 100$

$20 \quad + 100$

120

Write which operation is to be done first. Then compute.

1. $24 \div 6 - 2$
2. $50 - 5 \times 2^3$
3. $42 \div 6 + 1$
4. $8 + 2 \times 3$

Use the order of operations to compute.

5. $3 \times 6 - 1 + 4$
6. $16 \div 4 \times 3 - 6$
7. $12 \div 2 \div 6 + 3$
8. $11 - 1 \times 6 + 4^2$

9. $6 \times 5 + 10 \div 2$
10. $3^3 + 9 \div 3 + 5$
11. $8 + 5 \times 3 - 1$
12. $6 + 24 \div 8 \times 2$

Insert parentheses to make each number sentence true.

13. $245 \div 6^2 - 1 + 15 = 22$

14. $2 + 3 \times 6 + 4 \times 3 = 42$

15. $25 + 2^4 - 13 \times 2 = 31$

16. $14 + 6.6 \div 0.2 + 0.4 = 25$

Problem Solving Circle the letter of the correct mathematical expression to solve the problem. Then evaluate.

17. Sergei is saving to buy a bicycle.
He saves \$15 a week from his job.
His father gives him \$5 a week.
After 8 weeks how much money has
Sergei saved?

   a. $8 + \$15 \times 8 + \$5$
   b. $8 \times (\$15 + \$5)$
   c. $(8 \times \$15) + \$5$

Use with Lesson 4-1, pages 122–123 in the Student Book.
Then go to Lesson 4-1A, pages 207–208 in this Workbook.

Equations and Inequalities

A **closed equation** contains no variables and is either true or false. $4 \times 6 + 3 = 27 \leftarrow$ true $5 + 6 \times 2 = 22 \leftarrow$ false	An **open equation** contains a variable and is neither true nor false. $3n + 6 = 75$	An **inequality** can be open or closed, and uses $>$, $<$, $\geq$, $\leq$, or $\neq$. $45 + 54 > 90 \leftarrow$ closed $75 - n \leq 50 \longleftarrow$ open

Determine if the given value of the variable is the solution of the equation. Write *yes* or *no*.

1. $8d + 54 = 150$, when $d = 12$

   ____

2. $106 - 8h = 34$, when $h = 9$

   ____

3. $\frac{u}{4} + 9.9 = 16.9$, when $u = 24$

   ____

4. $25 - (9 - y) = 20.7$, when $y = 4.3$

   ____

5. $65 \div b + 8 \times 4 = 20$, when $b = 5$

   ____

6. $7.8 \times c + 3.4 = 19$, when $c = 2$

   ____

Write as an inequality. Then label each inequality *open* or *closed*. If the inequality is closed, write whether it is *true* or *false*.

7. Seven more than four times a number is less than or equal to six.

   ____

8. Sixty-five is greater than the product of seven and nine.

   ____

9. Eighteen is not equal to six times the sum of one and two.

   ____

10. The quotient of a number and 10 is greater than eighty-two.

   ____

Determine if the given value of the variable is a solution of the inequality. Write *yes* or *no*.

11. $80a + 11 < 121$, when $a = 2$ _______________

12. $9.8 + 41f - 13 > 200$, when $f = 5$ _______________

13. $(y + 23.2) - 5.8 \neq 482.24$, when $y = 2$ _______________

C Use with Lesson 4-4, pages 128–129 in the Student Book.
C Then go to Lessons 4-4A and 4-4B, pages 215–218 in this Workbook.

Addition Equations

Name ___________________________

Date ___________________________

> Solve: $38.6 = h + 5.7 + 19.8$
> $38.6 = h + 5.7 + 19.8$ ← Simplify by adding the numbers on one side.
> $38.6 = h + 25.5$
> $38.6 - 25.5 = h + 25.5 - 25.5$ ← Subtract 25.5 from both sides to isolate the variable.
> $13.1 = h$

Solve and check.

1. $7 + y = 25$

2. $1.5 = s + 0.3$

3. $p + 22 = 64$

4. $50 = b + 25$

5. $p + 86 = 100$

6. $x + 0.5 = 1$

7. $h + \$3.85 = \$7.50$

8. $k + 7 = 77$

9. $r + \$.80 = \$1.80$

10. $\$18.50 + a = \$30$

11. $1.09 + b = 4.6$

12. $d + 10.1 = 92$

13. $297 + e + 62 = 498$

14. $h + 55 + 1.93 = 98.7$

15. $7 + r = 18 + 23$

16. $0.5 + m = 3.2 + 0.9$

17. $12 + x + 25 = 553$

18. $14 + f = 68.9 + 6.8$

Write and solve an equation.

19. A number w increased by 5.9 is equal to 7.761.

20. When 177 is added to the sum of 66 and a number q, the result is 940.

21. The sum of a number c and 37 is equal to two hundred ninety-four.

22. Twenty-one hundredths more than a number t is equal to nine tenths.

Problem Solving Write an addition equation for each. Then solve.

23. There are 150 people at the soccer game. Of the people, 95 are students and the rest are parents. How many parents are at the game?

24. Dominic has 324 coins in a jar. There are 25 quarters and 112 dimes. The rest of the coins are nickels. How many nickels are in the jar?

40

Use with Lesson 4-5, pages 130–131 in the Student Book.
Then go to Lesson 4-6, pages 132–133 in the Student Book.

Subtraction Equations

Name _______________

Date _______________

Solve: $s - 23.5 = 82$

$s - 23.5 + 23.5 = 82 + 23.5$ ← Add 23.5 to both sides to isolate the variable.

$s = 105.5$

Check:

$105.5 - 23.5 = 82$

$82 = 82$ True

Solve and check.

1. $d - 6 = 33$

2. $12 = z - 10$

3. $\$45.58 - e = \$19.95$

4. $f - 4.1 = 8.6$

5. $j - \$2.10 = \$7.01$

6. $a - 15 = 0$

7. $h - 53 = 25$

8. $c - 72 = 34$

9. $b - 82.6 = 6.45$

10. $u - \$4.87 = \$.12$

11. $m - 19 = 11$

12. $v - (\$0.65 + \$5.74) = \$8.53$

13. $g - 4.7 = 5.91$

14. $y - 104 = 23$

15. $187 = t - (704 + 59)$

16. $73.4 = k - 62.7$

17. $h - 37 = 279$

18. $(6.13 + 2.46) - s = 3.86$

Write and solve an equation.

19. When a number g is decreased by 4.8, the result is 4.6443.

20. The difference between a number r and 38 is equal to six hundred five.

21. Seventeen hundredths less than a number n is equal to four tenths.

22. If the sum of 571 and 874 is subtracted from a number d, the result is 161.

Problem Solving Write a subtraction equation for each. Then solve.

23. At intermission, 19 people went home. Now there are 317 people in the theater. How many people were in the theater to begin with?

24. Alden has $68.72 saved for vacation. He had more saved, but spent $3.92 on a birthday card for a friend. How much had Alden saved before he bought the birthday card?

Use with Lesson 4-6, pages 132–133 in the Student Book.
Then go to Lesson 4-7, pages 134–135 in the Student Book.

Multiplication and Division Equations

Name ___________________________

Date ___________________________

Solve: $4n = 36$
- Divide both sides by 4 to isolate the variable.

$$4n \div 4 = 36 \div 4$$
$$n = 9$$

Solve: $x \div 5 = 3.45$
- Multiply both sides by 5 to isolate the variable.

$$x \div 5 \cdot 5 = 3.45 \cdot 5$$
$$x = 17.25$$

Solve and check.

1. $r \div 6 = 10$ _______

2. $8 \cdot w = 120$ _______

3. $15 = \dfrac{e}{0.5}$ _______

4. $8m = 40$ _______

5. $x \div 6 = 6$ _______

6. $9 = t \div 8$ _______

7. $12 = \frac{1}{2}x$ _______

8. $\dfrac{b}{5} = 15$ _______

9. $3 = \dfrac{s}{0.3}$ _______

10. $\dfrac{y}{19} = \$85$ _______

11. $\dfrac{\$385}{k} = \$5$ _______

12. $h \cdot \$250 = \$50$ _______

13. $720 = 9t$ _______

14. $4.15 = \dfrac{c}{0.13}$ _______

15. $4.52u = 31.64$ _______

16. $d \div 23 = 6.2$ _______

17. $9.12 \div s = 2.4$ _______

18. $324 = 4a$ _______

Write and solve an equation.

19. A number m divided by 3.25 is equal to 64.

____

20. Four tenths multiplied by a number z is equal to six and five tenths.

____

21. The quotient of a number n and seventeen is two hundred eighty-three.

____

22. The factors are twenty-one and g. The product is forty-eight and three tenths.

____

Problem Solving Write an equation for each. Then solve.

23. Hank bought 5 CDs for $64.75. If each CD cost the same price, how much did each cost?

____

24. It is 25.8 miles from Sandra's house to her grandparents' house. This is one fourth the distance from Sandra's house to her cousins' house. How far is it from Sandra's to her cousins'?

____

Use with Lesson 4-7, pages 134–135 in the Student Book.
Then go to Lesson 4-7A, pages 219–220 in this Workbook.

Use Formulas

Name ___________________

Date ___________________

Formula: a rule describing a mathematical relationship of two or more quantities.

Distance formula:	**Perimeter of a rectangle formula:**

Distance formula:
distance = rate × time
d = r × t

Perimeter of a rectangle formula:
Perimeter = twice the sum of length and width
$P = 2(\ell + w)$

Solve for r, when $d = 150$ miles and $t = 2.5$ hours.

$$d = r \times t$$
$$150 = r \times 2.5$$
$$150 \div 2.5 = 2.5r \div 2.5$$
$$60 = r$$

So $r = 60$ miles per hour.

Solve for P, when $\ell = 37$ ft and $w = 23$ ft.

$$P = 2(\ell + w)$$
$$P = 2(37 + 23)$$
$$P = 2(60)$$
$$P = 120$$

So $P = 120$ ft.

Use the Volume formula, $V = \ell \times w \times h$, to find each missing dimension.

1. $V = 5600$ ft^3, $\ell = 35$ ft, $w = 8$ ft,

    $h = $ _______ ft

2. $V = 5915$ cm^3, $\ell = 91$ cm,

    $w = $ _______ cm, $h = 5$ cm

3. $V = 2184$ in.^{3}, $\ell = $ _______ in.,

    $w = 7$ in., $h = 8$ in.

4. $V = 4928$ yd^3, $\ell = 56$ yd, $w = 2$ yd,

    $h = $ _______ yd

Describe the formula and solve for the missing measure.
Use the formulas at the back of this book.

5. $A = \frac{1}{2}bh$, when $A = 360$ m and
    $h = 12$ m

    ____

6. $V = e^3$, when $e = 7$ cm

    ____

7. $a + b + c = 180°$, when $a = 87°$ and
    $c = 32°$

    ____

8. $P = 4s$, when $P = 76$ in.

    ____

9. $A = bh$, when $A = 288$ mm^2 and
    $b = 24$ mm

    ____

10. $S = 2(\ell w + \ell h + wh)$, when $\ell = 6$ ft,
    $w = 3$ ft, $h = 5$ ft

    ____

Problem Solving Write the formula you would use to solve the problem. Then solve it.

11. A bus travels at a rate of 55 miles per
    hour. How far does it travel in 8 hours?

    ____

12. How many yards of fencing are needed to
    enclose a 14-yd-long by 8-yd-wide garden?

    ____

Explore Order of Operations with a Calculator

Name ___________________

Date ___________________

Evaluate the expression $(3 + 24n) + 5^3$, when $n = 2$.
Check your computation using a calculator.

> Most scientific calculators automatically follow the correct order of operations.

The value of $(3 + 24n) + 5^3$, when $n = 2$ is 176.

Evaluate. Use a calculator to check your work.

1. $62 + 9 \times 7^2$

2. $4 \times (9 - 3)^3 + 15$

3. $10^5 \times (15 + 5) \div 4$

4. $67 - 27 \div 3^2$

5. $6 \times (5 - 2)^3 + 13$

6. $(5)^4 - 10 + (25 + 5 \times 3)$

7. $(4 \times 2)^2 + 56 \div 2$

8. $252 \div 7 \times 4^3 - 104$

9. $45 + 23 - (60 + 2^3)$

10. $64^2 - 318 + (44 + 14 + 11) \div 3$

11. $93 + 16^3 \div 32 + 9 \times 17$

Compare. Write <, =, or >.

12. $45^2 - 6 \times 19$ _____ $(45^2 - 6) \times 19$

13. $(25 + 75) \div 5^2$ _____ $25 + 75 \div 5^2$

14. $17 + 63 \div 10 + 5^3$ _____ $(17 + 63) \div 10 + 5^3$

15. $(85 \times 4) + 55 \times 2^4$ _____ $85 \times 4 + (55 \times 2^4)$

16. $(264 + 126) \times 6 \div (5 + 8)$ _____ $264 + 126 \times 6 \div 5 + 8$

Problem Solving Circle the letter of the correct expression to solve the problem. Then evaluate the expression.

17. Maggie drove 9 miles to the store and then drove back home. Then she drove 19 miles to the park, 6 miles to the gym, and 23 miles back home. How far did Maggie drive?

a. $9 \times (2 + 19) + 6 + 23$
b. $9 \times (2 + 19 + 6 + 23)$
c. $(9 \times 2) + 19 + 6 + 23$

Use with Lesson 4-9, pages 138–139 in the Student Book.
Then go to Lesson 4-10, pages 140–141 in the Student Book.

Problem-Solving Strategy: Use More Than One Step

Ms. Hayashi buys 5 lb of chicken at $2.19 a pound, 2 lb of fresh green beans at $1.20 a pound, and a 64-ounce bottle of apple juice for $1.49. How much did she spend in all?

Ms. Hayashi spent $14.84 in all.

Step 1: Find the cost of the chicken.
$5 \times \$2.19 = \$10.95$

Step 2: Find the cost of the green beans.
$2 \times \$1.20 = \$2.40$

Step 3: Add to find the total cost of the three items.
$\$10.95 + \$2.40 + \$1.49 = \$14.84$

Solve. Do your work on a separate sheet of paper.

1. Yoshi buys a T-shirt for $15.95 and socks for $7.95. He pays with a gift card that has $31.19 left on it. What will the new balance on the gift card be?

2. If Bettinia drove for 3.8 hours at a constant speed of 56 mph and Willis drove for 4.1 hours at a constant speed of 52 mph, who drove farther? How much farther?

3. Pat wants to buy a CD player that costs $86.50. He has saved $60. He earns $5.30 an hour working after school and can save half of his total earnings. How many hours will he have to work to buy the CD player?

4. On Saturdays Diego works 8.25 hours and earns $6.50 an hour. Sabrina works 6.75 hours and earns $8.95 an hour. Who earns more? How much more?

5. Natasha needs to save $479.58 for a vacation. She has saved $149.88, and earns $7.85 an hour helping at the playground. How many hours must she work to meet her goal?

6. The price of a 6-ounce can of Kitty Kat turkey is $0.52. The price of a 4-ounce can of Cougar Cat turkey is $0.32. Which is the better buy?

7. Kathy runs 3.25 miles every Monday, 2.75 miles every Wednesday, and 3.5 miles every Friday. Last month she ran 5.5 miles and 6.25 miles on two Saturdays. How many miles did she run last month if there were 4 Mondays, 5 Wednesdays, and 5 Fridays?

8. Yoko buys a pen for $1.19 and 2 paperback books. Each book costs $5.95. She gives the clerk a 20-dollar bill and receives $7.91 in change. Does she receive the correct amount of change? Justify your answer.

Use with Lesson 4-10, pages 140–141 in the Student Book.
Then go to Lesson 4-11, pages 142–143 in the Student Book.

Problem-Solving Applications: Mixed Review

Name ______________________

Date ______________________

Solve each problem and explain the method you used. If needed, do all your work on a separate sheet of paper.

Read ▸ **Plan** ▸ **Solve** ▸ **Check**

1. Josh and three friends went out for lunch. His friends spent $9.62, $6.97, and $3.40. The total bill was $27.22. How much did Josh spend on his lunch?

2. There are 68 pairs of sneakers in the storeroom. This is 7 less than 3 times the number of pairs of flip-flops. How many pairs of flip-flops are there?

3. Colin weighs 6 pounds more than 4 times his baby brother's weight. If Colin weighs 54 pounds, how much does his baby brother weigh?

4. Each week, Julie saves $\frac{1}{10}$ more than she did the week before. If she saves $20 the first week, how much will she save the seventh week?

5. For every 7 cups of hot chocolate that Lisa orders, one of them is free. Each cup of hot chocolate costs $1.95. How much does Lisa pay for 23 cups of hot chocolate for her classmates?

Use the table for problems 6–9.

6. Shay buys 12 oz of sliced ham. What is the cost per ounce? Round to the nearest cent.

7. Derek has $15. He wants to buy $\frac{1}{2}$ lb of sliced roast beef and three times as much shaved roast beef. Does he have enough money?

8. Hilda is making a sandwich with 4 ounces of shaved meat. Which meat would be least expensive to use?

9. Use the table to write a problem modeled on exercise 8 above. Have a classmate solve it.

Meat	Quantity	Price
Roast Beef	8 oz sliced	$3.75
	$1\frac{1}{2}$ lb shaved	$10.50
Ham	12 oz sliced	$4.30
	1 lb shaved	$5.60
Turkey	$\frac{1}{2}$ lb sliced	$2.45
	16 oz shaved	$4.90
Pastrami	$\frac{3}{4}$ lb sliced	$3.60
	20 oz shaved	$5.75

Use with Lesson 4-11, pages 142–143 in the Student Book.

Integers

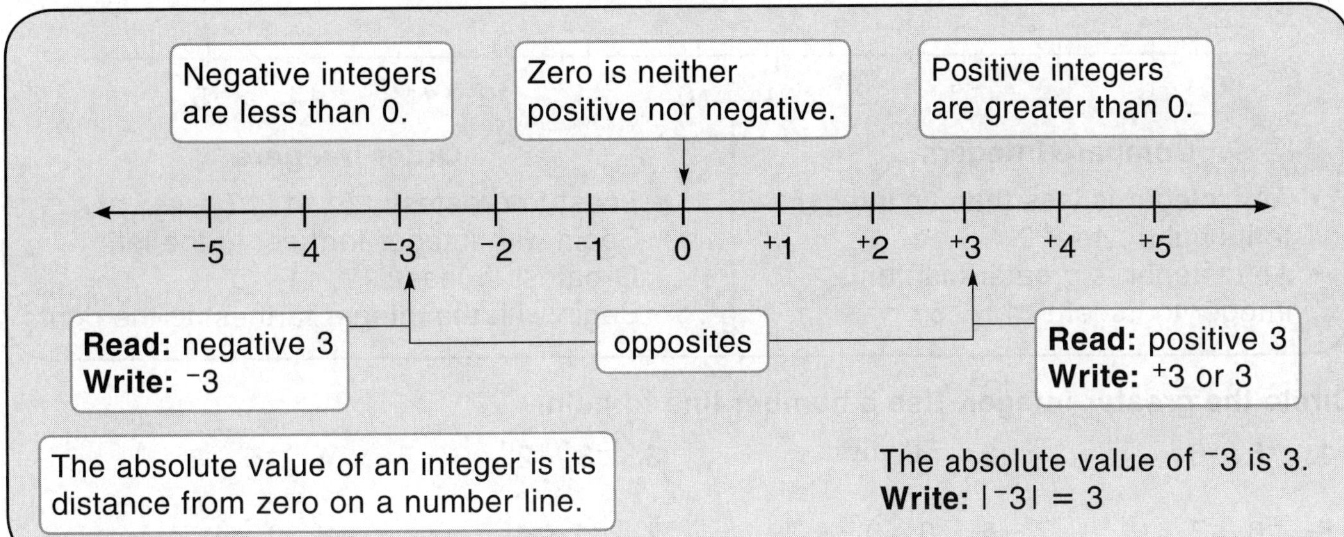

Write the opposite of each integer.

1. $^-6$ _______   **2.** $^-4$ _______   **3.** $^+5$ _______   **4.** $^-9$ _______   **5.** $^+12$ _______

6. $^-24$ _______   **7.** $^+33$ _______   **8.** $^-17$ _______   **9.** $^+99$ _______   **10.** $^-7$ _______

Identify the point that corresponds to the integer on the number line.

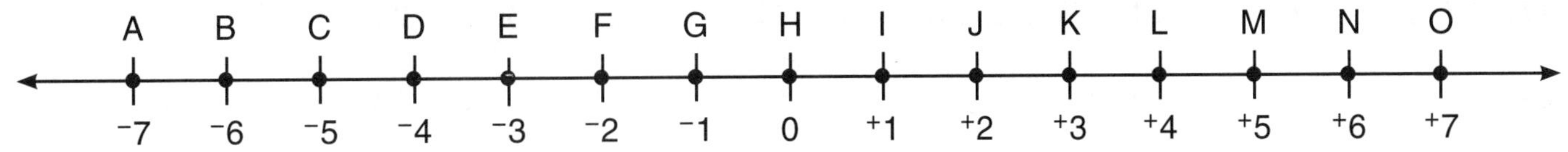

11. $^-6$ _______   **12.** $^-2$ _______   **13.** $^+2$ _______   **14.** $^+6$ _______   **15.** $^-3$ _______

16. $^-7$ _______   **17.** $^+4$ _______   **18.** 0 _______   **19.** $^+3$ _______   **20.** $^-4$ _______

Write the integer that is just before and just after each given number on a number line.

21. $^+10$ _________   **22.** $^-8$ _________   **23.** $^-1$ _________   **24.** $^+6$ _________

25. $^-5$ _________   **26.** $^+1$ _________   **27.** $^+12$ _________   **28.** $^-25$ _________

Write the integer to represent each situation. Then describe the opposite situation and write the integer to represent it.

29. 52 feet below sea level _______

30. 10° above zero _______

31. 15-yard loss _______

32. withdrawal of $18 _______

Write the absolute value of the integer.

33. $|^+32|$ _______   **34.** $|^-7|$ _______   **35.** $|^-18|$ _______   **36.** $|^+153|$ _______

C Use with Lesson 5-1, pages 150–151 in the Student Book.
C Then go to Lesson 5-1A, pages 221–222 in this Workbook.

Compare and Order Integers

Name _______________________

Date _______________________

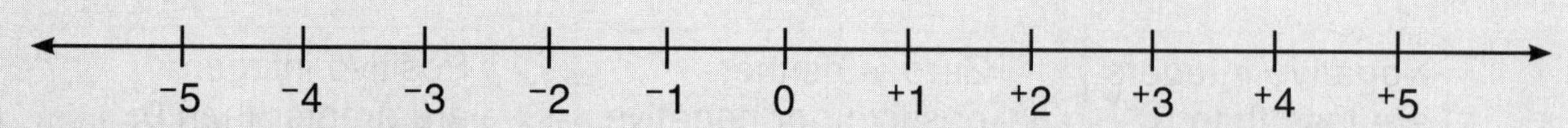

Compare integers	Order integers
• Any integer is less than an integer to its right: ⁻4 < ⁻2 • Any integer is greater than an integer to its left: ⁻1 > ⁻5	• Least to greatest: ⁻5, ⁻1, ⁺2 Begin with integer farthest to the left. • Greatest to least: ⁺2, ⁻1, ⁻5 Begin with the integer farthest to the right.

Circle the greater integer. Use a number line to help.

1. ⁺8, ⁺6   **2.** ⁻1, ⁻4   **3.** ⁻3, ⁺2   **4.** ⁺5, ⁻5

5. ⁻6, ⁻7   **6.** ⁻3, 0   **7.** ⁺1, ⁻4   **8.** 0, ⁺4

Compare. Write <, =, or >.

9. ⁺6 ____ ⁺10   **10.** ⁻6 ____ ⁻3   **11.** ⁺10 ____ ⁺10   **12.** ⁻2 ____ 0

13. ⁺5 ____ 0   **14.** ⁻7 ____ ⁺7   **15.** ⁺4 ____ ⁻4   **16.** ⁺3 ____ ⁻1

17. ⁺7 ____ ⁻4   **18.** ⁺9 ____ 0   **19.** ⁻5 ____ ⁺2   **20.** 0 ____ 0

21. ⁺2 ____ ⁺8   **22.** ⁻5 ____ ⁻1   **23.** ⁻6 ____ ⁻3   **24.** ⁺4 ____ 0

Write in order from least to greatest.

25. 0, ⁻2, ⁺4   _______________

26. ⁻4, ⁺6, ⁺5   _______________

27. ⁺10, ⁻2, ⁺6   _______________

28. ⁻1, ⁻9, ⁻8, ⁺2   _______________

29. ⁻7, 0, ⁻3, ⁺2   _______________

30. ⁺4, ⁻1, ⁻6   _______________

31. ⁻2, ⁻8, ⁻6, ⁻3   _______________

32. ⁺7, ⁺5, ⁺1, ⁺3   _______________

Write in order from greatest to least.

33. ⁻7, ⁺4, ⁻5   _______________

34. ⁻9, ⁻10, ⁻4   _______________

35. 0, ⁻6, ⁻11   _______________

36. ⁺3, ⁺5, ⁺9   _______________

37. ⁺2, ⁻5, ⁺8, ⁻1   _______________

38. ⁻3, ⁺8, 0, ⁻1   _______________

39. 0, ⁻17, ⁺2, ⁻5   _______________

40. ⁺1, ⁻8, ⁺9, ⁻6   _______________

Use with Lesson 5-2, pages 152–153 in the Student Book.
Then go to Lesson 5-2A, pages 223–224 in this Workbook.

Add Integers

Name _______________________

Date _______________________

Add with **like signs**: $^-1 + {}^-3$.	Add with **unlike signs**: $^-6 + {}^+3$.
• Add the absolute value of the addends.	• Subtract the absolute values.
$\|^-1\| + \|^-3\| = 1 + 3 = 4$	$\|^-6\| - \|^+3\| = 6 - 3 = 3$
• Use the sign of the addends for the sum.	• Use the sign of the addend with the greater absolute value for the sum.
$^-1 + {}^-3 = {}^-4$	$^-6 + {}^+3 = {}^-3$

Add. Use a number line to help.

1. $^+6 + {}^+6 =$ _______
2. $^+3 + {}^+5 =$ _______
3. $^-4 + {}^-5 =$ _______
4. $^-1 + {}^-1 =$ _______
5. $^-3 + {}^-6 =$ _______
6. $^+9 + {}^+9 =$ _______
7. $^-20 + {}^-42 =$ _______
8. $^+17 + {}^+5 =$ _______
9. $^+11 + {}^+12 =$ _______
10. $^-5 + {}^+7 =$ _______
11. $^-4 + {}^+3 =$ _______
12. $^+5 + {}^-5 =$ _______
13. $^+1 + {}^-11 =$ _______
14. $^-8 + {}^+4 =$ _______
15. $^+13 + {}^-6 =$ _______
16. $^-4 + {}^+6 =$ _______
17. $^-15 + {}^+16 =$ _______
18. $^-23 + {}^+7 =$ _______

Find the value of the variable.

19. $^+6 + x = {}^+19$ _______________
20. $^-3 + y = {}^+11$ _______________
21. $^-24 + s = {}^-16$ _______________
22. $t + {}^-7 = {}^-20$ _______________
23. $^+5 + u = {}^-1$ _______________
24. $^+10 + v = {}^+3$ _______________
25. $^-12 + j = {}^-2$ _______________
26. $^-6 + k = {}^-10$ _______________
27. $^+8 + w = {}^-4$ _______________
28. $h + {}^+4 = {}^+15$ _______________

Problem Solving

29. A submarine was 10 ft below sea level. It went down 20 more feet. Write its new depth as an integer. _______________

30. In April, Derek gained 2 pounds. In May, he lost 5 pounds. Write his total gain or loss in April and May as an integer. _______________

31. The West Town football team gained 18 yd on one play and lost 5 yd on the next play. Write the team's net gain or loss for the two plays as an integer. _______________

32. An anchor hung against the side of a boat 5 ft above sea level. A sailor lowered the anchor 22 ft. Write its depth as an integer. _______________

Use with Lesson 5-3, pages 154–155 in the Student Book.
Then go to Lesson 5-4, pages 156–157 in the Student Book.

Subtract Integers

Name ___________________________________

Date ___________________________________

Subtract: $^-6 - {}^+7$.
- Find the opposite of the subtrahend.
- Rewrite as an addition sentence. Then add.

$$^-6 - {}^+7 = n$$
$$^-6 + {}^-7 = {}^-13$$
$$n = {}^-13$$

> Subtracting an integer is the same as *adding the opposite* of that integer.

Subtract. Use a number line to help.

1. $^+10 - {}^+5 =$ _______
2. $^-4 - {}^-4 =$ _______
3. $^-9 - {}^-15 =$ _______
4. $^+7 - {}^-8 =$ _______
5. $^+7 - {}^+10 =$ _______
6. $^-10 - {}^-12 =$ _______
7. $^+12 - {}^-16 =$ _______
8. $^-13 - {}^+11 =$ _______
9. $^-5 - {}^-4 =$ _______
10. $^-5 - {}^-10 =$ _______
11. $^-6 - {}^-8 =$ _______
12. $^+6 - {}^+4 =$ _______
13. $^+7 - {}^-17 =$ _______
14. $^+4 - {}^+9 =$ _______
15. $^-8 - {}^-7 =$ _______
16. $^+5 - {}^-8 =$ _______
17. $^-9 - {}^-16 =$ _______
18. $^+10 - {}^-10 =$ _______
19. $^+17 - {}^+15 =$ _______
20. $^-6 - {}^+56 =$ _______
21. $^-1 - {}^-5 =$ _______

Find the value of the variable.

22. $^+8 - x = {}^+20$ ___________
23. $^+6 - y = {}^+16$ ___________
24. $s - {}^-2 = {}^+3$ ___________
25. $t - {}^-3 = 0$ ___________
26. $u - {}^+11 = {}^+14$ ___________
27. $^+17 - v = {}^+13$ ___________
28. $^-12 - j = {}^-2$ ___________
29. $k - {}^-16 = {}^+5$ ___________
30. $^+8 - w = {}^-4$ ___________
31. $h - {}^+4 = {}^+15$ ___________

Problem Solving

32. Dave was exploring coral 3 ft below sea level. Then he swam to an underwater cave with an entrance 15 ft below sea level. What is the difference in depth between the cave entrance and the coral? ___________

33. Death Valley is 282 feet below sea level. The Caspian Sea is 92 feet below sea level. What is the difference of the two depths written as an integer? ___________

34. Mr. Gray drilled down 6 feet looking for water. Ms. Ruiz drilled down 4 feet looking for water. How many feet farther did Mr. Gray drill? ___________

Use with Lesson 5-4, pages 156–157 in the Student Book.
Then go to Lesson 5-5, pages 158–159 in the Student Book.

Multiply Integers

Name ______________________

Date ______________________

The product of two integers is *positive* if they have *like* signs. $^+4 \times {}^+2 = {}^+8$ $^-4 \times {}^-2 = {}^+8$	The product of two integers is *negative* if they have *unlike* signs. $^-4 \times {}^+2 = {}^-8$ $^+4 \times {}^-2 = {}^-8$	The product of two integers is *zero* if one or both is *zero*. $0 \times {}^-4 = 0$ $0 \times {}^+4 = 0$ $0 \times 0 = 0$

Find the product.

1. $^-5 \times {}^+3$ ____

2. $^-6 \times 0$ ____

3. $^+11 \times {}^-3$ ____

4. $^-8 \times {}^-5$ ____

5. $^-5 \times {}^+5$ ____

6. $^+3 \times {}^+3$ ____

7. $^-5 \times {}^-5$ ____

8. $0 \times {}^+2$ ____

9. $^-8 \times {}^-3$ ____

10. $^+9 \times {}^+3$ ____

11. $^-3 \times {}^+5$ ____

12. $^+10 \times {}^+3$ ____

13. $^-16 \times {}^+9$ ____

14. $^+12 \times {}^-18$ ____

15. $^+5 \times {}^+24$ ____

16. $^-13 \times {}^-14$ ____

17. $^+11 \times {}^-12$ ____

18. $^-36 \times 0$ ____

19. $^-12 \times {}^-12$ ____

20. $0 \times {}^+48$ ____

What is the sign of the underlined factor for the given product?
Write $^-$ or $^+$.

21. $^-2 \times \underline{5} = {}^-10$ ____

22. $^+9 \times \underline{8} = {}^+72$ ____

23. $^+8 \times \underline{11} = {}^-88$ ____

24. $\underline{6} \times {}^+5 = {}^-30$ ____

25. $\underline{8} \times {}^-8 = {}^+64$ ____

26. $\underline{3} \times {}^-7 = {}^-21$ ____

27. $^+13 \times \underline{11} = {}^+143$ ____

28. $\underline{12} \times {}^-15 = {}^-180$ ____

29. $^+8 \times \underline{27} = {}^-216$ ____

30. $\underline{16} \times {}^-16 = {}^-256$ ____

31. $^-7 \times \underline{23} = {}^-161$ ____

32. $\underline{18} \times {}^+26 = {}^-468$ ____

Problem Solving

33. Write a number sentence with integers that shows how to get the result of each transaction in the table.

Transaction	Sentence	Result
3 deposits of $75		$^+\$225$
2 withdrawals of $35		$^-\$70$

34. A computer stock drops 2 points each day for ten days. What is the change over the ten days, written as an integer?

____

35. A tank was pumping out gasoline at a rate of 35 gallons an hour. What was the output of gas over an eight-hour period, written as an integer?

____

Divide Integers

Name _________________________

Date _________________________

The quotient of two integers is *positive* if the integers have *like* signs.	The quotient of two integers is *negative* if the integers have *unlike* signs.	The quotient of two integers is *zero* if the dividend is *zero*.
$^+18 \div {}^+9 = {}^+2$ $^-18 \div {}^-9 = {}^+2$	$^-14 \div {}^+2 = {}^-7$ $^+14 \div {}^-2 = {}^-7$	$0 \div {}^+8 = 0$ $0 \div {}^-8 = 0$ $0 \div 0$ is impossible.

Find each quotient.

1. $^+24 \div {}^-8$ _______
2. $^-20 \div {}^-2$ _______
3. $^+36 \div {}^-9$ _______
4. $^-32 \div {}^-4$ _______

5. $^-48 \div {}^+6$ _______
6. $0 \div {}^-1$ _______
7. $^+10 \div {}^-2$ _______
8. $^+99 \div 0$ _______

9. $\dfrac{^-16}{^-4}$ _______
10. $\dfrac{^+72}{^-9}$ _______
11. $\dfrac{0}{^-10}$ _______
12. $\dfrac{^-50}{^-5}$ _______

13. $\dfrac{^-64}{^+8}$ _______
14. $\dfrac{^-54}{^-9}$ _______
15. $\dfrac{^-1}{0}$ _______
16. $\dfrac{^-85}{^+5}$ _______

Divide to complete each chart. Then write the rule.

17.

IN	OUT
$^+12$	$^+4$
$^+36$	$^+12$
$^+18$	$^+6$
$^-21$	
$^-30$	
	$^-11$

Rule: IN $\div$ __ = OUT

18.

IN	OUT
$^-30$	$^+6$
$^-45$	$^+9$
$^-40$	$^+8$
$^+20$	
$^+25$	
	$^+15$

Rule: IN $\div$ __ = OUT

Compare. Write <, =, or >.

19. $^-8 \div {}^-4$ _______ $^-24 \div {}^+3$

20. $^+21 \div {}^-3$ _______ $^+20 \div {}^+4$

21. $^-12 \div {}^+3$ _______ $^-18 \div {}^+3$

22. $^+30 \div {}^-6$ _______ $^+40 \div {}^-5$

23. $^-45 \div {}^-5$ _______ $^-50 \div {}^+10$

24. $^-64 \div {}^+4$ _______ $^-32 \div {}^+2$

Problem Solving

25. A stock dropped 32 points in 8 days. If the stock dropped at the same rate each day, what is the rate per day?

____

26. A diver is at a depth of 350 meters. If she ascends at a rate of 5 meters per minute, how long will it take her to reach the surface?

____

52

Use with Lesson 5-6, pages 160–161 in the Student Book. Then go to Lesson 5-7, pages 162–163 in the Student Book.

Integers and Order of Operations

Evaluate the expression: $^+75 + {}^-84 \div {}^+3 + (^-8)^2$.

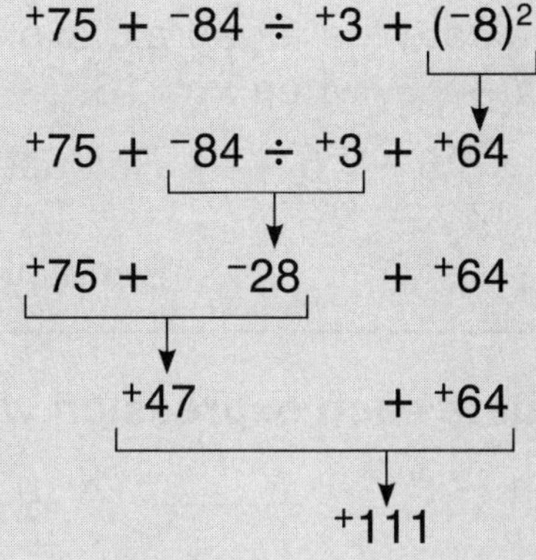

Order of Operations
1. Grouping symbols
2. Exponents
3. Multiply or divide from left to right.
4. Add or subtract from left to right.

Name the first step to simplify. Then evaluate the expression.

1. $^+56 + {}^-90 \times {}^+2 - {}^-17$ ________

2. $(^-21 + {}^+7)^2 \times {}^+12 \div {}^-6$ ________

3. $^+8 \times {}^-6^3 - {}^-100 \div {}^-20$ ________

4. $^-3 \times {}^+71 + {}^+95 \div {}^-5 + {}^+315$ ________

5. $^-37 - {}^-21 + {}^+39 \div {}^+13 \times {}^-23$ ________

6. $^+4 \times (^-56 - {}^-53)^2 + {}^+32 \times {}^-9$ ________

Compute. Watch the order of operations.

7. $^+78 \div {}^-3 + {}^+7^2 - {}^-9$ ________

8. $^-5 \times (^+4 + {}^-35) + (^-2)^5$ ________

9. $^+14 \times (^-3)^4 + {}^-75 \div {}^+5$ ________

10. $^+73 + {}^-59 - {}^-151 + {}^+211 \times {}^+2$ ________

11. $^-878 + (^+4 + {}^+7)^2 - {}^-95$ ________

12. $^+83 - {}^-95 \times {}^+7 + {}^+72 \div {}^-9$ ________

13. $^+5^3 + {}^-30 \div {}^+3 - {}^+99$ ________

14. $^+44 \div {}^-11 + (^+9 - {}^-5) \times {}^+15$ ________

Problem Solving Write an expression to solve each. Then compute.

15. Bill raises a flag 15 feet above the ground. Then he lowers it 8 feet and raises it another 2 feet. How far above the ground is the flag now?

____

16. A sea turtle descends 28 feet from the surface of the ocean and then ascends 5 feet. Then it descends 9 feet and repeats this descent 4 times. How many feet below the surface is the turtle then?

____

Expressions and Equations with Integers

Name _______________________

Date _______________________

Evaluate the algebraic expression: $^{+}7x - {}^{-}5$, when $x = {}^{+}6$.

$^{+}7 \times {}^{+}6 - {}^{-}5$ ⟵ Replace x with $^{+}6$.

$\quad ^{+}42 - {}^{-}5$

$\qquad ^{+}47$ ⟵ Simplify.

Solve the equation: $y \div {}^{-}12 = {}^{+}72$.

$y \div {}^{-}12 \times {}^{-}12 = {}^{+}72 \times {}^{-}12$ ⟵ Isolate the variable.

$\qquad y = {}^{-}864$ ⟵ Simplify.

Evaluate each expression when $a = {}^{+}9$, $b = {}^{-}6$, $c = {}^{-}8$, and $d = {}^{+}3$.

1. $a - d$ _______
2. $b \div d$ _______
3. $a + b - c$ _______
4. $a \cdot b - c$ _______

5. $a \cdot b \div d$ _______
6. $b + c \cdot d$ _______
7. $cd - ab$ _______
8. $bc(a + d)$ _______

Solve each equation. Use the replacement set $\{^{+}9, {}^{-}9, {}^{+}4, {}^{-}4\}$.

9. $n + {}^{+}20 = {}^{+}11$ _______
10. $n + {}^{+}20 = {}^{+}24$ _______
11. $^{+}4n = {}^{-}36$ _______

12. $\dfrac{^{-}16}{n} = {}^{+}4$ _______
13. $^{+}7 + n \cdot {}^{-}6 = {}^{+}31$ _______
14. $^{-}5n \div {}^{-}10 = {}^{+}2$ _______

Solve and check.

15. $k + {}^{-}9 = {}^{-}15$ _______
16. $c - {}^{+}12 = {}^{-}6$ _______
17. $^{+}14r = {}^{-}98$ _______

18. $\dfrac{^{+}189}{g} = {}^{-}21$ _______
19. $^{+}13 = \dfrac{^{-}65}{a}$ _______
20. $^{-}26m = {}^{-}546$ _______

Write and solve an equation for the variable used.

21. A number u divided by 6 equals $^{-}38$.

____

22. The product of a number w and $^{-}16$ is $^{+}128$.

____

23. A number y increased by 37 is $^{-}8$.

____

24. $^{-}11$ less than a number q is $^{+}29$.

____

Problem Solving

25. The temperature yesterday afternoon was $^{-}6°C$. It fell 14 degrees by midnight. What was the temperature then?

____

26. The water level in a bucket decreased by 62 cm in March. What was the average amount the water level decreased each day?

____

Use with Lesson 5-8, pages 164–165 in the Student Book.
Then go to Lesson 5-9, pages 166–167 in the Student Book.

Temperature

Name _______________________

Date _______________________

| The temperature was ⁻6°C. It rose 23 degrees. What was the new temperature? $^-6 + {}^+23 = n$ $\qquad {}^+17 = n$ The new temperature was 17°C. | The temperature was 5°F. It dropped to ⁻10°F. How many degrees did the temperature drop? $^-10 - {}^+5 = x$ $^-10 + {}^-5 = x$ $\qquad ^-15 = x$ The temperature dropped 15°F. | You can use formulas to **estimate** °C as °F and °F as °C. $°C \approx (°F - 30) \div 2$ $°F \approx 2°C + 30$ |

Compute the new temperature.

1. 23°C; falls 5° _____

2. 14°C; rises 8° _____

3. ⁻10°F; rises 6° _____

4. 0°F; drops 15° _____

5. ⁻13°C; falls 5° _____

6. ⁻7°C; climbs 12° _____

7. ⁻40°C; climbs 14° _____

8. ⁻18°C; rises 15° _____

9. 25°F; drops 29° _____

10. ⁻23°F; rises 12° _____

11. 16°C; falls 20° _____

12. ⁻5°F; climbs 7° _____

Estimate the temperature in °C or °F.
Watch for the degree unit.

13. 60°C _______

14. ⁻4°C _______

15. 18°F _______

16. ⁻12°F _______

17. ⁻20°F _______

18. 10°C _______

19. 70°F _______

20. 30°C _______

21. 78°F _______

22. ⁻20°C _______

23. ⁻40°F _______

24. ⁻15°C _______

Problem Solving

25. At 8:00 A.M. the temperature was 6°C. At noon it was ⁻12°C. How many degrees did the temperature drop? _______________________

26. What is the difference between normal body temperature, 37°C, and a cold winter day, ⁻10°C? _______________________

27. At 6:00 A.M. the temperature was ⁻18°F. By noon it was 25°F. How many degrees did the temperature rise? _______________________

28. The temperature was ⁻22°F. About how many degrees Celsius was it? _______________________

Problem-Solving Strategy: Make a Table

Name _______________________

Date _______________________

> Anthony is making rose-and-iris bouquets. He is using 3 roses for every 4 irises. How many roses will be in a bouquet of 42 flowers?
>
> - Make a table.
> - Add to find the number of roses in a 42-flower bouquet.
>
> | Irises | 4 | 8 | 12 | 16 | 20 | 24 |
> |---|---|---|---|---|---|---|
> | Roses | 3 | 6 | 9 | 12 | 15 | 18 |
> | Total Flowers | 7 | 14 | 21 | 28 | 35 | 42 |
>
> A bouquet of 42 flowers will have 18 roses.

Solve. Do your work on a separate sheet of paper.

1. Luanne inspected light bulbs. She found 3 out of every 95 light bulbs to be defective. How many defective light bulbs could she expect to find out of 760 light bulbs?

2. Theo recorded the temperature at 6:00 A.M. It was ⁻8°F. What would be the temperature at noon if it rose 7° every hour?

3. Steve conducted a survey and found that 48 out of 192 people bought Power Peanut Butter. How many people out of 1536 would you expect to buy Power Peanut Butter?

4. Tim is mixing blue and white paint to make a pale blue paint. He uses 2 quarts of blue for every 3 quarts of white paint. How many quarts of each color will he need to get 35 quarts of pale blue paint?

5. Every week Rochelle saves $12 in an envelope. Every other week she takes out $5 to spend on entertainment. How many weeks will it take her to have $76 in the envelope?

6. Sue Ellen is making a design using squares and circles. She uses 3 squares for every 5 circles. How many shapes in all will she use for her design if she uses 45 circles?

7. Mary had $150 in her savings account. She decided to add to it each week. The first week she added $5. For each week after that she added $3 more than the preceding week. How many weeks did it take her to save $335?

8. A recipe for one loaf of blueberry bread calls for 3 cups of flour, 2 cups of blueberries, and $\frac{1}{4}$ cup molasses. How much of each ingredient is needed for 10 loaves of blueberry bread?

Use with Lesson 5-10, pages 168–169 in the Student Book.
Then go to Lesson 5-11, pages 170–171 in the Student Book.

Problem-Solving Applications: Mixed Review

Name _______________

Date _______________

Solve each problem and explain the method you used. If needed, do all your work on a separate sheet of paper.

Read ▶ Plan ▶ Solve ▶ Check

1. The temperature at 8:00 P.M. was 88°F. It dropped 5°F every 2 hours until 6:00 A.M., and then rose 3°F every 2 hours until noon. What was the temperature then?

2. Owen quadrupled a number and added ⁻32 to it. His answer was ⁺36. What was his number?

3. A jeweler has 126 rings. Each display holds 12 rings. How many displays does the jeweler need?

4. A goose started on the ground and rose 22 feet in the air. The goose descended 6 feet and then rose another 9 feet. What was the goose's altitude after the last 9-foot ascent?

5. Ms. Siegel spent $99.65 on books. Paperbacks cost $7.95 each and hard covers cost $18.95 each. If Ms. Siegel bought 4 hard covers, how many paperbacks did she buy?

Use the table for problems 6–9.

6. What was the difference between Monday's low temperature and Sunday's low temperature?

7. How much did the temperature drop from Friday's high temperature to its low temperature?

High and Low Temperatures Last Week		
Day	**High**	**Low**
Monday	13°F	9°F
Tuesday	18°F	7°F
Wednesday	15°F	10°F
Thursday	9°F	0°F
Friday	5°F	⁻2°F
Saturday	⁻1°F	?
Sunday	⁻5°F	⁻12°F

8. Saturday's low temperature was 8° lower than the high temperature. What was Saturday's low temperature?

9. Write a problem that uses the data in the table. Have someone solve it.

Divisibility

You can use the divisibility rules to help you determine if one number is divisible by another number.

A number is **divisible** by another number if there is no remainder when you divide.

Divisibility Rules	
A number is divisible by:	**if . . .**
2	it is an even number (ends in 0, 2, 4, 6, or 8)
3	the sum of its digits is divisible by 3
4	the last two digits form a number divisible by 4
5	the ones digit is 0 or 5
6	it is divisible by both 2 and 3
8	the last three digits form a number divisible by 8
9	the sum of its digits is divisible by 9
10	the last digit is 0

Tell whether the number is divisible by 2, 3, 4, 5, 6, 8, 9, and/or 10.

1. 198

2. 524

3. 486

4. 345

5. 3273

6. 7055

7. 5840

8. 3102

9. 334,366

10. 825,723

11. 629,288

12. 928,480

Find the missing digit or digits that would make each number divisible by the given number.

13. 325☐ ; by 10

14. 29☐9; by 9

15. 647☐ ; by 4

16. 517,13☐ ; by 5

17. 17☐,684; by 3

18. 799,8☐8; by 8

19. 896,87☐ ; by 6

20. 699,19☐ ; by 2 and 4

21. ☐48,611; by 3

Problem Solving

22. Dr. Davis wants to divide 8487 tongue depressors evenly among some containers. She has 10 containers, but does not need to use them all. How many containers could she use so there are no tongue depressors left over?

23. Mr. Russo has 2856 raffle tickets that he will distribute evenly to some of his neighbors. He wants to give the tickets to at least 3 but no more than 10 neighbors. To how many neighbors can he give raffle tickets so there are none left over? How many tickets will each neighbor get?

Use with Lesson 6-1, pages 178–179 in the Student Book.
Then go to Lesson 6-2, pages 180–181 in the Student Book.

Prime and Composite Numbers

Name _______________

Date _______________

> | A **prime number** is a whole number greater than 1 that has exactly two factors, itself and 1. | A **composite number** is a whole number greater than 1 that has more than two factors. |
> |---|---|
> | $1 \times 7 = 7$ Factors of 7: 1, 7

 7 is a prime number. | $1 \times 6 = 6$
 $2 \times 3 = 6$ Factors of 6: 1, 2, 3, 6

 6 is a composite number. |

Write whether each is *prime*, *composite*, or *neither*.

1. 6 _______________   2. 11 _______________   3. 15 _______________

4. 5 _______________   5. 38 _______________   6. 79 _______________

7. 1 _______________   8. 24 _______________   9. 56 _______________

10. 23 _______________   11. 2 _______________   12. 16 _______________

13. 90 _______________   14. 0 _______________   15. 3 _______________

Write *true* or *false* for each statement. Give an example to justify your answer.

16. The greatest prime number between 1 and 100 is 99. _______________

17. All even numbers are composite numbers. _______________

18. No prime numbers are odd numbers. _______________

19. The least prime number is 2. _______________

20. The numbers 23, 31, 37, and 41 are all prime numbers. _______________

21. There are no composite numbers between 70 and 80. _______________

Use the numbers in the box. Identify the numbers that . . .

22. have exactly four factors. _______________

23. have more than four factors. _______________

24. are prime numbers. _______________

25. have both 2 and 4 as factors. _______________

26. have both 1 and 3 as factors. _______________

8	10	12	13	15
17	18	19	20	21
24	26	29	30	

Use with Lesson 6-2, pages 180–181 in the Student Book.
Then go to Lesson 6-3, pages 182–183 in the Student Book.

Prime Factorization

Name ___________________________

Date ___________________________

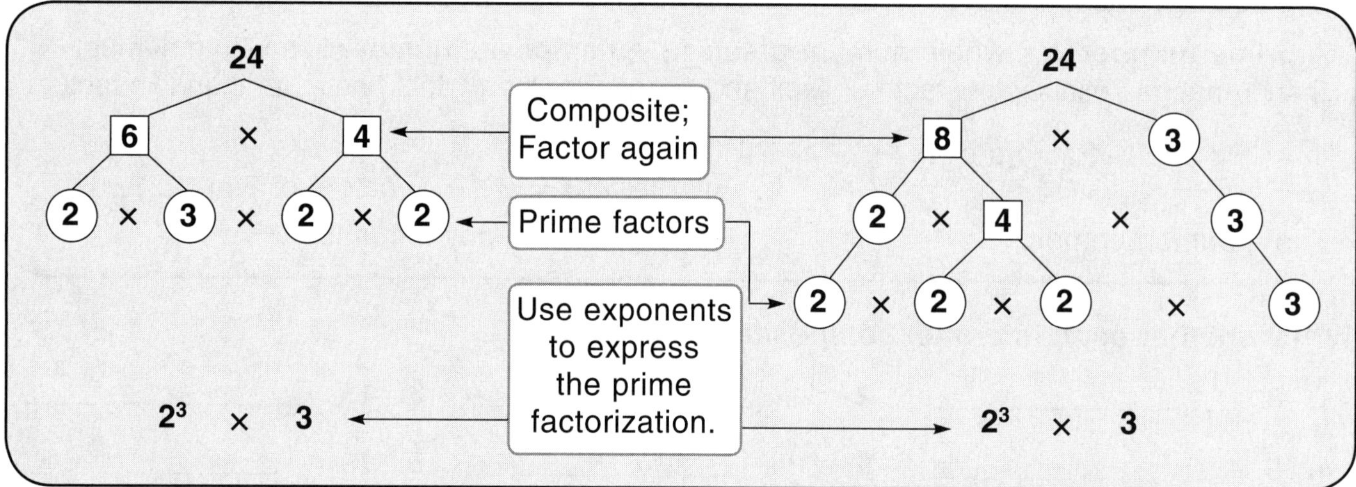

Express each in exponential form. Then find the product.

1. $7 \times 2 \times 7$

2. $3 \times 3 \times 3 \times 5 \times 5$

3. $5 \times 2 \times 5 \times 2$

____

Find the prime factorization and write in exponential form.

4. 98

5. 81

6. 75

7. 54

8. 90

9. 84

10. 32

11. 63

Find the prime factorization. Use the divisibility rules and a factor tree to help.

12. 56

13. 279

14. 560

15. 225

16. 490

17. 728

18. 405

19. 1665

Solve for y to complete the prime factorization.

20. $2 \times y \times 7 = 42$

21. $11y = 55$

22. $40 = 2^3 \times y$

23. $2^3 \times y = 56$

24. $90 = y \times 3^2 \times 5$

25. $2^2 \times 3^2 \times y = 396$

Use with Lesson 6-3, pages 182–183 in the Student Book.
Then go to Lesson 6-4, pages 184–185 in the Student Book.

Equivalent Fractions

Name _______________________

Date _______________________

Equivalent fractions name the same part of a whole or set.
To find equivalent fractions, multiply or divide the fraction
by a fraction equal to 1.

$$\frac{7}{8} = \frac{7 \times 4}{8 \times 4} = \frac{28}{32} \qquad\qquad \frac{9}{45} = \frac{9 \div 9}{45 \div 9} = \frac{1}{5}$$

$$\frac{7}{8} = \frac{28}{32} \leftarrow \text{equivalent fractions} \qquad\qquad \frac{9}{45} = \frac{1}{5} \leftarrow \text{equivalent fractions}$$

**Which two figures show equivalent fractions?
Explain your answer.**

1. ___________ **a.** 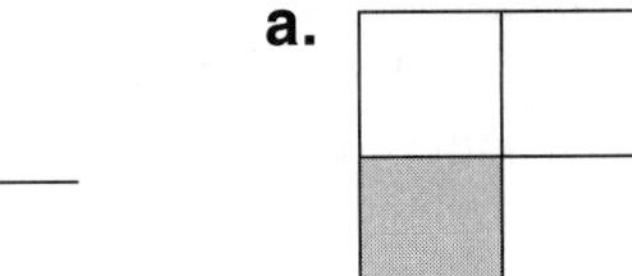 **b.** 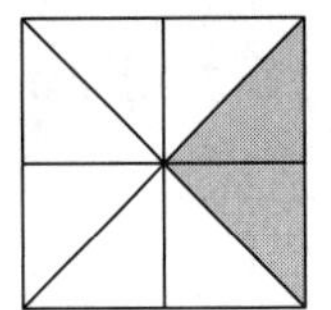 **c.** 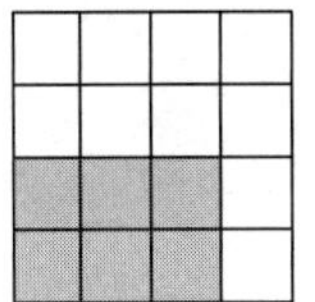 **d.** 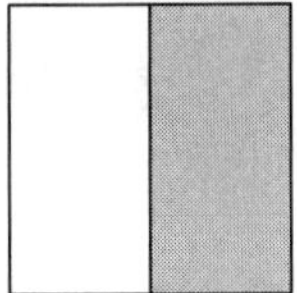

Write the missing term to complete the equivalent fraction.

2. $\dfrac{3}{5} = \dfrac{12}{}$ **3.** $\dfrac{7}{12} = \dfrac{21}{}$ **4.** $\dfrac{1}{6} = \dfrac{}{18}$ **5.** $\dfrac{5}{11} = \dfrac{35}{}$ **6.** $\dfrac{3}{10} = \dfrac{33}{}$

7. $\dfrac{24}{56} = \dfrac{}{7}$ **8.** $\dfrac{3}{8} = \dfrac{}{40}$ **9.** $\dfrac{3}{33} = \dfrac{1}{}$ **10.** $\dfrac{9}{} = \dfrac{1}{3}$ **11.** $\dfrac{13}{26} = \dfrac{1}{}$

Write two equivalent fractions for each fraction.

12. $\dfrac{4}{9}$ ______ **13.** $\dfrac{5}{50}$ ______ **14.** $\dfrac{5}{8}$ ______ **15.** $\dfrac{12}{16}$ ______ **16.** $\dfrac{8}{11}$ ______

17. $\dfrac{8}{12}$ ______ **18.** $\dfrac{7}{9}$ ______ **19.** $\dfrac{1}{14}$ ______ **20.** $\dfrac{3}{5}$ ______ **21.** $\dfrac{5}{9}$ ______

Complete the equivalent fractions.

22. $\dfrac{1}{2} = \dfrac{}{4} = \dfrac{}{8}$ **23.** $\dfrac{2}{3} = \dfrac{}{6} = \dfrac{8}{}$ **24.** $\dfrac{2}{5} = \dfrac{}{15} = \dfrac{18}{}$

25. $\dfrac{1}{3} = \dfrac{3}{} = \dfrac{}{27}$ **26.** $\dfrac{4}{7} = \dfrac{8}{} = \dfrac{16}{}$ **27.** $\dfrac{5}{6} = \dfrac{}{12} = \dfrac{20}{}$

28. $\dfrac{20}{24} = \dfrac{}{12} = \dfrac{}{6}$ **29.** $\dfrac{18}{27} = \dfrac{6}{} = \dfrac{}{3}$ **30.** $\dfrac{32}{64} = \dfrac{}{16} = \dfrac{2}{}$

Use with Lesson 6-4, pages 184–185 in the Student Book.
Then go to Lesson 6-5, pages 186–187 in the Student Book.

Greatest Common Factor

Name _______________________

Date _______________________

Find the greatest common factor (GCF) of 6, 9, and 12.
List the factors of each number.

6: **1**, 2, **3**, 6
9: **1**, **3**, 9
12: **1**, 2, **3**, 4, 6, 12

Common Factors: 1 and 3
Greatest Common Factor: 3

The greatest common factor can also be referred to as the greatest common divisor (GCD).

Write all the common factors for each set of numbers.

1. 10 and 45

2. 12 and 32

3. 24 and 36

4. 9 and 54

5. 15 and 75

6. 60 and 24

7. 4, 8, and 16

8. 7, 13, and 23

9. 8, 20, and 34

Find the GCF (or GCD) for each set of numbers.

10. 8 and 16

11. 6 and 10

12. 12 and 20

13. 14 and 42

14. 7 and 35

15. 9 and 15

16. 5 and 30

17. 8 and 25

18. 7, 28, and 35

19. 4, 12, and 24

20. 13, 26, and 65

21. 18, 51, and 81

Find the GCF (or GCD). Use prime factorization.

22. 36 and 60

23. 40 and 65

24. 28 and 63

25. 70 and 105

26. 26 and 91

27. 33 and 75

28. 56 and 84

29. 81 and 99

30. 15, 45, and 60

31. 34, 85, and 102

32. 16, 64, and 96

33. 56, 64, and 104

Find the pairs of numbers:

34. between 8 and 18 that have 5 as their GCF. _______________

35. between 15 and 30 that have 7 as their GCF. _______________

Ⓒ Use with Lesson 6-5, pages 186–187 in the Student Book.
Ⓒ Then go to Lesson 6-5A, pages 225–226 in this Workbook.

Fractions in Simplest Form

Name _______________________

Date _______________________

Rename $\frac{21}{56}$ in simplest form, or lowest terms.

Find the GCF of the numerator and the denominator.	Divide the numerator and the denominator by their GCF.

21: 1, 3, **7**, 21
56: 1, 2, 4, **7**, 8, 14, 28, 56

$$\frac{21}{56} = \frac{21 \div 7}{56 \div 7} = \frac{3}{8}$$

The simplest form of $\frac{21}{56}$ is $\frac{3}{8}$.

Circle the letter of the GCF of the numerator and the denominator of each fraction.

1. $\frac{9}{12}$ **a.** 6   **b.** 3   **c.** 2   **d.** 9

2. $\frac{4}{8}$ **a.** 1   **b.** 2   **c.** 0   **d.** 4

3. $\frac{16}{40}$ **a.** 2   **b.** 4   **c.** 8   **d.** 16

Is the fraction in lowest terms? Write *yes* or *no*. If *no*, rename the fraction in simplest form.

4. $\frac{3}{8}$ _______   5. $\frac{4}{10}$ _______   6. $\frac{5}{16}$ _______   7. $\frac{2}{4}$ _______

8. $\frac{12}{27}$ _______   9. $\frac{5}{12}$ _______   10. $\frac{8}{32}$ _______   11. $\frac{11}{33}$ _______

Rename each as a fraction in simplest form.

12. $\frac{10}{15}$ 13. $\frac{21}{28}$ 14. $\frac{35}{40}$ 15. $\frac{18}{81}$

_______   _______   _______   _______

16. $\frac{15}{18}$ 17. $\frac{28}{56}$ 18. $\frac{9}{30}$ 19. $\frac{8}{88}$

_______   _______   _______   _______

20. $\frac{15}{25}$ 21. $\frac{14}{63}$ 22. $\frac{10}{16}$ 23. $\frac{32}{40}$

_______   _______   _______   _______

Problem Solving

Write the answer as a fraction in simplest form.

24. The movie theater sold 28 matinee tickets and 56 tickets to the evening show. What fractional part of the tickets sold were for the matinee?

____

Use with Lesson 6-6, pages 188–189 in the Student Book.
Then go to Lesson 6-7, pages 190–191 in the Student Book.

Mixed Numbers and Improper Fractions

Name _______________________

Date _______________________

Rename $2\frac{1}{4}$ as an improper fraction.

$$2\frac{1}{4} = \frac{(4 \times 2) + 1}{4} = \frac{9}{4}$$

Rename $\frac{30}{8}$ as a mixed number.

$$\frac{30}{8} = 8\overline{)30} \quad 3\text{ R6}$$

$$\frac{30}{8} = 3\frac{6}{8}$$

$$= 3\frac{3}{4}$$

Write the word name for each mixed number.

1. $4\frac{2}{3}$ _______________________

2. $1\frac{1}{2}$ _______________________

3. $38\frac{5}{12}$ _______________________

4. $16\frac{7}{10}$ _______________________

Write as a mixed number.

5. two and four fifths __________

6. six and nine tenths __________

7. three and nine twentieths __________

8. eleven and eight fifteenths __________

Express each as an improper fraction.

9. $1\frac{5}{8}$ __________   10. $2\frac{5}{6}$ __________   11. $3\frac{1}{2}$ __________   12. $5\frac{1}{3}$ __________

13. $7\frac{3}{4}$ __________   14. $1\frac{5}{7}$ __________   15. $10\frac{1}{8}$ __________   16. $2\frac{2}{5}$ __________

17. $3\frac{1}{6}$ __________   18. $9\frac{3}{10}$ __________   19. $4\frac{3}{4}$ __________   20. $11\frac{7}{8}$ __________

21. $1\frac{2}{9}$ __________   22. $10\frac{3}{4}$ __________   23. $8\frac{3}{5}$ __________   24. $3\frac{5}{12}$ __________

Express each as a whole number or a mixed number in simplest form.

25. $\frac{7}{4}$ __________   26. $\frac{9}{8}$ __________   27. $\frac{12}{6}$ __________   28. $\frac{25}{10}$ __________

29. $\frac{26}{5}$ __________   30. $\frac{84}{7}$ __________   31. $\frac{9}{2}$ __________   32. $\frac{4}{3}$ __________

33. $\frac{7}{2}$ __________   34. $\frac{48}{5}$ __________   35. $\frac{32}{9}$ __________   36. $\frac{64}{10}$ __________

37. $\frac{22}{4}$ __________   38. $\frac{66}{8}$ __________   39. $\frac{39}{3}$ __________   40. $\frac{72}{10}$ __________

Use with Lesson 6-7, pages 190–191 in the Student Book.
Then go to Lesson 6-8, pages 192–193 in the Student Book.

Fraction Sense

Name _______________________

Date _______________________

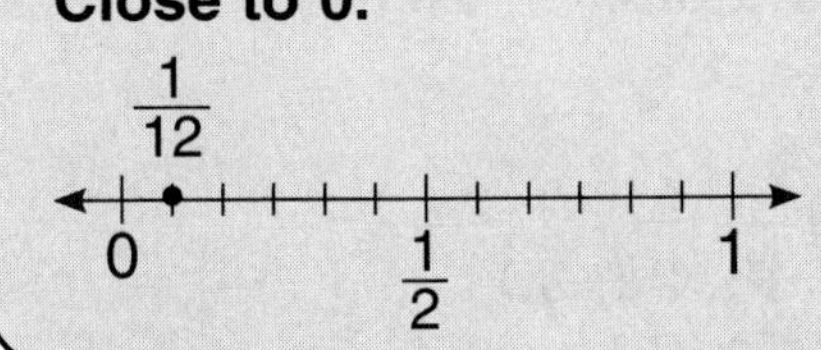

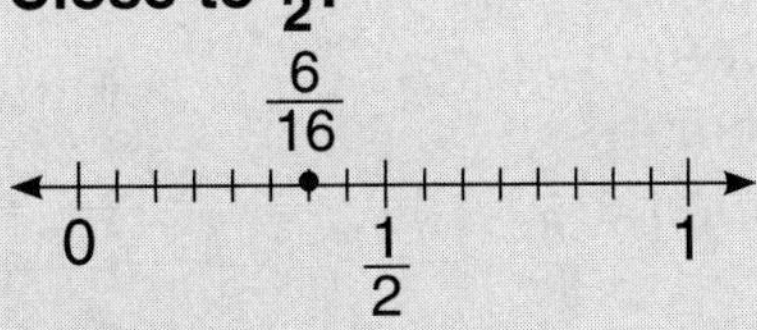

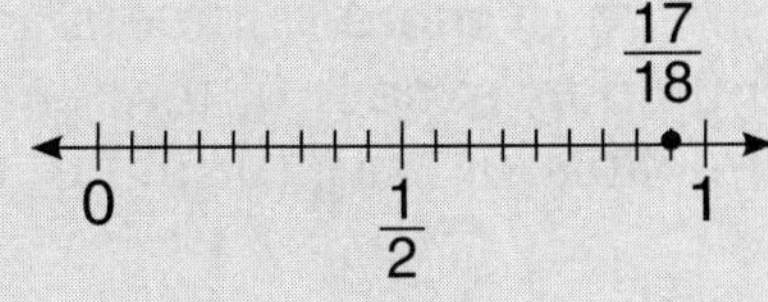

Write the fraction that names each point.
Tell whether the fraction is close to 0, $\frac{1}{2}$, or 1.

1.
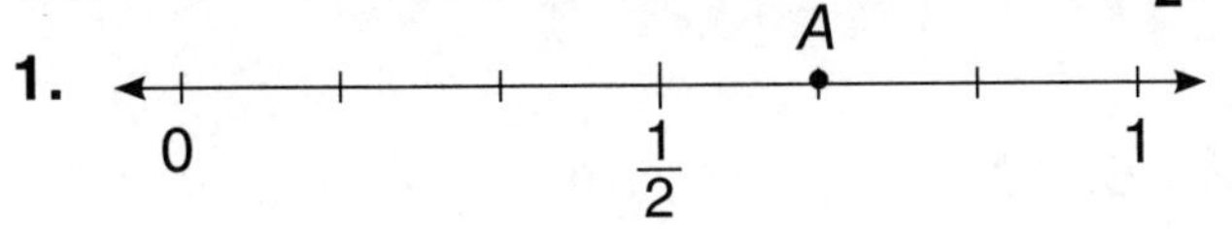

____

2.
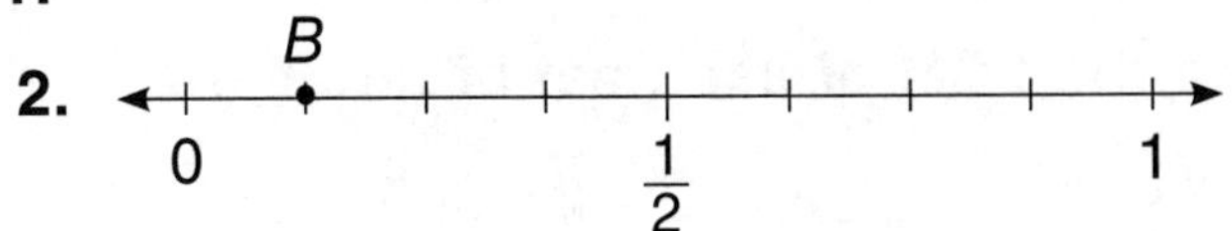

____

3.
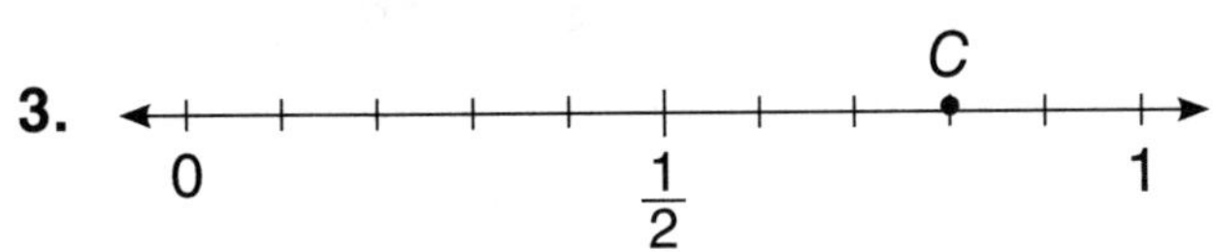

____

4.
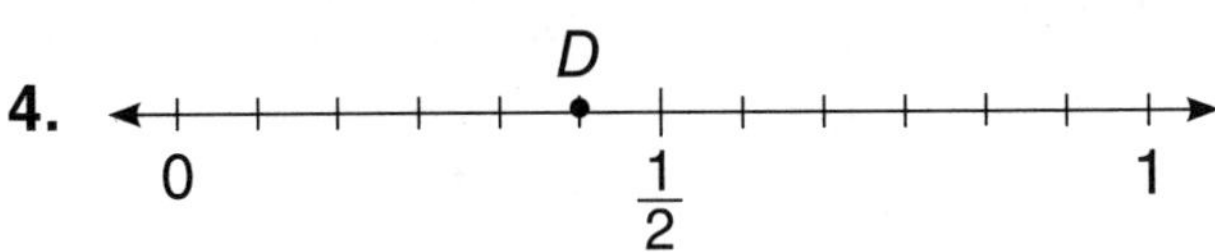

____

5.
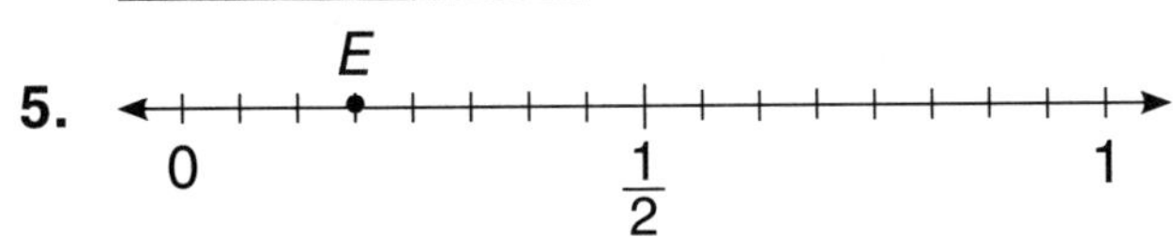

____

6.
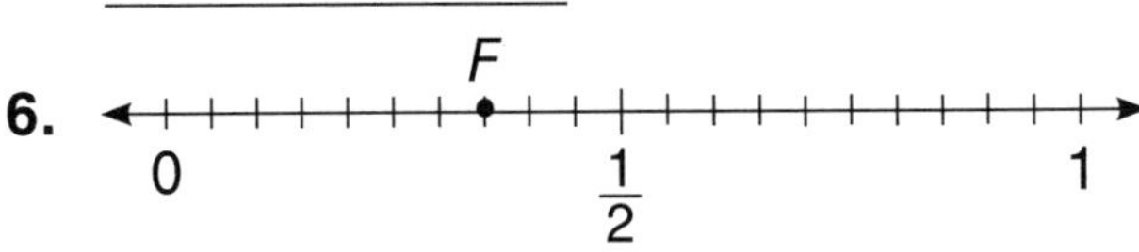

____

Tell whether the fraction is close to 0, $\frac{1}{2}$, or 1.

7. $\frac{1}{5}$ _____   **8.** $\frac{9}{14}$ _____   **9.** $\frac{8}{11}$ _____   **10.** $\frac{12}{28}$ _____   **11.** $\frac{10}{12}$ _____

12. $\frac{7}{16}$ _____   **13.** $\frac{12}{30}$ _____   **14.** $\frac{4}{9}$ _____   **15.** $\frac{30}{40}$ _____   **16.** $\frac{22}{66}$ _____

17. $\frac{60}{72}$ _____   **18.** $\frac{9}{24}$ _____   **19.** $\frac{55}{100}$ _____   **20.** $\frac{8}{80}$ _____   **21.** $\frac{90}{100}$ _____

Complete. For each exercise write a fraction that is close to 0,
a fraction that is close to $\frac{1}{2}$, and a fraction that is close to 1.

22. $\frac{a}{16}$ _____ _____ _____   **23.** $\frac{25}{b}$ _____ _____ _____   **24.** $\frac{c}{19}$ _____ _____ _____

25. $\frac{d}{24}$ _____ _____ _____   **26.** $\frac{e}{11}$ _____ _____ _____   **27.** $\frac{3}{f}$ _____ _____ _____

28. $\frac{8}{g}$ _____ _____ _____   **29.** $\frac{h}{28}$ _____ _____ _____   **30.** $\frac{5}{j}$ _____ _____ _____

Is the fraction a little more than $\frac{1}{2}$? Write *yes* or *no*. Explain.

31. $\frac{12}{28}$ _______________________

C Use with Lesson 6-8, pages 192–193 in the Student Book.
C Then go to Lesson 6-9, pages 194–195 in the Student Book.

Least Common Multiple

Name _______________________

Date _______________________

> The **least common multiple (LCM)** of two or more numbers is the least number, except 0, that is a common multiple of both (or all) of the numbers.
>
> What is the LCM of 4, 6, and 8?
>
> **Multiples**
>
> 4: 4, 8, 12, 16, 20, **24** . . .
> 6: 6, 12, 18, **24**, 30 . . .
> 8: 8, 16, **24**, 32 . . .
>
> **Least Common Multiple (LCM): 24**

Find the LCM of each set of numbers.

1. 4, 7 _______   **2.** 3, 5 _______   **3.** 6, 12 _______   **4.** 5, 7 _______

5. 4, 24 _______   **6.** 7, 11 _______   **7.** 6, 15 _______   **8.** 9, 30 _______

9. 5, 8 _______   **10.** 1, 17 _______   **11.** 8, 48 _______   **12.** 3, 12 _______

13. 32, 48 _______   **14.** 2, 35 _______   **15.** 16, 64 _______   **16.** 10, 12 _______

17. 9, 36 _______   **18.** 14, 42 _______   **19.** 7, 8 _______   **20.** 11, 12 _______

21. 5, 10, and 15 _______   **22.** 3, 6, and 9 _______   **23.** 4, 8, and 12 _______

24. 2, 3, and 5 _______   **25.** 3, 4, and 6 _______   **26.** 4, 6, and 9 _______

27. 3, 5, and 9 _______   **28.** 3, 4, and 7 _______   **29.** 4, 7, and 8 _______

30. 4, 6, and 32 _______   **31.** 5, 8, and 20 _______   **32.** 3, 4, and 18 _______

Find the LCM of each pair of numbers. Use prime factorization.

33. 4, 10 _______   **34.** 2, 16 _______   **35.** 9, 27 _______   **36.** 5, 9 _______

37. 5, 25 _______   **38.** 4, 12 _______   **39.** 7, 11 _______   **40.** 2, 13 _______

Problem Solving

41. Tasha lists all the multiples of 3 from 3 to 99. Tony lists all the multiples of 5 from 5 to 100. What is the first number that is on both lists? the second?

____

Use with Lesson 6-9, pages 194–195 in the Student Book.
Then go to Lesson 6-10, pages 196–197 in the Student Book.

Compare Fractions

Name ______________________

Date ______________________

Compare: $\frac{7}{12}$? $\frac{11}{12}$	**Compare:** $\frac{2}{3}$? $\frac{3}{5}$
$\frac{7}{12}$? $\frac{11}{12}$ $\longrightarrow$ $7 < 11$ So $\frac{7}{12} < \frac{11}{12}$.	$\frac{2}{3}$? $\frac{3}{5}$ LCD is 15. $\frac{2}{3} = \frac{?}{15} \longrightarrow \frac{2 \times 5}{3 \times 5} = \frac{10}{15}$ $\frac{3}{5} = \frac{?}{15} \longrightarrow \frac{3 \times 3}{5 \times 3} = \frac{9}{15}$ $10 > 9$ $\frac{10}{15} > \frac{9}{15}$ so $\frac{2}{3} > \frac{3}{5}$.

The LCD of two fractions is the LCM of their denominators.

Compare. Write <, =, or >.

1. $\frac{2}{5}$ ____ $\frac{3}{5}$ 2. $\frac{3}{8}$ ____ $\frac{7}{8}$ 3. $\frac{11}{12}$ ____ $\frac{11}{12}$ 4. $\frac{9}{10}$ ____ $\frac{4}{10}$ 5. $\frac{14}{25}$ ____ $\frac{21}{25}$

6. $\frac{5}{7}$ ____ $\frac{1}{7}$ 7. $\frac{21}{28}$ ____ $\frac{24}{28}$ 8. $\frac{17}{18}$ ____ $\frac{7}{18}$ 9. $\frac{20}{30}$ ____ $\frac{25}{30}$ 10. $\frac{9}{11}$ ____ $\frac{5}{11}$

Write the LCD of each pair of fractions. Then rename the fractions so they have the LCD as their denominator.

11. $\frac{3}{4}, \frac{2}{12}$ __________   12. $\frac{7}{8}, \frac{1}{2}$ __________   13. $\frac{2}{5}, \frac{3}{10}$ __________

14. $\frac{1}{4}, \frac{1}{5}$ __________   15. $\frac{1}{2}, \frac{3}{7}$ __________   16. $\frac{3}{8}, \frac{5}{12}$ __________

17. $\frac{5}{9}, \frac{1}{8}$ __________   18. $\frac{2}{3}, \frac{9}{10}$ __________   19. $\frac{4}{5}, \frac{1}{18}$ __________

Compare. Write <, =, or >.

20. $\frac{3}{4}$ ____ $\frac{3}{7}$ 21. $\frac{7}{8}$ ____ $\frac{2}{5}$ 22. $\frac{1}{4}$ ____ $\frac{3}{10}$

23. $\frac{2}{3}$ ____ $\frac{8}{12}$ 24. $\frac{1}{2}$ ____ $\frac{5}{12}$ 25. $\frac{4}{5}$ ____ $\frac{7}{9}$

26. $\frac{9}{12}$ ____ $\frac{3}{8}$ 27. $\frac{14}{30}$ ____ $\frac{7}{15}$ 28. $\frac{2}{5}$ ____ $\frac{15}{25}$

Problem Solving

29. Mrs. Johnson bought $\frac{5}{8}$ yd of gingham and $\frac{2}{3}$ yd of calico. Did she buy more gingham or more calico? __________

Use with Lesson 6-10, pages 196–197 in the Student Book.
Then go to Lesson 6-11, pages 198–199 in the Student Book.

Order Fractions

Name _______________________

Date _______________________

Order from greatest to least: $3\frac{1}{3}$, $3\frac{9}{15}$, $\frac{17}{5}$ $\boxed{\frac{17}{5} = 3\frac{2}{5}}$

- Compare the whole numbers. $3 = 3 = 3$

- Rename each fraction using the LCD. $3\frac{5}{15}$, $3\frac{9}{15}$, $3\frac{6}{15}$ $\boxed{LCD = 15}$

- Compare numerators. $\frac{9}{15} > \frac{6}{15} > \frac{5}{15}$

- Write the numbers from greatest to least. $3\frac{9}{15}$, $\frac{17}{15}$, $3\frac{1}{3}$

Write in order from least to greatest.

1. $\frac{5}{12}$, $\frac{1}{12}$, $\frac{7}{12}$ 2. $\frac{8}{15}$, $\frac{11}{15}$, $\frac{4}{15}$ 3. $\frac{3}{4}$, $\frac{1}{8}$, $\frac{5}{8}$ 4. $\frac{5}{9}$, $\frac{1}{3}$, $\frac{2}{9}$

5. $\frac{3}{10}$, $\frac{1}{2}$, $\frac{3}{5}$ 6. $\frac{1}{6}$, $\frac{1}{9}$, $\frac{1}{3}$ 7. $\frac{3}{4}$, $\frac{5}{6}$, $\frac{7}{9}$ 8. $\frac{3}{10}$, $\frac{1}{4}$, $\frac{2}{5}$

9. $5\frac{2}{3}$, $5\frac{5}{9}$, $5\frac{11}{15}$ 10. $1\frac{1}{3}$, $1\frac{3}{5}$, $1\frac{3}{10}$ 11. $7\frac{5}{12}$, $7\frac{1}{2}$, $7\frac{3}{8}$ 12. $4\frac{9}{10}$, $4\frac{3}{4}$, $4\frac{5}{8}$

Write in order from greatest to least.

13. $\frac{3}{8}$, $\frac{7}{8}$, $\frac{5}{8}$ 14. $\frac{7}{10}$, $\frac{3}{10}$, $\frac{9}{10}$ 15. $\frac{4}{15}$, $\frac{4}{5}$, $\frac{3}{5}$ 16. $\frac{7}{12}$, $\frac{1}{4}$, $\frac{5}{12}$

17. $\frac{11}{12}$, $\frac{7}{8}$, $\frac{5}{6}$ 18. $\frac{3}{7}$, $\frac{1}{4}$, $\frac{5}{14}$ 19. $\frac{4}{9}$, $\frac{1}{3}$, $\frac{1}{2}$ 20. $\frac{2}{3}$, $\frac{8}{15}$, $\frac{7}{12}$

21. $8\frac{3}{10}$, $8\frac{7}{20}$, $8\frac{2}{5}$ 22. $\frac{31}{7}$, $\frac{13}{14}$, $\frac{21}{7}$ 23. $1\frac{2}{9}$, $1\frac{2}{5}$, $1\frac{1}{3}$ 24. $4\frac{1}{4}$, $\frac{38}{8}$, $4\frac{1}{2}$

Problem Solving

25. Recipe A calls for $\frac{2}{3}$ c cornmeal, recipe B calls for $\frac{5}{8}$ c cornmeal, and recipe C calls for $\frac{1}{2}$ c cornmeal. Which recipe uses the most cornmeal? _______________________

Use with Lesson 6-11, pages 198–199 in the Student Book.
Then go to Lesson 6-12, pages 200–201 in the Student Book.

Relate Fractions to Decimals

Name _______________________

Date _______________________

What decimal is equivalent to $\frac{13}{100}$?

- Read the given fraction. $\frac{13}{100} \rightarrow$ thirteen hundredths
- Determine the decimal place.   hundredths $\rightarrow$ *two* decimal places
- Write an equivalent decimal.   thirteen hundredths = 0.13

You can also rename mixed numbers as decimals.

$6\frac{5}{100} = 6.05$

Write the letter of the equivalent decimal or fraction.

1. $\frac{9}{10}$ _____   **a.** 0.9   **b.** 0.09   **c.** 0.009   **d.** 9

2. $8\frac{17}{100}$ _____   **a.** 0.817   **b.** 0.0817   **c.** 8.17   **d.** 817

3. 0.012 _____   **a.** $\frac{12}{10}$ **b.** $\frac{12}{100}$ **c.** $\frac{12}{1000}$ **d.** $\frac{12}{10,000}$

4. 2.6139 _____   **a.** $\frac{26139}{10}$ **b.** $2\frac{6139}{1000}$ **c.** $26\frac{139}{100}$ **d.** $2\frac{6139}{10,000}$

Write the word name. Then write the equivalent decimal or fraction.

5. $8\frac{8}{100}$ _________________________ _______

6. $16\frac{114}{1000}$ _________________________ _______

7. 65.22 _________________________ _______

8. 12.0037 _________________________ _______

9. 0.005 _________________________ _______

10. 0.0004 _________________________ _______

Write the equivalent decimal or whole number.

11. $\frac{44}{10}$ _______   12. $\frac{190}{100}$ _______   13. $\frac{560}{10}$ _______   14. $\frac{70}{10}$ _______

15. $\frac{2550}{1000}$ _______   16. $\frac{399}{100}$ _______   17. $\frac{859}{100}$ _______   18. $\frac{1500}{1000}$ _______

19. $\frac{6124}{1000}$ _______   20. $\frac{18,123}{10,000}$ _______   21. $\frac{95,000}{10,000}$ _______   22. $\frac{42,500}{10,000}$ _______

Use with Lesson 6-12, pages 200–201 in the Student Book.
Then go to Lesson 6-13, pages 202–203 in the Student Book.

Rename Fractions as Decimals

To rename a mixed number or a fraction as a decimal:

- Separate the whole number and fraction parts.

$$3\tfrac{1}{4} = 3 + \tfrac{1}{4}$$

- Rename the fraction part as a decimal.

$$\tfrac{1}{4} \rightarrow 4\overline{)1.00} \quad 0.25$$

- Add the whole number part and the decimal.

$$3 + 0.25 = 3.25$$

Write each as a decimal.

1. $\dfrac{1}{2}$ 2. $\dfrac{3}{20}$ 3. $\dfrac{4}{50}$ 4. $\dfrac{6}{8}$

5. $\dfrac{6}{25}$ 6. $\dfrac{12}{15}$ 7. $\dfrac{3}{4}$ 8. $\dfrac{35}{40}$

9. $2\tfrac{1}{5}$ 10. $19\tfrac{3}{5}$ 11. $8\tfrac{2}{25}$ 12. $22\tfrac{3}{20}$

13. $15\tfrac{1}{8}$ 14. $30\tfrac{12}{50}$ 15. $61\tfrac{3}{10}$ 16. $10\tfrac{86}{100}$

Write each fraction or mixed number as a decimal. It may help you to rename the fractions as equivalent fractions with denominators that are powers of ten.

17. $\dfrac{6}{25}$ 18. $\dfrac{45}{50}$ 19. $\dfrac{14}{20}$ 20. $1\tfrac{2}{5}$

21. $9\tfrac{17}{50}$ 22. $3\tfrac{7}{25}$ 23. $7\tfrac{7}{50}$ 24. $34\tfrac{9}{20}$

Problem Solving

25. Lavonne has six and seven twentieths dollars. How much money does she have?

26. Julio has six twelfths of a dollar. How much money does he have?

Use with Lesson 6-13, pages 202–203 in the Student Book.
Then go to Lesson 6-14, pages 204–205 in the Student Book.

Rename Decimals as Fractions

Name _______________

Date _______________

Write 0.44 as a fraction in simplest form.

- Read the given decimal.
- Determine the denominator of the fraction.
- Write an equivalent fraction.
- Simplify if necessary.

$0.44 \longrightarrow$ forty-four hundredths

The denominator is 100.

forty-four hundredths $= \frac{44}{100}$

$\frac{44}{100} = \frac{11}{25}$

So $0.44 = \frac{11}{25}$.

Complete.

1. $0.8 = \frac{}{10} = \frac{}{5}$

2. $0.24 = \frac{24}{} = \frac{}{25}$

3. $0.009 = \frac{}{1000}$

4. $3.25 = 3\frac{25}{} = 3\frac{}{4}$

5. $8.063 = 8\frac{}{1000}$

6. $6.875 = 6\frac{}{}$

Write each decimal as a fraction in simplest form.

7. 0.3 _______

8. 0.17 _______

9. 0.009 _______

10. 0.387 _______

11. 0.125 _______

12. 0.0123 _______

13. 0.62 _______

14. 0.046 _______

15. 0.4 _______

16. 0.12 _______

17. 0.275 _______

18. 0.0025 _______

19. 0.099 _______

20. 0.5 _______

21. 0.48 _______

22. 0.0125 _______

Write each decimal as a mixed number in simplest form.

23. 5.04 _______

24. 9.12 _______

25. 8.133 _______

26. 6.01 _______

27. 7.625 _______

28. 2.25 _______

29. 1.325 _______

30. 10.6 _______

31. 3.08 _______

32. 2.0004 _______

33. 5.0125 _______

34. 9.42 _______

35. The newborn baby weighed 3.2 kilograms. _______

36. The newborn calf weighed 74.25 pounds. _______

Use with Lesson 6-14, pages 204–205 in the Student Book.
Then go to Lesson 6-15, pages 206–207 in the Student Book.

Terminating and Repeating Decimals

Name _______________________

Date _______________________

Terminating Decimals	Repeating Decimals
$\frac{1}{4}$ ⟶ $4\overline{)1.00}$ = 0.25	$\frac{1}{6}$ ⟶ $6\overline{)1.00000}$ = 0.16666 . . . ⟶ $0.1\overline{6}$
$\frac{5}{16}$ ⟶ $16\overline{)5.0000}$ = 0.3125	$\frac{3}{11}$ ⟶ $11\overline{)3.000000}$ = 0.272727 . . . ⟶ $0.\overline{27}$

Rewrite each repeating decimal with a bar over the part that repeats.

1. 0.12121 . . . _______

2. 0.63636 . . . _______

3. 0.1818 . . . _______

4. 2.54545 . . . _______

5. 5.3888 . . . _______

6. 1.2666 . . . _______

Write each repeating decimal showing eight decimal places.

7. $0.\overline{6}$ _______

8. $0.\overline{27}$ _______

9. $0.\overline{3125}$ _______

10. $4.0\overline{9}$ _______

11. $7.\overline{83}$ _______

12. $11.\overline{545}$ _______

13. $6.1\overline{6}$ _______

14. $9.\overline{1}$ _______

15. $2.08\overline{3}$ _______

Rename each as a terminating or repeating decimal.

16. $\frac{4}{5}$ _______

17. $\frac{2}{3}$ _______

18. $\frac{9}{11}$ _______

19. $\frac{7}{20}$ _______

20. $\frac{7}{18}$ _______

21. $\frac{1}{18}$ _______

22. $\frac{5}{8}$ _______

23. $\frac{7}{12}$ _______

24. $2\frac{1}{3}$ _______

25. $5\frac{1}{8}$ _______

26. $9\frac{1}{2}$ _______

27. $8\frac{5}{18}$ _______

28. $28\frac{1}{25}$ _______

29. $35\frac{2}{9}$ _______

30. $64\frac{7}{12}$ _______

31. $58\frac{9}{11}$ _______

Use with Lesson 6-15, pages 206–207 in the Student Book.
Then go to Lesson 6-16, pages 208–209 in the Student Book.

Rational Numbers

A **rational number** is a number that can be written in the form of a fraction $\frac{a}{b}$, where a and b are integers and $b \neq 0$.

All whole numbers are integers.
All integers are rational numbers.

The numbers $^-1\frac{1}{2}$ and $^+6\frac{1}{4}$ are *rational numbers*.

Positive and negative decimals, such as $^-3.75$ and $^+8.5$, are rational numbers. Zero is also a rational number.

Every rational number has an *opposite*.
$^-1\frac{1}{2}$ and $^+1\frac{1}{2}$ are opposites.
$^+0.25$ and $^-0.25$ are opposites.

Identify the rational number that corresponds to the point on the number line.

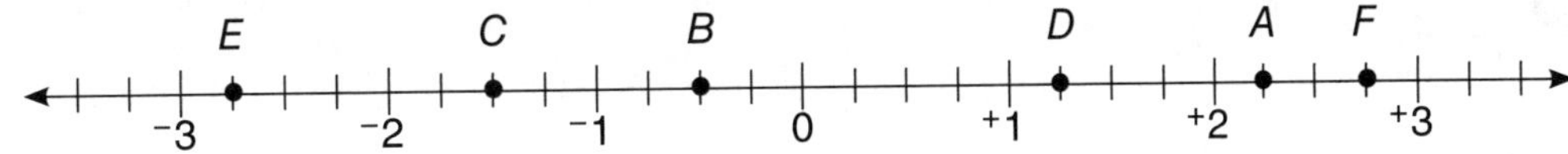

1. B _____ 2. A _____ 3. C _____ 4. F _____ 5. D _____ 6. E _____

Write a rational number for each point.

7. _____

8. _____

9. _____

10. _____

11. _____

12. _____

Write each rational number.

13. Express $^-5\frac{1}{4}$ as a decimal. _________

14. Express $^-1.75$ as a fraction. _________

Write the opposite of each.

15. $^+1\frac{1}{4}$ _____

16. $^-8.5$ _____

17. $^+13$ _____

18. $^+0.5$ _____

Problem Solving

19. At the close of the stock market on Friday, the price of a stock dropped 3.75 points. Express this loss as a rational number in two ways.

____

20. When Aaron was sick, his temperature went from 98.6° to 100.1°, a rise of 1.5°. Express this rise in temperature as a rational number in two ways.

____

C Use with Lesson 6-16, pages 208–209 in the Student Book.
C Then go to Lesson 6-17, pages 210–211 in the Student Book.

Compare and Order Rational Numbers

Name ______________________

Date ______________________

<table>
<tr><td>

Compare rational numbers

Compare: $^-3$ and $^-2\frac{1}{4}$

Use a number line. The number farther to the right is the greater number.

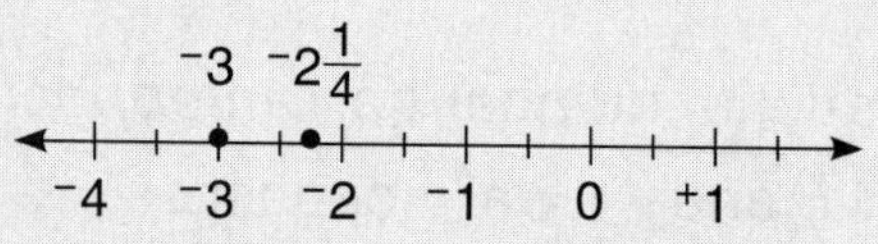

$^-2\frac{1}{4}$ is farther to the right.

So $^-3 < {}^-2\frac{1}{4}$.

</td><td>

Order rational numbers

Order from least to greatest: $^-1.5$, $^-1\frac{3}{4}$, $^-\frac{1}{2}$

Write all the numbers as either decimals or fractions. Then use a number line.

The numbers as fractions: $^-1\frac{1}{2}$, $^-1\frac{3}{4}$, $^-\frac{1}{2}$

The numbers as decimals: $^-1.5$, $^-1.75$, $^-0.5$

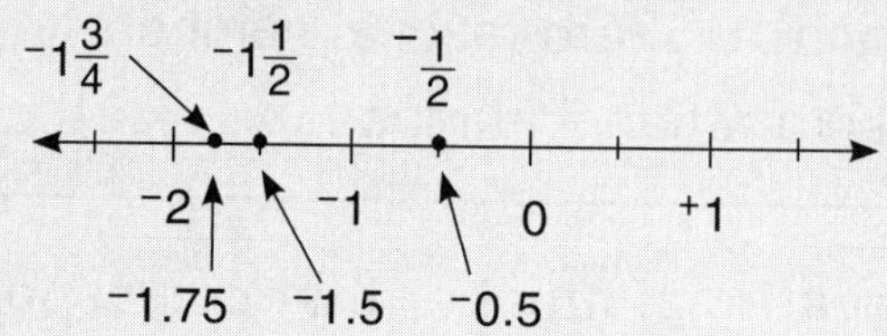

From least to greatest: $^-1\frac{3}{4}$, $^-1.5$, $^-\frac{1}{2}$

</td></tr>
</table>

Compare. Write <, =, or >. Use the number line.

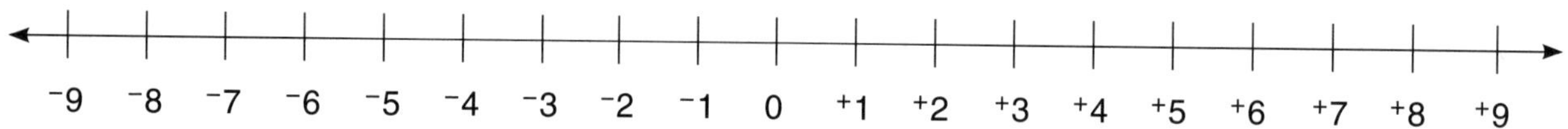

1. $^-6\frac{1}{4}$ _____ $^+3\frac{1}{2}$ 2. $^-9\frac{1}{4}$ _____ $^-1\frac{3}{4}$ 3. 0 _____ $^-3.5$ 4. $^-1.75$ _____ $^-1.5$

5. $^-6\frac{1}{4}$ _____ $^-6.25$ 6. $^-3\frac{1}{4}$ _____ $^-1.25$ 7. $^-3.5$ _____ $^+3\frac{3}{4}$ 8. $^+0.5$ _____ 0

Write in order from least to greatest. Use the number line above to help you.

9. $^-5\frac{1}{5}$, 0, $^-5\frac{1}{2}$

10. $^-9.7$, $^-1.4$, $^+1.4$

11. $^-5\frac{1}{2}$, $^+2.5$, $^-2\frac{1}{2}$

12. $^+1\frac{1}{3}$, $^+1\frac{1}{2}$, $^-6$

13. $^-8\frac{1}{5}$, $^-\frac{1}{2}$, 0

14. $^+6\frac{1}{4}$, 0, $^+6.75$

Problem Solving

15. Over a 5-day period, a share of stock showed these changes:

$$^-2\frac{1}{4}, \ ^+1, \ ^-\frac{1}{2}, \ ^+2\frac{1}{2}, \text{ and } ^-1$$

What was the greatest gain? What was the greatest loss?

16. Over a 5-day period, the temperatures in degrees Celsius were as follows:

$$^-3°, \ ^-3.5°, \ ^-2.75°, \ ^-1°, \text{ and } ^-1.25°$$

What was the warmest temperature? the coldest temperature?

74

Use with Lesson 6-17, pages 210–211 in the Student Book.
Then go to Lesson 6-18, pages 212–213 in the Student Book.

Problem-Solving Strategy: Find a Pattern

There are 8 people in a room. If each person shakes hands with each other person in the room, how many handshakes will there be?

Make a table and look for a pattern.

People	2	3	4	5	6	7	8
Handshakes	1	3	6	10	15	21	28

+2 +3 +4 +5 +6 +7

There will be 28 handshakes.

Solve. Do your work on a separate sheet of paper.

1. Luella has designed a pattern like the one shown at the right. She wants to add more squares of dots around the pattern. If she continues the pattern for two more squares, how many dots will be in the largest square?

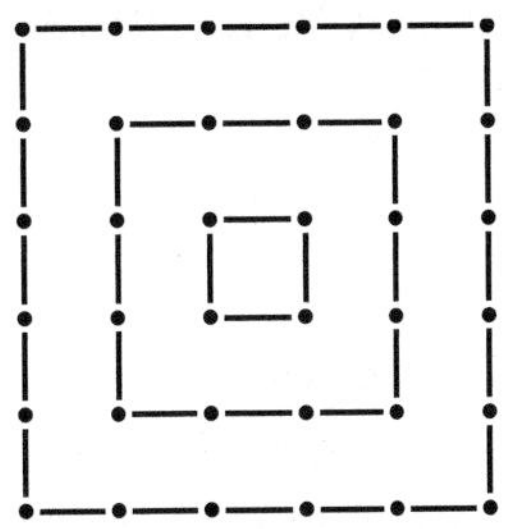

2. Ellis uses tiles to make the figures at the right. If he continues the pattern, how many tiles will he need to make the sixth figure?

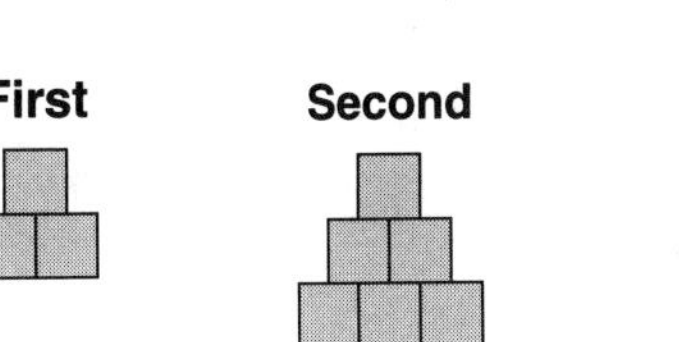

3. Write the next three terms in this sequence: 0.1, 0.3, 0.5, 0.7. What is the pattern?

4. There are 12 basketball teams in the league. Each team will play 1 game with each of the other teams. How many games will there be?

5. Don saves $1 the first week, $2 the second week, $3 the third week, and $4 the fourth week. If he continues in this way, how many weeks will it take before Don has saved at least $50?

6. Darryl is placing colored tiles around a swimming pool. He has started the pattern with red, white, blue, white, and red and then repeated the same color sequence. If he continues this pattern, what will be the color of the 43rd tile?

Problem-Solving Applications: Mixed Review

Name _______________

Date _______________

Solve each problem and explain the method you used. If needed, do all your work on a separate sheet of paper.

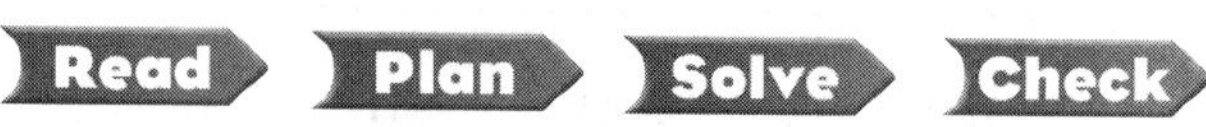

Strategy File

Use These Strategies
Guess and Test
Write an Equation
Use a Graph
Find a Pattern
Interpret the Remainder
Use More Than One Step

1. The rug in Ben's living room is 3.2 meters longer than it is wide. Its length is $5\frac{1}{4}$ meters. It has a 2-meter square in its center. What is the width of the rug?

2. Grant folds a sheet of paper in thirds, then in half, then in thirds again. Estimate into how many parts his sheet is divided. Check your answer by following the folds.

3. Celia uses $\frac{3}{8}$ of a 6-oz bag of flour to make her modeling clay. Jimmy uses $\frac{4}{5}$ of a 6-oz bag of flour to make his modeling clay. How many more ounces of flour does Jimmy use than Celia?

4. Rebecca makes the design shown. If she continues the pattern, what fractional part of the next square will be shaded?

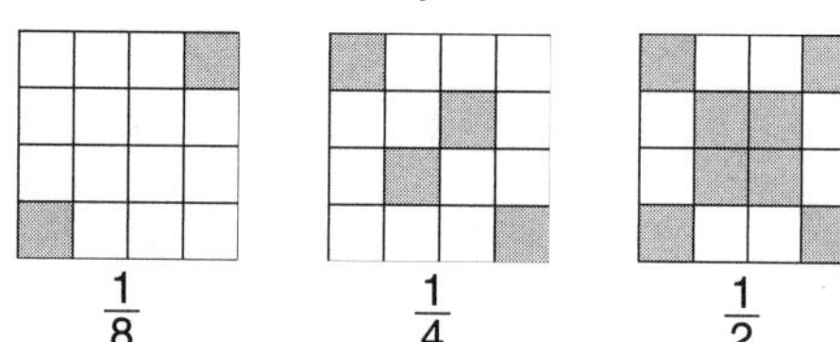

$\frac{1}{8}$ $\frac{1}{4}$ $\frac{1}{2}$

5. Every fifth day in June, Juan goes to the skate park. Every third day in June, Juan has swim team practice. On June 30 Juan goes to the skate park and also has swim team practice. On what other date or dates do both fall?

Use the circle graph for problems 6–9.

Linda's Produce Stand

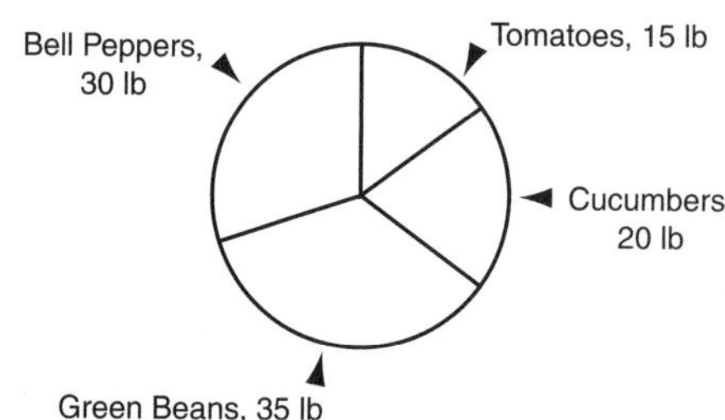

6. Of the total weight of all of the vegetables, what fractional part are the tomatoes?

7. What vegetable makes up $\frac{7}{20}$ of the total weight of the vegetables?

8. What vegetable makes up $\frac{1}{5}$ of the total weight of the vegetables?

9. When Linda adds 20 lb of peas to her produce stand, what fractional part of the total weight are the peas?

Use with Lesson 6-19, pages 214–215 in the Student Book.

Addition Properties: Fractions

Name _______________

Date _______________

<table>
<tr><td>Commutative Property

$\frac{1}{6} + \frac{4}{6} = \frac{4}{6} + \frac{1}{6}$

$\frac{5}{6} = \frac{5}{6}$</td><td>Associative Property

$\left(\frac{1}{8} + \frac{2}{8}\right) + \frac{4}{8} = \frac{1}{8} + \left(\frac{2}{8} + \frac{4}{8}\right)$

$\frac{3}{8} + \frac{4}{8} = \frac{1}{8} + \frac{6}{8}$

$\frac{7}{8} = \frac{7}{8}$</td><td>Identity Property

$\frac{1}{2} + 0 = \frac{1}{2}$ or $0 + \frac{1}{2} = \frac{1}{2}$

Inverse Property

$\frac{1}{4} + \frac{-1}{4} = 0$</td></tr>
</table>

Write *true* or *false* for each equation. If *false*, explain why.

1. $\frac{5}{11} + 1 = \frac{5}{11}$ _______

2. $\left(\frac{1}{10} + \frac{3}{10}\right) + \frac{7}{10} = \frac{1}{10} + \left(\frac{3}{10} + \frac{7}{10}\right)$ _______

3. $\frac{6}{7} + \frac{3}{7} = \frac{3}{7} + \frac{6}{7}$ _______

4. $\left(\frac{2}{5} + \frac{-2}{5}\right) = \frac{4}{5}$ _______

Name the property shown.

5. $\frac{1}{5} + \frac{3}{5} = \frac{3}{5} + \frac{1}{5}$

6. $\left(\frac{1}{9} + \frac{3}{9}\right) + \frac{4}{9} = \frac{1}{9} + \left(\frac{3}{9} + \frac{4}{9}\right)$

7. $\frac{9}{10} + \frac{-9}{10} = 0$

____

____

____

8. $\left(\frac{1}{9} + \frac{2}{9}\right) + \frac{5}{9} = \frac{1}{9} + \left(\frac{2}{9} + \frac{5}{9}\right)$

9. $\frac{2}{3} + 0 = \frac{2}{3}$

10. $\frac{3}{10} + \frac{4}{10} = \frac{4}{10} + \frac{3}{10}$

____

____

____

Find the value of the variable. Use the properties of addition.

11. $\frac{3}{8} + \frac{1}{8} = \frac{1}{8} + e$ _______

12. $\frac{9}{12} + p = \frac{9}{12}$ _______

13. $\frac{2}{5} + \frac{4}{5} = y + \frac{2}{5}$ _______

14. $\left(\frac{3}{6} + \frac{5}{6}\right) + \frac{1}{6} = x + \left(\frac{5}{6} + \frac{1}{6}\right)$ _______

15. $\frac{5}{10} + h = 0$ _______

16. $\frac{5}{8} + \left(\frac{7}{8} + \frac{3}{8}\right) = \left(\frac{5}{8} + k\right) + \frac{3}{8}$ _______

17. $t + \frac{9}{15} = \frac{9}{15} + \frac{4}{15}$ _______

Problem Solving Write an equation to solve each problem.

18. Ricardo had red grapes and green grapes for sale. Three fifths of the grapes were red grapes; the rest were green grapes. If he sold all the red grapes and none of the green grapes, what fractional part of his grapes did he sell? _______________

19. Jeanine bought $\frac{3}{8}$ pound of peanuts and $\frac{1}{8}$ pound of cashews. Jeff bought $\frac{1}{8}$ pound of peanuts and $\frac{3}{8}$ pound of cashews. Who bought more nuts? _______________

Use with Lesson 7-1, pages 222–223 in the Student Book.
Then go to Lesson 7-2, pages 224–225 in the Student Book.

Estimate Sums and Differences

> Estimate: $\frac{2}{11} + \frac{5}{8}$
>
> $\downarrow \quad \downarrow$
>
> $0 + \frac{1}{2} = \frac{1}{2}$
>
> So $\frac{2}{11} + \frac{5}{8}$ is close to $\frac{1}{2}$.
>
> - For fractions, first round each fraction to 0, $\frac{1}{2}$, or 1.
> - For mixed numbers, first round each mixed number to the nearest whole number.
> - Then add or subtract the rounded numbers.
>
> Estimate: $7\frac{1}{2} - 4\frac{2}{5}$
>
> $\downarrow \quad \downarrow$
>
> $8 - 4 = 4$
>
> So $7\frac{1}{2} - 4\frac{2}{5}$ is close to 4.

Estimate the sum or difference.

1. $\frac{1}{4} + \frac{7}{13}$ _____

2. $\frac{6}{13} - \frac{1}{5}$ _____

3. $\frac{5}{9} + \frac{13}{15}$ _____

4. $\frac{8}{9} - \frac{10}{19}$ _____

5. $\frac{9}{11} + \frac{8}{9}$ _____

6. $\frac{7}{8} - \frac{5}{6}$ _____

7. $\frac{1}{7} + \frac{2}{11}$ _____

8. $\frac{8}{17} - \frac{7}{15}$ _____

9. $\frac{9}{10} - \frac{1}{7}$ _____

10. $\frac{10}{19} + \frac{1}{8} + \frac{3}{5}$ _____

11. $\frac{1}{10} + \frac{8}{15} + \frac{4}{9}$ _____

12. $\frac{7}{12} + \frac{2}{9} + \frac{11}{20} + \frac{8}{15}$ _____

13. $10\frac{1}{2}$
    $- \ 8\frac{3}{5}$

14. $5\frac{4}{7}$
    $+ \ 6\frac{1}{8}$

15. $12\frac{1}{8}$
    $+ \ 11\frac{5}{6}$

16. $15\frac{4}{9}$
    $- \ 3\frac{5}{8}$

17. $9\frac{1}{6}$
    $- \ 8\frac{7}{8}$

18. $11\frac{4}{5}$
    $+ \ 2\frac{1}{2}$

19. $13\frac{5}{11}$
    $- \ 1\frac{9}{12}$

20. $6\frac{7}{9}$
    $+ \ 14\frac{1}{12}$

Problem Solving — Use estimation.

21. Julio has a 12-inch strip of ribbon. He cuts off a strip that is $6\frac{3}{4}$ inches long. He needs another strip that is $6\frac{3}{4}$ inches long. Does he have enough ribbon? Explain. _____________

22. Joanne set a goal to hike 14 miles in 3 days. She hiked $3\frac{5}{6}$ miles on the first day, $5\frac{7}{9}$ miles on the second day, and $4\frac{2}{3}$ miles on the last day. Did she make her goal of 14 miles? Explain. _____________

Use with Lesson 7-2, pages 224–225 in the Student Book.
Then go to Lesson 7-3, pages 226–227 in the Student Book.

Add Fractions

Name ___________________________

Date ___________________________

Add: $\frac{3}{5} + \frac{7}{10} + \frac{1}{2}$

Find the LCD of the fractions.

Multiples of 5: 5, **10**, 15, 20, . . .
Multiples of 10: **10**, 20, 30, 40, . . .
Multiples of 2: 2, 4, 6, 8, **10**, . . .

The LCD is 10.

Rename each fraction.

$$\frac{3}{5} = \frac{3 \times 2}{5 \times 2} = \frac{6}{10}$$

$$\frac{7}{10} = \frac{7}{10}$$

$$+ \frac{1}{2} = \frac{1 \times 5}{2 \times 5} = \frac{5}{10}$$

Add. Then simplify.

$$\frac{6}{10}$$
$$\frac{7}{10}$$
$$+ \frac{5}{10}$$
$$\frac{18}{10} = 1\frac{8}{10} = 1\frac{4}{5}$$

Find the LCD for each set of fractions.

1. $\frac{3}{4}, \frac{5}{16}$ _____

2. $\frac{3}{5}, \frac{1}{9}$ _____

3. $\frac{5}{6}, \frac{7}{9}, \frac{2}{3}$ _____

4. $\frac{3}{8}, \frac{1}{4}, \frac{5}{6}$ _____

Estimate and then add. Write each answer in simplest form.

5. $\frac{1}{8}$ $+ \frac{3}{4}$

6. $\frac{4}{7}$ $+ \frac{3}{5}$

7. $\frac{1}{6}$ $+ \frac{7}{8}$

8. $\frac{2}{3}$ $+ \frac{5}{12}$

9. $\frac{5}{14}$ $+ \frac{3}{7}$

10. $\frac{9}{24}$ $+ \frac{5}{12}$

11. $\frac{5}{6}$ $+ \frac{7}{18}$

12. $\frac{4}{5}$ $+ \frac{7}{12}$

13. $\frac{7}{12}$ $+ \frac{7}{9}$

14. $\frac{8}{9}$ $+ \frac{1}{2}$

15. $\frac{5}{9}$ $\frac{7}{12}$ $+ \frac{1}{3}$

16. $\frac{3}{8}$ $\frac{1}{6}$ $+ \frac{3}{4}$

17. $\frac{7}{9}$ $\frac{1}{2}$ $+ \frac{1}{6}$

18. $\frac{3}{4}$ $\frac{5}{6}$ $+ \frac{3}{8}$

19. $\frac{1}{2}$ $\frac{1}{3}$ $+ \frac{1}{4}$

Compare. Write <, =, or >.

20. $\frac{1}{4} + \frac{3}{16}$ _____ $\frac{1}{2}$

21. $\frac{1}{8} + \frac{7}{12}$ _____ $\frac{2}{3}$

22. $\frac{2}{5} + \frac{4}{15}$ _____ $\frac{2}{3}$

23. $\frac{2}{3} + \frac{3}{4}$ _____ $1\frac{1}{4}$

24. $\frac{7}{10} + \frac{1}{3}$ _____ $1\frac{1}{30}$

25. $\frac{3}{4} + \frac{3}{8}$ _____ $\frac{7}{8}$

Use with Lesson 7-3, pages 226–227 in the Student Book.
Then go to Lesson 7-4, pages 228–229 in the Student Book.

79

Add Mixed Numbers

Name _______________________

Date _______________________

Add: $2\frac{4}{5} + 3\frac{2}{5}$

- Add the fractions.
- Add the whole numbers.
- Simplify.

$$2\frac{4}{5}$$
$$+\ 3\frac{2}{5}$$
$$\overline{5\frac{6}{5} = 6\frac{1}{5}}$$

Add: $2\frac{4}{10} + 3\frac{2}{5}$ LCD: 10

- Rename each fraction.
- Add.
- Simplify.

$$2\frac{4}{10} + 3\frac{4}{10}$$
$$2\frac{4}{10} + 3\frac{4}{10} = 5\frac{8}{10}$$
$$5\frac{8}{10} = 5\frac{4}{5}$$

Complete the addition.

1. $\quad 9\frac{1}{4} = 9\frac{}{20}$

$\quad +\ 1\frac{3}{5} = 1\frac{}{20}$

$\quad\quad\overline{10\frac{}{20}}$

2. $\quad 12\frac{4}{7}$

$\quad +\ \ 3\frac{3}{7}$

$\quad\quad\overline{15\frac{}{} = \underline{}}$

3. $\quad 10\frac{5}{18} = 10\frac{5}{}$

$\quad +\ 11\frac{1}{6} = 11\frac{3}{}$

$\quad\quad\overline{21\frac{8}{} = \underline{}}$

Add. Estimate to help.

4. $\quad 4\frac{1}{4}$
$\quad +\ 5\frac{3}{4}$

5. $\quad 1\frac{3}{4}$
$\quad +\ 3\frac{5}{8}$

6. $\quad 4\frac{5}{6}$
$\quad +\ 6\frac{7}{18}$

7. $\quad 7\frac{1}{2}$
$\quad +\ 9\frac{1}{4}$

8. $2\frac{3}{7} + 4 = \underline{}$

9. $8\frac{3}{5} + 7\frac{2}{5} = \underline{}$

10. $5\frac{1}{2} + 4\frac{3}{10} = \underline{}$

11. $15\frac{1}{3} + 10\frac{5}{6} = \underline{}$

12. $12\frac{9}{10} + 1\frac{7}{15} = \underline{}$

13. $1\frac{3}{5} + 3\frac{2}{3} = \underline{}$

14. $3\frac{1}{8} + 6\frac{3}{8} + 2\frac{5}{8} = \underline{}$

15. $8\frac{1}{2} + 9\frac{3}{4} + 2\frac{1}{8} = \underline{}$

16. $5\frac{1}{3} + 7\frac{2}{5} + 3\frac{2}{3} = \underline{}$

17. $6\frac{1}{5} + 1\frac{4}{5} + 5\frac{3}{10} = \underline{}$

18. $2\frac{1}{6} + 1\frac{3}{8} + 8\frac{1}{4} = \underline{}$

19. $1\frac{3}{4} + 2\frac{2}{5} + 3\frac{1}{10} = \underline{}$

Problem Solving Express your answer in simplest form.

20. On a weekend hike, a group walked $5\frac{1}{10}$ miles on Saturday and $4\frac{5}{10}$ miles on Sunday. How many miles did they hike both days? ________________

21. Malik rode his bicycle $4\frac{1}{2}$ miles in the morning. In the afternoon he rode $3\frac{3}{4}$ miles. How many miles did he ride in all? ________________

Use with Lesson 7-4, pages 228–229 in the Student Book.
Then go to Lesson 7-5, pages 230–231 in the Student Book.

Subtract Fractions

Name ___________________________

Date ___________________________

Subtract: $\frac{5}{6} - \frac{2}{8}$

Find the LCD of the fractions.

Multiples of 6: 6, 12, 18, **24**, . . .
Multiples of 8: 8, 16, **24**, . . .

The LCD is 24.

Rename each fraction.

$$\frac{5}{6} = \frac{5 \times 4}{6 \times 4} = \frac{20}{24}$$
$$-\frac{2}{8} = \frac{2 \times 3}{8 \times 3} = \frac{6}{24}$$

Subtract. Then simplify.

$$\frac{20}{24}$$
$$-\frac{6}{24}$$
$$\frac{14}{24} = \frac{7}{12}$$

Estimate and then subtract. Write each answer in simplest form.

1. $\frac{5}{8}$
   $-\frac{1}{8}$

2. $\frac{2}{3}$
   $-\frac{1}{9}$

3. $\frac{3}{4}$
   $-\frac{5}{12}$

4. $\frac{3}{7}$
   $-\frac{2}{5}$

5. $\frac{1}{2}$
   $-\frac{3}{16}$

6. $\frac{1}{6}$
   $-\frac{1}{9}$

7. $\frac{3}{4}$
   $-\frac{2}{3}$

8. $\frac{11}{12}$
   $-\frac{7}{12}$

9. $\frac{7}{8}$
   $-\frac{1}{4}$

10. $\frac{4}{5}$
    $-\frac{4}{10}$

11. $\frac{3}{4} - \frac{4}{9} =$ _______

12. $\frac{5}{6} - \frac{4}{7} =$ _______

13. $\frac{5}{6} - \frac{3}{5} =$ _______

Use a related sentence to find the missing fraction or whole number.

14. $n + \frac{4}{5} = \frac{7}{8}$

    ____

15. $z - \frac{2}{7} = \frac{3}{14}$

    ____

16. $\frac{5}{9} = y + \frac{1}{3}$

    ____

17. $\frac{1}{4} = x - \frac{1}{16}$

    ____

18. $b - 2\frac{1}{3} = 2\frac{2}{3}$

    ____

19. $h - 0 = \frac{1}{8}$

    ____

20. $t - \frac{8}{9} = 8\frac{1}{9}$

    ____

21. $\frac{3}{8} = a + \frac{5}{24}$

    ____

22. $\frac{4}{7} = c + \frac{11}{21}$

    ____

Problem Solving

23. Patty lives $\frac{5}{8}$ mile from school. Frank lives $\frac{3}{5}$ mile from school. How much farther from school does Patty live?

    ____

Use with Lesson 7-5, pages 230–231 in the Student Book.
Then go to Lesson 7-6, pages 232–233 in the Student Book.

Subtract Mixed Numbers

Name _______________________

Date _______________________

Subtract: $8\frac{7}{10} - 3\frac{3}{10}$

- Subtract the fractions.
- Subtract the whole numbers.
- Simplify.

$$8\frac{7}{10}$$
$$-\ 3\frac{3}{10}$$
$$5\frac{4}{10} = 5\frac{2}{5}$$

Subtract: $8\frac{1}{10} - 2\frac{4}{5}$ $\boxed{\text{LCD: 10}}$

- Rename the subtrahend. $2\frac{4}{5} = 2\frac{8}{10}$
- Rename the minuend. $8\frac{1}{10} = 7\frac{11}{10}$
- Subtract. $7\frac{11}{10} - 2\frac{8}{10} = 5\frac{3}{10}$

Estimate and then subtract. Write each answer in simplest form.

1. $6\frac{3}{4}$
   $-\ 3\frac{1}{4}$

2. $5\frac{11}{15}$
   $-\ 4\frac{8}{15}$

3. $10\frac{7}{8}$
   $-\ 5\frac{2}{3}$

4. $8\frac{1}{6}$
   $-\ 4\frac{5}{12}$

5. $14\frac{1}{2}$
   $-\ 9\frac{5}{8}$

6. $20\frac{3}{8}$
   $-\ 17\frac{1}{2}$

7. 19
   $-\ 12\frac{2}{5}$

8. $15\frac{4}{9}$
   $-\ 12$

9. $6 - 2\frac{7}{8} =$ _______

10. $12\frac{2}{3} - 9 =$ _______

11. $12 - 10\frac{1}{9} =$ _______

12. $8\frac{1}{5} - \frac{2}{3} =$ _______

13. $5\frac{2}{9} - 4\frac{1}{5} =$ _______

14. $10\frac{1}{2} - 6\frac{1}{3} =$ _______

15. $18\frac{1}{3} - 9\frac{4}{5} =$ _______

16. $7 - 2\frac{7}{9} =$ _______

17. $5\frac{1}{4} - 2\frac{1}{2} + 1\frac{5}{6} =$ _______

18. $9\frac{3}{8} - 3\frac{1}{12} - 6\frac{1}{4} =$ _______

Problem Solving

19. Larry lives 3 mi from the library. Jalen lives $1\frac{5}{8}$ mi from the library. How much farther from the library does Larry live than Jalen?

    ____

20. Jane baked $8\frac{1}{4}$ dozen cupcakes. She sold all but $\frac{5}{6}$ dozen. How many dozen cupcakes did she sell?

    ____

Use with Lesson 7-6, pages 232–233 in the Student Book.
Then go to Lesson 7-7, pages 234–235 in the Student Book.

Mental Math: Addition and Subtraction

Name _______________________

Date _______________________

Compute the whole-number part, then the fraction part.	Look for sums of 1.	Compensate by "adding on" and then subtracting.
$7\frac{1}{5} + 8\frac{2}{5} = n$	$2\frac{3}{8} + 7\frac{5}{8} = c$	$15 - 2\frac{2}{9} = a$
$7 + 8 = 15$ $\quad$ $\frac{1}{5} + \frac{2}{5} = \frac{3}{5}$	$\frac{3}{8} + \frac{5}{8} = 1$	$2\frac{2}{9} + \frac{7}{9} = 3$ Subtract 3, then add $\frac{7}{9}$. $15 - 3 = 12$ and $12 + \frac{7}{9} = 12\frac{7}{9}$
$7\frac{1}{5} + 8\frac{2}{5} = 15\frac{3}{5}$	$2\frac{3}{8} + 7\frac{5}{8} = 10$	$15 - 2\frac{2}{9} = 12\frac{7}{9}$

Compute mentally. Find the whole-number part and then the fraction part.

1. $5\frac{1}{4} + 2\frac{1}{4}$ _______

2. $6\frac{7}{9} - 2\frac{2}{9}$ _______

3. $8\frac{5}{11} - 6\frac{4}{11}$ _______

4. $6\frac{1}{8} + 5\frac{3}{8} + 7$ _______

5. $8\frac{5}{9} + 6\frac{1}{9} - 3$ _______

6. $17\frac{9}{10} - 7\frac{3}{10} - 5$ _______

Compute mentally. Look for sums of 1.

7. $4\frac{2}{5} + 6\frac{3}{5}$ _______

8. $11\frac{7}{8} + 5\frac{1}{8}$ _______

9. $9\frac{1}{4} + 4\frac{3}{4}$ _______

10. $8\frac{3}{4} + 3\frac{1}{4} + 2\frac{1}{4} + 6$ _______

11. $3\frac{3}{8} + 3\frac{3}{8} + 5\frac{1}{8} + 4\frac{1}{8}$ _______

12. $7\frac{2}{5} + 3\frac{1}{10} + 7\frac{1}{2} + 10$ _______

13. $9\frac{5}{8} + 7\frac{1}{3} + 10\frac{3}{8}$ _______

Compensate to compute mentally.

14. $7 - 2\frac{3}{8}$ _______

15. $12 - 8\frac{3}{5}$ _______

16. $9 - 2\frac{1}{3}$ _______

17. $3\frac{1}{9} - 1\frac{4}{9}$ _______

18. $7\frac{1}{4} - 3\frac{3}{4}$ _______

19. $12\frac{7}{10} - 5\frac{9}{10}$ _______

Problem Solving

20. Jesse skis for $4\frac{3}{4}$ hours Monday, $3\frac{1}{2}$ hours Tuesday, and $5\frac{1}{4}$ hours Wednesday. Does he ski for more than 13 hours? Explain. _______

21. Cristina has a 7-pound bag of soil for planting flowers. She uses $4\frac{2}{3}$ pounds of the soil. How much soil is left in the bag? _______

Use with Lesson 7-7, pages 234–235 in the Student Book.
Then go to Lesson 7-8, pages 236–237 in the Student Book.

Addition and Subtraction Expressions with Fractions

Name _______________

Date _______________

Evaluate: $a + 3\frac{1}{2} + b + 2\frac{3}{5}$, when $a = 3\frac{4}{5}$ and $b = 5\frac{1}{2}$.

- Replace a with $3\frac{4}{5}$ and b with $5\frac{1}{2}$.

$$3\frac{4}{5} + 3\frac{1}{2} + 5\frac{1}{2} + 2\frac{3}{5}$$

- Use the Commutative and Associative Properties.

$$\left(3\frac{4}{5} + 2\frac{3}{5}\right) + \left(3\frac{1}{2} + 5\frac{1}{2}\right)$$

- Simplify using the order of operations.

$$6\frac{2}{5} + 9$$

$$15\frac{2}{5}$$

Evaluate each expression for the given values. Use the properties of addition.

1. $6\frac{3}{5} + m$, when $m = 3\frac{3}{10}$ _______

2. $8\frac{7}{9} + g$, when $g = 3$ _______

3. $6\frac{2}{7} + p$, when $p = 6\frac{5}{7}$ _______

4. $y - 4\frac{1}{2} + z$, when $y = 8\frac{4}{5}$ and $z = 3\frac{1}{5}$ _______

5. $e - 0$, when $e = 23\frac{6}{11}$ _______

6. $h + 1 + 8\frac{1}{6} + 2\frac{3}{4}$, when $h = 2\frac{5}{6}$ _______

Simplify each expression. Use mental math and the properties of addition.

7. $8\frac{1}{6} + 5\frac{5}{6} + 3\frac{1}{10}$ _______

8. $6\frac{3}{8} + 0 + 9\frac{1}{8}$ _______

9. $7\frac{2}{5} + 9 + 2\frac{1}{10}$ _______

10. $3\frac{4}{7} + 5\frac{5}{7} + 13$ _______

11. $5\frac{1}{3} + 6\frac{1}{6} + 5\frac{1}{9}$ _______

12. $4\frac{1}{3} + 3\frac{5}{8} + 7\frac{5}{6}$ _______

13. $\left(6\frac{3}{4} + 3\frac{1}{5}\right) + 10\frac{1}{4}$ _______

14. $9\frac{2}{11} + \left(2\frac{4}{7} + 7\frac{9}{11}\right)$ _______

15. $5\frac{1}{9} + \left(6\frac{2}{3} - 6\frac{2}{3}\right)$ _______

16. $\left(5\frac{5}{6} - 5\frac{5}{6}\right) + \left(9\frac{2}{3} + 3\frac{2}{5}\right)$ _______

Problem Solving Write and evaluate an expression for each situation.

17. Halle used $3\frac{2}{5}$ yards of red ribbon, some white ribbon, and $2\frac{3}{10}$ yards of blue ribbon to make a bulletin board border. If she used $3\frac{1}{5}$ yards of white ribbon, how much ribbon did she use altogether?

____

18. Len has $4\frac{3}{4}$ pounds of cans to recycle. He collects another $2\frac{1}{8}$ pounds of cans, and his sister collects $1\frac{1}{4}$ pounds of cans. How many pounds of cans do Len and his sister have altogether?

____

Use with Lesson 7-8, pages 236–237 in the Student Book.
Then go to Lesson 7-9, pages 238–239 in the Student Book.

Addition and Subtraction Equations with Fractions

Name _______________

Date _______________

Solve: $d + 3\frac{1}{9} + 5\frac{4}{9} = 10\frac{8}{9}$

- Simplify by adding the numbers on one side.
- Subtract $8\frac{5}{9}$ from both sides to isolate the variable.
- Simplify.

$$d + 8\frac{5}{9} = 10\frac{8}{9}$$

$$d + 8\frac{5}{9} - 8\frac{5}{9} = 10\frac{8}{9} - 8\frac{5}{9}$$

$$d = 2\frac{3}{9} = 2\frac{1}{3}$$

> Solve equations with fractions the same way as with whole numbers.

Solve and check.

1. $6\frac{2}{9} + x = 12\frac{2}{3}$

2. $5\frac{1}{6} - u = 2\frac{3}{4}$

3. $g + 9\frac{3}{4} = 15\frac{1}{2}$

4. $h - 9\frac{6}{7} = 5\frac{3}{7}$

5. $6\frac{2}{9} + r = 10\frac{1}{2}$

6. $s - \frac{5}{6} = 9\frac{2}{5}$

7. $2\frac{2}{3} + a = 7\frac{1}{8}$

8. $n - 6\frac{1}{4} = 3\frac{5}{6}$

9. $c + 1\frac{7}{8} = 12\frac{1}{2}$

10. $20\frac{3}{8} - d = 18\frac{5}{8}$

11. $m + 3\frac{4}{5} = 11\frac{1}{4}$

12. $b - \frac{2}{5} - \frac{1}{3} = 5\frac{4}{15}$

Problem Solving

Circle the letter of the correct equation to solve each problem. Then solve.

13. Stephen has some navy beans and $1\frac{3}{8}$ pounds of kidney beans. He has a total of $3\frac{1}{8}$ pounds of beans. How many pounds of navy beans does Stephen have?

a. $n + 3\frac{1}{8} = 1\frac{3}{8}$

b. $n + 1\frac{3}{8} = 3\frac{1}{8}$

c. $n = 1\frac{3}{8} + 3\frac{1}{8}$

14. The perimeter of a triangular garden is 14 yards. Two of the sides measure $3\frac{1}{4}$ yards and $4\frac{1}{2}$ yards. How long is the third side of the garden?

a. $14 = 3\frac{1}{4} + 4\frac{1}{2} + s$

b. $14 + 3\frac{1}{4} + 4\frac{1}{2} = s$

c. $14 + 3\frac{1}{4} = 4\frac{1}{2} + s$

Use with Lesson 7-9, pages 238–239 in the Student Book.
Then go to Lesson 7-10, pages 240–241 in the Student Book.

Problem-Solving Strategy: Work Backward

Aunt Martha says, "If you subtract 8 from my age and divide the result by 2, you will get the number of eggs in a dozen." How old is Aunt Martha?

- Start with the number of eggs in a dozen.　　12
- Multiply by 2.　　$2 \times 12 = 24$
- Add 8.　　$24 + 8 = 32$

Aunt Martha is 32 years old.

Solve. Do your work on a separate sheet of paper.

1. Shawna had to decorate 3 gift packages with ribbon. She used $1\frac{1}{3}$ yards of ribbon for the first package, $1\frac{1}{2}$ yards of ribbon for the second package, and $1\frac{2}{3}$ yards to decorate the third package. Shawna had $3\frac{1}{3}$ yards of ribbon left over. How much ribbon did she start with?

2. Paulina gets on an elevator. At the first stop, 4 people get off and 3 get on. At the second stop, 5 people get off and one gets on. At the third stop, Paulina gets off. If 4 people are still in the elevator when Paulina gets off, how many people were on the elevator when she got on?

3. From one piece of wood, Sam cut two $9\frac{1}{2}$ in. strips for 2 sides of a frame. He cut two $11\frac{3}{4}$ in. strips each for the other 2 sides. Sam had $5\frac{1}{2}$ in. of wood left. How long was the piece of wood when he started?

4. Jeanine used $2\frac{1}{2}$ cups of flour to make muffins and $1\frac{3}{4}$ cups of flour to make biscuits. After borrowing $\frac{1}{4}$ cup of flour, she had $2\frac{1}{4}$ cups left to make bread. How much flour did she have to begin with?

5. Simon added $4.50 to the money in his bank. Then his father agreed to double Simon's money, which gave him $33. How much money did Simon have to begin with?

6. Franklin was paid for doing yard work. He spent $4.45 of his pay for a sandwich and fruit drink and $2.95 for a magazine. He had $8.55 left. How much was Franklin paid for the yard work?

7. Chita is $3\frac{3}{4}$ years younger than Pablo. If you multiply Chita's age by 4, the answer is 43. How old is Pablo?

8. Duwayne wrote a two-digit number. He multiplied it by 3, added 18, and divided by 8. His final answer was 9. What number did Duwayne write?

Use with Lesson 7-10, pages 240–241 in the Student Book.
Then go to Lesson 7-11, pages 242–243 in the Student Book.

Problem-Solving Applications: Mixed Review

Name _______________________

Date _______________________

Solve each problem and explain the method you used. If needed, do all your work on a separate sheet of paper.

Read ▸ Plan ▸ Solve ▸ Check

1. George started with a 24-inch piece of leather. He cut one $8\frac{1}{6}$-inch piece and one $7\frac{1}{3}$-inch piece. Does he have enough left over to cut two $4\frac{1}{4}$-inch pieces?

2. Laura cut leather strips to make key chains. She cut three $5\frac{3}{10}$-in. strips and one $6\frac{1}{5}$-in. strip. She has $3\frac{1}{2}$ in. of leather left over. How much leather did she start with?

3. Write the next five numbers in this series: $\frac{1}{2}$, $\frac{5}{8}$, $\frac{3}{4}$, $\frac{7}{8}$, 1, $1\frac{1}{8}$, . . .

4. Muhammad cashed a check from his uncle. He then spent $7.40 on taxis and $40.20 at a restaurant. He deposited the $97.75 he had left. What was the total amount of Muhammad's check?

5. Irene has 3 puppies. The black puppy weighs 12 pounds. The white puppy weighs $1\frac{1}{4}$ pounds more than the black puppy. The tan puppy weighs $2\frac{3}{8}$ pounds less than the white puppy. How much does the tan puppy weigh?

Use the diagram for problems 6–9.

6. How much longer is the checkered ribbon than the plain ribbon?

7. What is the total length of the three pieces of ribbon?

8. Lisa has a piece of polka-dot ribbon that is as long as 5 pieces of the striped ribbon. How long is Lisa's polka-dot ribbon?

9. Write and solve a problem like problem 8. Have a classmate solve it.

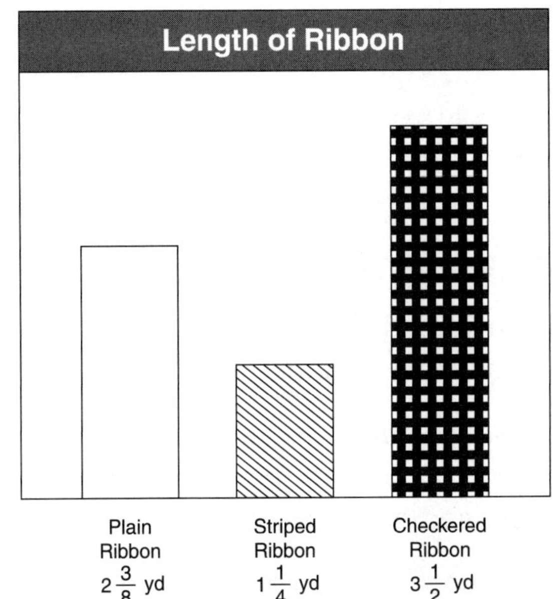

Use with Lesson 7-11, pages 242–243 in the Student Book.

Multiply Fractions by Fractions

Name _______________________

Date _______________________

Multiply: $\frac{3}{4} \times \frac{8}{15}$

- Divide any numerator and denominator by their GCF.

- Multiply the numerators. Then multiply the denominators. The product will be in simplest form.

$$\frac{3}{4} \times \frac{8}{15} = \frac{\overset{1}{\cancel{3}}}{\underset{1}{\cancel{4}}} \times \frac{\overset{2}{\cancel{8}}}{\underset{5}{\cancel{15}}}$$

GCF of 3 and 15: 3
GCF of 4 and 8: 4

$$= \frac{1 \times 2}{1 \times 5}$$

$$= \frac{2}{5}$$

simplest form

Multiply. Use the GCF to simplify whenever possible.

1. $\frac{2}{7} \times \frac{3}{7} =$ _______

2. $\frac{3}{8} \times \frac{1}{4} =$ _______

3. $\frac{1}{3} \times \frac{2}{5} =$ _______

4. $\frac{7}{12} \times \frac{4}{5} =$ _______

5. $\frac{6}{10} \times \frac{4}{5} =$ _______

6. $\frac{12}{15} \times \frac{3}{4} =$ _______

7. $\frac{3}{4} \times \frac{6}{8} =$ _______

8. $\frac{18}{20} \times \frac{5}{10} =$ _______

9. $\frac{12}{14} \times \frac{2}{7} =$ _______

10. $\frac{8}{21} \times \frac{3}{12} =$ _______

11. $\frac{22}{70} \times \frac{10}{11} =$ _______

12. $\frac{7}{16} \times \frac{12}{28} =$ _______

13. $\frac{1}{5} \times \frac{3}{7} \times \frac{5}{9} =$ _______

14. $\frac{3}{4} \times \frac{10}{12} \times \frac{6}{9} =$ _______

15. $\frac{5}{6} \times \frac{1}{10} \times \frac{6}{9} =$ _______

16. $\frac{1}{2} \times \frac{3}{4} \times \frac{2}{5} =$ _______

17. $\frac{4}{5} \times \frac{2}{6} \times \frac{5}{10} =$ _______

18. $\frac{3}{4} \times \frac{4}{9} \times \frac{1}{8} =$ _______

19. $\frac{3}{5} \times \frac{10}{35} \times \frac{7}{20} =$ _______

20. $\frac{2}{9} \times \frac{3}{12} \times \frac{4}{5} =$ _______

21. $\frac{4}{15} \times \frac{5}{8} \times \frac{3}{5} =$ _______

Problem Solving

22. Philip had $\frac{5}{8}$ yd of paper toweling. He used $\frac{2}{3}$ of it. How long was the toweling Philip used?

____

23. Janelle purchased a piece of wood that measured $\frac{5}{6}$ yd. She used only $\frac{3}{5}$ of it. How long was the unused piece of wood?

____

24. A punch recipe calls for $\frac{3}{4}$ cup of grape juice. If Carlos wants to cut the recipe in half, how much grape juice should he use?

____

Use with Lesson 8-1, pages 250–251 in the Student Book.
Then go to Lesson 8-2, pages 252–253 in the Student Book.

Multiply Fractions and Whole Numbers

Name _______________________

Date _______________________

Multiply: $5 \times \frac{3}{8}$

$5 \times \frac{3}{8} = \frac{5}{1} \times \frac{3}{8}$

Rename the whole number as a fraction with a denominator of 1.

$= \frac{5 \times 3}{1 \times 8}$

$= \frac{15}{8} = 1\frac{7}{8}$

Find: $\frac{2}{3}$ of \$84

"of" means "times"

$\frac{2}{3} \times 84 = \frac{2}{\overset{}{\underset{1}{3}}} \times \frac{\overset{28}{84}}{1}$

$= \frac{2 \times 28}{1 \times 1} = \frac{56}{1} = \$56$

Multiply.

1. $3 \times \frac{2}{3} =$ _______

2. $9 \times \frac{5}{6} =$ _______

3. $14 \times \frac{2}{7} =$ _______

4. $8 \times \frac{1}{7} =$ _______

5. $24 \times \frac{5}{8} =$ _______

6. $15 \times \frac{3}{5} =$ _______

7. $18 \times \frac{3}{4} =$ _______

8. $25 \times \frac{4}{15} =$ _______

9. $\frac{7}{8} \times 56 =$ _______

10. $\frac{4}{9} \times 18 =$ _______

11. $\frac{3}{4} \times 10 =$ _______

12. $\frac{4}{5} \times 8 =$ _______

Find the product.

13. $\frac{1}{8}$ of 32 = _______

14. $\frac{1}{5}$ of 25 = _______

15. $\frac{1}{8}$ of 12 = _______

16. $\frac{2}{3}$ of 18 = _______

17. $\frac{2}{9}$ of 3 = _______

18. $\frac{3}{10}$ of 5 = _______

19. $\frac{1}{8}$ of 4 = _______

20. $\frac{2}{3}$ of 14 = _______

21. $\frac{3}{4}$ of \$24 = _______

22. $\frac{2}{3}$ of \$27 = _______

23. $\frac{1}{5}$ of \$3.50 = _______

24. $\frac{3}{7}$ of \$4.20 = _______

Problem Solving

25. David lives $\frac{7}{8}$ mi from school. If he walks to school but does not walk home from school each day, how many miles does he walk in a 5-day school week? _______________________

26. Susan baked 12 muffins. Her family ate $\frac{5}{6}$ of them. How many muffins were left? _______________________

27. Joshua rode his bicycle 16 miles. He stopped for a rest after riding $\frac{3}{4}$ of the way. How many miles did he ride after resting? _______________________

Use with Lesson 8-2, pages 252–253 in the Student Book.
Then go to Lesson 8-3, pages 254–255 in the Student Book.

Properties of Multiplication

Name ___________________________

Date ___________________________

Commutative Property	Identity Property	Associative Property
$\frac{3}{8} \times \frac{4}{7} = \frac{4}{7} \times \frac{3}{8}$	$1 \times \frac{2}{9} = \frac{2}{9}$ $\frac{2}{9} \times 1 = \frac{2}{9}$	$(\frac{1}{3} \times \frac{1}{4}) \times 7 = \frac{1}{3} \times (\frac{1}{4} \times 7)$
Zero Property	Inverse Property	Distributive Property Over Addition
$0 \times \frac{8}{9} = 0$ $\frac{8}{9} \times 0 = 0$	$\frac{2}{3} \times \frac{3}{2} = 1$ reciprocals	$\frac{1}{3} \times (\frac{1}{7} + \frac{2}{7}) = (\frac{1}{3} \times \frac{1}{7}) + (\frac{1}{3} \times \frac{2}{7})$

Find the value of *n*. Use the properties of multiplication.

1. $\frac{1}{8} \times \frac{2}{5} = \frac{2}{5} \times n$ ______

2. $\frac{5}{12} \times 0 = n$ ______

3. $\frac{4}{5} \times n = \frac{4}{5}$ ______

4. $\frac{1}{9} \times \frac{2}{3} = n \times \frac{1}{9}$ ______

5. $n \times \frac{3}{7} = \frac{3}{7}$ ______

6. $n \times \frac{3}{10} = 0$ ______

7. $(\frac{2}{5} \times \frac{1}{11}) \times \frac{1}{6} = \frac{2}{5} \times (n \times \frac{1}{6})$ ______

8. $\frac{4}{5} \times (12 \times n) = (\frac{4}{5} \times 12) \times \frac{1}{6}$ ______

9. $(\frac{1}{6} \times n) \times \frac{3}{8} = \frac{1}{6} \times (\frac{1}{3} \times \frac{3}{8})$ ______

10. $(n \times \frac{6}{3}) \times 2 = \frac{3}{5} \times (\frac{6}{3} \times 2)$ ______

Write the reciprocal of each number.

11. 3 ______

12. 23 ______

13. $\frac{1}{4}$ ______

14. $\frac{13}{24}$ ______

15. $\frac{9}{7}$ ______

16. $\frac{15}{8}$ ______

Compute. Use the properties of multiplication.

17. $\frac{4}{7} \times \frac{2}{3} \times 6$ ______

18. $0 \times \frac{7}{12} \times \frac{10}{11}$ ______

19. $(\frac{1}{5} \times \frac{3}{8}) \times 15$ ______

20. $(\frac{2}{5} \times \frac{1}{3}) \times 3$ ______

21. $\frac{4}{3} \times (\frac{3}{4} \times \frac{15}{28})$ ______

22. $(\frac{5}{6} \times \frac{2}{3}) \times \frac{6}{5}$ ______

23. $\frac{2}{5} \times \frac{1}{6} \times \frac{5}{8}$ ______

24. $\frac{4}{9} \times 8 \times 18$ ______

25. $\frac{5}{24} \times \frac{12}{25} \times \frac{24}{5}$ ______

26. $(\frac{9}{5} \times \frac{3}{7}) \times \frac{5}{9}$ ______

27. $\frac{7}{21} \times \frac{13}{18} \times \frac{21}{7}$ ______

28. $\frac{3}{5} \times (\frac{17}{35} \times \frac{5}{3})$ ______

Use with Lesson 8-3, pages 254–255 in the Student Book.
Then go to Lesson 8-4, pages 256–257 in the Student Book.

Multiply Mixed Numbers

Name _______________________

Date _______________________

Multiply: $4\frac{2}{3} \times 14\frac{1}{4}$

- Rename both factors as fractions greater than or equal to one.

- Simplify using the GCF.

- Multiply the numerators and then the denominators.

- Rename the product as a mixed number.

$$4\frac{2}{3} \times 14\frac{1}{4} = \frac{14}{3} \times \frac{57}{4}$$

$$= \frac{\overset{7}{\cancel{14}}}{\underset{1}{\cancel{3}}} \times \frac{\overset{19}{\cancel{57}}}{\underset{2}{\cancel{4}}}$$

GCF of 14 and 4: 2
GCF of 3 and 57: 3

$$= \frac{7 \times 19}{1 \times 2} = \frac{133}{2}$$

$$= 66\frac{1}{2}$$

Estimate each product by rounding.

1. $3\frac{5}{6} \times 8\frac{2}{7} =$ _______

2. $6\frac{1}{5} \times 4\frac{3}{4} =$ _______

3. $7 \times 9\frac{7}{8} =$ _______

4. $93\frac{5}{6} \times \frac{6}{7} =$ _______

5. $15\frac{1}{3} \times 2\frac{1}{4} =$ _______

6. $\frac{4}{5} \times 28\frac{2}{3} =$ _______

Multiply. Estimate to help you.

7. $4\frac{2}{3} \times 18 =$ _______

8. $1\frac{1}{6} \times 4\frac{4}{5} =$ _______

9. $2\frac{3}{4} \times 3\frac{1}{5} =$ _______

10. $\frac{3}{7} \times 8\frac{1}{6} =$ _______

11. $5\frac{1}{3} \times 3\frac{3}{8} =$ _______

12. $1\frac{1}{8} \times 10\frac{2}{3} =$ _______

13. $21 \times 3\frac{2}{3} =$ _______

14. $1\frac{1}{5} \times 5\frac{2}{3} \times 5 =$ _______

15. $1\frac{4}{5} \times 2\frac{1}{3} \times 1\frac{7}{8} =$ _______

Compare. Write <, =, or >.

16. $1\frac{1}{2} \times 3\frac{1}{4}$ _______ $1\frac{1}{4} \times 3\frac{1}{2}$

17. $2\frac{3}{5} \times 1\frac{1}{5}$ _______ $1\frac{4}{5} \times 1\frac{2}{3}$

18. $2\frac{1}{6} \times 1\frac{1}{4}$ _______ $1\frac{5}{8} \times 2\frac{1}{3}$

19. $4\frac{2}{3} \times 3\frac{6}{7}$ _______ $4\frac{5}{7} \times 3\frac{2}{3}$

Find the value of *n*. Use the properties of multiplication.

20. $n \times 4\frac{2}{5} = 0$ _______

21. $1\frac{1}{2} \times n = \frac{3}{4} \times 1\frac{1}{2}$ _______

22. $1 \times n = 7\frac{4}{5}$ _______

23. $\left(\frac{2}{3} \times \frac{1}{4}\right) \times 4\frac{1}{3} = \frac{2}{3} \times \left(n \times 4\frac{1}{3}\right)$ _______

24. $\frac{7}{8} \times \left(n \times 3\frac{1}{2}\right) = \left(\frac{7}{8} \times 4\right) \times 3\frac{1}{2}$ _______

Problem Solving

25. A group hiked $2\frac{3}{4}$ miles in one hour. At that rate, how far could it hike in $2\frac{1}{2}$ hours?

____

26. Sean is $15\frac{1}{2}$ years old. Kathy is $1\frac{1}{3}$ times as old. How old is Kathy?

____

Meaning of Division

Name ______________________

Date ______________________

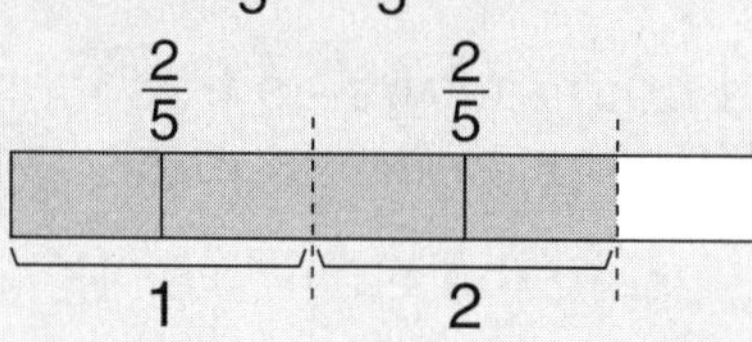

Divide: $4 \div \frac{1}{6}$

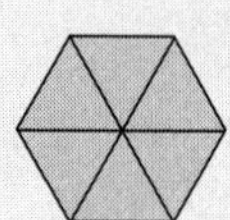 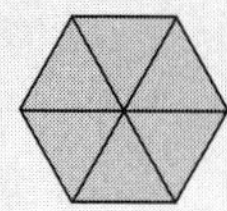 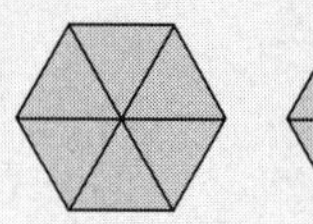 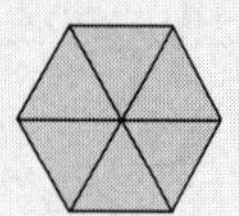

How many $\frac{1}{6}$s are in 4?

4 wholes divided into sixths make 24 equal parts.

Division sentence: $4 \div \frac{1}{6} = 24$.

Divide: $\frac{4}{5} \div \frac{2}{5}$

How many $\frac{2}{5}$s are in $\frac{4}{5}$?

1 whole is divided into fifths.

There are two $\frac{2}{5}$s in $\frac{4}{5}$.

Division sentence: $\frac{4}{5} \div \frac{2}{5} = 2$.

Write a division sentence for each diagram.

1. 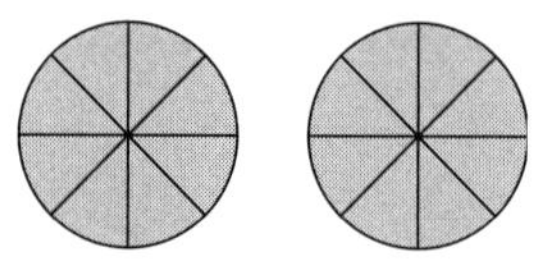

____

2. 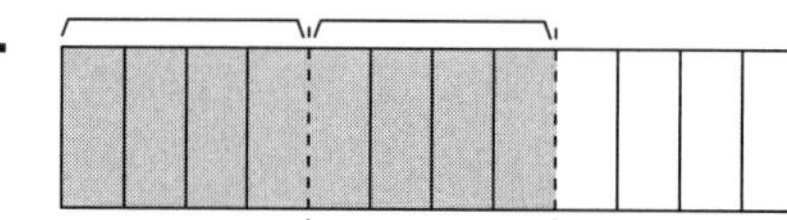

____

3. 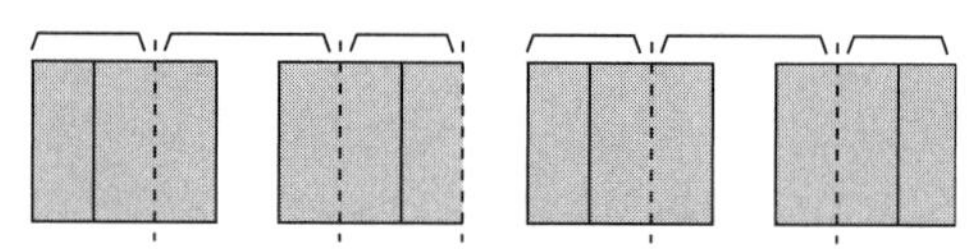

____

4. 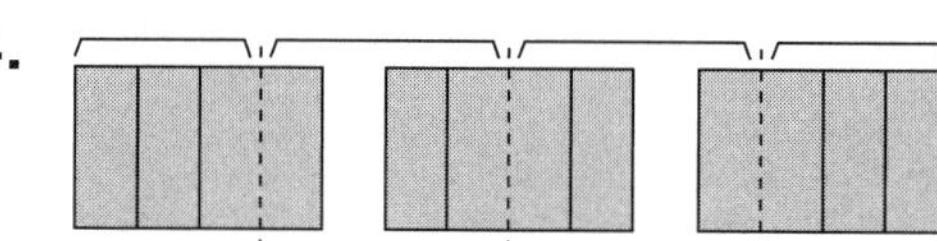

____

5. 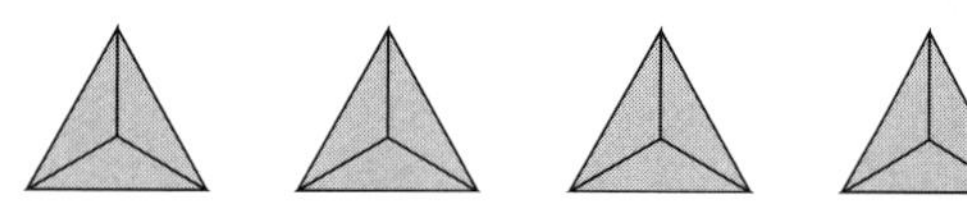

____

6. 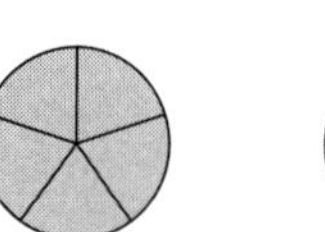 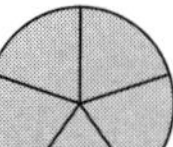 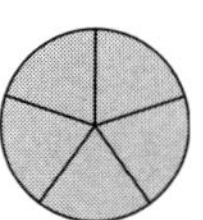

____

7. 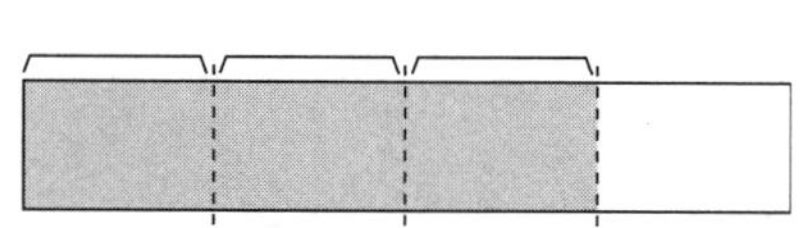

____

8. 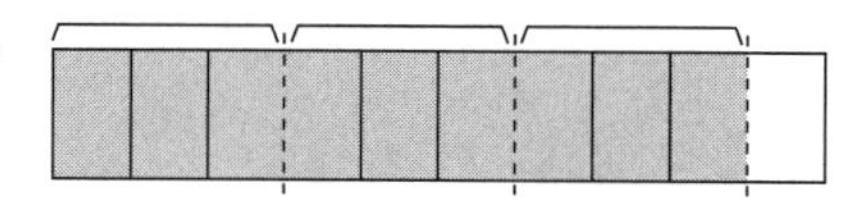

____

Draw a diagram to show each division. Write each quotient. Explain how your drawing illustrates the division. Do your work on a separate sheet of paper.

9. $5 \div \frac{1}{2}$ ______

10. $\frac{4}{6} \div \frac{1}{6}$ ______

11. $3 \div \frac{1}{4}$ ______

12. $\frac{8}{9} \div \frac{2}{9}$ ______

13. $6 \div \frac{1}{2}$ ______

14. $\frac{8}{10} \div \frac{4}{10}$ ______

Use with Lesson 8-5, pages 258–259 in the Student Book.
Then go to Lesson 8-5A, pages 227–228 in this Workbook.

Divide Fractions by Fractions

Name _______________________

Date _______________________

Divide: $\frac{3}{4} \div \frac{5}{8}$

$$\frac{3}{4} \div \frac{5}{8} = \frac{3}{\overset{1}{\cancel{4}}} \times \frac{\overset{2}{\cancel{8}}}{5} = \frac{6}{5} = 1\frac{1}{5}$$

reciprocals

Multiply by the reciprocal of the divisor.

Simplify using the GCF, where possible.

Divide: $\frac{2}{3} \div \frac{1}{6}$

$$\frac{2}{3} \div \frac{1}{6} = \frac{2}{\overset{1}{\cancel{3}}} \times \frac{\overset{2}{\cancel{6}}}{1} = 4$$

reciprocals

Write the value of each variable.

1. $\frac{4}{7} \div \frac{2}{3} = \frac{4}{7} \times \frac{3}{2} = a$ ______

2. $\frac{8}{15} \div \frac{16}{25} = \frac{8}{15} \times \frac{25}{16} = m$ ______

3. $\frac{5}{6} \div \frac{5}{24} = \frac{5}{6} \times \frac{24}{5} = h$ ______

4. $\frac{3}{4} \div \frac{1}{16} = \frac{3}{4} \times \frac{16}{1} = s$ ______

Solve for _n_. Draw a diagram to help you.

5. $\frac{1}{2} \div \frac{1}{8} = n$ ______

6. $\frac{4}{5} \div \frac{1}{15} = n$ ______

7. $n = \frac{3}{4} \div \frac{3}{16}$ ______

Find the quotient.

8. $\frac{7}{12} \div \frac{7}{9} =$ ______

9. $\frac{1}{8} \div \frac{1}{7} =$ ______

10. $\frac{20}{21} \div \frac{5}{14} =$ ______

11. $\frac{7}{8} \div \frac{21}{32} =$ ______

12. $\frac{16}{21} \div \frac{4}{7} =$ ______

13. $\frac{8}{9} \div \frac{14}{15} =$ ______

Problem Solving Write a division sentence.

14. How many $\frac{1}{8}$s are there in $\frac{3}{4}$?

____

15. How many $\frac{1}{20}$s are there in $\frac{1}{5}$?

____

16. If $\frac{2}{3}$ is divided by a certain fraction $\frac{m}{n}$, the result is $\frac{3}{5}$. What is $\frac{m}{n}$?

____

Use with Lesson 8-6, pages 260–261 in the Student Book.
Then go to Lesson 8-7, pages 262–263 in the Student Book.

Estimate Quotients of Fractions and Mixed Numbers

Name ___________________

Date ___________________

When the dividend is greater than the divisor, the quotient is greater than 1.

$$\frac{3}{7} \div \frac{1}{7} = 3$$

$$\frac{3}{7} > \frac{1}{7} \qquad 3 > 1$$

When the dividend is less than the divisor, the quotient is less than 1.

$$\frac{1}{6} \div \frac{5}{6} = \frac{1}{5}$$

$$\frac{1}{6} < \frac{5}{6} \qquad \frac{1}{5} < 1$$

Use the nearest compatible whole numbers to estimate quotients of mixed numbers.

$$4\frac{2}{3} \div 14\frac{1}{2}$$

$4\frac{2}{3} < 14\frac{1}{2}$, so the quotient is less than 1.

$$4\frac{2}{3} \div 14\frac{1}{2}$$
$$5 \div 15 = \frac{1}{3} \leftarrow \text{estimated quotient}$$

Compare the dividend and the divisor to determine whether the quotient _is less than 1_ or _is greater than 1_. Write < or >. Then find the quotient.

1. $\frac{1}{3} \div \frac{2}{3}$ _______

2. $\frac{5}{9} \div \frac{2}{9}$ _______

3. $\frac{1}{4} \div \frac{1}{12}$ _______

4. $\frac{1}{11} \div \frac{1}{10}$ _______

5. $\frac{2}{7} \div \frac{2}{5}$ _______

6. $\frac{5}{8} \div \frac{5}{12}$ _______

7. $\frac{3}{4} \div \frac{1}{3}$ _______

8. $\frac{3}{4} \div \frac{7}{8}$ _______

9. $\frac{1}{3} \div \frac{5}{12}$ _______

10. $\frac{13}{24} \div \frac{7}{12}$ _______

11. $\frac{3}{10} \div \frac{7}{15}$ _______

12. $\frac{3}{8} \div \frac{6}{7}$ _______

13. $1 \div \frac{1}{4}$ _______

14. $\frac{1}{5} \div \frac{1}{2}$ _______

15. $\frac{2}{3} \div \frac{7}{8}$ _______

16. $\frac{4}{5} \div \frac{2}{7}$ _______

Use the nearest compatible whole numbers to estimate each quotient.

17. $3\frac{3}{5} \div 1\frac{7}{8}$ _______

18. $9\frac{1}{4} \div 2\frac{3}{4}$ _______

19. $7 \div 2\frac{1}{3}$ _______

20. $15 \div 1\frac{9}{10}$ _______

21. $3\frac{4}{5} \div 16\frac{1}{7}$ _______

22. $8\frac{2}{7} \div 11\frac{2}{3}$ _______

Compare. Write < or >. Use estimation to help you.

23. $12\frac{1}{7} \div 2\frac{1}{3}$ _______ 1

24. $32 \div 8$ _______ $32 \div 7\frac{4}{9}$

25. $\frac{3}{5} \div 9\frac{1}{4}$ _______ $9\frac{1}{4} \div \frac{3}{5}$

Problem Solving

26. About how much will each person get if 8 people share $1\frac{2}{3}$ qt of lemonade?

____

94

Use with Lesson 8-7, pages 262–263 in the Student Book.
Then go to Lesson 8-8, pages 264–265 in the Student Book.

Divide with Whole and Mixed Numbers

Name _______________________

Date _______________________

Divide: $9 \div \frac{4}{7}$

$9 \div \frac{4}{7} = \frac{9}{1} \div \frac{4}{7}$

> Rename the whole numbers and mixed numbers as fractions.

$= \frac{9}{1} \times \frac{7}{4}$

> Multiply by the reciprocal. Simplify, using the GCF where possible.

$= \frac{63}{4}$

$= 15\frac{3}{4}$ ←———— simplest form ————→ $= 2\frac{1}{4}$

Divide: $7\frac{7}{8} \div 3\frac{1}{2}$

$7\frac{7}{8} \div 3\frac{1}{2} = \frac{63}{8} \div \frac{7}{2}$

$= \frac{\overset{9}{\cancel{63}}}{8} \times \frac{\overset{1}{\cancel{2}}}{\cancel{7}}$

$= \frac{9 \times 1}{4 \times 1} = \frac{9}{4}$

$= 2\frac{1}{4}$

Find the value of each variable to complete the division.

1. $\frac{1}{9} \div 5 = \frac{a}{9} \div \frac{b}{1}$

$= \frac{a}{9} \times \frac{1}{b} = n$

____

2. $9\frac{1}{3} \div 1\frac{1}{3} = \frac{28}{3} \div \frac{g}{h}$

$= \frac{28}{3} \times \frac{h}{g} = y$

____

Divide. Estimate to help you.

3. $6 \div \frac{1}{4} =$ _______

4. $8 \div \frac{1}{8} =$ _______

5. $3 \div \frac{2}{7} =$ _______

6. $4 \div \frac{2}{5} =$ _______

7. $\frac{1}{3} \div 2 =$ _______

8. $24 \div \frac{8}{9} =$ _______

9. $\frac{3}{4} \div 4\frac{1}{5} =$ _______

10. $6\frac{2}{3} \div 5\frac{5}{8} =$ _______

11. $2\frac{1}{7} \div \frac{5}{14} =$ _______

12. $2\frac{2}{5} \div 4 =$ _______

13. $2 \div 1\frac{1}{3} =$ _______

14. $6\frac{1}{9} \div \frac{5}{6} =$ _______

Compare. Write <, =, or >.

15. $15 \div \frac{5}{7}$ ____ $14 \div \frac{2}{3}$

16. $\frac{1}{6} \div 8$ ____ $\frac{2}{3} \div 3\frac{1}{3}$

17. $2\frac{2}{7} \div 6$ ____ $2\frac{2}{7} \div 4$

18. $63 \div 2\frac{5}{8}$ ____ $9\frac{1}{3} \div \frac{7}{12}$

19. $5\frac{3}{5} \div 1\frac{3}{4}$ ____ $4\frac{5}{9} \div 2\frac{2}{9}$

20. $6\frac{2}{3} \div 2\frac{2}{5}$ ____ $6\frac{1}{4} \div 1\frac{3}{4}$

Problem Solving

21. One batch of honey-nut muffins requires $\frac{2}{3}$ cup of honey. How many batches can Mindy make with 3 cups of honey?

____

22. Allen drove 90 miles in $2\frac{1}{4}$ hours. If he drove at a constant rate of speed, how many miles did he drive in one hour?

____

Order of Operations with Fractions

Name _______________________

Date _______________________

<table>
<tr><td colspan="2">Order of Operations</td><td colspan="2">Distributive Property Over Subtraction</td></tr>
</table>

Order of Operations

- Grouping symbols.

$$\left(\tfrac{1}{4} + \tfrac{1}{4}\right)^2 + 4\tfrac{1}{2} \times \tfrac{1}{6}$$

- Exponents.

$$\left(\tfrac{1}{2}\right)^2 + 4\tfrac{1}{2} \times \tfrac{1}{6}$$

- Multiply or divide from left to right.

$$\tfrac{1}{4} + \tfrac{9}{2} \times \tfrac{1}{6}$$

- Add or subtract from left to right.

$$\tfrac{1}{4} + \tfrac{3}{4}$$

$$1$$

Distributive Property Over Subtraction

$$\tfrac{3}{7} \times \left(2 - \tfrac{7}{5}\right) = \left(\tfrac{3}{7} \times 2\right) - \left(\tfrac{3}{7} \times \tfrac{7}{5}\right)$$

$$\tfrac{3}{7} \times \tfrac{3}{5} = \left(\tfrac{3}{7} \times \tfrac{2}{1}\right) - \left(\tfrac{3}{7} \times \tfrac{7}{5}\right)$$

$$\tfrac{9}{35} = \tfrac{6}{7} - \tfrac{3}{5}$$

$$\tfrac{9}{35} = \tfrac{9}{35}$$

Use the order of operations to simplify. Check with a calculator.

1. $\tfrac{4}{7} \div 1\tfrac{1}{7} + 5$ _____

2. $1\tfrac{3}{4} - 0.25 - 1$ _____

3. $2\tfrac{1}{3} + 1\tfrac{1}{3} \times 2$ _____

4. $1 - \tfrac{1}{8} + 1\tfrac{5}{8}$ _____

5. $2\tfrac{1}{6} + 1\tfrac{5}{6} - 2\tfrac{1}{3}$ _____

6. $\left(\tfrac{1}{5}\right)^2 + \tfrac{1}{5} \div \tfrac{1}{4}$ _____

7. $1\tfrac{3}{8} \div \left(\tfrac{1}{3} + \tfrac{1}{6}\right)^2$ _____

8. $4 \times \tfrac{5}{8} \div \tfrac{1}{3}$ _____

9. $8 \times \tfrac{1}{4} \div 0.5$ _____

10. $\tfrac{3}{8} \div \left(\tfrac{1}{2} + 1\tfrac{1}{4}\right)$ _____

11. $\left(6\tfrac{1}{3} - 4\right) \div \tfrac{3}{4}$ _____

12. $1\tfrac{3}{4} \times \tfrac{1}{7} \div \tfrac{2}{3}$ _____

13. $\tfrac{3}{5} + 0.8 \times \tfrac{1}{2}$ _____

14. $10 \times \tfrac{2}{5} \div \tfrac{3}{5}$ _____

15. $2\tfrac{1}{2} \times \tfrac{1}{4} - \left(\tfrac{1}{4}\right)^2$ _____

16. $\tfrac{1}{2} \times \left(\tfrac{2}{3} - \tfrac{1}{6}\right)^2$ _____

17. $\tfrac{5}{9} - \tfrac{1}{3} \div (3)^2$ _____

18. $\left(\tfrac{2}{7} + \tfrac{1}{3}\right) \times 12$ _____

Simplify using the Distributive Property.

19. $\tfrac{2}{5} \times \left(11 - \tfrac{1}{4}\right)$ _____

20. $\tfrac{1}{3} \times \left(6 - \tfrac{2}{3}\right)$ _____

21. $\tfrac{5}{8} \times \left(10 - \tfrac{3}{4}\right)$ _____

22. $\tfrac{4}{5} \times \left(15 - \tfrac{3}{5}\right)$ _____

23. $\tfrac{1}{6} \times \left(12 - \tfrac{1}{3}\right)$ _____

24. $\tfrac{1}{2} \times \left(14 - \tfrac{1}{4}\right)$ _____

Use with Lesson 8-9, pages 266–267 in the Student Book.
Then go to Lesson 8-10, pages 268–269 in the Student Book.

Fractions with Money

Name _______________________

Date _______________________

Find: $\frac{2}{5}$ of \$1.40

$$\frac{2}{5} \text{ of } \$1.40 = \frac{2}{5} \times \frac{\$1.40}{1}$$

$$= \frac{2}{\overset{5}{\underset{1}{5}}} \times \frac{\overset{\$.28}{\cancel{\$1.40}}}{1}$$

$$= \frac{\$.56}{1}$$

$$= \$.56$$

Divide: $\$4.60 \div 1\frac{1}{3}$

$$\$4.60 \div 1\frac{1}{3} = \frac{\$4.60}{1} \div \frac{4}{3}$$

$$= \frac{\$4.60}{1} \times \frac{3}{4}$$

$$= \frac{\overset{\$1.15}{\cancel{\$4.60}}}{1} \times \frac{3}{\underset{1}{\cancel{4}}}$$

$$= \frac{\$3.45}{1} = \$3.45$$

Compute. Round to the nearest cent when necessary.

1. $\frac{1}{3}$ of \$36 _______

2. $\frac{1}{4}$ of \$3.20 _______

3. $\frac{1}{8}$ of \$8.56 _______

4. $\frac{1}{6}$ of \$7.20 _______

5. $\frac{2}{3}$ of \$52 _______

6. $\frac{3}{5}$ of \$72 _______

7. $\frac{5}{8}$ of \$12.40 _______

8. $\$23.45 \div 1\frac{2}{3}$ _______

9. $\$2.70 \div 1\frac{1}{5}$ _______

10. $\$4.50 \div 1\frac{1}{4}$ _______

11. $\$9.90 \div 1\frac{3}{8}$ _______

12. $\frac{3}{4}$ of \$22.50 _______

13. $\$18.60 \div 2\frac{1}{4}$ _______

14. $\$25.55 \div 1\frac{2}{5}$ _______

15. $\$42 \div 1\frac{3}{4}$ _______

16. $\$28.75 \div \frac{5}{8}$ _______

17. $\frac{3}{4}$ of \$24 _______

18. $\$24 \div \frac{3}{4}$ _______

19. $\frac{2}{5}$ of \$50 _______

20. $\$50 \div \frac{2}{5}$ _______

21. $\$12.32 \div \frac{4}{5}$ _______

Problem Solving

22. Francis wants a camera that costs \$48. He has saved $\frac{2}{3}$ of the cost. How much has Francis saved? _______

23. Sally paid \$8.55 for $4\frac{1}{2}$ yards of cloth. How much was the cloth per yard? _______

24. Pedro promised to raise \$75 for a charity. He has raised $\frac{3}{5}$ of that amount. How much more money does he need to raise? _______

Multiplication and Division Expressions with Fractions

Name _______________

Date _______________

Evaluate: $\frac{y}{8}$, when $y = 2\frac{1}{9}$.

$\frac{y}{8} = \frac{2\frac{1}{9}}{8}$ ← fraction bar means ÷

$2\frac{1}{9} \div 8 = \frac{19}{9} \div \frac{8}{1}$

$= \frac{19}{9} \times \frac{1}{8}$

$= \frac{19 \times 1}{9 \times 8} = \frac{19}{72}$ ← value

Evaluate: $t + 1\frac{1}{4} \div u$, when $t = \frac{11}{12}$ and $u = \frac{2}{9}$.

$t + 1\frac{1}{4} \div u = \frac{11}{12} + \frac{5}{4} \div \frac{2}{9}$

$= \frac{11}{12} + \frac{5}{4} \times \frac{9}{2}$

$= \frac{11}{12} + \frac{45}{8} = \frac{157}{24}$

$= 6\frac{13}{24}$ ← value

Evaluate each expression.

1. $\frac{3}{10}h$, when $h = \frac{3}{7}$ ____

2. $b \div \frac{6}{7}$, when $b = \frac{6}{35}$ ____

3. $5\frac{4}{9}m$, when $m = \frac{18}{49}$ ____

4. $a \div \frac{3}{5}$, when $a = 3\frac{3}{10}$ ____

5. $9j$, when $j = \frac{13}{36}$ ____

6. $n \div \frac{4}{7}$, when $n = 18$ ____

7. $9\frac{1}{5}c$, when $c = \frac{5}{11}$ ____

8. $1\frac{7}{8} \div f$, when $f = 2\frac{13}{16}$ ____

9. $8\frac{3}{4}e$, when $e = 1\frac{11}{35}$ ____

10. $(w + x) \div \frac{1}{4}$, when $w = \frac{1}{2}$ and $x = \frac{3}{16}$ ____

11. $d + \frac{4}{7}s$, when $d = 9\frac{1}{3}$ and $s = \frac{7}{9}$ ____

12. $(j - k)l \div k$, when $j = \frac{9}{10}$, $k = \frac{7}{10}$, and $l = \frac{5}{16}$ ____

13. $g + (h + i) \div i$, when $g = 1\frac{1}{2}$, $h = 2\frac{1}{2}$, and $i = 3\frac{1}{4}$ ____

Problem Solving

Write and evaluate an expression that could be used to solve the problem.

14. Two fifths of Eileen's money is in a savings account, and the rest is in a checking account. If Eileen has \$1015, how much is in her savings account?

____

15. Oscar has $12\frac{3}{4}$ pounds of clay. He makes bowls using $\frac{3}{4}$ pound of clay for each. How many bowls can Oscar make?

____

16. Julio has a pine board that is $3\frac{3}{5}$-meters long. How many $\frac{3}{5}$-meter pieces can he make from the board?

____

Ⓒ Use with Lesson 8-11, pages 270–271 in the Student Book.
Ⓒ Then go to Lesson 8-12, pages 272–273 in the Student Book.

Multiplication and Division Equations with Fractions

Name _______________________

Date _______________________

Solve: $d \div \frac{4}{5} = 12\frac{1}{2}$

$d \div \frac{4}{5} \times \frac{4}{5} = 12\frac{1}{2} \times \frac{4}{5}$ ← Isolate the variable.

$d = \frac{25}{2} \times \frac{4}{5}$ ← Compute to solve.

$d = \frac{\overset{5}{\cancel{25}}}{\cancel{2}_{1}} \times \frac{\overset{2}{\cancel{4}}}{\cancel{5}_{1}} = \frac{10}{1}$

$d = 10$

Solve: $\frac{2}{5}f + \frac{2}{5}f = \frac{9}{10}$

$\frac{4}{5}f = \frac{9}{10}$ ← Combine like terms.

$\frac{4}{5}f \div \frac{4}{5} = \frac{9}{10} \div \frac{4}{5}$ ← Isolate the variable.

$f = \frac{9}{10} \times \frac{5}{4}$ ← Compute to solve.

$f = \frac{9}{\cancel{10}_{2}} \times \frac{\overset{1}{\cancel{5}}}{4} = \frac{9}{8}$

$f = 1\frac{1}{8}$

Solve for x.

1. $\frac{2}{5}x = 48$ _______

2. $35x = \frac{7}{10}$ _______

3. $x \div \frac{7}{8} = 64$ _______

4. $x \div 8\frac{8}{9} = 9$ _______

5. $6\frac{1}{3}x = 2\frac{1}{2}$ _______

6. $x \div 1\frac{1}{4} = 3\frac{3}{5}$ _______

7. $\frac{6}{11}x = 7\frac{1}{5}$ _______

8. $x \div 3\frac{3}{4} = 1\frac{7}{25}$ _______

9. $\frac{4}{9}x = \frac{8}{27}$ _______

10. $5\frac{5}{7}x + 2\frac{1}{7}x = 1\frac{11}{14}$ _______

11. $3x + \frac{3}{5}x = 2\frac{1}{10}$ _______

12. $x \div 9\frac{1}{5} = 12\frac{1}{2}$ _______

Use the formulas at the right to convert the temperature to °C or °F. Watch for the degree unit.

13. $41°F$ _____

14. $^{-}15°C$ _____

15. $14°F$ _____

16. $45°C$ _____

17. $^{-}4°F$ _____

18. $35°C$ _____

$$°C = \frac{5}{9}(°F - 32)$$
$$°F = \frac{9}{5}°C + 32$$

Problem Solving

19. Tosha hiked $2\frac{2}{3}$ times as far this weekend as she did last weekend. If she hiked $8\frac{2}{3}$ miles this weekend, how far did she hike last weekend?

____

20. Jake divided a bag of sunflower seeds into $\frac{3}{4}$-cup servings. If he made 15 servings, how many cups of sunflower seeds did he have to begin with?

____

Probability

Name _______________________

Date _______________________

<table>
<tr><td>

Theoretical probability

$$P(E) = \frac{\text{number of favorable outcomes}}{\text{total number of possible outcomes}}$$

Experimental probability

$$\text{Exp } P(E) = \frac{\text{number of favorable outcomes}}{\text{number of trials in the experiment}}$$

</td><td>

Complementary events cannot occur at the same time.

$$P(E) + P(\text{not E}) = 1$$

Mutually exclusive events have no outcomes in common.

$$P(A \text{ or } B) = P(A) + P(B)$$

</td></tr>
</table>

Use the spinner to find the probability of each event. Are the events in exercises 4, 5, 7, and 10 mutually exclusive? If not, tell why.

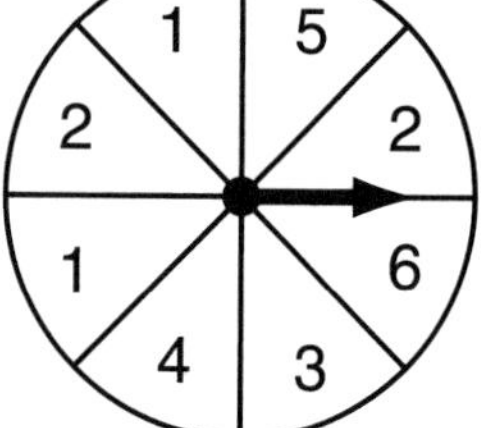

1. $P(2)$ _______________

2. $P(3)$ _______________

3. $P(4)$ _______________

4. $P(1 \text{ or } 2)$ _______________

5. $P(\text{odd or even number})$ _______________

6. $P(\text{not } 2)$ _______________

7. $P(5 \text{ or odd number})$ _______________

8. $P(\text{even number})$ _______________

9. $P(\text{odd number})$ _______________

10. $P(1 \text{ or } 6)$ _______________

One crayon is picked at random from a box containing 2 red crayons, 3 green crayons, 1 purple crayon, 1 blue crayon, and 1 yellow crayon. Find the probability of each event. Then find the probability of its complement.

11. $P(\text{yellow})$ _______________

12. $P(\text{blue or green})$ _______________

13. $P(\text{green})$ _______________

14. $P(\text{not blue})$ _______________

15. $P(\text{red or green})$ _______________

16. $P(\text{not red})$ _______________

17. $P(\text{green, purple, blue, or yellow})$ _______________

Find the experimental probability of each event. Then compare it with the theoretical probability.

Experiment:
Roll a 1–6 number cube.

Outcome	1	2	3	4	5	6
No. of Times	12	18	10	16	10	14

18. Exp $P(3)$

19. Exp $P(4)$

20. Exp $P(6)$

21. Exp $P(1 \text{ or } 2)$

_______________ _______________ _______________ _______________

Use with Lesson 8-13, pages 274–275 in the Student Book.
Then go to Lesson 8-14, pages 276–277 in the Student Book.

Compound Events

Name _______________________

Date _______________________

<table>
<tr><td>

The Counting Principle

If one event has *m* possible outcomes and a second event has *n* possible outcomes, then there are $m \times n$ total possible outcomes for the two events together.

</td><td>

If A and B are **independent events**,

$$P(A, B) = P(A) \times P(B).$$

If A and B are **dependent events**,

$$P(A, B) = P(A) \times P(B \text{ after } A).$$

</td></tr>
</table>

On a separate sheet of paper draw a tree diagram or make a table and use the Counting Principle to find the number of possible outcomes. List all possible outcomes.

1. Roll a 1–6 number cube and spin the spinner.

 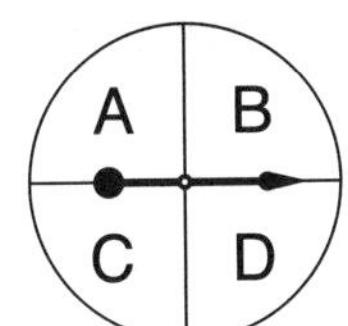

2. Toss a coin and choose a marble without looking.

____

3. Order a 1-topping, 1-cheese pizza given 3 types of cheese and 7 toppings from which to choose.

4. Build a sundae of one flavor of ice cream and one topping, given 5 flavors of ice cream and 4 toppings from which to choose.

____

5. Select a math, science, and history teacher given 5 math, 3 science, and 4 history teachers from which to choose.

6. Select a theater, art, and music elective given 4 theater, 6 art, and 4 music classes from which to choose.

____

Find the probability: (a) if the first choice is replaced; and (b) if the first choice is not replaced.

Experiment: Pick one tile from a bag containing 5 red (R), 3 blue (B), and 2 white (W) tiles. Then pick a second tile.

7. $P(R, B)$ 8. $P(R, W)$ 9. $P(W, R \text{ or } B)$

____

Permutations and Combinations

Three teachers from a team of 5 will coach track.
How many combinations of teachers can be formed?

| Find the number of permutations of the items. Use the Counting Principle. | Find the number of arrangements for each combination. | Divide to eliminate duplicate combinations. |

$5 \times 4 \times 3 = 60$

$3 \times 2 \times 1 = 6$

$60 \div 6 = 10$

Ten combinations of teachers can be formed.

**Tell whether or not order matters in each situation.
Write *yes* or *no*. If yes, explain why.**

1. three toppings selected for a pizza

2. five ingredients needed for a recipe

3. three numbers needed to open a lock

4. seven coins put into a parking meter

5. four kinds of fruit to make a smoothie

6. six students to be ushers at the school play

7. two students to give one opening and one closing speech at graduation

Tell how many permutations and combinations can be made.

8. four of the digits 4, 6, 9, 1, and 3

9. three of the digits 1, 3, 5, 7, and 9

10. three of the letters A, B, C, D, E, F, and G

11. two of the letters A, B, C, D, E, and F

Problem Solving

12. Eight members of the track team run the 800-meter race. Trophies are awarded for first, second, and third place. How many ways can 3 of the track team members win a trophy?

Use with Lesson 8-15, pages 278–279 in the Student Book.
Then go to Lesson 8-16, pages 280–281 in the Student Book.

Predictions and Probability

Name ______________________

Date ______________________

Use theoretical probability to make predictions.

In 500 spins, predict how many times the spinner will land on 2.

$$\frac{1}{\overset{}{\underset{1}{\cancel{5}}}} \times \frac{\overset{100}{\cancel{500}}}{1} = 100$$

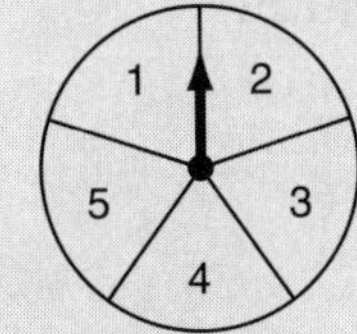

Based on a probability of $\frac{1}{5}$, you can predict the spinner will land on 2 about 100 times.

Odds in favor of an event:

$$\frac{\text{number of favorable outcomes}}{\text{number of unfavorable outcomes}}$$

Odds against an event:

$$\frac{\text{number of unfavorable outcomes}}{\text{number of favorable outcomes}}$$

In 1000 spins, predict the number of times the spinner above would land on each of the following.

1. number < 4 ______
2. number > 4 ______
3. odd number ______
4. even number ______

Use the experimental results to predict how many times you can expect to randomly select the marble given the number of selections.

Marbles	Times Selected
White	15
Red	35
Blue	26
Green	24

5. White marble, 40 times

6. Green marble, 350 times

7. Blue marble, 250 times

8. Red marble, 740 times

Find the odds in favor of and the odds against spinning the given number on the spinner at the right.

9. an even number

10. a multiple of 3

11. a factor of 18

12. an odd number

13. number 3

14. a multiple of 4

15. a number greater than 3

16. a number less than 4

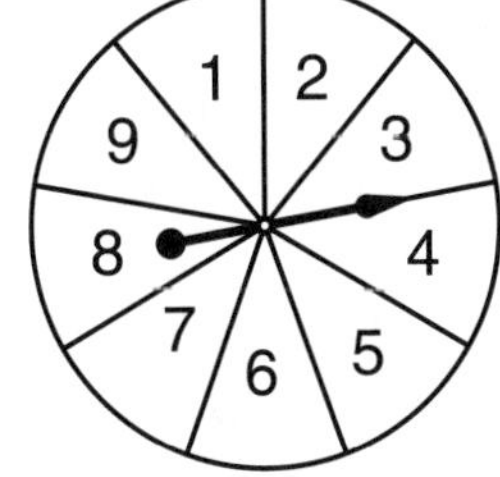

Problem Solving

17. Out of 25 light bulbs tested, 1 was found to be defective. Out of 2000 light bulbs, how many would you expect to be defective? ______

18. In a sample of 200 people, 150 said they would vote for Davis. What are the odds against Davis winning the election? ______

19. What are the odds in favor of rolling a 5 if you roll a 1–6 number cube? ______

Problem-Solving Strategy: Use a Diagram

Of 20 students, 10 are members of the Travel Club and 14 are members of the Drama Club. What fractional part of the 20 students are members of both clubs?

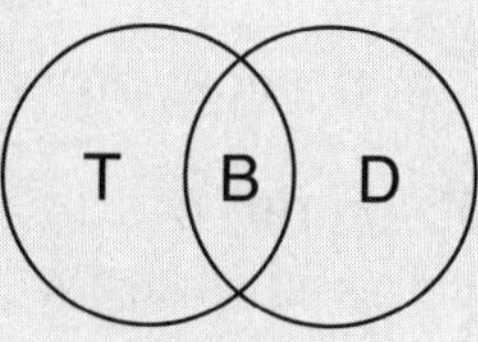

Make a Venn diagram to show the facts.
Let T represent Travel Club members.
Let D represent Drama Club members.
Let B represent members of both clubs.

Four students are members of both clubs.

So $\frac{4}{20}$ or $\frac{1}{5}$ of the students are in both clubs.

$T + B = 10$

$D + B = 14$

$10 + 14 = 24$

$T + B + D = 20$

$B = 24 - 20$

$B = 4$

Solve. Do your work on a separate sheet of paper.

1. Ten students play basketball and 16 students play baseball. If there are 18 students in all, how many students play both sports?

2. A bouquet of 41 flowers is all pink and white. Nine of the flowers are both pink and white and 18 are all pink. How many flowers are all white?

3. Of 30 students, 12 students belong to the Science Club only, and 15 students belong to the Math Club only. How many students belong to both clubs?

4. Of 45 students, five students speak only Spanish and 25 students speak both Spanish and English. What fractional part of the students speaks only English?

5. There are 36 students in the History Club who are planning to take a trip. Twenty-four of these students have visited Boston and 16 have visited Philadelphia. What fractional part of all the students have visited both cities?

6. Of 80 students who take music lessons, 45 play only a string instrument. Forty-three students play only a brass instrument. What fractional part of the students plays both a string instrument and a brass instrument?

7. There are 24 cans of vegetables in Victoria's cupboard. Four cans have only corn in them, 9 cans have only peas in them, and 7 cans have only carrots in them. What fractional part of the 24 cans contain at least two vegetables?

8. Twenty-five members of the Coin Club collect coins from the United States or from foreign countries. Twelve members collect only foreign coins. Eight members collect both foreign and United States coins. How many members collect only coins from the United States?

Use with Lesson 8-17, pages 282–283 in the Student Book.
Then go to Lesson 8-18, pages 284–285 in the Student Book.

Problem-Solving Applications: Mixed Review

Name _______________

Date _______________

Solve each problem and explain the method you used. If needed, do all your work on a separate sheet of paper.

Strategy File

Use These Strategies
Use More Than One Step
Use Simpler Numbers
Use a Diagram
Work Backward

1. Carol has 2 As, 6 Bs, and 8 Cs left at the bottom of her bowl of alphabet soup. If she dips her spoon in without looking, what is the probability that she will get a C?

____

2. Liz has 8 more salted pretzels than unsalted pretzels in a bag. If the probability of randomly selecting an unsalted pretzel is $\frac{4}{16}$, how many salted and unsalted pretzels are in Liz's bag?

____

3. At the deli, Alfredo bought $2\frac{1}{2}$ lb roast beef for $7.75. Cecilia bought $1\frac{3}{4}$ lb roast beef at the market for $5.39. Who spent more per pound on roast beef?

____

4. Michel has $\frac{3}{4}$ bag of dog food. He sends $\frac{1}{4}$ of the food to doggie daycare with his dog. What part of the bag of dog food is left?

____

5. At the end of the picnic, Selma had $\frac{3}{4}$ pound of hamburger meat left. During the picnic she cooked six $\frac{1}{4}$-pound hamburgers and Josiah brought her 4 ounces of hamburger meat. How many pounds of hamburger meat did Selma have at the beginning of the picnic?

____

6. Shrimp is on sale for $9.95 per pound. Do $3\frac{1}{4}$ pounds of shrimp cost more than $30?

____

Use the diagram for problems 7–9.

7. Which students have only sisters?

____

8. How many students have brothers?

____

9. Who has both brothers and sisters?

____

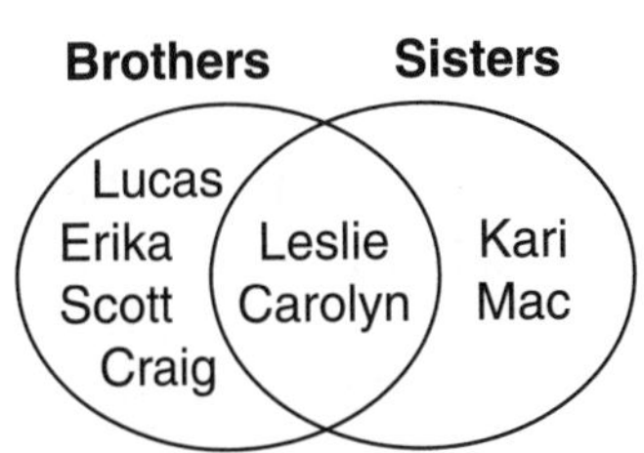

Use with Lesson 8-18, pages 284–285 in the Student Book.

Surveys

Name _______________________

Date _______________________

**The bar graph shows the results of a survey about making a bicycle route.
Use the bar graph to answer the questions.**

1. Write a survey question that could be used to obtain the data.

   ____

   ____

2. How many people are in favor of a bicycle route?

   ____

3. How many more people are in favor of a bicycle route
   than are against it? _______________________

4. How many people in all were surveyed?

   ____

5. What fractional part of those surveyed are in favor
   of a bicycle route? _______________________

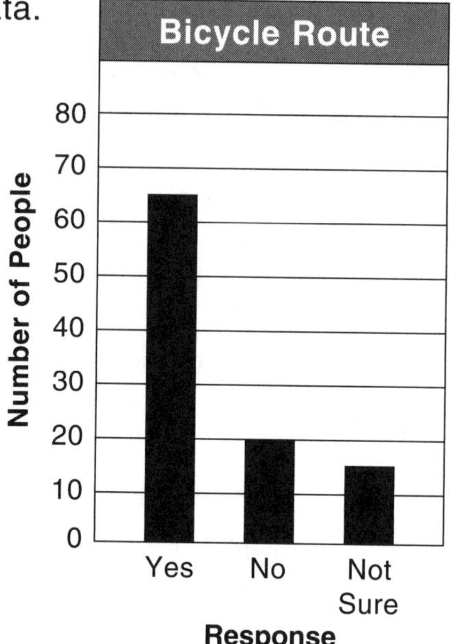

**The pictograph shows the results of a florist's survey about favorite flowers.
Use the graph to answer the questions.**

6. Write a survey question that could be used
   to obtain the data.

   ____

   ____

7. How many people in all were surveyed?

   ____

8. How many of those surveyed did not choose
   either rose or tulip as their favorite flower?

   ____

9. Which flower was the favorite of 12 people?

   ____

10. What fractional part of those surveyed chose
    either iris or tulip?

11. Based on the results of the survey, about how
    many people out of 1000 would you expect to
    choose rose as their favorite flower?

Use with Lesson 9-1, pages 292–293 in the Student Book.
Then go to Lesson 9-2, pages 294–295 in the Student Book.

Samples

Name

Date

Population: the set of all individuals being considered for a survey

Sample: a small part of the population

Representative sample: a sample that has characteristics similar to the population

Use Samples to Predict Data

| sample | population |

$$\frac{9 \text{ boys}}{20 \text{ students in all}} = \frac{n \text{ boys}}{360 \text{ students in all}}$$

$$\frac{9 \times 18}{20 \times 18} = \frac{162}{360} \longrightarrow n = 162$$

Out of 360 students, about 162 are boys.

For each survey question, tell whether you would survey the *population* or use a *sample*. Explain.

1. What is the most popular song in the country this week?

2. What ice cream flavor should be served at the family picnic?

3. Who should be elected mayor of the city?

4. What is the most popular brand of sneakers of the students in your school?

5. What is the favorite lunch meat of the people at Anna's bus stop?

6. What is the favorite ride of the people at an amusement park?

Tell whether the sample is *likely* or *unlikely* to be a representative sample of the whole population. If *unlikely*, explain why.

7. Pedro wants to know how many hours people on his block spend listening to music. He asks the adults who live on the block.

8. Sophie wants to know the favorite song of the members of the marching band. She writes each member's name on a card and chooses 25 names randomly.

Predict the number of *yes* responses from the population.

9. population: 1500 people
   sample: 250 people
   yes responses from sample: 25

10. population: 800 teachers
    sample: 100 teachers
    yes responses from sample: 90

Use with Lesson 9-2, pages 294–295 in the Student Book.
Then go to Lesson 9-3, pages 296–297 in the Student Book.

Bias in Surveys

Name _______________________

Date _______________________

> Alexa wants to survey people to get their opinions about the most beautiful city in the United States.
>
> | unbiased question |
>
> What is the most beautiful city in the U.S.?
>
> | biased question |
>
> Isn't San Francisco the most beautiful city in the U.S.?
>
> | unbiased sample |
>
> people from each state in the U.S.
>
> | biased sample |
>
> people from San Francisco

Tell whether you would be likely to find a biased sample at the location listed for each survey. Write *yes* or *no*. Explain.

1. Favorite author; high school cafeteria

____

2. Most popular vehicle; monster truck show

____

3. Favorite sport to watch; rodeo

____

4. Most popular movie; beach

____

Write whether the question is *biased* or *unbiased*. Explain.

5. Do you think rabbits make the best pets?

____

6. Do you think tennis is the best summer sport?

____

7. Who is your favorite singer?

____

8. What is your favorite meal?

____

On a separate sheet of paper, explain how the data displays can influence how the results are interpreted.

9.

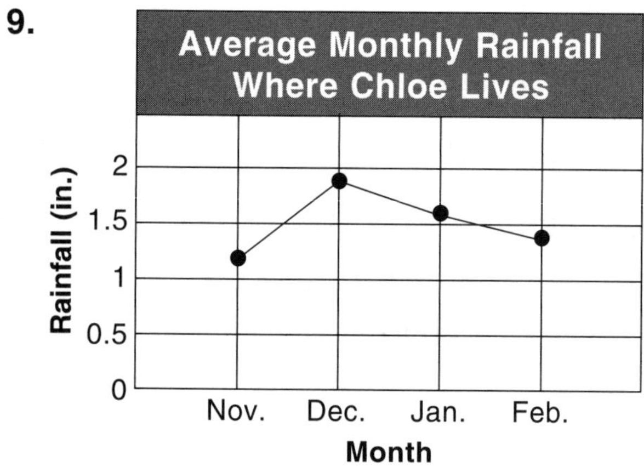

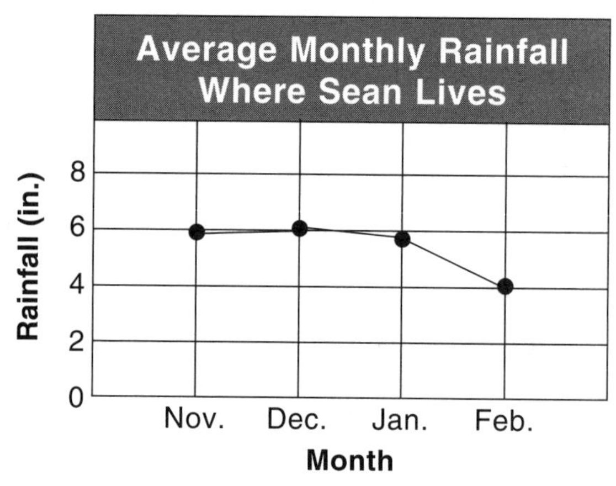

Use with Lesson 9-3, pages 296–297 in the Student Book.
Then go to Lesson 9-3A, pages 229–230 in this Workbook.

Record and Interpret Data

Name _______________________

Date _______________________

The frequency table shows the heights of a pediatrician's patients.

1. Complete the table.

2. How many heights were recorded? _______________________

3. Within which range are the greatest number of heights?

____

Heights (meters)	Tally	Frequency	Cumulative Frequency
1.21–1.30	III		3
1.31–1.40		6	9
1.41–1.50		7	
1.51–1.60	III		
1.61–1.70	I		

4. How many more patients were from 1.31 m to 1.40 m tall than were less than 1.31 m tall? _______________________

5. Write a conclusion about the data in the table.

____

The data in the table below shows the speeds, in seconds, for the 100-meter dash at the Regional Championship Finals.

100-Meter Dash: Regional Championship Finals									
13.5	13.6	13.7	13.8	13.6	13.9	13.7	13.6	13.8	13.7
13.8	13.7	13.7	13.9	13.5	13.6	13.7	13.8	13.7	13.6

6. Use the data to complete the ungrouped frequency table.

Speed (seconds)	13.5				
Tally	II				
Frequency	2				
Relative Frequency	0.10				

$2 \div 20 = 0.10$

7. How many runners had a speed of exactly 13.8 seconds? _______________________

8. Which time was run the most often? _______________________

9. Which time was run by exactly 5 runners? _______________________

10. How many times were recorded? _______________________

11. How many more runners had a time of 13.7 seconds than a time of 13.5 seconds? _______________________

Apply Measures of Central Tendency and Range

Name ______________________

Date ______________________

In six basketball games, Griffin scored 18, 16, 19, 16, 15, and 21 points. Find the mean, median, mode, and range of his scores. Which measure most accurately reflects the data: the mean, median, or mode?

Mean: $18 + 16 + 19 + 16 + 15 + 21 = 105 \longrightarrow 105 \div 6 = 17.5$

Median: 15, 16, 16, 18, 19, 21 $\longrightarrow 16 + 18 = 34 \longrightarrow 34 \div 2 = 17$

Mode: 16   **Range:** $21 - 15 = 6$

Since there are an equal number of scores that are greater than or less than the mean (17.5) or median (17), either the mean or the median best describes the data.

Find the mean, median, mode, and range for each set of data. Then use each measure to describe the data set.

1.

Ages of Children at the Doctor's Office							
5	6	7	7	9	10	12	16

2.

Number of Cars in the Parking Lot					
25	30	40	25	50	40

For each data set, find the mean, median, and mode. Tell which measure is most useful for describing the data. Explain why.

3. Over five weeks, Mike's Diner sold 223, 228, 473, 230, and 236 sandwiches. Mike wants to know how much bread to order from the bakery.

4. The museum is open from Monday to Saturday. In the first 6 weeks of the year, the museum had 2075, 2200, 2150, 2115, 2200, and 2160 visitors. Melissa wants to show that the museum should start opening on Sundays.

Problem Solving

5. The table shows how many of his dog toys Theo has chewed through. Find the mean, median, and mode for the data. How would those measures change if Year 1 was not included?

Number of Toys Chewed Through								
Year	1	2	3	4	5	6	7	8
Toys	33	52	38	40	46	39	54	46

Use with Lesson 9-5, pages 300–301 in the Student Book.
Then go to Lesson 9-6, pages 302–303 in the Student Book.

Analyze Data

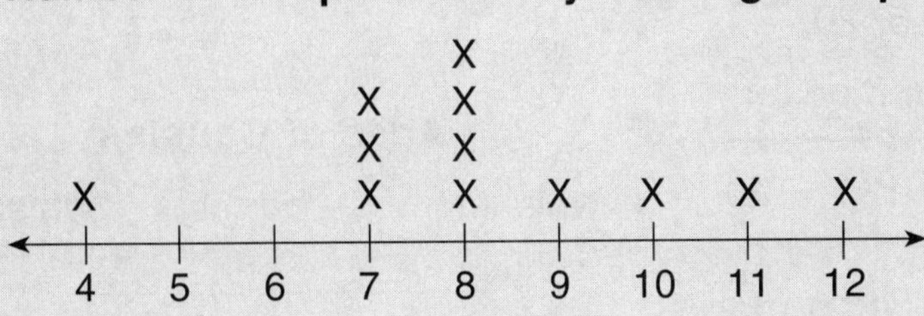

Number of People in Library Reading Groups

mean: 8.25

median: 8

mode: 8

cluster: 7 to 8

gap: between 4 and 7

outlier: 4

Use the line plot for exercises 1–6.

1. What age is an outlier?

2. Is there a gap in the data? Where?

3. Around what age do the data cluster?

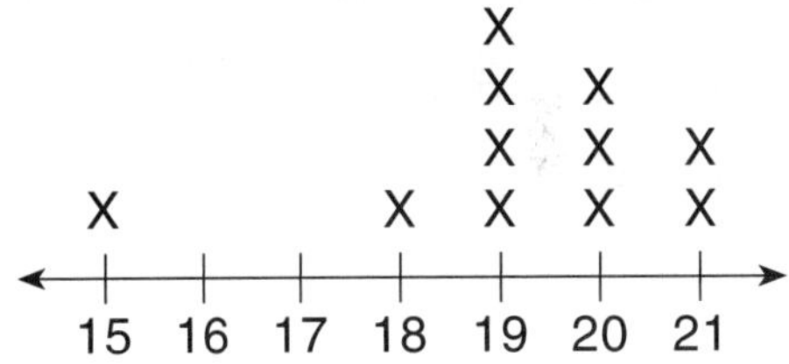

**Ages of People
at the Racquetball Courts**

4. Find the mean, median, and mode of the data set. Round to the nearest tenth.

5. Find the mean, median, and mode of the data without the outlier.

6. What effect does the outlier have on the mean, median, and mode?

On a separate sheet of paper, make a line plot for each set of data. Identify any clusters, gaps, and outliers.

7.

Number of Swim Meets
6 5 7 1 8 6 8 5
7 6 6 7 6 8

cluster: ___________

gaps: ___________

outliers: ___________

8.

Video Game Scores
150 175 100 325 125 150
150 200 175 150

cluster: ___________

gaps: ___________

outliers: ___________

C Use with Lesson 9-6, pages 302–303 in the Student Book.
C Then go to Lessons 9-6A and 9-6B, pages 231–234 in this Workbook.

Box-and-Whisker Plots

Name _______________________

Date _______________________

You can use a box-and-whisker plot to display data.

Ages of cousins: 12, 14, 10, 16, 18, 15, 20

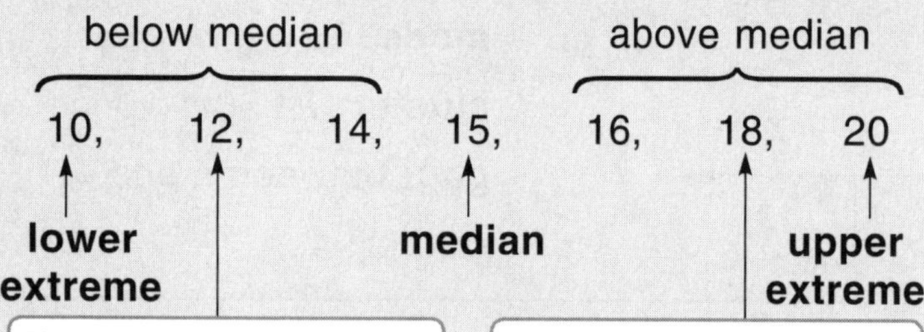

below median

above median

10,   12,   14,   15,   16,   18,   20

lower extreme

median

upper extreme

The **lower quartile** is the median of the data below the median.

The **upper quartile** is the median of the data above the median.

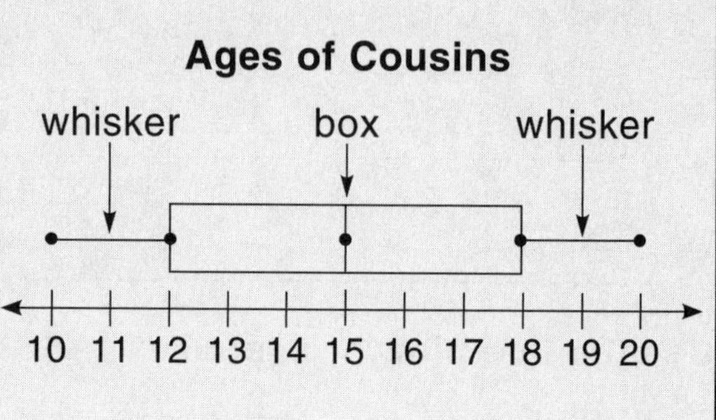

Ages of Cousins

Use the box-and-whisker plot for exercises 1–4.

1. What are the extremes of the data?

   ____

2. What is the median of the data?

   ____

3. What are the upper and lower quartiles?

   ____

4. What is the range of the data?

   ____

On a separate sheet of paper, make a box-and-whisker plot for each set of data.

5.

Number of Tickets Sold				
35	45	30	55	25
25	45	60	70	45	45

6.

Daily Temperatures (°F)		
24°	22°	18°
34°	28°	20°

Problem Solving The box-and-whisker plot shows how many miles from the state capital each of 15 families live.

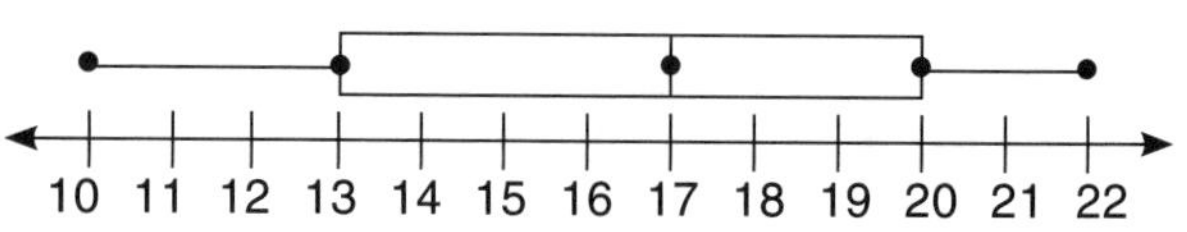

7. What does each part of the plot represent, including the points and each part of the box?

   ____

   ____

8. Write 15 possible distances from the capital that the families could live to equal the amounts that the box-and-whisker plot represents.

   ____

   ____

Use with Lesson 9-7, pages 304–305 in the Student Book.
Then go to Lesson 9-7A, pages 235–236 in this Workbook.

Stem-and-Leaf Plots

Name ______________________

Date ______________________

Make a stem-and-leaf plot for the following daily high-temperature (°F) data: 95°, 88°, 88°, 75°, 82°, 73°, 69°, 89°, 94°, 95°, 84°.

- Draw a chart and label two columns as *Stem* and *Leaf.*
- The tens digits are the stems. The ones digits are the *leaves*. Write the stems and leaves in order in the corresponding columns.
- Write a title and a key for the plot.

Daily High Temperatures

Stem	Leaf
6	9
7	3 5
8	2 4 8 8 9
9	4 5 5

Key: 6|9 represents 69.

The data shows daily low temperatures (°F) for Miami, Florida during a two-week period. Complete the stem-and-leaf plot. Then answer questions 2–4.

1.

Stem	Leaf
4	
5	
6	

48°	53°	59°	56°	58°	59°	49°
60°	60°	55°	59°	57°	54°	61°

2. What is the range, median, and mode of the data? ______________________

3. How many days was the temperature below 50°F? ______________________

4. Write a statement that summarizes what the stem-and-leaf plot shows. ______________________

The data shows the heights (numbers of floors) of some tall buildings in Detroit, Michigan. Use the data to answer questions 5–8.

47	40	71	28	28	40	39	35	32	32	40
38	32	27	27	27	28	25	34	26	25	19

5. Make a stem-and-leaf plot for the data.

6. What is the range, median, and mode of the data?

____

7. How many buildings have a height of 40 stories

or more? ______________________

8. Write a statement that summarizes what the stem-and-leaf plot shows about the tallest building.

____

Line Graphs

Name _______________________

Date _______________________

Complete the graph to show the data in the table.

1.

Profits Earned by the Beach Company	
Month	**Profit**
June	$45,000
July	$50,000
August	$55,000
September	$65,000
October	$35,000
November	$35,000
December	$20,000

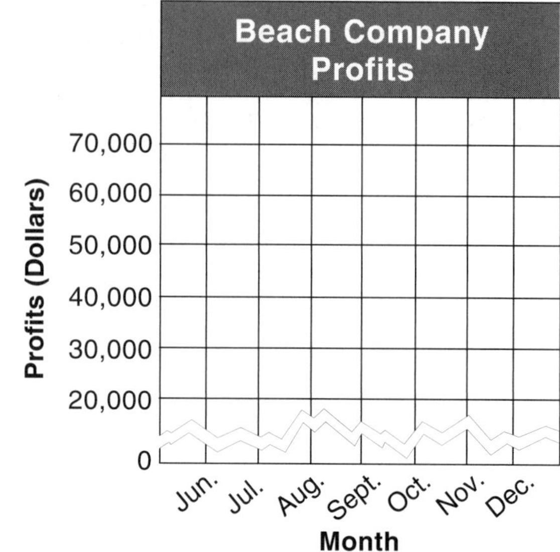

Use the completed line graph for exercises 2–5.

2. How much money does each interval on the vertical scale represent?

____

3. What trend does the graph show?

____

4. By how much did profits decrease from July to November?

____

5. What is the range of the profits? the median profit?

____

6. In the first 75 games Mario played, the time it took him to complete a game decreased by 10 seconds for every 5 games. Draw a line graph of the data and determine if the line slopes upward or downward. Explain why this happens.

Games Played	5	10	15	20	25
Time to Complete Game (seconds)	180	170	160	150	140

____

____

7. Shamika's watch gains 5 minutes every 18 hours. Complete the table below. Then draw a line graph of the data and determine if the line slopes upward or downward. Explain why this happens.

Hours	18	36			90
Minutes Gained	5		15		

____

____

Use with Lesson 9-9, pages 308–309 in the Student Book.
Then go to Lesson 9-10, pages 310–311 in the Student Book.

Double Line Graphs

Name ______________________

Date ______________________

Use the double line graph for problems 1–4.

1. How much more rain fell in Houston than in St. Louis during September? ______________________

2. What can you say about the rainfall in St. Louis between January and April? ______________________

3. In which city did the amount of rainfall stay the same for two consecutive months? ______________________

4. When was the difference between the amount of rainfall in Houston and in St. Louis the greatest?

____

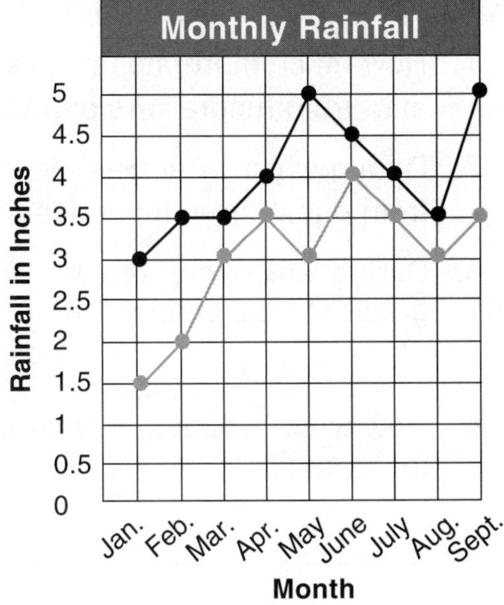

Use the double line graph for problems 5–8.

5. Whose bean sprout was 6 cm tall on Wednesday? How do you know?

____

6. On which day was the difference in heights of Jared's and Mia's bean sprouts greatest? Explain how you found your answer.

____

7. On which day or days was the difference in heights 1 cm?

____

8. Whose bean sprout grew the most from Monday to Friday? How do you know?

____

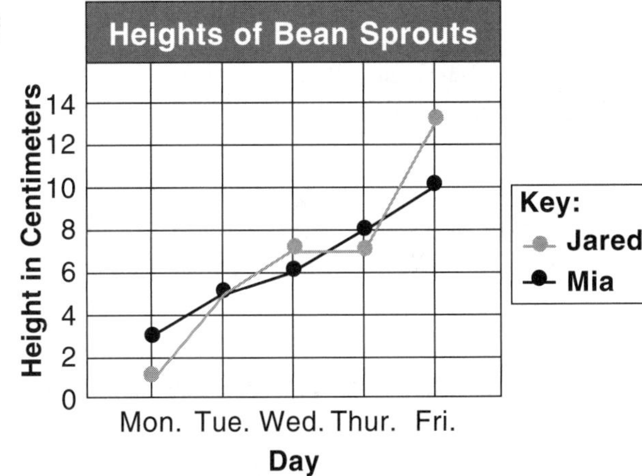

On a separate sheet of paper, make a double line graph for each data set.

9.

Betty's Bookstore Sales		
Month	Children's	Adult's
Apr.	130	150
May	125	140
June	120	145
July	95	120
Aug.	100	110

10.

Mountain School Enrollment		
Year	Boys	Girls
2002	70	60
2003	70	70
2004	75	85
2005	85	90
2006	100	95

Use with Lesson 9-10, pages 310–311 in the Student Book.
Then go to Lesson 9-11, pages 312–313 in the Student Book.

Double Bar Graphs

Name _______________

Date _______________

Use the double bar graph for problems 1–4.

1. How much more money was made from dues than from fundraisers during 2002? _______

2. During which year was the most money made from dues? from fundraisers? _______

3. During which year did the club earn the greatest total amount? the least total amount?

   ____

4. How would you summarize the data in the graph?

   ____

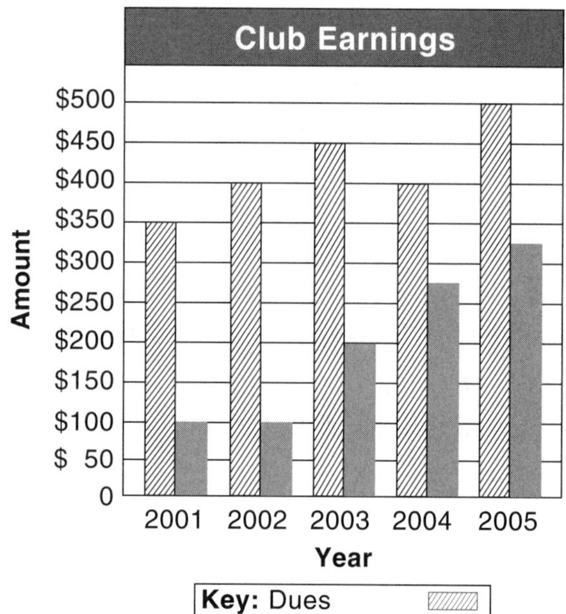

Use the double bar graph for problems 5–8.

5. Which sport was the favorite of 6 girls?

   ____

6. How many students chose football? Explain how you found your answer.

   ____

7. Which was the least favorite sport overall? How do you know?

   ____

8. How would you summarize the data in the graph?

   ____

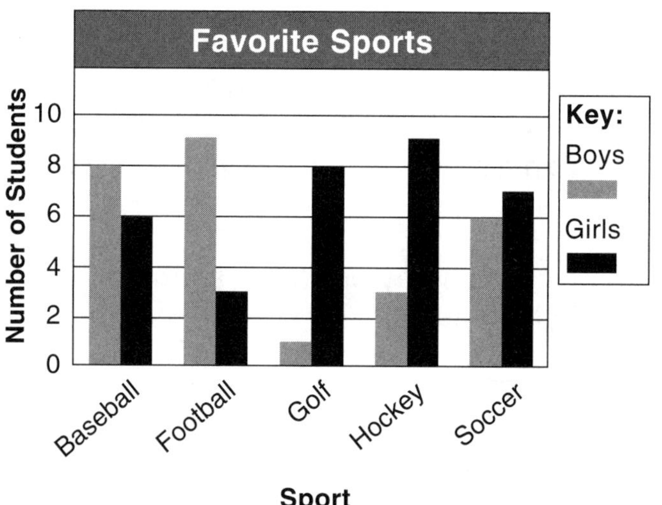

On a separate sheet of paper, make a double bar graph for each data set.

9.

High and Low Math Scores		
Test	**High Score**	**Low Score**
Test 1	95	60
Test 2	89	65
Test 3	90	70
Test 4	95	75
Test 5	85	68

10.

Number of School Lunches Sold		
Day	**6th Graders**	**7th Graders**
Mon.	90	30
Tues.	40	70
Wed.	30	80
Thurs.	70	60
Fri.	50	50

Use with Lesson 9-11, pages 312–313 in the Student Book.
Then go to Lesson 9-12, pages 314–315 in the Student Book.

Misleading Graphs and Statistics

The table and graph show the heights of buildings.

Building	Height (floors)
Prestige Plaza	55
Lincoln Tower	110
Americas Center	75
Century Tower	100

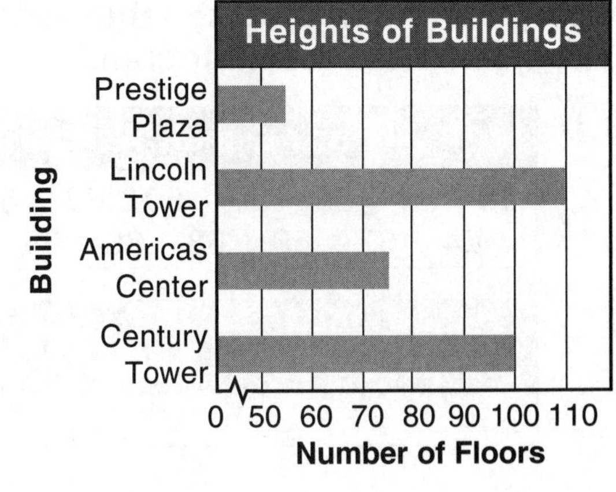

1. According to the graph which building appears to be about half as tall as the Lincoln Tower?

2. Which building actually is about half as tall? ___________

3. What makes this graph misleading? ___________

The graphs show the number of books sold over a 5-month period.

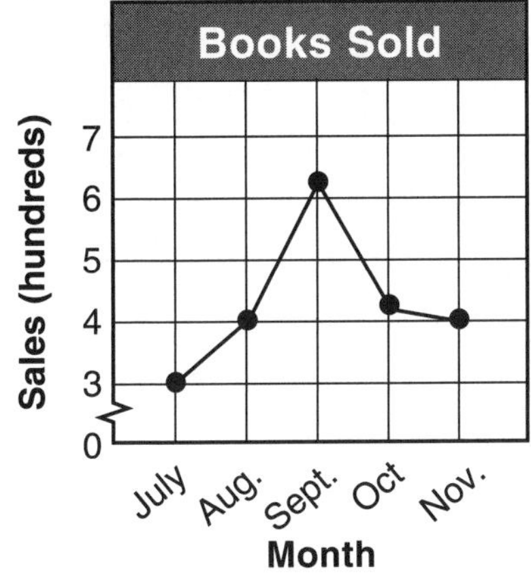

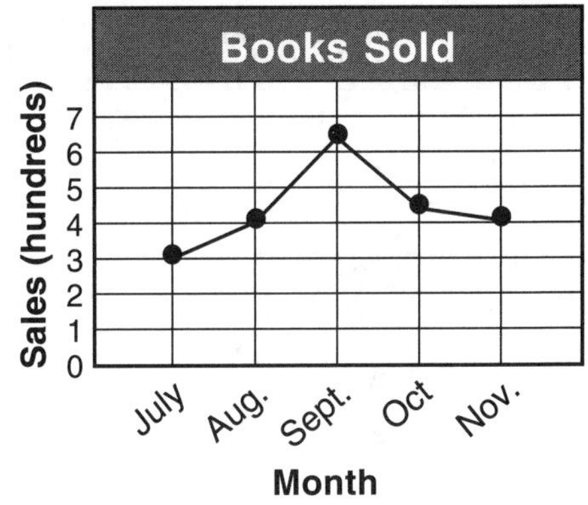

4. Do both graphs show the same data? ___________

5. How are the graphs different? ___________

The graph at the right shows the attendance at the Hiker's Club yearly business meeting.

6. Was there a steady increase or a steady decrease in attendance? ___________

7. Does the graph give the impression that the change in attendance over the last 4 years is small or great? Which is it? ___________

8. How would you change the graph to make it represent the data better? ___________

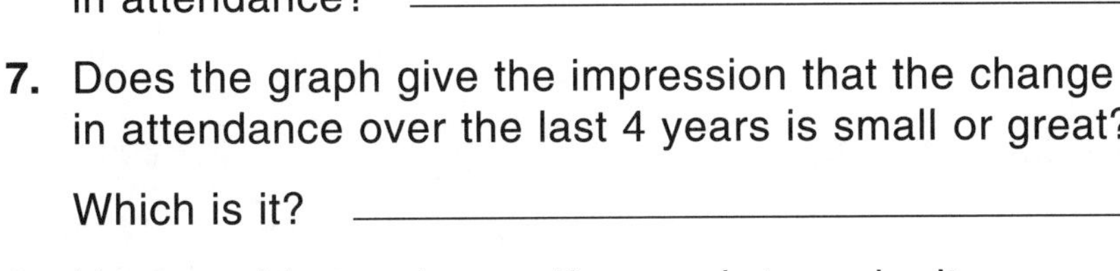

Histograms

Name _______________

Date _______________

**Complete the frequency table for the given data.
Then complete the histogram.**

1.

Daily Ocean Temperatures (°F)									
58	57	58	59	60	62	65	66	61	63
64	67	68	68	66	65	63	61	59	

Daily Ocean Temperatures	Tally	Frequency

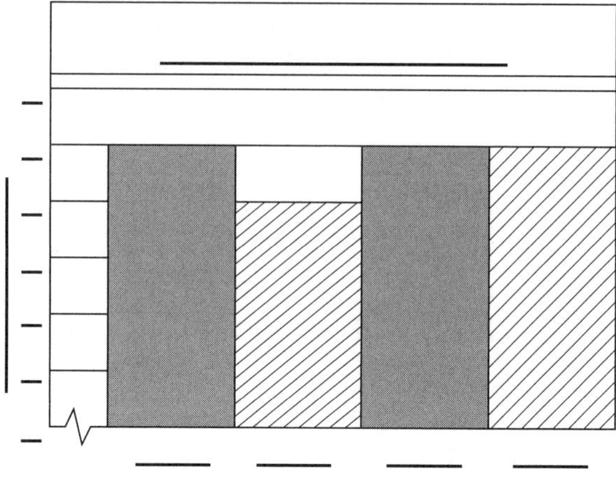

**Complete the frequency table for the given data.
Then make a histogram.**

2.

Badges Earned by Troop 818 Scouts									
13	22	5	22	9	3	13	3	14	6
24	1	19	15	11	2	12	14	24	

Badges Earned	Tally	Frequency

Problem Solving Use the histogram for exercises 3–6.

3. How many students were surveyed?

____

4. Which interval of days did most students
spend reading last month?

____

5. Which interval had the least frequency?

____

6. How many students spent 10–14 days reading
last month?

____

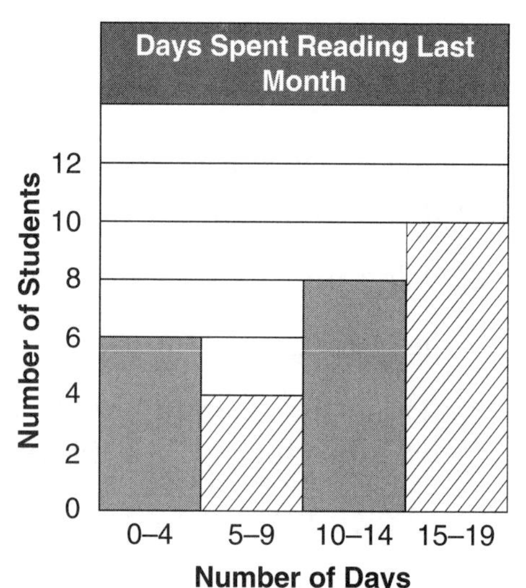

Use with Lesson 9-13, pages 316–317 in the Student Book.
Then go to Lesson 9-14, pages 318–319 in the Student Book.

Interpret Circle Graphs

Name _______________

Date _______________

Use the circle graph at the right to complete the table.

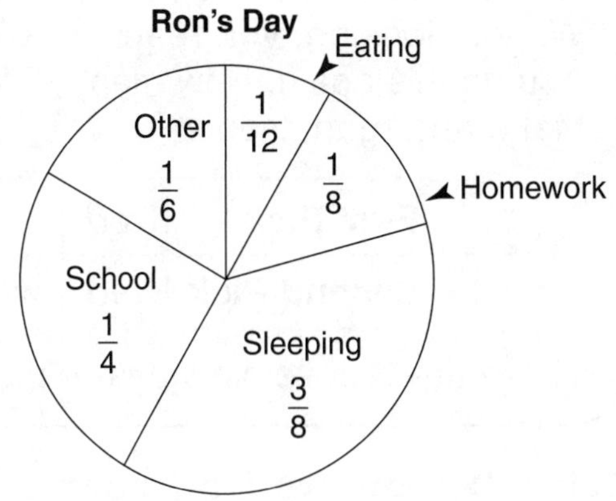

	Activity	Fraction	Hours
1.	Sleeping		
2.	Eating		
3.	School		
4.	Homework		
5.	Other		

Use the circle graph at the right for problems 6–9.

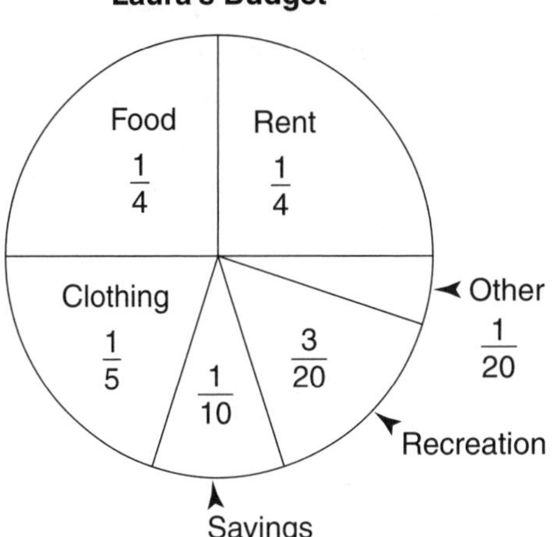

6. Laura's budget is $200 per week. How much can she spend on clothing each week?

____

7. For which two items has Laura budgeted the same amount of money? how much money?

____

8. What fractional part of Laura's budget is spent on items other than savings? _______________

9. How would the circle graph look if Laura spent $10 more on rent and $10 less on food?

____

____

Use the circle graph at the right for problems 10–13.

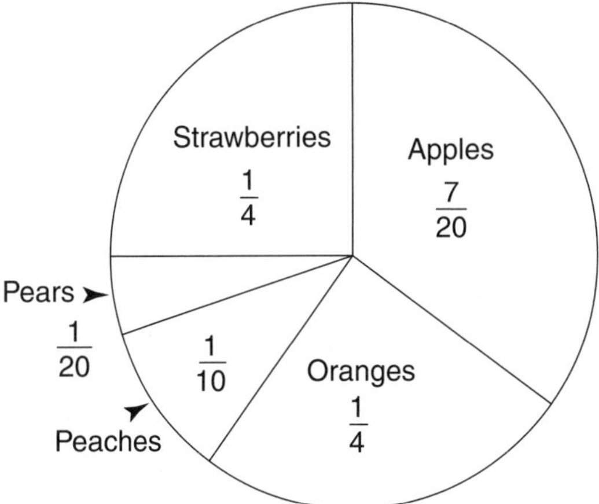

10. What fractional part of sales is peaches and pears?

____

11. What fractional part of the fruit sold is not apples?

____

12. If 600 bushels of fruit are sold weekly, how many bushels are oranges? _______________

13. If 600 bushels of fruit are sold weekly, how many bushels are pears? _______________

Use with Lesson 9-14, pages 318–319 in the Student Book.
Then go to Lesson 9-15, pages 320–321 in the Student Book.

Problem-Solving Strategy: Make an Organized List

Name _______________________

Date _______________________

A bag holds a red marble, a white marble, and a blue marble.
Without looking, you reach in, pick a marble, note its color, and put it back.
You do this again. How many different ways of picking two marbles are possible?
Make an organized list.

First Pick	red	red	red	white	white	white	blue	blue	blue
Second Pick	red	white	blue	red	white	blue	red	white	blue

There are 9 possible ways of picking two marbles.

Solve. Do your work on a separate sheet of paper.

1. Zev has 5 T-shirts in a drawer: 1 blue, 1 white, 1 red, 1 green, and 1 yellow. Without looking, he reaches in and takes out one shirt, and then he reaches in and takes out another shirt. How many different ways can he take out two shirts?

2. Leda needs to choose one letter and one digit from the following: X, Y, Z, 0, 1, 2, 3. She must place the letter first to form a 2-character code. How many different 2-character codes are there from which Leda can choose?

3. How many different 3-digit numbers can you make with the digits 1, 2, and 3 if repetition is permitted?

4. Ben has 5 tulip bulbs and 3 window boxes. In how many ways can he plant all the bulbs so that each window box has at least one bulb?

5. Al has a red shirt, a white shirt, and a yellow shirt. He has a pair of brown slacks, a pair of black slacks, and a pair of blue slacks. How many different outfits can he make?

6. In a multiplication game you spin the spinner twice and find the product of the two numbers. How many different products are possible if the spinner is divided into 4 equal sections numbered 1, 2, 3, 4 respectively?

7. Victoria is spending her vacation in Washington, D.C. She wants to visit the Capitol Building, the White House, the Lincoln Memorial, and the Washington Monument. In how many different orders can she visit all four places?

8. A library has a front door, a door on the left side of the building, another door on the right side, and two rear doors. Victor can enter the library through the front door and leave through any door. In how many different ways can he do this?

Use with Lesson 9-15, pages 320–321 in the Student Book.
Then go to Lesson 9-16, pages 322–323 in the Student Book.

Problem-Solving Applications: Mixed Review

Name _______________

Date _______________

Solve each problem and explain the method you used. If needed, do all your work on a separate sheet of paper.

Strategy File

Use These Strategies
Write an Equation
Make an Organized List
Use a Graph
Use More Than One Step
Guess and Test

1. Six people meet for dinner at a restaurant. If each person shakes every other person's hand, how many pairs of people shake hands?

2. The number of sixth-grade students at Miguel's school is 5 more than twice the number of fifth-grade students. If there are 275 sixth-grade students, how many fifth-grade students are there?

3. Over seven days, Adrianna did the following number of jumping jacks: 38, 57, 72, 81, 37, 75, and 60. How many must she do on the eighth day to keep the mean and median the same?

Use the bar graph for problems 4–6.

4. Which school had more people in the talent show in 2005?

5. How many more people from East School than West School entered the talent show in 2004?

6. How many people altogether entered the talent show in 2003?

Use the circle graph for problems 7–9.

7. What fractional part of the fruit salad is apples and bananas?

8. Which two fruits together make up about $\frac{1}{4}$ of the fruit salad?

9. Suppose Rhonda added 2 more bananas to the salad. What fractional part of the new salad would apples be?

Talent Show Entries

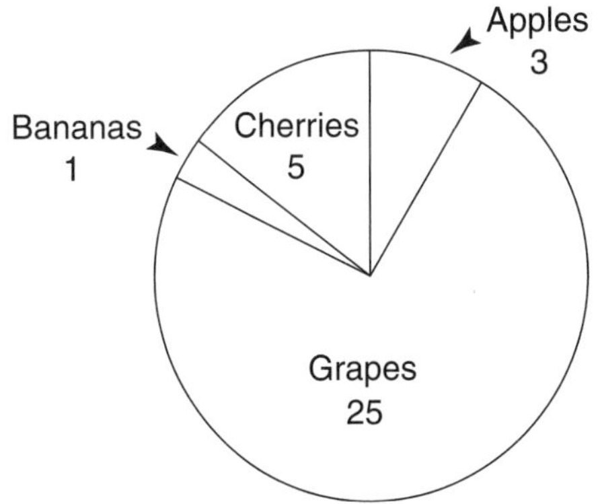

Rhonda's Fruit Salad

Measure and Draw Angles

Name _______________________

Date _______________________

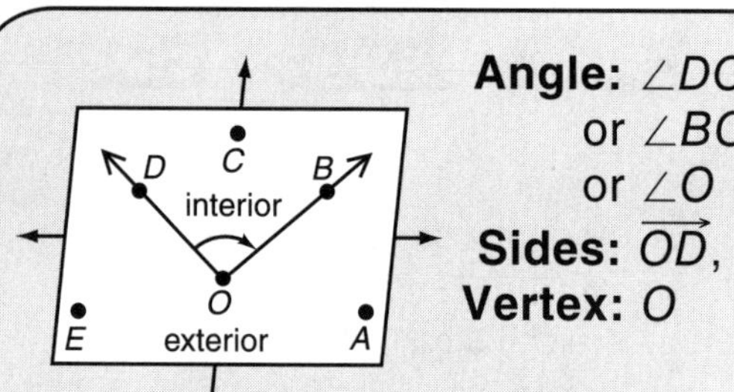

Angle: ∠DOB
or ∠BOD
or ∠O
Sides: $\overrightarrow{OD}$, $\overrightarrow{OB}$
Vertex: O

Plane *EAC* contains ∠DOB.
Point *C* is in the interior of ∠DOB.
Points *E* and *A* are in the
exterior of ∠DOB.

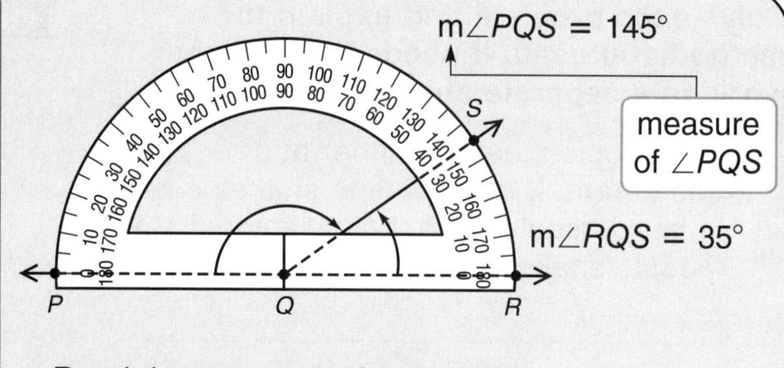

m∠PQS = 145°

measure
of ∠PQS

m∠RQS = 35°

Read the measure of each angle
where $\overrightarrow{QS}$ crosses the protractor.

Name the points that are in the interior and the points that are in the exterior of the given angle. Then find the measure of the angle.

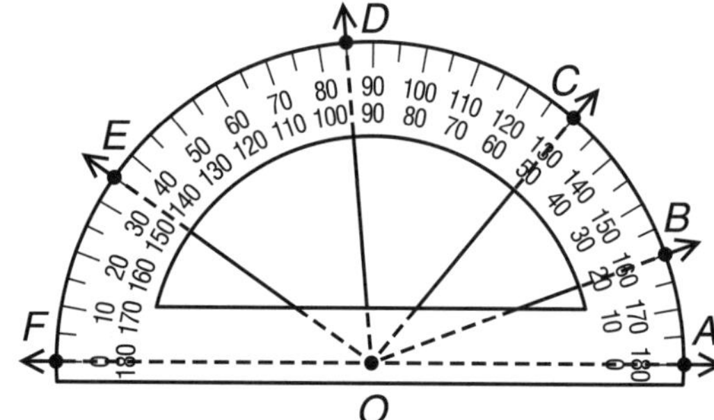

1. ∠AOE _______________________

2. ∠AOC _______________________

3. ∠AOD _______________________

4. ∠FOC _______________________

5. ∠FOD _______________________

Estimate the measure of each angle. Then use a protractor to find the exact measure.

6. 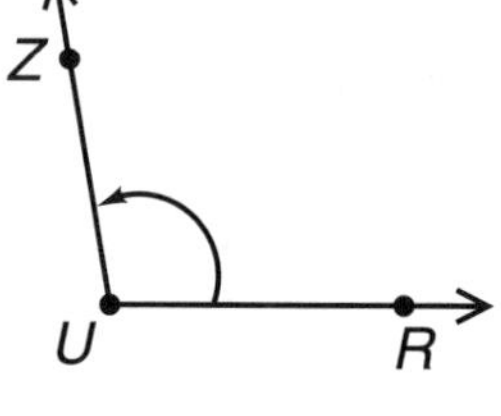

____

7. 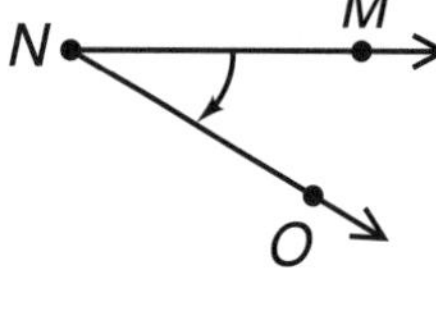

____

8. 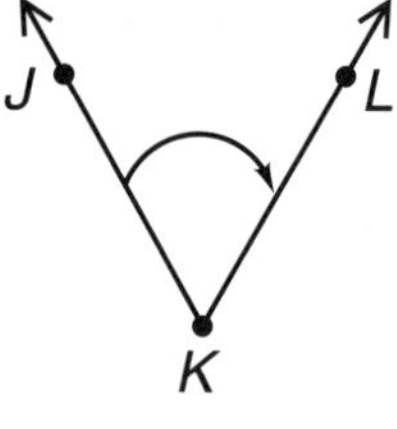

____

Use a protractor to draw each angle.

9. 15°

10. 150°

11. 65°

12. 135°

13. 55°

14. 110°

Use with Lesson 10-1, pages 330–331 in the Student Book.
Then go to Lesson 10-2, pages 332–333 in the Student Book.

Lines and Angles

Name _______________________

Date _______________________

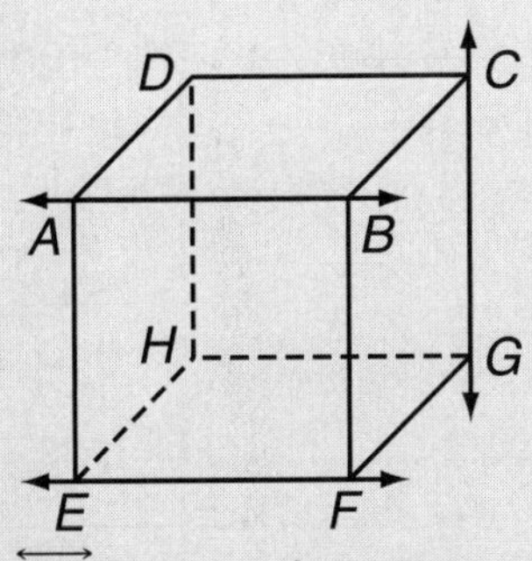

$\overleftrightarrow{AB}$ and $\overleftrightarrow{EF}$ are in the same plane.
$\overleftrightarrow{AB}$ and $\overleftrightarrow{EF}$ are parallel lines.
$\overleftrightarrow{AB}$ and $\overleftrightarrow{CG}$ are in different planes.
$\overleftrightarrow{AB}$ and $\overleftrightarrow{CG}$ are skew lines.

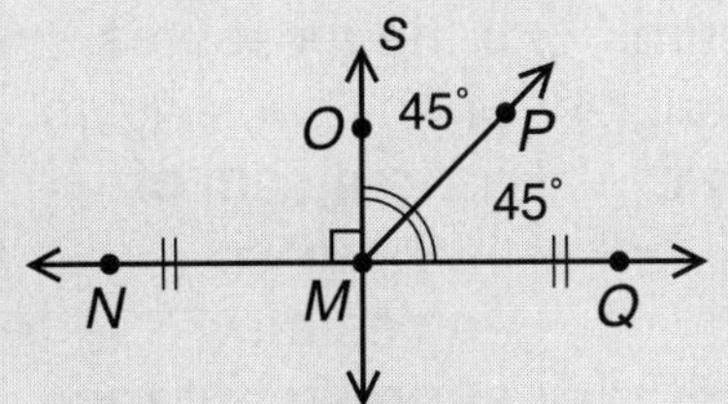

M is the midpoint of $\overline{NQ}$.
$\overline{NM} \cong \overline{QM}$ is congruent to

Line s is a perpendicular bisector of $\overline{NQ}$.
$\overrightarrow{MP}$ is the angle bisector of $\angle OMQ$.
$\angle OMP \cong \angle PMQ$

Use the figure at the right.

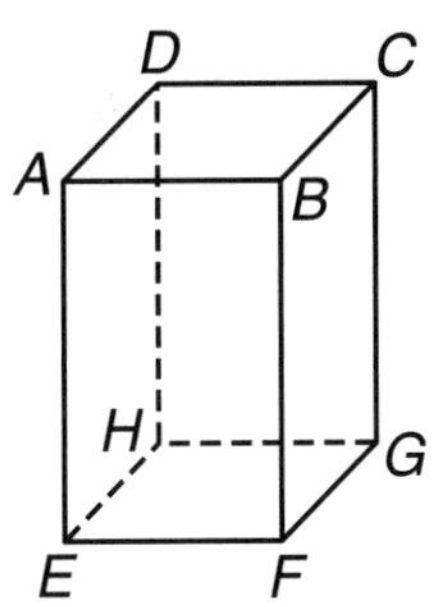

1. Name a line that is parallel to the given line.

   a. $\overleftrightarrow{FG}$ _________   **b.** $\overleftrightarrow{AB}$ _________

2. Name the lines that form a pair of skew lines with $\overleftrightarrow{DC}$.

____

Classify each angle as *right, acute, obtuse,* or *straight.* Use a protractor to check.

3. 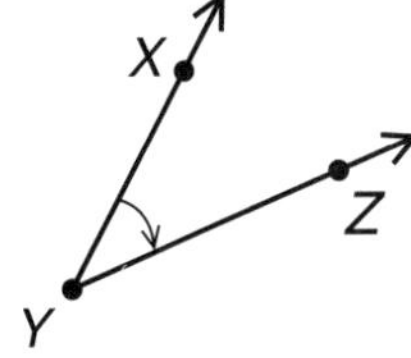

4. 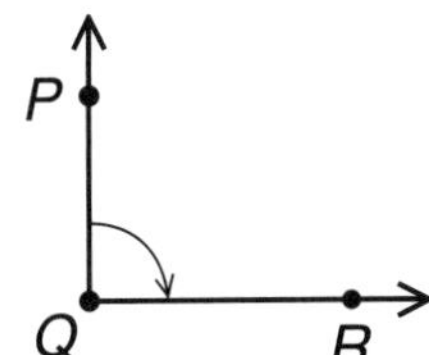

5. 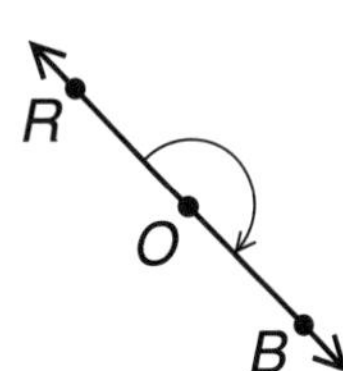

6. 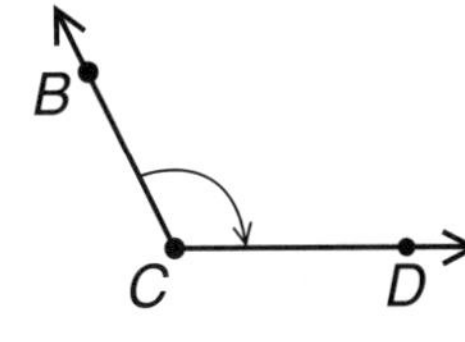

_________   _________   _________   _________

Write *true* or *false.* If *false,* explain why. Use the figure at the right.

7. $\overrightarrow{JF} \perp \overrightarrow{EI}$

8. $\overrightarrow{EI}$ bisects $\angle JEG$.

____

9. $\angle JEH \cong \angle FEG$

10. $\overrightarrow{EH} \perp \overrightarrow{EF}$

____

11. $\overleftrightarrow{HG} \parallel \overleftrightarrow{JF}$

12. E is the midpoint of $\overline{HG}$

____

Draw a figure for each description. Use a separate sheet of paper.

13. $\angle ABC$ is bisected by $\overrightarrow{BX}$.

14. $\overleftrightarrow{KL} \parallel \overleftrightarrow{RS}$

15. $\overline{MN}$ bisects $\overline{OP}$ at Y.

16. $\overleftrightarrow{BC} \perp \overleftrightarrow{FG}$

Use with Lesson 10-2, pages 332–333 in the Student Book.
Then go to Lesson 10-3, pages 334–335 in the Student Book.

Angle Pairs

Name ______________________

Date ______________________

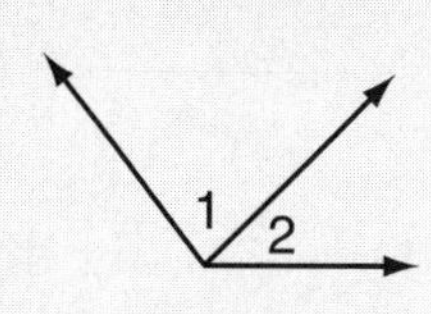
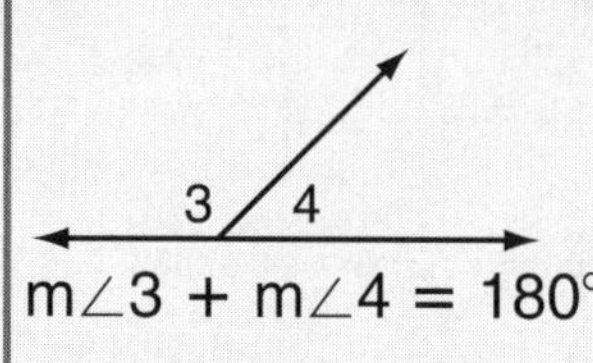
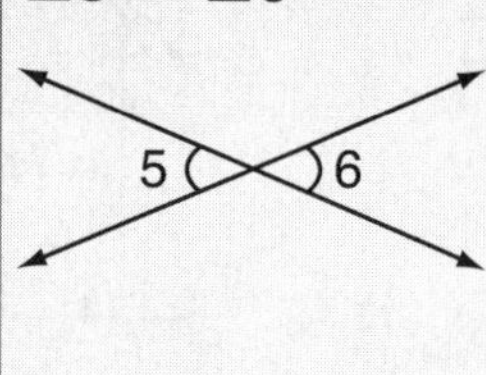

If the measures of any two angles have a sum of 90°, those angles are **complementary angles.**	If the measures of any two angles have a sum of 180°, those angles are **supplementary angles.**	∠1 and ∠2 are **adjacent angles.**	∠3 and ∠4 form a **linear pair.** m∠3 + m∠4 = 180°	∠5 and ∠6 are **vertical angles.** ∠5 ≅ ∠6

Are ∠1 and ∠2 adjacent angles? Write *yes* or *no*. If no, explain why.

1. 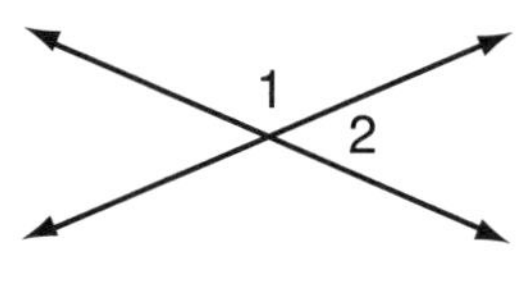

2. 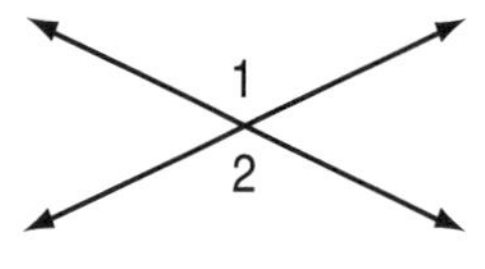

3. 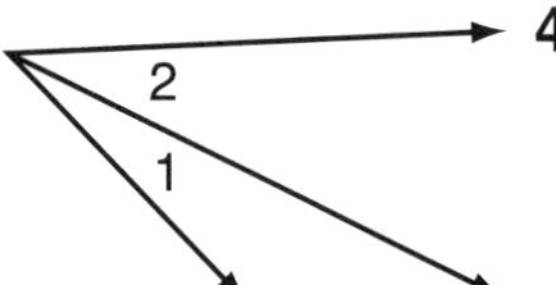

4. 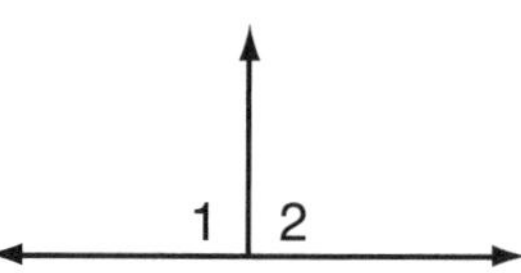

_______________   _______________   _______________

Are ∠1 and ∠2 vertical angles? Write *yes* or *no*. If no, explain why.

5. 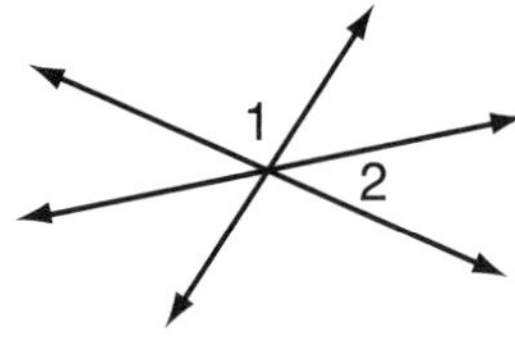

6. 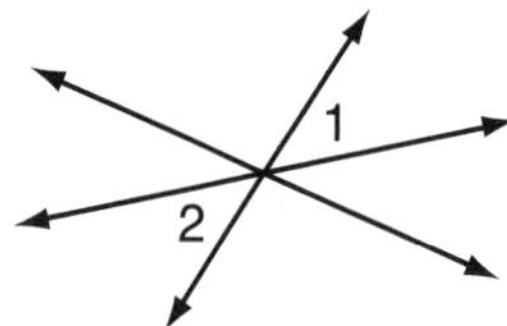

7. 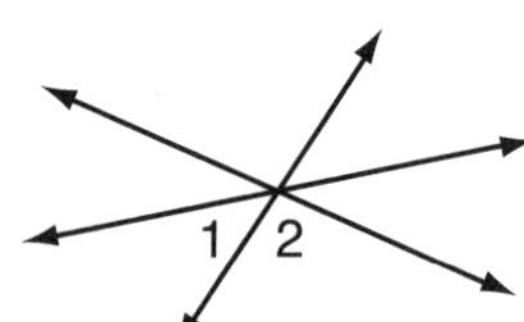

8. 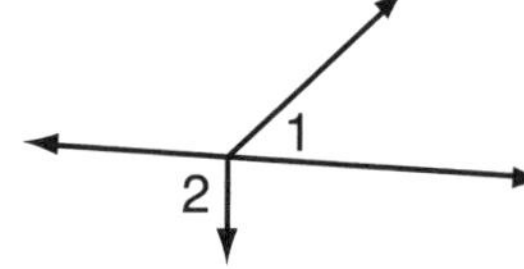

_______________   _______________   _______________

Write whether the angle pairs are *complementary angles*, *supplementary angles*, or *neither*.

9. 45°, 45° ______________________   **10.** 73°, 107° ______________________

11. 35°, 65° ______________________   **12.** 170°, 10° ______________________

13. 87°, 83° ______________________   **14.** 62°, 28° ______________________

15. 89°, 1° ______________________   **16.** 95°, 85° ______________________

Find the value of x.

17. 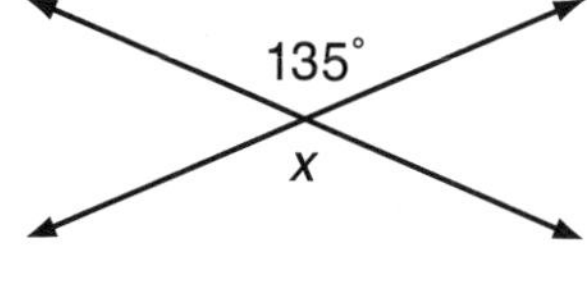

18. 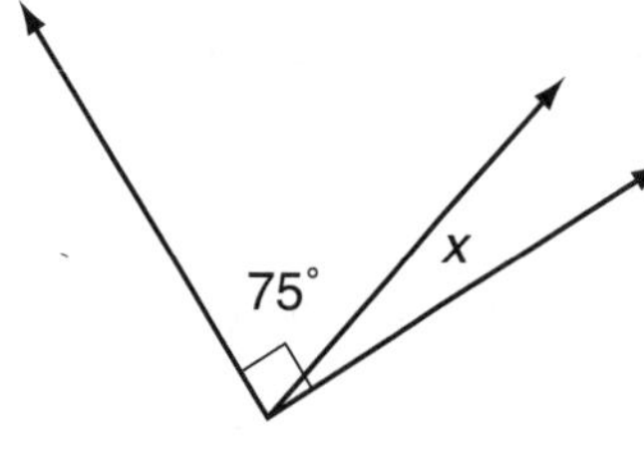

19. 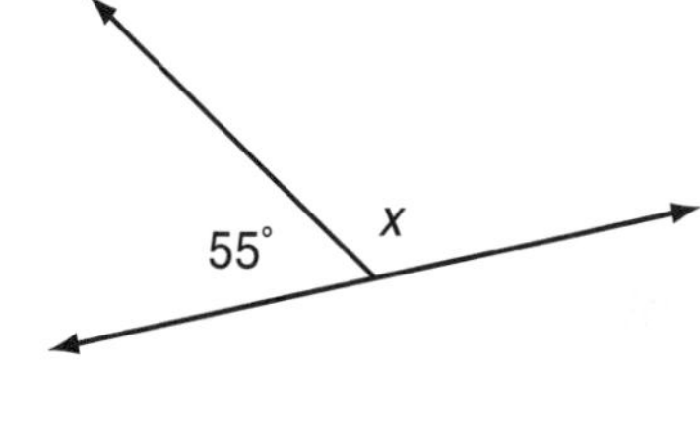

_______________   _______________   _______________

Use with Lesson 10-3, pages 334–335 in the Student Book.
Then go to Lesson 10-4, pages 336–337 in the Student Book.

Angles of Parallel Lines

Name _______________________

Date _______________________

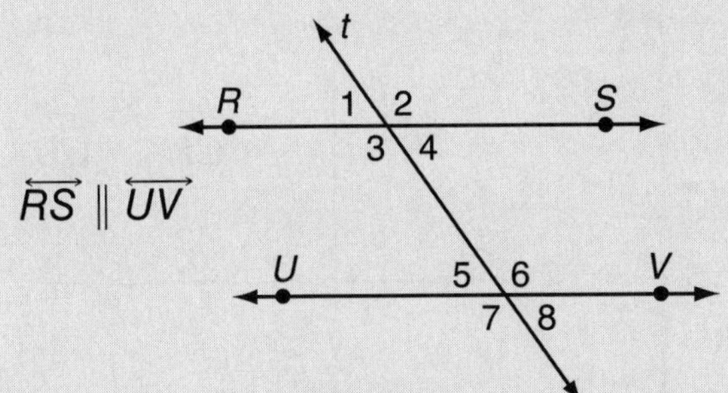

A *transversal* intersects two or more lines at different points. Line *t* is a transversal.

$\overrightarrow{RS} \parallel \overrightarrow{UV}$

A transversal forms pairs of angles with special names.

Corresponding angles:

∠1 and ∠5; ∠2 and ∠6; ∠3 and ∠7; ∠4 and ∠8

∠1 ≅ ∠5; ∠2 ≅ ∠6; ∠3 ≅ ∠7; ∠4 ≅ ∠8

Alternate interior angles:

∠3 and ∠6; ∠4 and ∠5

∠3 ≅ ∠6; ∠4 ≅ ∠5

Alternate exterior angles:

∠1 and ∠8; ∠2 and ∠7

∠1 ≅ ∠8; ∠2 ≅ ∠7

Identify each pair of angles as *alternate interior, alternate exterior, corresponding,* or *none of these*.

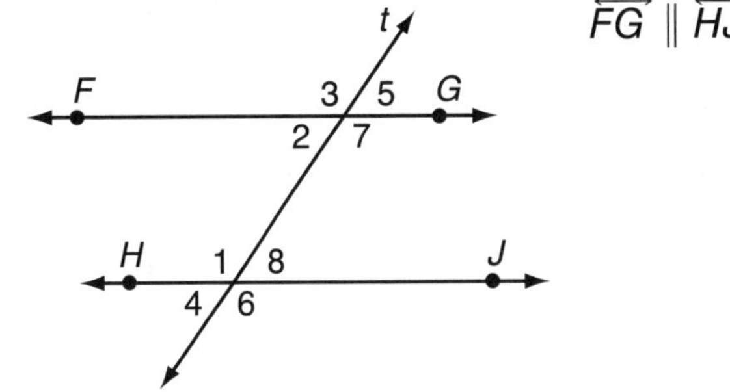

$\overrightarrow{FG} \parallel \overrightarrow{HJ}$

1. ∠1 and ∠2 _______________________

2. ∠3 and ∠6 _______________________

3. ∠2 and ∠8 _______________________

4. ∠6 and ∠7 _______________________

Use the figure above to find each measure.

5. m∠4 when m∠2 = 45° _________

6. m∠7 when m∠8 = 45° _________

7. m∠3 when m∠6 = 135° _________

8. m∠1 when m∠5 = 45° _________

Problem Solving In the figure at the right, $\overrightarrow{LM} \parallel \overrightarrow{PQ}$. $\overrightarrow{TU}$ and $\overrightarrow{VW}$ are transversals. Also, m∠3 = 75° and m∠12 = 35°. Use the figure for exercises 9–11.

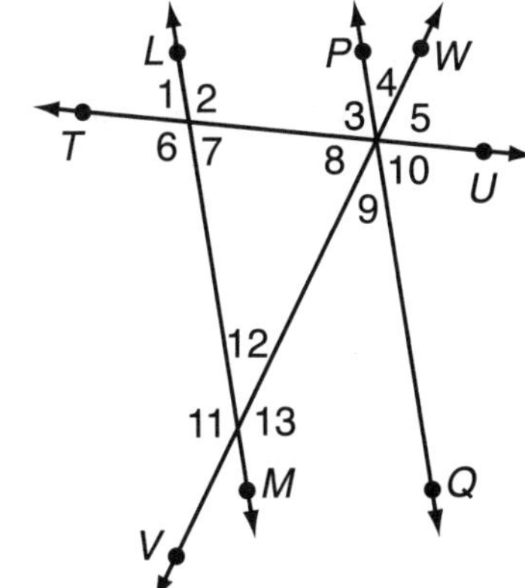

9. What is the measure of ∠8? Explain your answer.

____

10. What is the measure of ∠5? Explain your answer.

____

11. What is the measure of ∠1? Explain your answer.

____

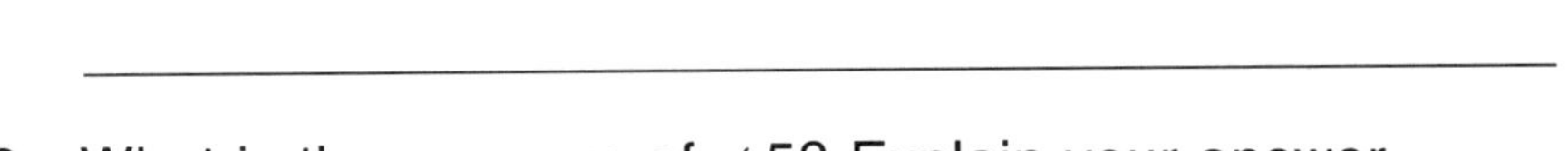

Use with Lesson 10-4, pages 336–337 in the Student Book.
Then go to Lesson 10-5, pages 338–339 in the Student Book.

Line Constructions

Name ______________________

Date ______________________

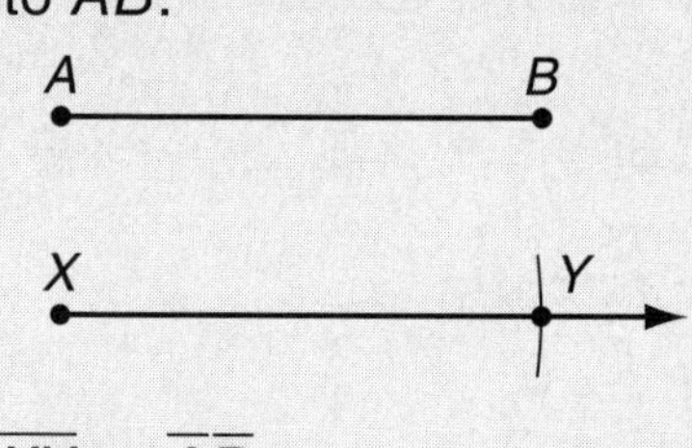

Construct $\overline{XY}$ congruent to $\overline{AB}$.

$\overline{XY} \cong \overline{AB}$

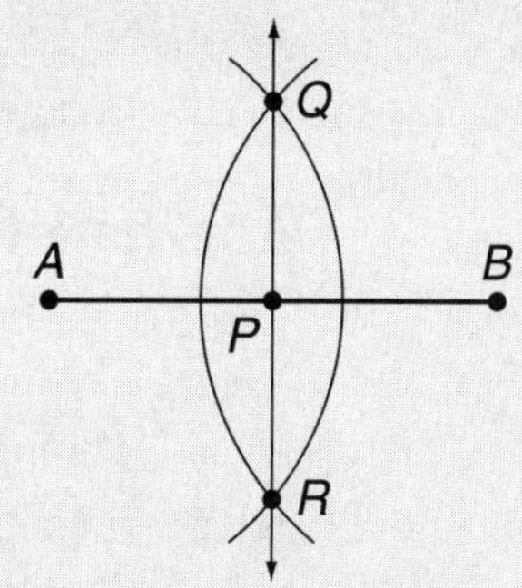

Construct the perpendicular bisector of $\overline{AB}$.

$\overrightarrow{QR} \perp \overline{AB}$

$\overrightarrow{QR}$ bisects $\overline{AB}$.

Point P is the midpoint of $\overline{AB}$.

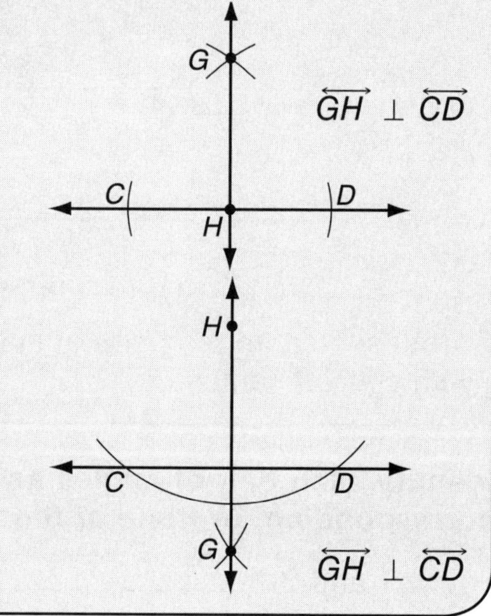

Construct line GH perpendicular to line CD at H.

$\overleftrightarrow{GH} \perp \overleftrightarrow{CD}$

$\overleftrightarrow{GH} \perp \overleftrightarrow{CD}$

Construct a line segment congruent to each.

1.

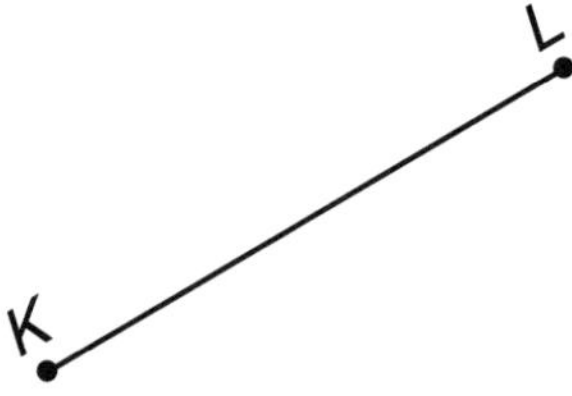

2.

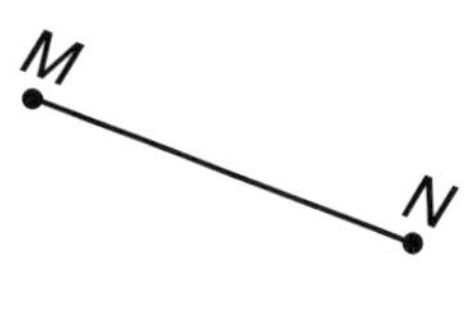

3.

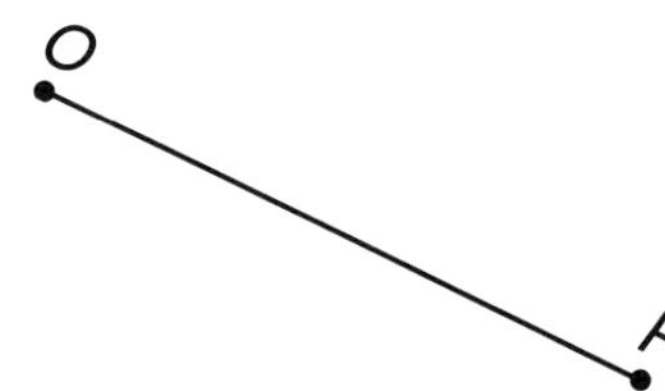

Construct the perpendicular bisector of each line segment.

4.

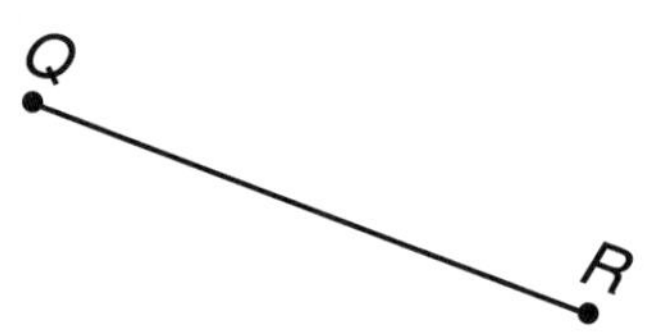

5.

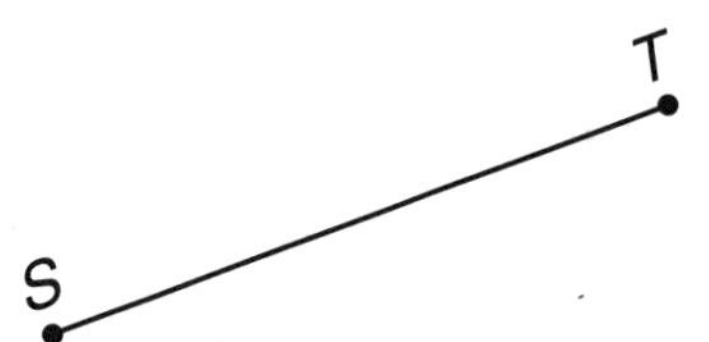

6.

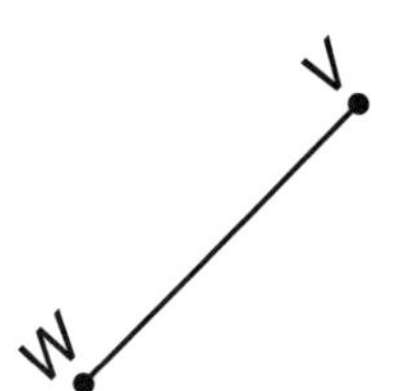

Construct a line perpendicular to ℓ through P.

7.

8.

Use with Lesson 10-5, pages 338–339 in the Student Book.
Then go to Lesson 10-6, pages 340–341 in the Student Book.

Constructions With Angles

Name _______________________

Date _______________________

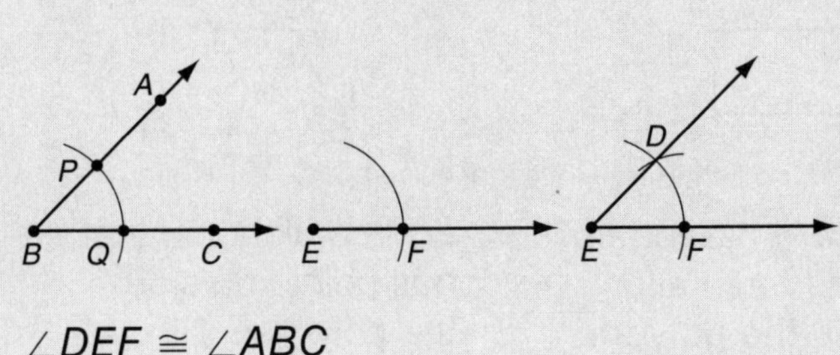

Construct ∠*DEF* congruent to ∠*ABC*.

∠*DEF* ≅ ∠*ABC*

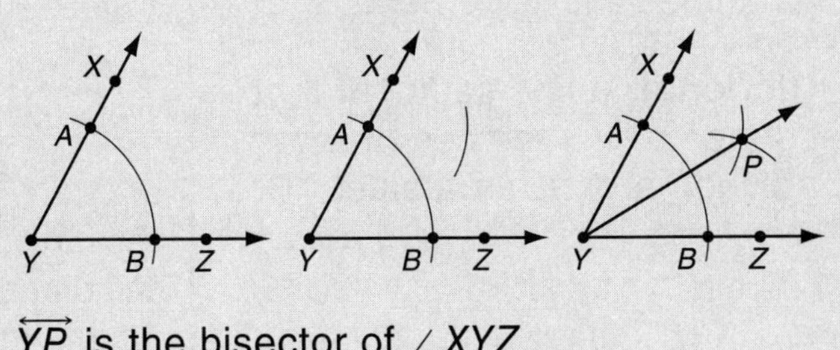

Construct the bisector of ∠*XYZ*.

$\overrightarrow{YP}$ is the bisector of ∠*XYZ*.

Construct an angle congruent to each angle.

1.

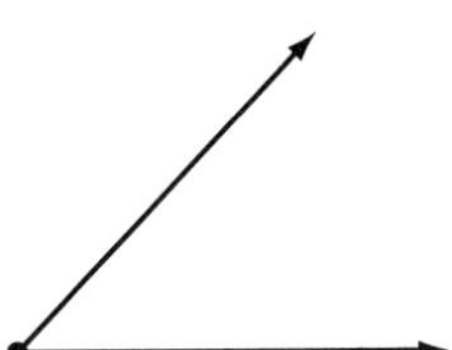

2.

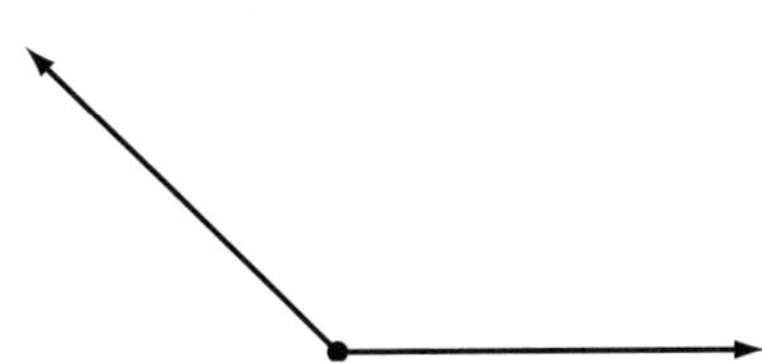

3.

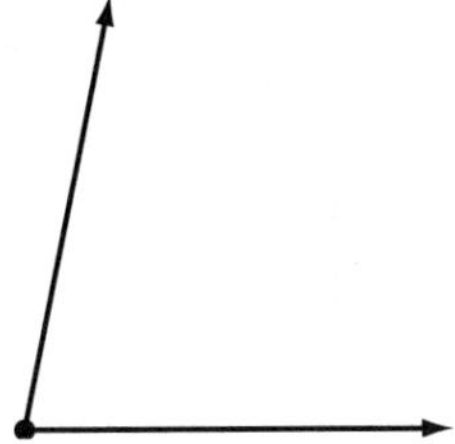

Construct the bisector of each angle.

4.

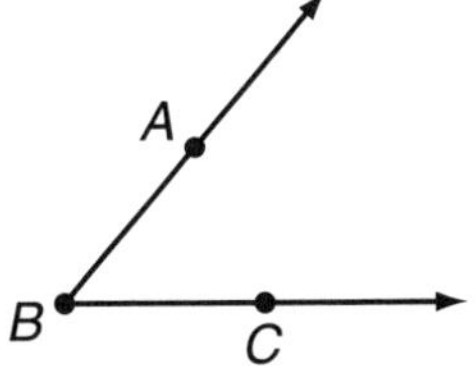

5.

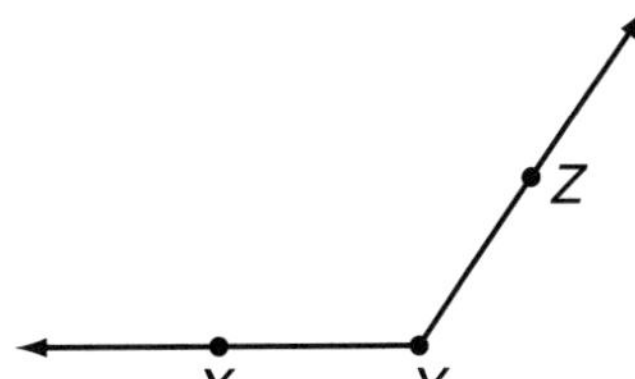

6.

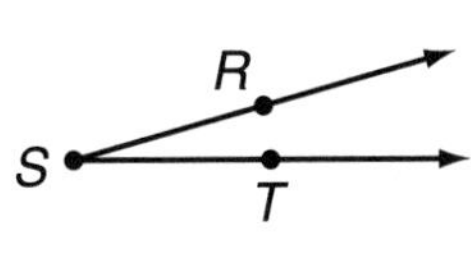

Draw each angle described. Then construct the angle bisector of each.

7. 120°

8. 70°

9. 40°

Use with Lesson 10-6, pages 340–341 in the Student Book.
Then go to Lesson 10-7, pages 342–343 in the Student Book.

Polygons

Name _______________________

Date _______________________

Regular polygon: all sides and all angles are congruent.

Diagonal: a line segment that connects two vertices of a polygon and is *not* a side.

Convex Polygon

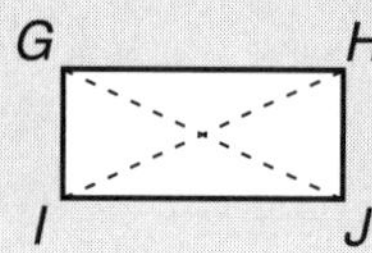

$\overline{GJ}$ and $\overline{HI}$ are diagonals. All diagonals have all points inside the polygon.

Concave Polygon

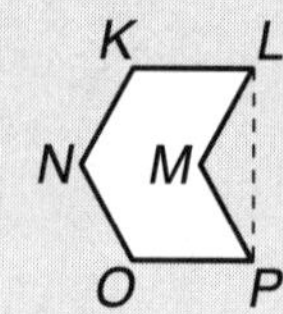

$\overline{LP}$ is a diagonal that has points outside the polygon.

Write *regular* or *not regular* for each polygon. Then write whether the polygon is *convex* or *concave*.

1. 

2. 

3. 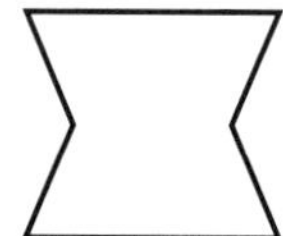

4. 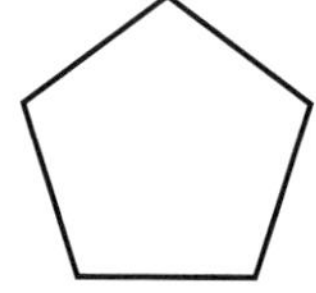

_______________   _______________   _______________   _______________

_______________   _______________   _______________   _______________

Draw each polygon. Write the number of sides and vertices for each.

5. pentagon   6. decagon   7. quadrilateral   8. heptagon

_______________   _______________   _______________   _______________

Find the number of diagonals for each convex polygon.

9. rhombus _______   10. hexagon _______   11. pentagon _______   12. triangle _______

On a separate sheet of paper draw the polygon described. Then draw and name its diagonals.

13. quadrilateral *ABCD* with no right angles

14. concave pentagon *MNRST*

Use with Lesson 10-7, pages 342–343 in the Student Book. Then go to Lesson 10-8, pages 344–345 in the Student Book.

Triangles

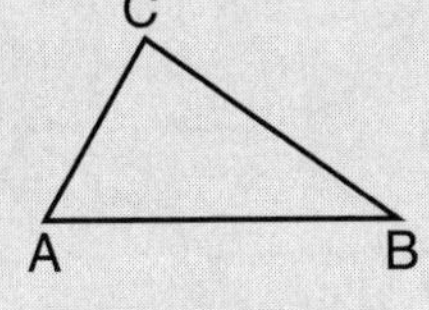 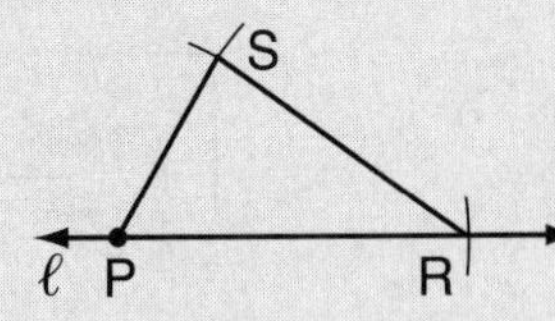

Construct △PRS congruent to △ABC.

• Draw $\overline{PR} \cong \overline{AB}$ on line ℓ.

• Measure $\overline{AC}$. From point P construct an arc. Measure $\overline{BC}$. From point R construct an arc.

• Label point S. Draw $\overline{PS}$ and $\overline{RS}$. △PRS ≅ △ABC

Classify each triangle by the measure of its sides and by the measure of its angles.

1. 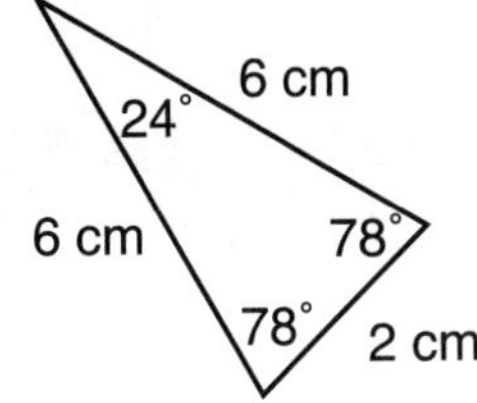

____

2. 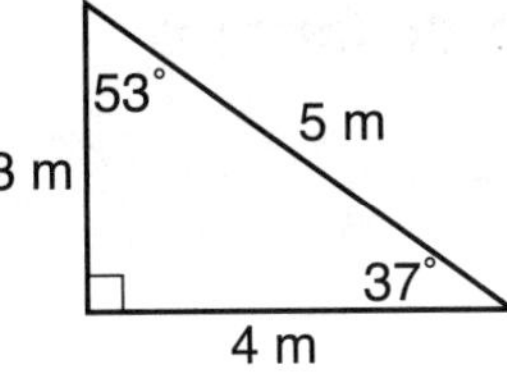

____

3. 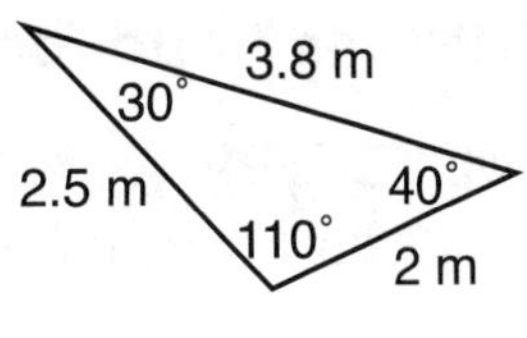

____

4. 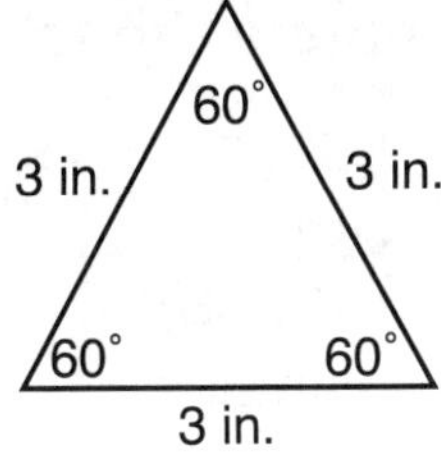

____

Use a protractor and a centimeter ruler to measure the sides and angles of each triangle. Then classify the triangle by its sides and angles.

5. 

____

6. 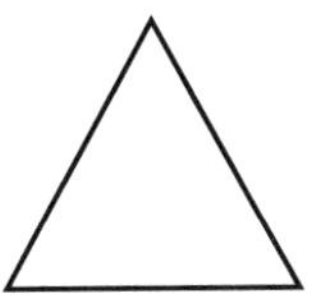

____

7. 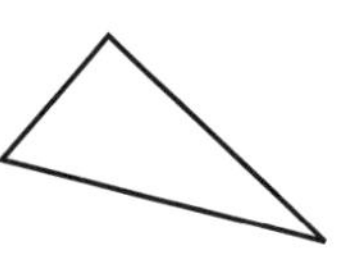

____

8. 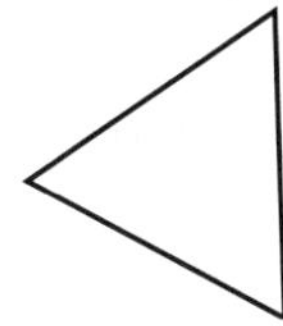

____

9. 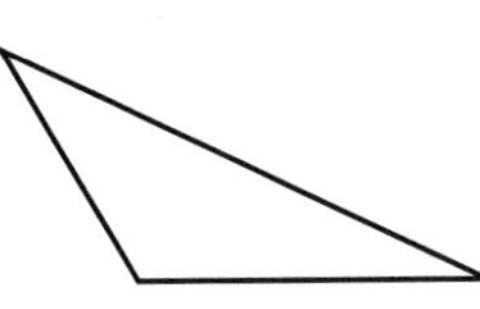

____

10. 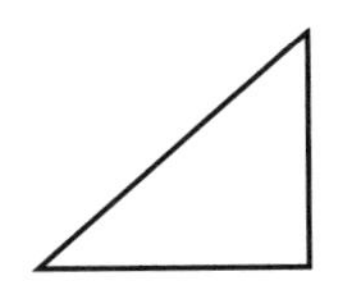

____

11. 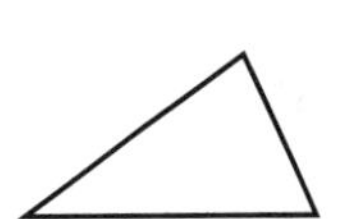

____

12. 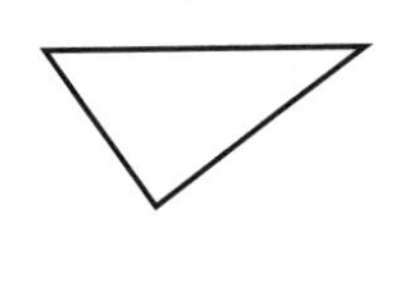

____

Draw the triangle indicated. Then construct a triangle congruent to it.

13. scalene △RST

14. acute △CDE

15. isosceles △OPQ

Quadrilaterals

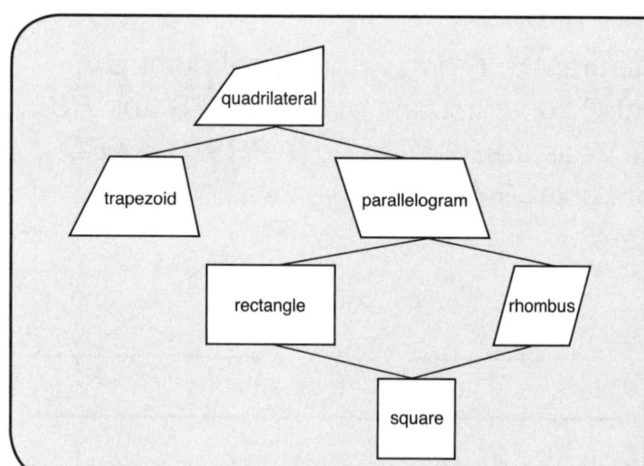

Construct parallelogram *MNOP*.

1. Draw $\overline{MN}$ and $\overline{MP}$.
2. From *P* and *N*, construct arcs.
3. Label *O*. Draw $\overline{NO}$ and $\overline{OP}$.

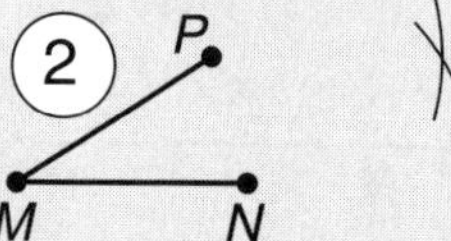
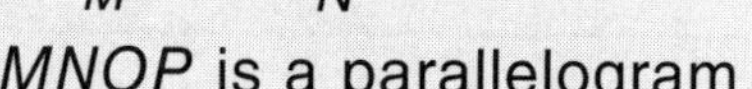
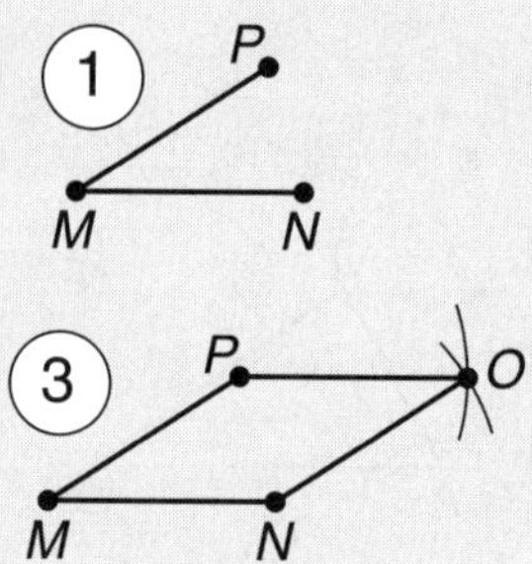

MNOP is a parallelogram.

Complete the table. Write *yes* or *no* for each description.

	Description	Rhombus	Square	Rectangle	Parallelogram	Trapezoid
1.	4 right angles					
2.	opposite sides parallel					
3.	all sides congruent					

Write whether each statement is *true* or *false*. Explain.

4. Some rectangles are trapezoids.

5. All rectangles are parallelograms.

6. Some parallelograms are rectangles.

7. All rhombuses are squares.

Construct the figure described.

8. parallelogram *ABCD*

9. rhombus *RSTU* with each side 2 cm long

Use with Lesson 10-9, pages 346–347 in the Student Book.
Then go to Lesson 10-10, pages 348–349 in the Student Book.

Angles of Triangles and Quadrilaterals

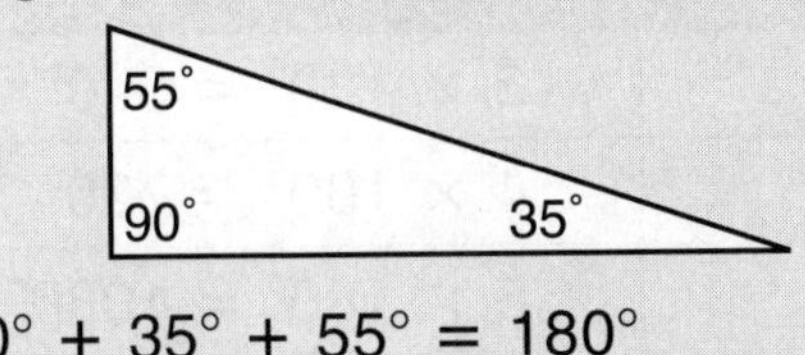

The sum of the measures of the interior angles of a triangle is 180°.

$$90° + 35° + 55° = 180°$$

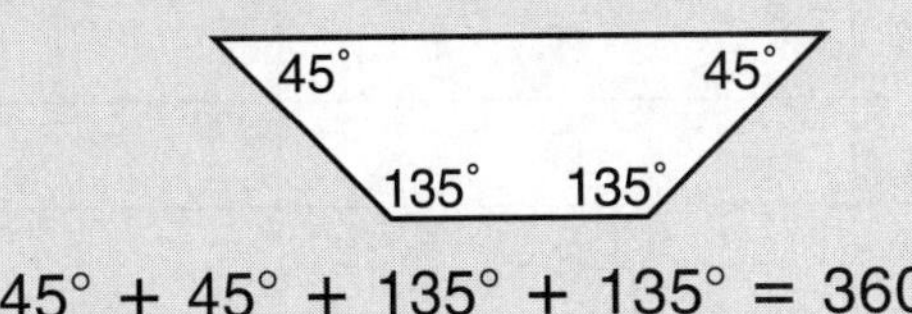

The sum of the measures of the interior angles of a quadrilateral is 360°.

$$45° + 45° + 135° + 135° = 360°$$

Find the measure of the third angle of each triangle.

1.

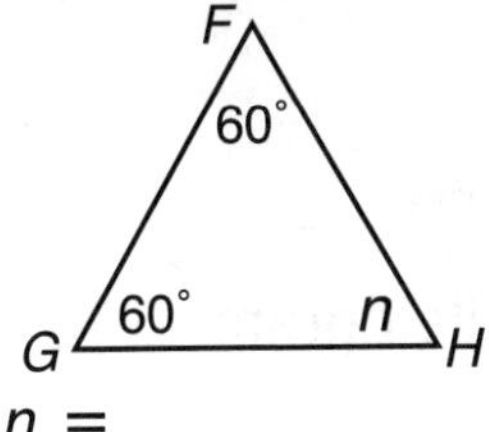

$n =$ _______

2.

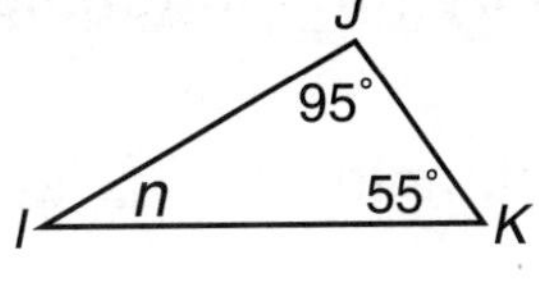

$n =$ _______

3.

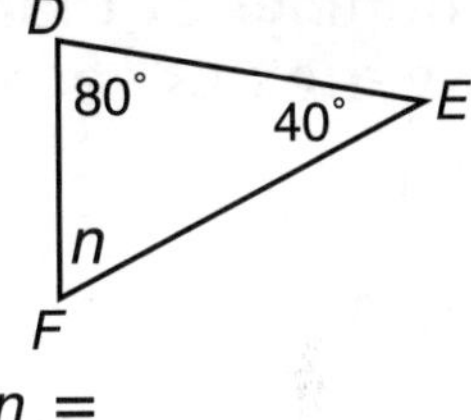

$n =$ _______

4. $\angle K = 38°$, $\angle L = 89°$, $\angle M =$ _______

5. $\angle X = 85°$, $\angle Y = 49°$, $\angle Z =$ _______

Find the measure of the fourth angle of each quadrilateral.

6. $\angle E = 99°$, $\angle F = 47°$, $\angle G = 79°$, $\angle H =$ _______

7. $\angle J = 23°$, $\angle K = 109°$, $\angle L = 97°$, $\angle M =$ _______

8. $\angle Q = 88°$, $\angle R = 93°$, $\angle S = 97°$, $\angle T =$ _______

Find the value of n in each quadrilateral.

9.

____

10.

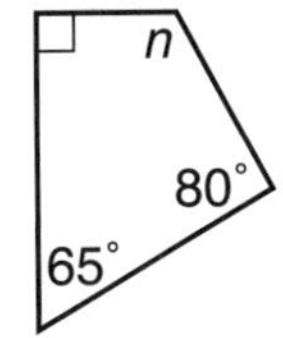

____

11.

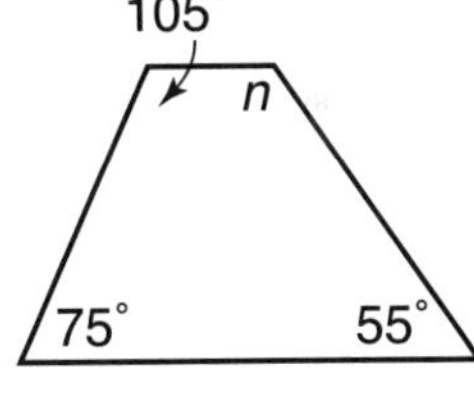

____

Find the value of each variable.

12.

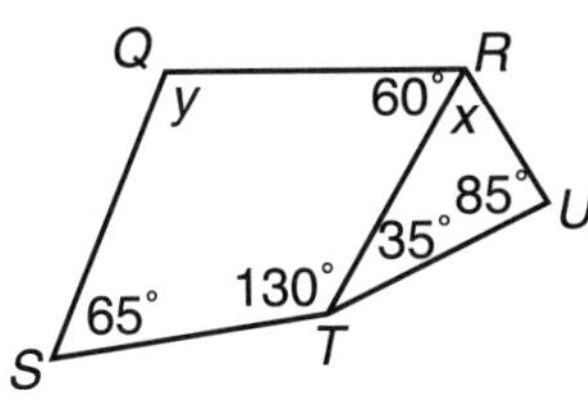

____

13.

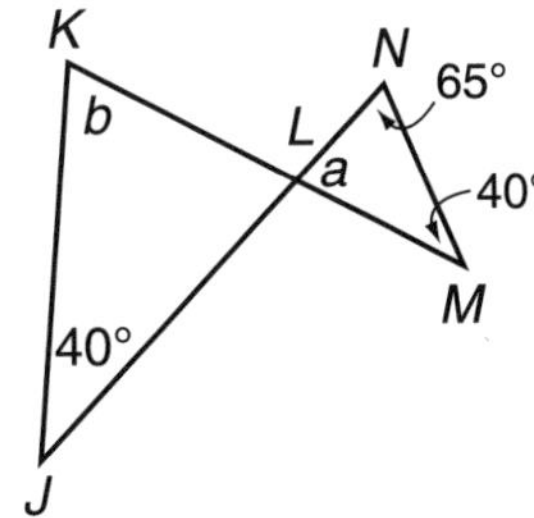

____

14.

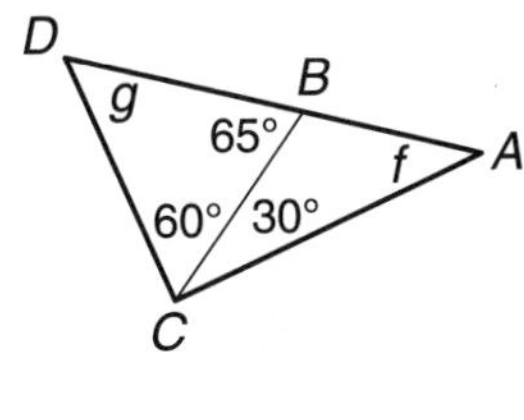

____

Problem Solving

15. Trapezoid *EFGH* has two pairs of congruent angles. One of the angles measures 124°. What are the measures of the other angles? _______________________

Angles of Polygons

Name _______________________

Date _______________________

Polygon	Number of Sides	Number of Triangles Formed by Diagonals from One Vertex	Sum of the Measures of the Interior Angles
pentagon	5	$5 - 2 = 3$	$3 \times 180° = 540°$
hexagon	6	$6 - 2 = 4$	$4 \times 180° = 720°$
octagon	8	$8 - 2 = 6$	$6 \times 180° = 1080°$
n-gon	n	$n - 2$	$(n - 2) \times 180°$

Find the number of triangles formed by the diagonals from one vertex of each polygon.

1. 14-gon _______________

2. rectangle _______________

3. 19-gon _______________

4. nonagon _______________

5. 12-gon

6. parallelogram _______________

Find the sum of the measures of the interior angles of each polygon.

7. 14-gon

8. rhombus

9. 19-gon

____

____

____

10. nonagon

11. 12-gon

12. heptagon

____

____

____

Find the value of the variable in each polygon.

13.

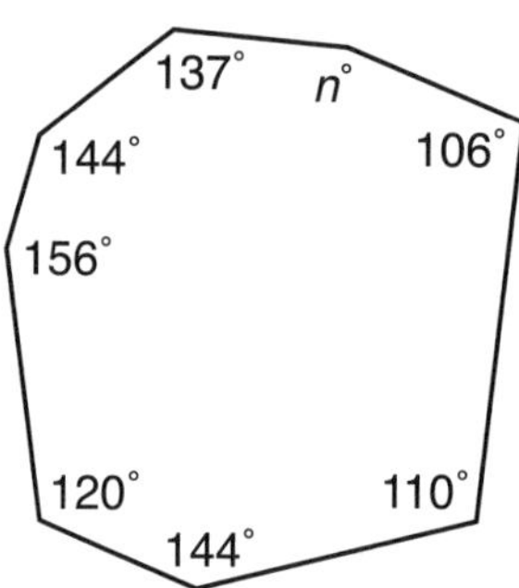

14.

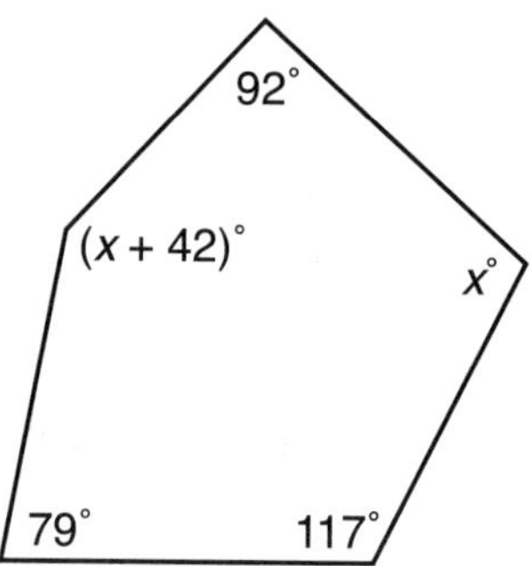

____

____

Problem Solving

15. Derek draws a polygon. The sum of its interior angles is 1440°. What kind of polygon does Derek draw?

16. Four of the interior angles of Fiona's hexagon measure 167°, 105°, 145°, and 135°. The other interior angles are congruent to each other. What are the measures of the other angles?

____

____

Use with Lesson 10-11, pages 350–351 in the Student Book.
Then go to Lesson 10-12, pages 352–353 in the Student Book.

Circles

Name _______________________

Date _______________________

Point *M* is the center of circle *M*.

$\overline{MA}$ is a radius.

$\overline{AN}$ is a diameter.

$\overline{AC}$ is a chord.

$\angle AMC$ is a central angle.

$\overset{\frown}{ACN}$ is a semicircle. m$\overset{\frown}{ACN}$ = 180°

$\overset{\frown}{ABC}$ is a minor arc. m$\overset{\frown}{ABC}$ < 180°

$\overset{\frown}{CON}$ is a major arc. m$\overset{\frown}{CON}$ > 180°

Construct a regular hexagon by using a circle.

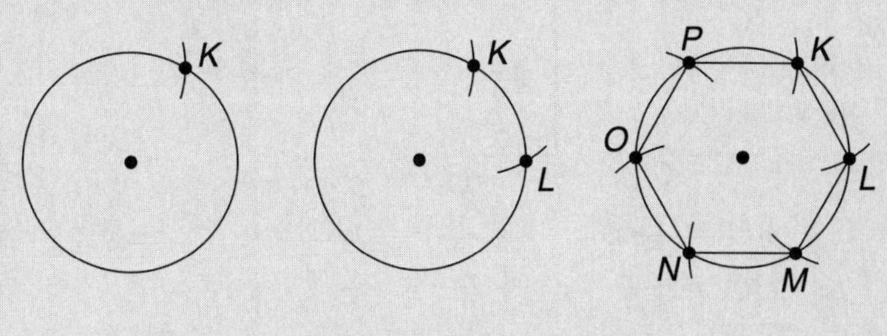

KLMNOP is a regular hexagon.

**Use a compass to construct a circle with a radius of 2 cm.
Then draw and label each of the following:**

1. center: point *O*

2. radius: $\overline{OR}$

3. central angle: $\angle ROT$

4. diameter: $\overline{XY}$

5. chord: $\overline{RS}$

6. chord: $\overline{YZ}$

Use circle *M* in the display above for exercises 7–9.

7. Name one semicircle other than $\overset{\frown}{ACN}$: _______________________

8. Name one minor arc other than $\overset{\frown}{ABC}$: _______________________

9. Name one major arc other than $\overset{\frown}{CON}$: _______________________

For each statement, write *always*, *sometimes*, or *never*.

10. One endpoint of every radius of a circle is the center of the circle.

____

11. Chords pass through the center of a circle.

____

12. A diameter forms a straight angle.

____

13. A central angle of a circle has its vertex on the circle.

____

**Construct each regular polygon by using a circle.
Explain your process.**

14. an octagon

15. a hexagon

16. a nonagon

Congruent and Similar Polygons

Name ___________________________

Date ___________________________

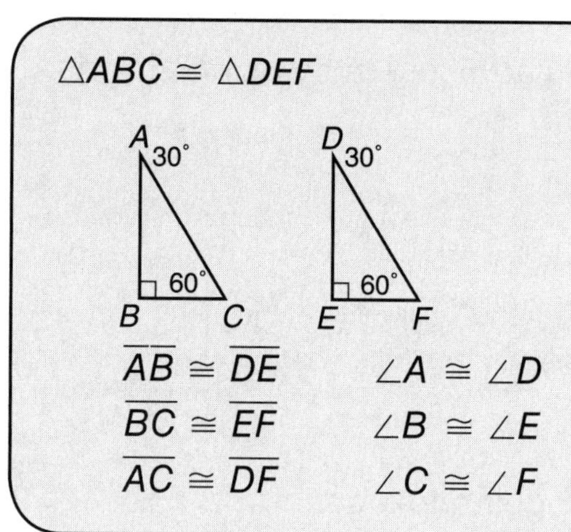

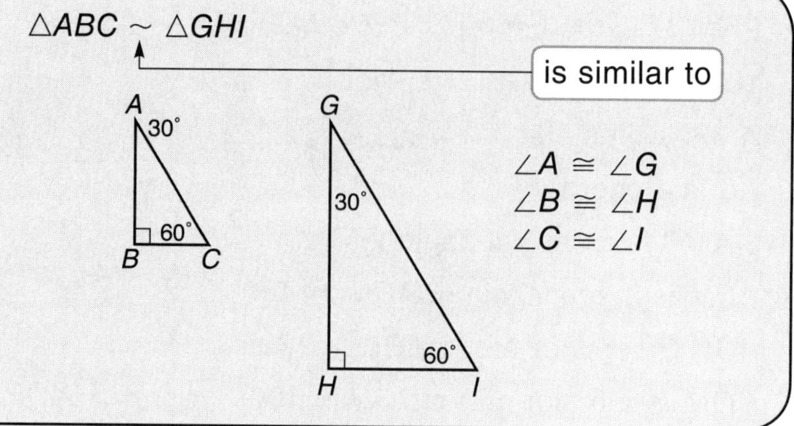

Do the polygons appear to be *congruent*, *similar*, or *neither*?

1. 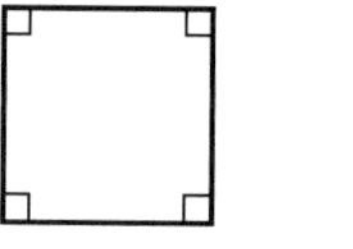 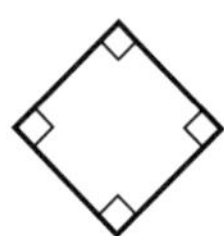

____

2. 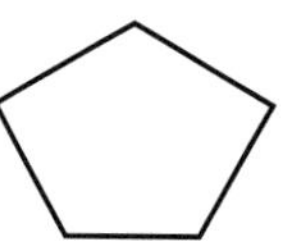 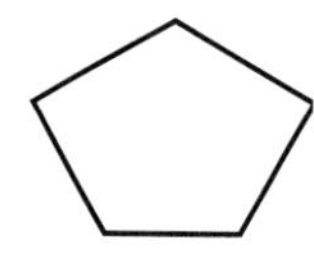

____

3. 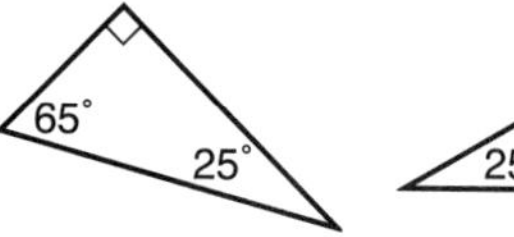

____

4. 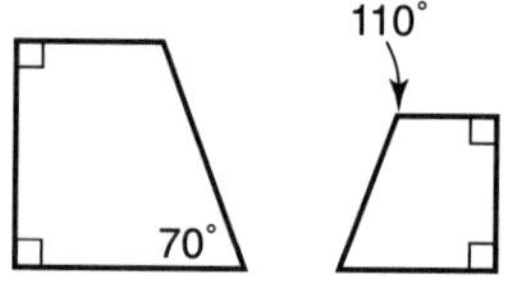

____

5. 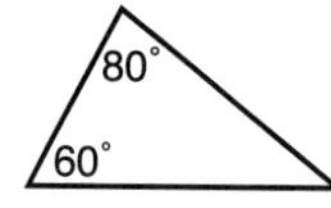

____

6. 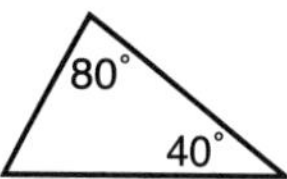 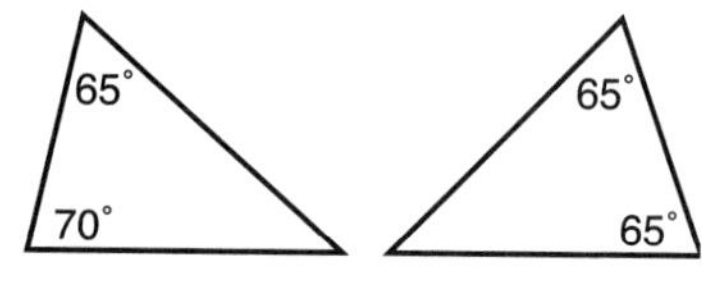

____

Name the corresponding congruent parts.

Parallelogram *ABCD* ~ Parallelogram *EFGH*

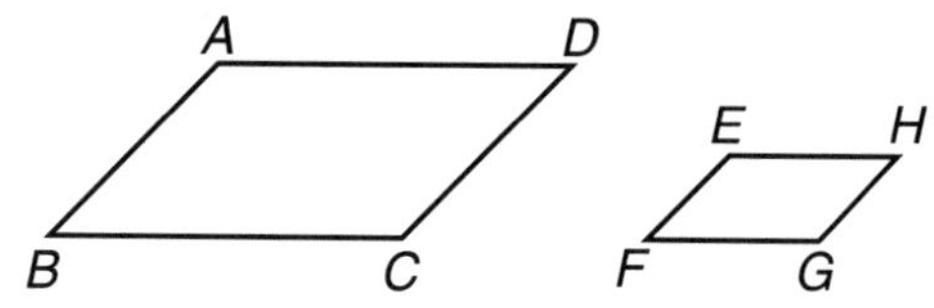

Trapezoid *PQRS* ≅ Trapezoid *JKLM*

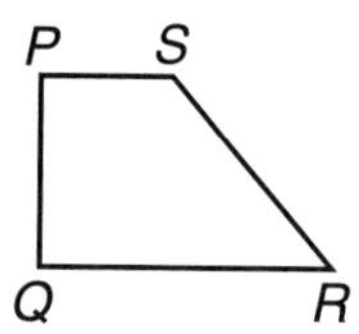 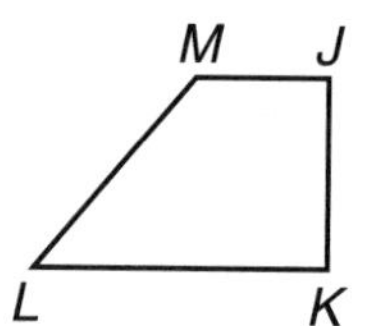

7. ∠A ≅ _______   **8.** ∠C ≅ _______

9. ∠H ≅ _______   **10.** ∠B ≅ _______

11. PS ≅ _______   **12.** JK ≅ _______

13. RS ≅ _______   **14.** ∠L ≅ _______

15. ∠Q ≅ _______   **16.** ∠M ≅ _______

Problem Solving

17. In the figures at the right, *KLMN* ≅ *WXYZ*.
Find the measure of ∠Y and ∠W
and the lengths of XY and WX.

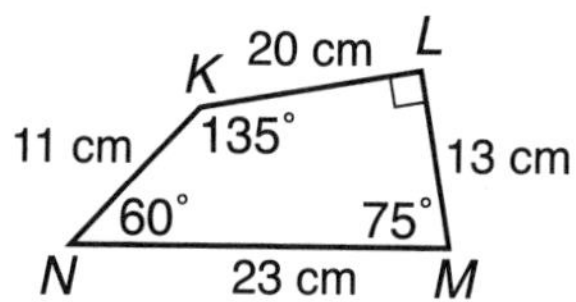 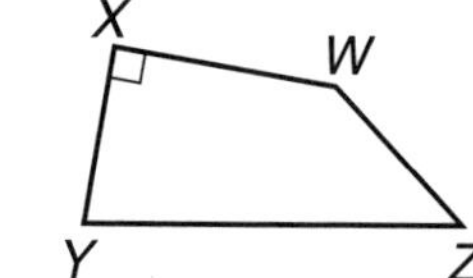

____

Use with Lesson 10-13, pages 354–355 in the Student Book.
Then go to Lesson 10-14, pages 356–357 in the Student Book.

Transformations

Name _______________

Date _______________

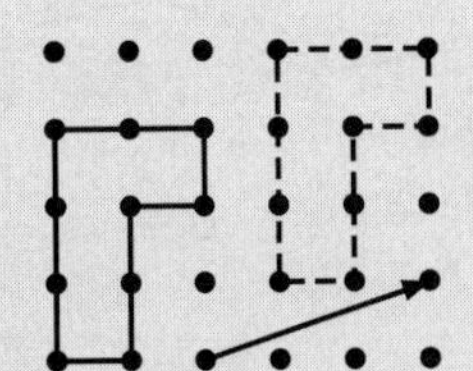 **Translation (Slide)**   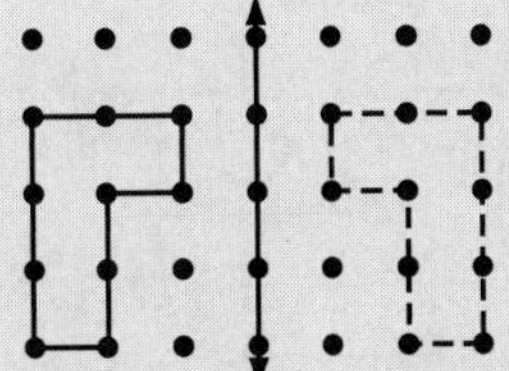 **Reflection (Flip)**   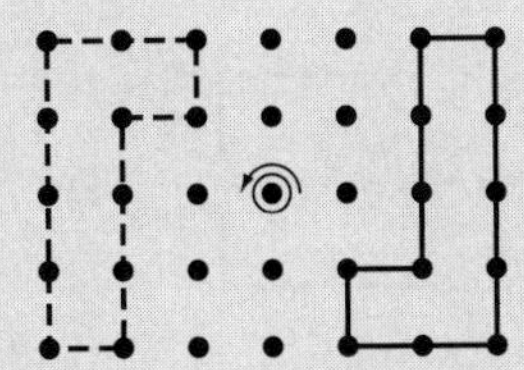 **Rotation (Turn)**

Draw a translation, reflection, and rotation image of each figure.

1. Translation   Reflection   Rotation

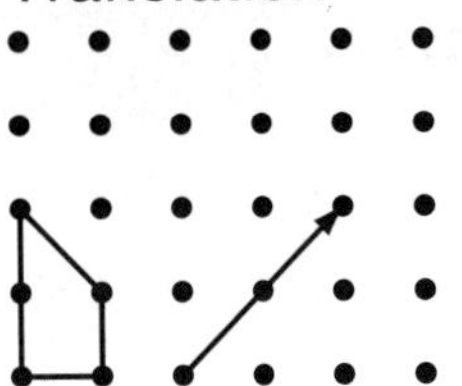 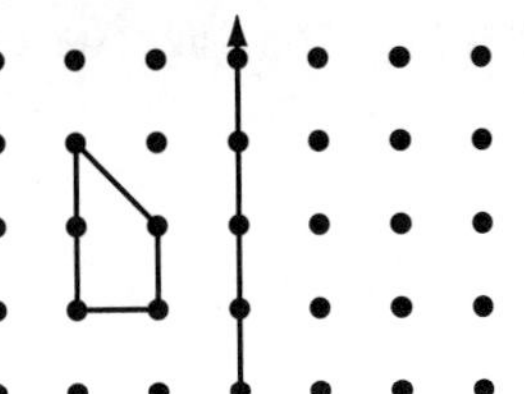 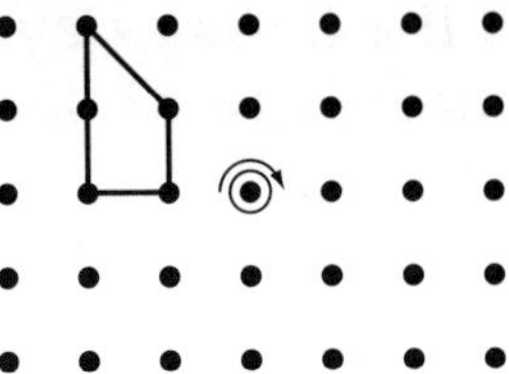

2. Translation   Reflection   Rotation

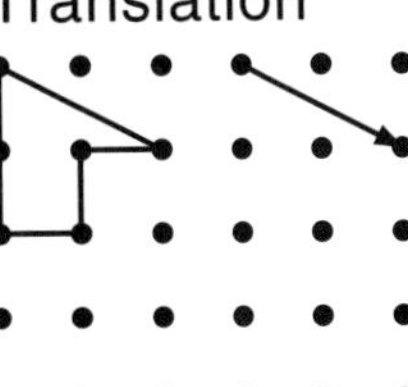 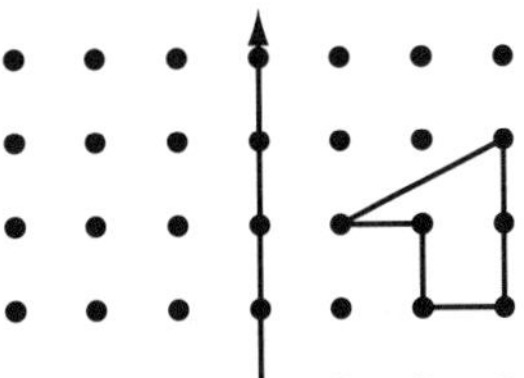 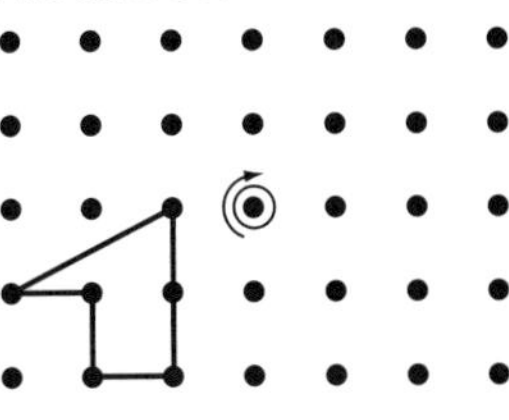

Write *true* or *false* for each statement. If *false,* explain why. Draw transformations on dot paper to help.

3. A figure rotated 360° around a point will result in a reflection of the original figure.

____

4. A figure and its reflection image are similar but not congruent.

____

5. The translation image of a figure is always congruent to the original figure, regardless of how far the figure is moved.

____

6. A figure rotated 180° around a point clockwise will look the same as the same figure rotated 180° counterclockwise.

____

Problem Solving

7. Draw a 180° clockwise rotation of the figure.

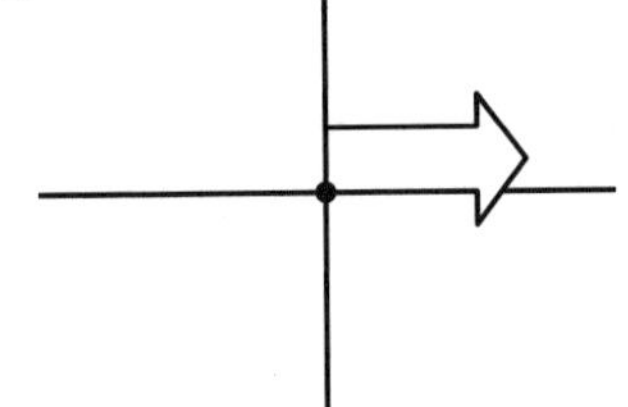

8. Describe this transformation.

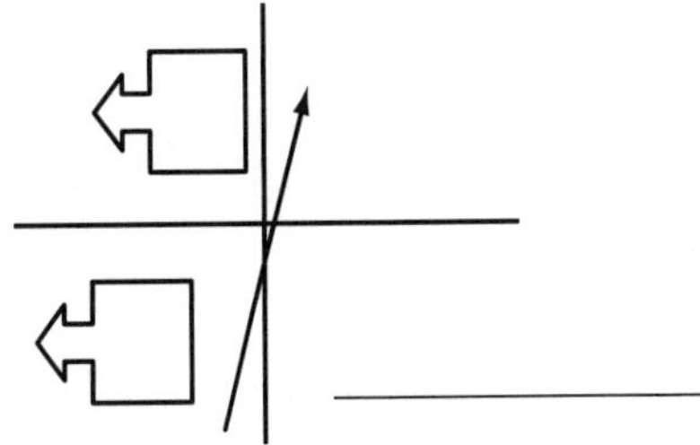

Use with Lesson 10-14, pages 356–357 in the Student Book.
Then go to Lesson 10-15, pages 358–359 in the Student Book.

135

Symmetry

Name _______________________

Date _______________________

Reflection Symmetry	Rotational Symmetry	Point Symmetry
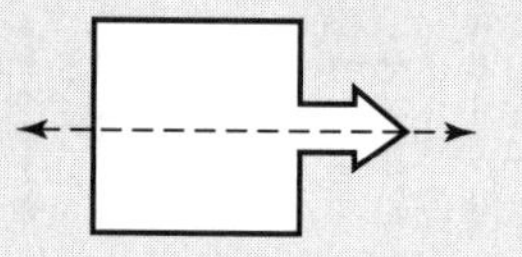	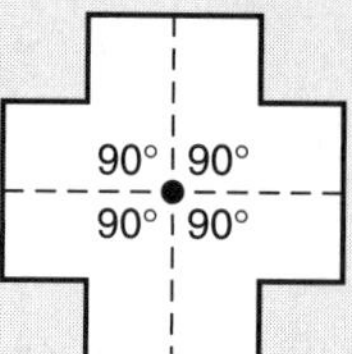	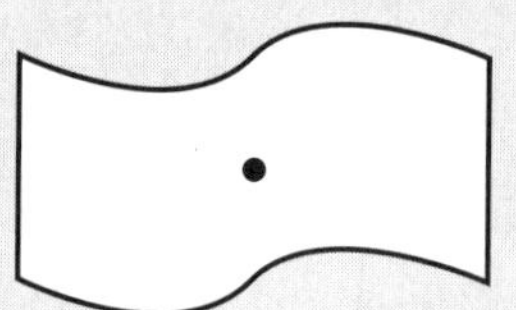
horizontal line of symmetry	90° ($\frac{1}{4}$-turn) rotational symmetry	180°-rotational symmetry is also point symmetry.

Name all the lines of symmetry for each figure. Write *vertical*, *horizontal*, or *diagonal*. Draw all lines of symmetry.

1. 

2. 

3. 

_______________   _______________   _______________

Each figure has rotational symmetry about point O. Tell the smallest turn, or the number of degrees, that will rotate the figure onto itself.

4. 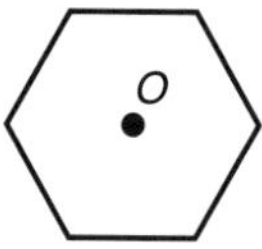

5. 

6. 

_______________   _______________   _______________

Tell whether the figure has point symmetry. Write *yes* or *no*.

7. 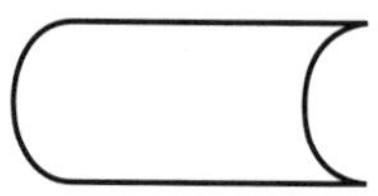

8. 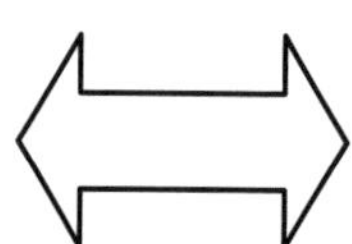

9. 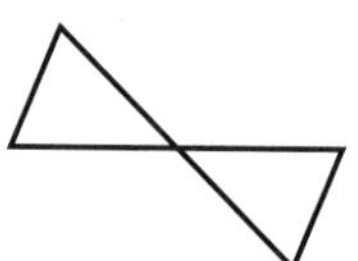

_______________   _______________   _______________

Tell which words and numbers have *reflection*, *rotational*, or *point* symmetry.

10. **WOW**   11. **NOON**   12. **DEED**   13. **99066**

_______________   _______________   _______________

Use with Lesson 10-15, pages 358–359 in the Student Book.
Then go to Lesson 10-16, pages 360–361 in the Student Book.

Tessellations

A tessellation is made from congruent figures that completely cover a surface without overlapping or leaving gaps.

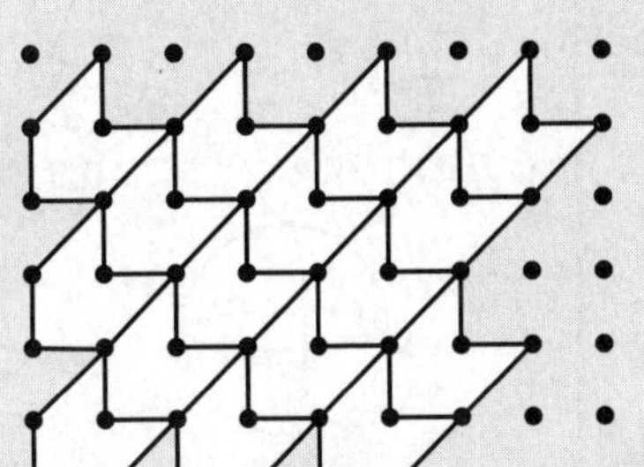

These figures tessellate.

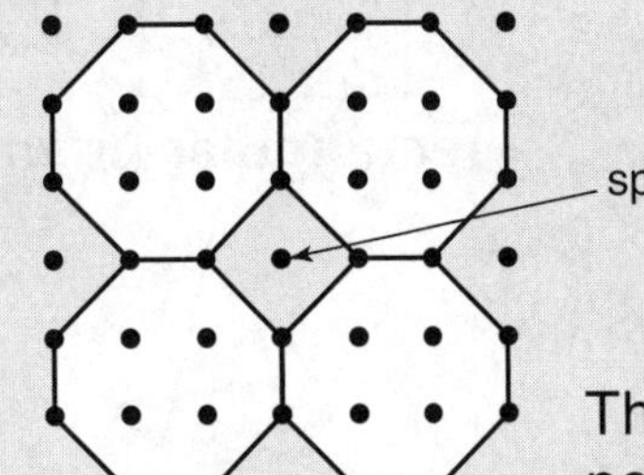

These figures do not tessellate.

**Try to make a tessellation using each polygon.
Does the polygon tessellate? Write *yes* or *no*.**

1. 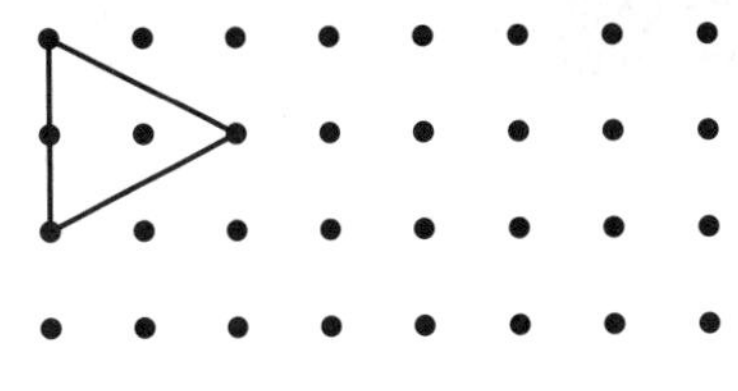

____

2. 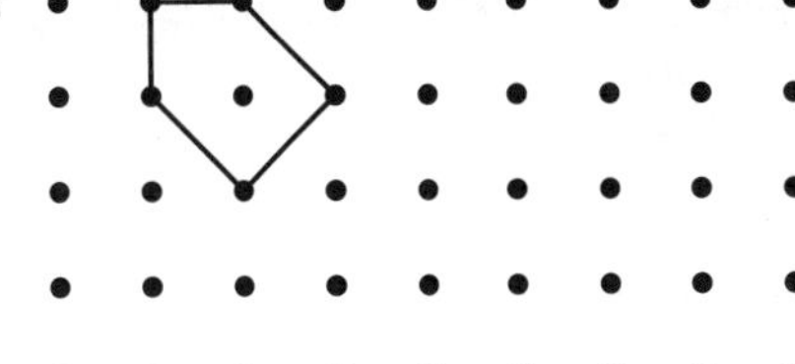

____

3. 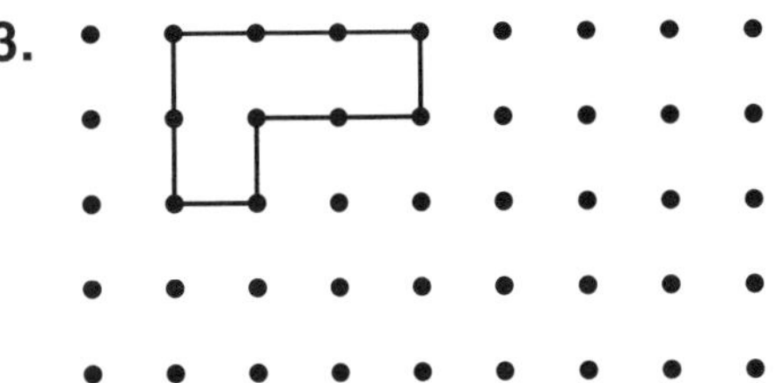

____

4. 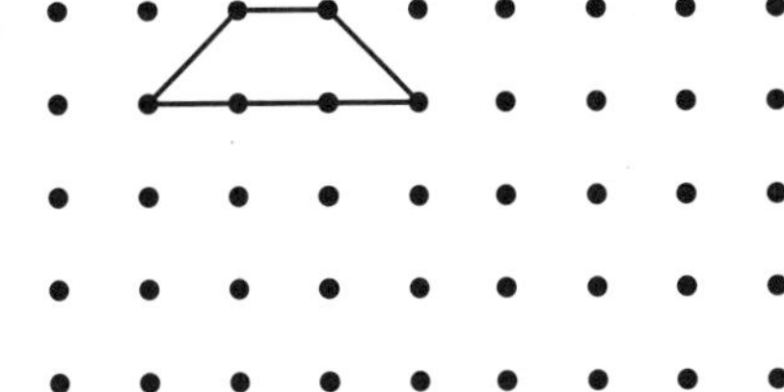

____

5. Tessellate the plane using both squares and hexagons.

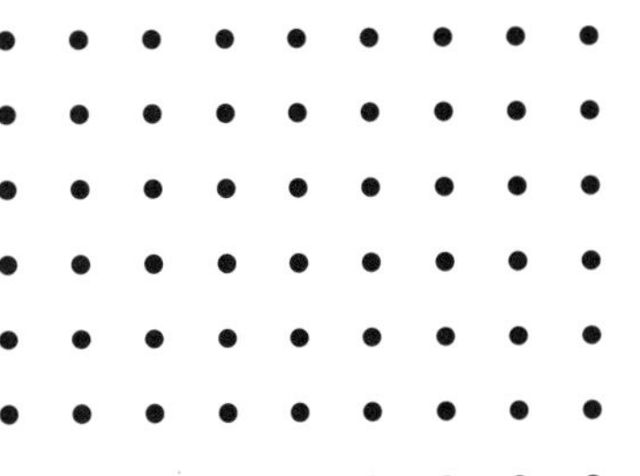

6. Tessellate the plane using both squares and trapezoids.

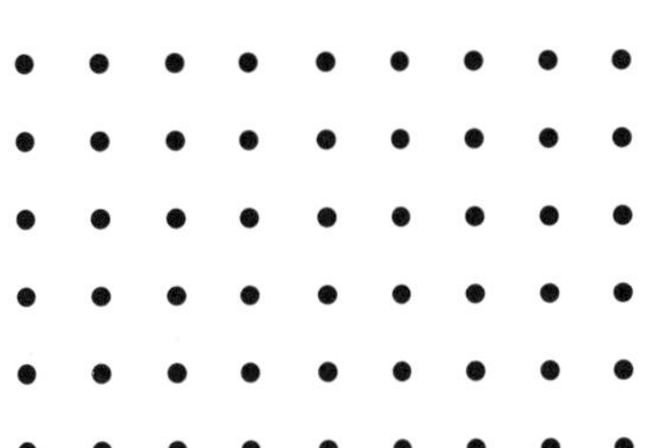

7. Circle the names of shapes that tessellate.

squares	triangles	regular pentagons	regular hexagons
regular octagons	parallelograms	trapezoids	rectangles

Solid Figures

Name _______________________

Date _______________________

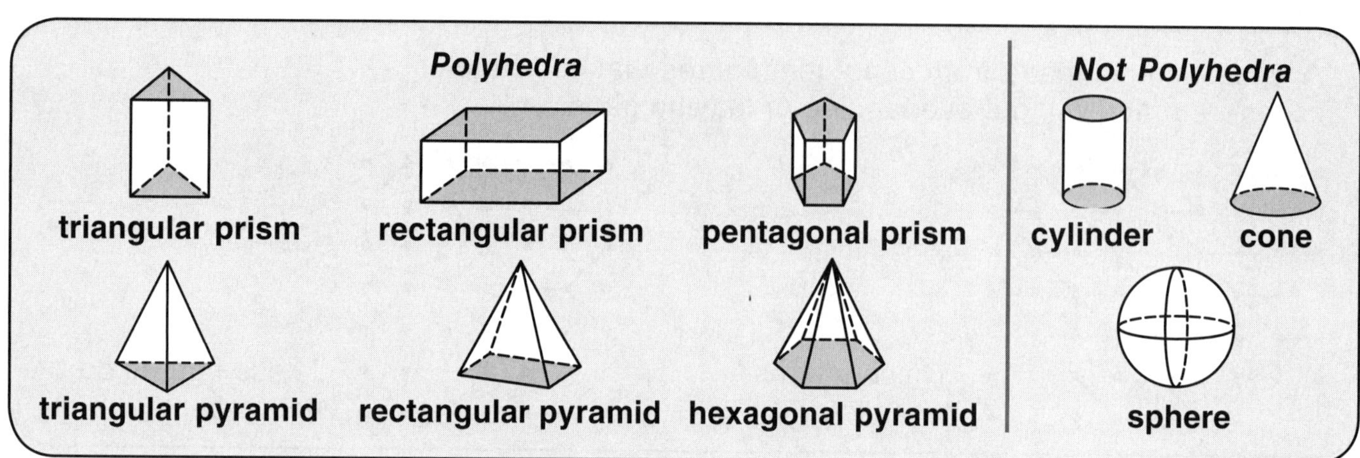

Complete the table. Write the number of faces, vertices, and edges of each space figure.

	Solid Figure	Faces	Vertices	Edges
1.	triangular prism			
2.	rectangular prism			
3.	pentagonal prism			
4.	triangular pyramid			
5.	rectangular pyramid			
6.	hexagonal pyramid			

Write which solid figure(s) can have a base like the one shown.

7. 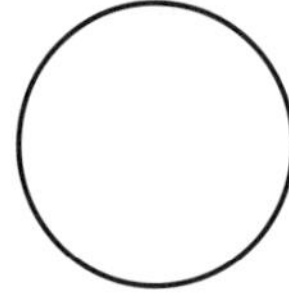

8. 

9. 

10. 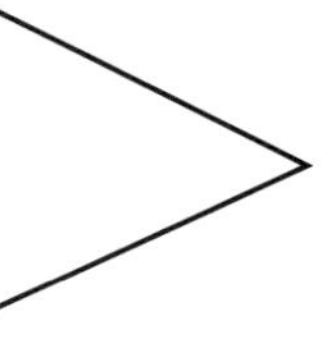

____________________   ____________________   ____________________   ____________________

____________________   ____________________   ____________________   ____________________

Problem Solving

11. A net of a solid figure has 1 rectangular base and 4 triangular faces. Which solid figure is it? How many edges does it have? How many vertices?   _______________________

12. Is it true or false that all cones are polyhedra? Explain.   _______________________

Use with Lesson 10-17, pages 362–363 in the Student Book.
Then go to Lesson 10-18, pages 364–365 in the Student Book.

Views of Solid Figures

Name _______________________

Date _______________________

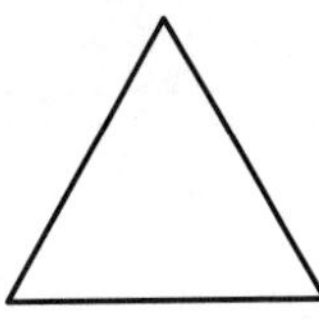 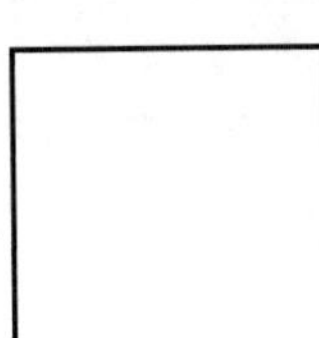 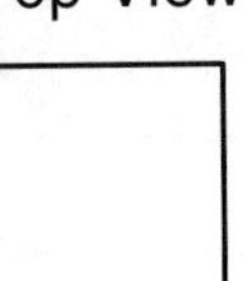 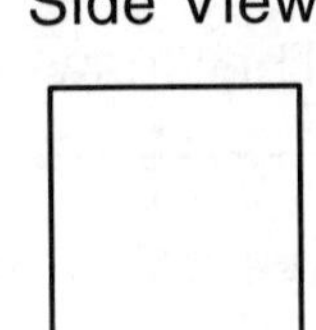

Solid Figure   **Top View**   **Front View**   **Side View**

The different views show that the figure is a rectangular prism.

Name the solid figure that has these views.

1. Top View   Front View

____

2. Top View   Front View   Side View

____

Draw the top, front, and side views of each figure.

3.

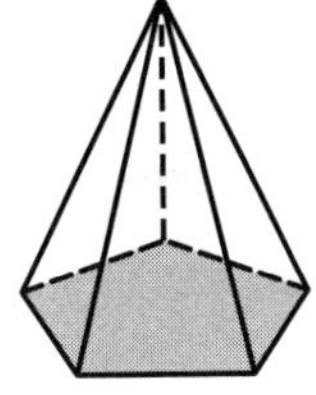

Top	Front	Side

4.

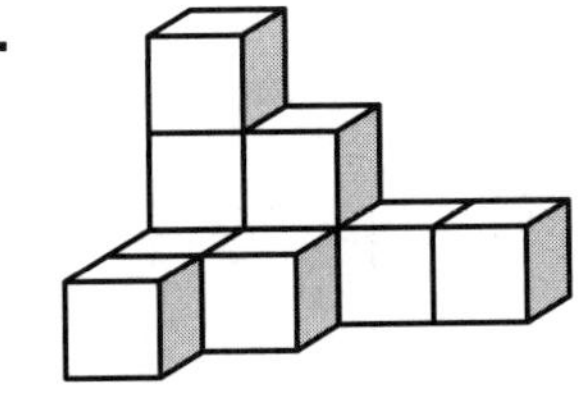

Top	Front	Side

Problem Solving

5. Leanne builds a base that is 3 cubes wide by 2 cubes long. On top of that she places another base that is 2 cubes wide by 2 cubes long. On top of that she places a third base that is 2 cubes wide by 1 cube long. Draw the top, front, and side views of Leanne's building.

Use with Lesson 10-18, pages 364–365 in the Student Book.
Then go to Lesson 10-19, pages 366–367 in the Student Book.

Problem-Solving Strategy: Logical Reasoning

Name ___________________

Date ___________________

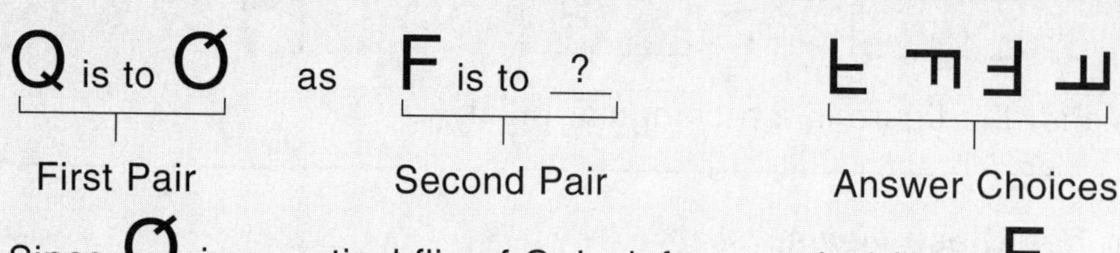

A statement that tells the way in which two pairs of things are alike is an analogy. Choose the correct answer to make an analogy out of this incomplete statement.

Q is to Ό   as   F is to _?_   Ⴌ ⊤┐ ⊥ ⊥┌

First Pair   Second Pair   Answer Choices

Since Ό is a vertical flip of Q, look for a vertical flip of F.

The answer is Ⴌ.

Solve each problem. Use logical reasoning to help you.

1. Rod and Cami make designs that follow the same pattern. Rod's design uses squares and Cami's uses circles. Rod's design is shown below. Draw Cami's design and explain how it is like Rod's.

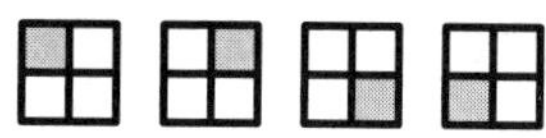

____

2. Maria has a triangle, square, pentagon, hexagon, and octagon. She places them in a row so that no two figures with an even number of sides and no two figures with an odd number of sides are next to each other. When the numbers of sides are listed, no two numbers are in counting order. How could Maria arrange the figures?

3. Find two ways Adrian can complete this analogy: 7 is to 28 as 4 is to _?_ .

____

4. 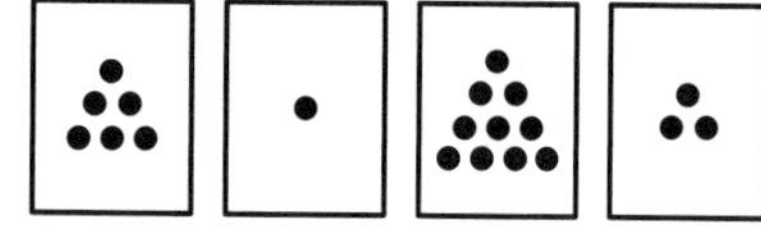

Tina rearranges these cards in a row to form a pattern. Draw the new arrangement, including a 5th card. Then describe the pattern.

____

5. 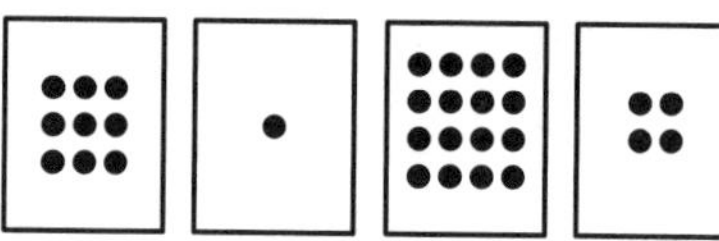

Jed rearranges these cards in a row to form a pattern. Draw the new arrangement, including a 5th card. Then describe the pattern.

____

140

Use with Lesson 10-19, pages 366–367 in the Student Book.
Then go to Lesson 10-20, pages 368–369 in the Student Book.

Problem-Solving Applications: Mixed Review

Solve each problem and explain the method you used. If needed, do all your work on a separate sheet of paper.

1. Julio drew a design that has 7 line segments. His design contains two right triangles, one equilateral triangle, a square, and a pentagon. Draw a picture that shows what Julio's design could look like.

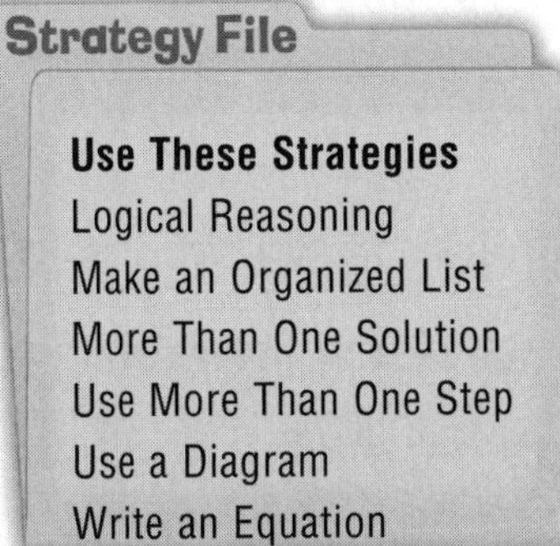

2. ◯ is to ⊖ as ☐ is to __?__ .

3. Susan is choosing a 3-digit combination for her locker. She can not use any digit more than once, and the order of the digits does matter. How many different codes can Susan make using the digits 1–9?

4. Darnell draws a polygon with all congruent angles. The sum of the measures of the interior angles is 1260°. What is the measure of each interior angle?

5. Each isosceles triangle in the figure below has an area of 8 square centimeters. Each right triangle has an area of 5.6 square centimeters. What is the area of the entire figure?

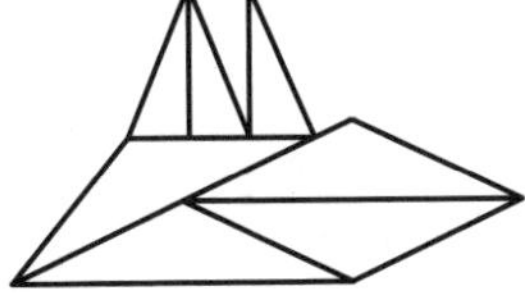

6. A right angle, an acute angle, an obtuse angle, and a straight angle are drawn on the board. $\angle A$ is less than 90°. $\angle B$ is not a 90° angle. The measure of $\angle C$ is 180°. What type of angle is $\angle D$?

Use the diagram for problems 7–9.

7. What is the measure of $\angle ECB$? Explain how you know.

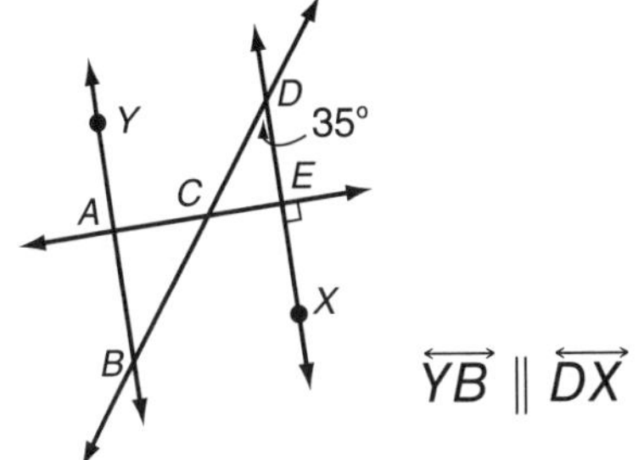

8. What is the measure of $\angle ACD$?

9. Which angle is congruent to $\angle CDE$? Why?

Ratio

Name _______________________

Date _______________________

A **ratio** is a way of comparing two numbers or quantities by division.
A ratio can compare a part to a part, a part to a whole, or a whole to a part.

Ben has 10 rabbits: 3 are white, 5 are black, and 2 are brown.

	Word Form	Ratio Form	Fraction Form
Part to part: brown rabbits to black rabbits	2 to 5	2:5	$\frac{2}{5}$
Part to whole: white rabbits to total rabbits	3 to 10	3:10	$\frac{3}{10}$
Whole to part: total rabbits to brown rabbits	10 to 2	10:2	$\frac{10}{2}$
simplest form →	5 to 1	5:1	$\frac{5}{1}$

Use the bar graph. Write each ratio three ways.

1. mysteries to history books _______________

2. history books to science fiction books _______________

3. nature books to sports books _______________

4. sports books to all books _______________

5. history books to nature books _______________

6. all books to nature and history books _______________

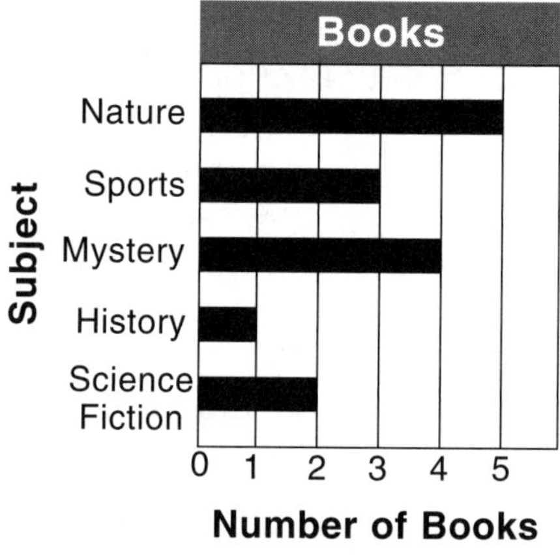

Write each ratio in simplest form.

7. 9 to 15 _______   8. 12:3 _______   9. $\frac{4}{10}$ _______   10. $\frac{21}{78}$ _______

11. 6:15 _______   12. $\frac{3}{9}$ _______   13. $\frac{15}{30}$ _______   14. $\frac{56}{48}$ _______

15. $\frac{28}{35}$ _______   16. $\frac{9}{21}$ _______   17. $\frac{40}{16}$ _______   18. $\frac{60}{45}$ _______

Find the baseball batting average to complete the table. Use a calculator to help.

4 8 ÷ 1 4 5 Enter = | 0.3310345 | ⟶ 0.331

19.

Hits	48	28	35	78	90	29	188
Times at Bat	145	112	170	286	295	113	599
Average	0.331						

Use with Lesson 11-1, pages 376–377 in the Student Book.
Then go to Lesson 11-2, pages 378–379 in the Student Book.

Equivalent Ratios

Name ___________________________

Date ___________________________

Equivalent ratios have the same value and can be written as equivalent fractions.

Write an equivalent ratio for 6 to 8.

| Write the ratio as a fraction. | Multiply or divide the numerator and denominator by the same nonzero number. | Write the result as a fraction. |

$6 \text{ to } 8 = \dfrac{6}{8}$ $\qquad \dfrac{6 \times 4}{8 \times 4} \longrightarrow \dfrac{24}{32}$

$\text{OR} \quad \dfrac{6 \div 2}{8 \div 2} \longrightarrow \dfrac{3}{4}$

Write three equivalent ratios for each.

1. $\dfrac{3}{8}$ ___________

2. $\dfrac{18}{24}$ ___________

3. $\dfrac{4}{10}$ ___________

4. $\dfrac{8}{16}$ ___________

5. $\dfrac{15}{9}$ ___________

6. $\dfrac{1}{2}$ ___________

Circle the letter of the ratio that is equivalent to the given ratio.

7. $\dfrac{2}{3}$ **a.** $\dfrac{5}{6}$ **b.** $6:9$ **c.** 1 to 6   **d.** 6 to 2

8. 4 to 12   **a.** $12:24$ **b.** $\dfrac{1}{4}$ **c.** $5:13$ **d.** 1 to 3

9. $10:2$ **a.** 5 to 1   **b.** $\dfrac{5}{2}$ **c.** $1:5$ **d.** $\dfrac{10}{5}$

10. 12 to 8   **a.** $\dfrac{2}{3}$ **b.** $\dfrac{3}{2}$ **c.** $\dfrac{6}{3}$ **d.** $10:6$

Which ratios are equivalent? Write = or ≠.

11. $\dfrac{3}{5}$ ____ $\dfrac{6}{10}$ **12.** $\dfrac{9}{2}$ ____ $\dfrac{18}{1}$ **13.** $\dfrac{5}{6}$ ____ $\dfrac{25}{30}$ **14.** $\dfrac{3}{4}$ ____ $\dfrac{24}{32}$

15. $\dfrac{2}{3}$ ____ $\dfrac{4}{8}$ **16.** $\dfrac{7}{8}$ ____ $\dfrac{21}{25}$ **17.** $\dfrac{7}{2}$ ____ $\dfrac{14}{49}$ **18.** $\dfrac{8}{2}$ ____ $\dfrac{24}{6}$

Find the value of each variable.

19. $\dfrac{9}{18} = \dfrac{n}{2}$ ____   **20.** $\dfrac{4}{8} = \dfrac{8}{a}$ ____   **21.** $\dfrac{3}{c} = \dfrac{9}{15}$ ____   **22.** $\dfrac{4}{6} = \dfrac{x}{3}$ ____

23. $\dfrac{8}{20} = \dfrac{4}{d}$ ____   **24.** $\dfrac{5}{3} = \dfrac{25}{f}$ ____   **25.** $\dfrac{14}{m} = \dfrac{2}{3}$ ____   **26.** $\dfrac{5}{r} = \dfrac{10}{8}$ ____

Problem Solving

27. There are 24 videotapes in 8 identical packages. How many videotapes are in one package? ___________

28. There are 12 books in one carton. How many books are in 5 cartons that are the same size? ___________

Use with Lesson 11-2, pages 378–379 in the Student Book.
Then go to Lessons 11-2A and 11-2B, pages 237–240 in this Workbook.

Rates

Name ______________________________

Date ______________________________

> A **rate** is a ratio that compares two quantities with different units of measure.
>
> A **unit rate** is a rate that has 1 unit as its second term, or denominator.
>
> $$\frac{80 \text{ breaths}}{2 \text{ minutes}} = \frac{x \text{ breaths}}{1 \text{ minute}} \longrightarrow \frac{80 \div 2}{2 \div 2} = \frac{40}{1}$$
>
> 40 breaths in 1 minute is called a unit rate.

Write each as a unit rate.

1. $\dfrac{64 \text{ feet}}{2 \text{ seconds}} = \dfrac{\text{feet}}{1 \text{ second}}$

2. $\dfrac{12 \text{ apples}}{4 \text{ children}} = \dfrac{\text{apples}}{1 \text{ child}}$

3. $\dfrac{24 \text{ crayons}}{3 \text{ boxes}} = \dfrac{\text{crayons}}{1 \text{ box}}$

4. $\dfrac{150 \text{ pages}}{2 \text{ hours}} = \dfrac{\text{pages}}{\text{hour}}$

5. $\dfrac{8 \text{ quarts}}{16 \text{ pints}} = \dfrac{\text{quart}}{\text{pints}}$

6. $\dfrac{165 \text{ miles}}{3 \text{ hours}} = \dfrac{\text{miles}}{\text{hour}}$

Find the unit rate or unit price.

7. 40 meters in 5 seconds __________

8. 135 miles in 3 hours __________

9. 6 pears for $2.10 __________

10. 3 books for $8.85 __________

11. 24 pens in 2 boxes __________

12. $44 for 8 hours __________

Use the unit rate or the unit price to complete.

13. $4 for 1 ticket

 __________ for 3 tickets

14. 30 miles in 1 hour

 __________ in 5 hours

15. 1 pencil for 20¢

 3 pencils for __________

16. 80 words in 1 minute

 __________ in 5 minutes

17. 1 book for $3.50

 4 books for __________

18. 32 miles on 1 gallon

 __________ on 12 gallons

Problem Solving

19. A pilot flew his plane 225 mi in 45 minutes. What was his speed per minute? __________

20. A 3-lb loaf of bread costs $5.25. At the same rate per pound, how much would a 1-lb loaf cost? __________

21. Maria earns $6.50 per hour. How much does she earn working 15 hours? __________

Ⓒ Use with Lesson 11-3, pages 380–381 in the Student Book.
Ⓒ Then go to Lesson 11-3A, pages 241–242 in this Workbook.

Proportions

A **proportion** is an equation that shows two ratios are equivalent.
Two ratios form a proportion if their cross products are equal.

Are $3:12$ and $5:20$ equivalent ratios?

The product of the extremes is equal to the product of the means.

extremes

$$3:12 \quad = \quad 5:20$$

means

$$3 \times 20 \stackrel{?}{=} 12 \times 5$$
$$60 = 60$$

So $3:12$ and $5:20$ are equivalent ratios. They form a proportion.

Use equivalent fractions or the cross-products rule to determine if the ratios form a proportion. Write *yes* or *no*.

1. $\dfrac{2}{5} \stackrel{?}{=} \dfrac{5}{2}$ _____

2. $\dfrac{4}{7} \stackrel{?}{=} \dfrac{8}{14}$ _____

3. $\dfrac{9}{4} \stackrel{?}{=} \dfrac{12}{27}$ _____

4. $\dfrac{6}{4} \stackrel{?}{=} \dfrac{12}{8}$ _____

5. $\dfrac{6}{10} \stackrel{?}{=} \dfrac{3}{5}$ _____

6. $\dfrac{2}{9} \stackrel{?}{=} \dfrac{12}{54}$ _____

7. $\dfrac{24}{18} \stackrel{?}{=} \dfrac{4}{2}$ _____

8. $\dfrac{16}{6} \stackrel{?}{=} \dfrac{3}{8}$ _____

9. $\dfrac{12}{50} \stackrel{?}{=} \dfrac{7}{25}$ _____

10. $\dfrac{3}{8} \stackrel{?}{=} \dfrac{9}{24}$ _____

11. $\dfrac{1}{4} \stackrel{?}{=} \dfrac{25}{100}$ _____

12. $\dfrac{24}{30} \stackrel{?}{=} \dfrac{4}{5}$ _____

Find the missing term to form a proportion.

13. $\dfrac{3}{7} = \dfrac{9}{a}$ _____

14. $\dfrac{2}{5} = \dfrac{4}{x}$ _____

15. $\dfrac{6}{b} = \dfrac{9}{15}$ _____

16. $\dfrac{6}{12} = \dfrac{d}{36}$ _____

17. $\dfrac{7}{3} = \dfrac{28}{f}$ _____

18. $\dfrac{12}{54} = \dfrac{n}{9}$ _____

19. $\dfrac{3}{5} = \dfrac{c}{45}$ _____

20. $\dfrac{18}{24} = \dfrac{n}{4}$ _____

21. $\dfrac{5}{8} = \dfrac{r}{48}$ _____

22. $\dfrac{10}{3} = \dfrac{40}{h}$ _____

23. $\dfrac{20}{100} = \dfrac{1}{e}$ _____

24. $\dfrac{25}{75} = \dfrac{w}{3}$ _____

**Circle the letters of the two equivalent ratios.
Then write a proportion.**

25. **a.** $\dfrac{1}{3}$ **b.** $\dfrac{3}{6}$ **c.** $\dfrac{5}{15}$ _____________________

26. **a.** $\dfrac{21}{28}$ **b.** $\dfrac{3}{4}$ **c.** $\dfrac{4}{3}$ _____________________

27. **a.** $\dfrac{2}{10}$ **b.** $\dfrac{4}{5}$ **c.** $\dfrac{24}{30}$ _____________________

28. **a.** $6:50$ **b.** $3:25$ **c.** $5:40$ _____________________

29. **a.** $48:12$ **b.** $20:5$ **c.** $12:4$ _____________________

30. **a.** $10:15$ **b.** $1:3$ **c.** $14:21$ _____________________

Use with Lesson 11-4, pages 382–383 in the Student Book.
Then go to Lessons 11-4A and 11-4B, pages 243–246 in this Workbook.

Solve Proportions

Solve the proportion: $\frac{n}{16} = \frac{5}{20}$.

Extremes   Means

$\frac{n}{16} \diagdown\!\!\!\!\diagup \frac{5}{20} \longrightarrow n \times 20 = 16 \times 5$

$20n = 80$

$20n \div 20 = 80 \div 20$

$n = 4$

Check:

$\frac{4}{16} \overset{?}{=} \frac{5}{20} \longrightarrow 4 \times 20 = 16 \times 5$

$80 = 80$

Complete to find the missing term in each proportion.

1. $\frac{n}{8} = \frac{30}{48} \longrightarrow n \times 48 = 8 \times 30$

$48n = 240$

$48n \div \underline{\quad} = 240 \div \underline{\quad}$

$n = \underline{\quad}$

2. $\frac{7}{n} = \frac{21}{30} \longrightarrow 7 \times 30 = n \times 21$

$210 = 21n$

$210 \div \underline{\quad} = 21n \div \underline{\quad}$

$\underline{\quad} = n$

Find the missing term in each proportion.

3. $\frac{n}{3} = \frac{10}{15}$ _____

4. $\frac{9}{10} = \frac{n}{40}$ _____

5. $\frac{n}{4} = \frac{9}{6}$ _____

6. $\frac{8}{40} = \frac{n}{20}$ _____

7. $\frac{6}{7} = \frac{n}{21}$ _____

8. $\frac{6}{9} = \frac{12}{n}$ _____

9. $\frac{8}{12} = \frac{n}{24}$ _____

10. $\frac{3}{n} = \frac{24}{16}$ _____

11. $\frac{n}{6} = \frac{35}{42}$ _____

12. $\frac{2}{n} = \frac{5}{10}$ _____

13. $\frac{3}{4} = \frac{n}{48}$ _____

14. $\frac{16}{20} = \frac{48}{n}$ _____

Find the value of a.

15. $4 : a = 16 : 24$ _____

16. $a : 7 = 7 : 49$ _____

17. $8 : 3 = a : 12$ _____

18. $5 : a = 15 : 21$ _____

19. $2 : 9 = 16 : a$ _____

20. $a : 12 = 15 : 60$ _____

21. $0.2 : 4 = a : 16$ _____

22. $a : 9 = 0.3 : 27$ _____

23. $15 : 5 = 4.5 : a$ _____

Circle the letters of the two ratios that form a proportion.

24. **a.** $\frac{1}{3}$ **b.** $\frac{1}{6}$ **c.** $\frac{2}{6}$

25. **a.** $\frac{3}{8}$ **b.** $\frac{5}{6}$ **c.** $\frac{10}{12}$

26. **a.** $\frac{5}{10}$ **b.** $\frac{10}{15}$ **c.** $\frac{1}{2}$

27. **a.** $\frac{12}{30}$ **b.** $\frac{2}{5}$ **c.** $\frac{6}{5}$

28. **a.** $\frac{7}{8}$ **b.** $\frac{21}{24}$ **c.** $\frac{14}{21}$

29. **a.** $\frac{28}{30}$ **b.** $\frac{35}{50}$ **c.** $\frac{7}{10}$

30. **a.** $\frac{18}{81}$ **b.** $\frac{3}{14}$ **c.** $\frac{2}{9}$

31. **a.** $\frac{4}{16}$ **b.** $\frac{1}{4}$ **c.** $\frac{1}{8}$

Use with Lesson 11-5, pages 384–385 in the Student Book.
Then go to Lesson 11-6, pages 386–387 in the Student Book.

Write Proportions

Name _______________________

Date _______________________

At the given rate, how much would Tyrell earn in 20 hours?

- Write a proportion.

earnings → $\dfrac{\$6.50}{1} = \dfrac{t}{20}$ ← earnings
hours →   ← hours

- Use cross products to solve.

$$\dfrac{\$6.50}{1} = \dfrac{t}{20}$$

$$\$6.50 \times 20 = 1 \times t$$

$$\$130 = t$$

Tyrell would earn $130 in 20 hours.

Hourly Wages	
Laura	$6.00
Tom	$5.75
Tyrell	$6.50
Teresa	$6.25
Wai Kai	$7.00

Be sure that the two equivalent ratios in the proportion compare similar things.

Use the table above to write and solve a proportion to find the total earnings for each number of hours worked.

1. Laura, 25 hours

2. Wai Kai, 16 hours

3. Tom, 31 hours

4. Teresa, 10 hours

5. Tyrell, 18 hours

6. Laura, 8 hours

Write and solve a proportion.

Speed or rate $(r) = \dfrac{\text{distance } (d)}{\text{time } (t)}$

7. Oscar gets 4 hits out of every 15 times he comes to bat. How many hits would you expect him to have in 60 at bats?

8. One out of every 37 pitches is hit into the stands. Out of 148 pitches, how many would you expect to be hit into the stands?

9. A sailfish can travel as fast as 68 miles per hour. At that rate, how far would a sailfish travel in 45 minutes?

10. A penguin travels up to 25 miles per hour. At that rate, how long would it take a penguin to travel 112.5 miles?

Use with Lesson 11-6, pages 386–387 in the Student Book.
Then go to Lesson 11-7, pages 388–389 in the Student Book.

Proportions and Similar Figures

Name ______________________

Date ______________________

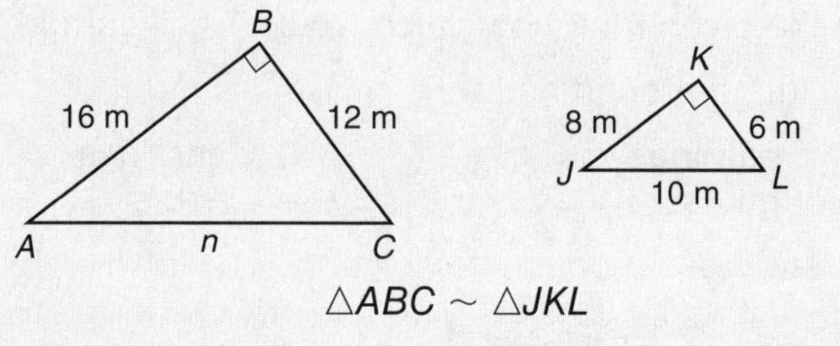

What is the length of $\overline{AC}$?
- Write a proportion.

$$\frac{n}{JL} = \frac{AB}{JK} \longrightarrow \frac{n}{10} = \frac{16}{8}$$

- Use cross products to solve.

$$n \times 8 = 10 \times 16$$
$$8n = 160$$
$$8n \div 8 = 160 \div 8$$
$$n = 20$$

The length of $\overline{AC}$ is 20 m.

$$\triangle ABC \sim \triangle JKL$$

Similar figures have the same shape and their corresponding angles are congruent.

The figures in each pair are similar. Write and solve a proportion to find the length of each missing side.

1. 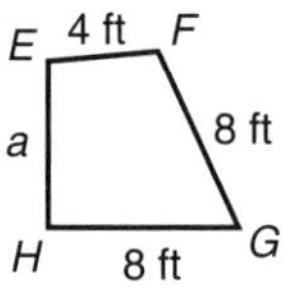 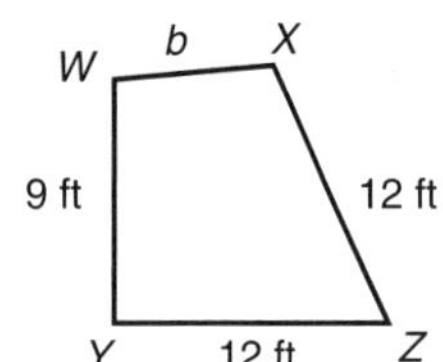

2. 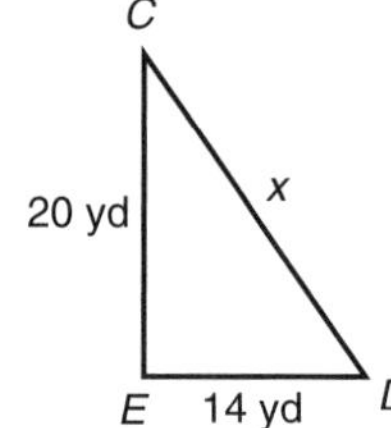

____

3. 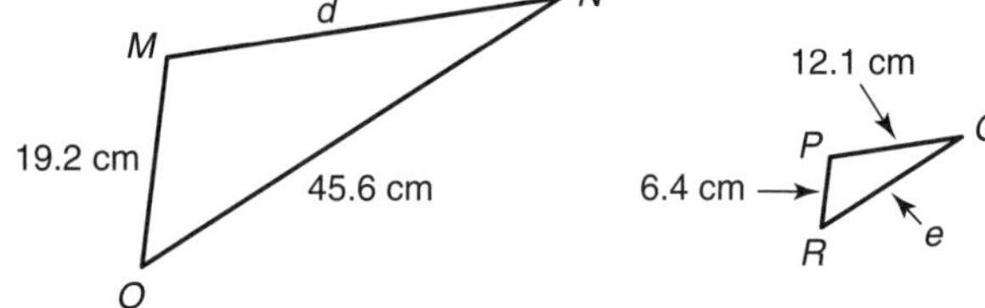

4. 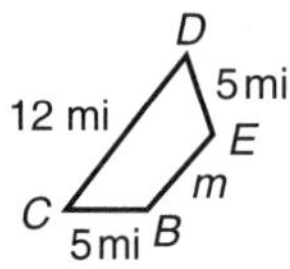

____

Problem Solving

5. Lisa draws two similar parallelograms. The lengths of the longer sides of the parallelograms are 4.6 in. and 6.9 in. If the length of the shorter side of the smaller parallelogram is 3.8 in., how long is the shorter side of the larger parallelogram?

6. Marco draws two trapezoids. The bases of the first trapezoid are 14 and 16 cm long, and its other two sides are 6 cm long. The bases of the second trapezoid are 7 and 8 cm long, and its sides are 4 cm long. Are the trapezoids similar? Explain.

7. $\triangle JKL \sim \triangle PQR$. $\overline{JK}$, $\overline{KL}$, and $\overline{PQ}$ are 5, 10, and 20 cm long, respectively. How many times the length of $\overline{JL}$ is $\overline{PR}$?

8. The lengths, in mm, of the sides of a rectangle are 57 and 87. If the shorter sides of a similar rectangle are 19 cm long, how long are its longer sides?

____

Use with Lesson 11-7, pages 388–389 in the Student Book.
Then go to Lesson 11-8, pages 390–391 in the Student Book.

Use Proportions

Jen is 4 ft tall. Her shadow is 3 ft long. She is standing near a vertical pole that casts a 6 ft shadow. How tall is the pole?

- Write a proportion.

$$\frac{3}{6} = \frac{4}{n}$$

- Use the cross-products rule to solve.

$$\frac{3}{6} \times \frac{4}{n}$$

$$3 \times n = 6 \times 4$$
$$3n \div 3 = 24 \div 3$$
$$n = 8$$

The pole is 8 ft tall.

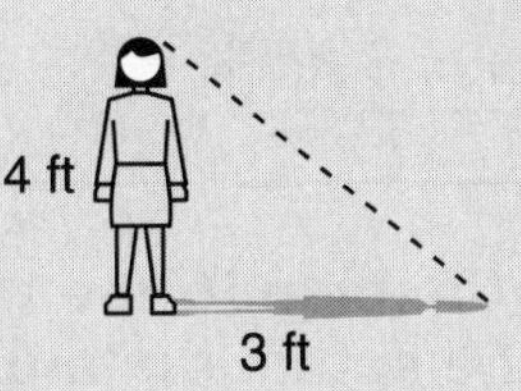

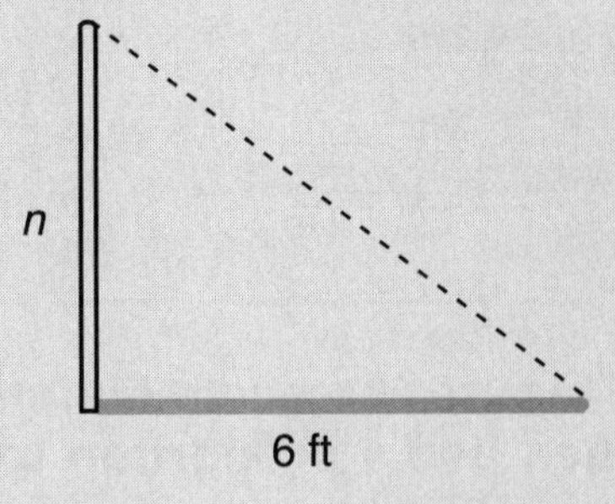

Write a proportion. Then solve.

1. Frank, who is 1.3 meter tall, casts a shadow that is 5.2 meters long. A lamppost near him is 6.5 meters tall. How long is the lamppost's shadow?

2. A triangular sail has sides of 12 ft, 28 ft, and 32 ft. If the longest side of a similar sail measures 28 ft, what is the measure of its shortest side?

3. A 9-foot pole casts a 15-foot shadow. At the same time, a tree casts a 24-foot shadow. How tall is the tree?

4. A surveyor determines the length of a pond by setting up similar triangles, as shown in the figure at the right. If CD represents the length of the pond, how long is the pond?

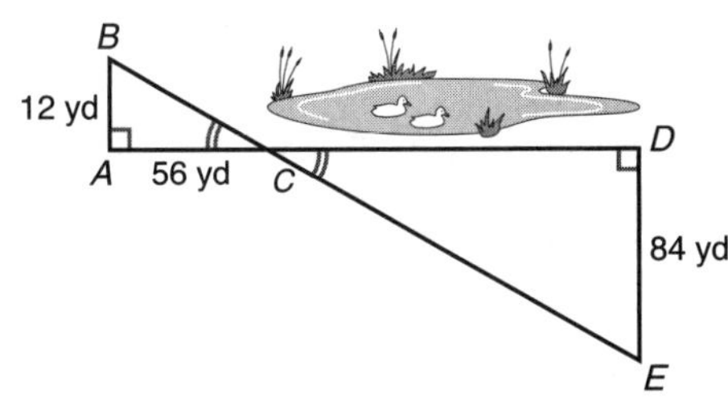

5. A fence post that is 2 meters tall casts a shadow 5 meters long. At the same time, a tree casts a shadow 108 meters. How tall is the tree?

6. Similar triangular sails are raised on two sailboats. If the larger sail is 24 ft tall and 18 ft wide, and the smaller sail is 12 ft wide, how tall is the smaller sail?

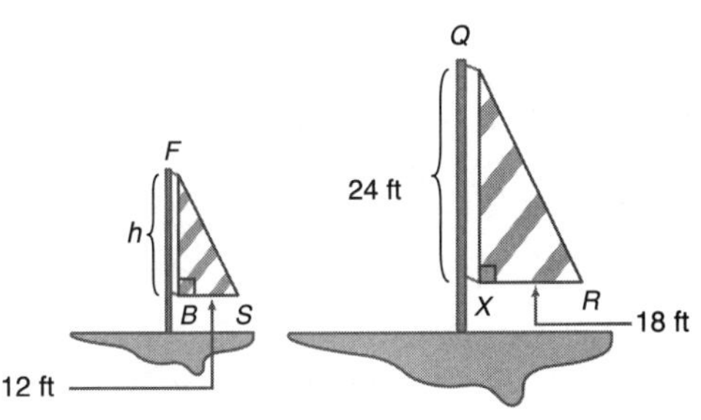

Use with Lesson 11-8, pages 390–391 in the Student Book.
Then go to Lesson 11-9, pages 392–393 in the Student Book.

Scale Drawings and Maps

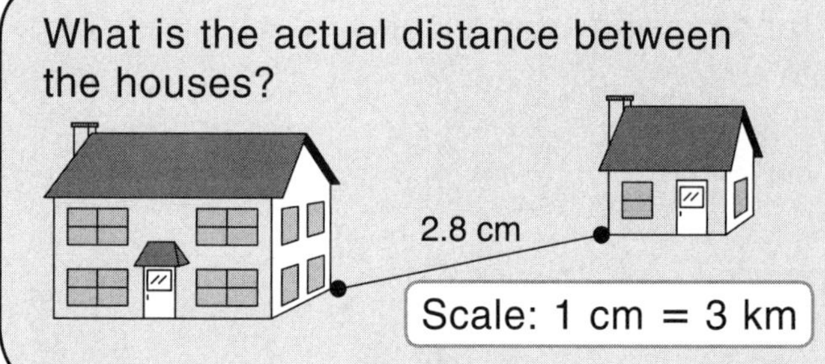

$$\frac{1 \text{ cm}}{3 \text{ km}} = \frac{2.8 \text{ cm}}{n \text{ km}} \longrightarrow \frac{1}{3} \times \frac{2.8}{n}$$

$$1 \times n = 3 \times 2.8$$

$$n = 8.4$$

The actual distance is 8.4 km.

Measure the scale distance on the map to the nearest 0.5 cm Then use a proportion to find the actual distance.

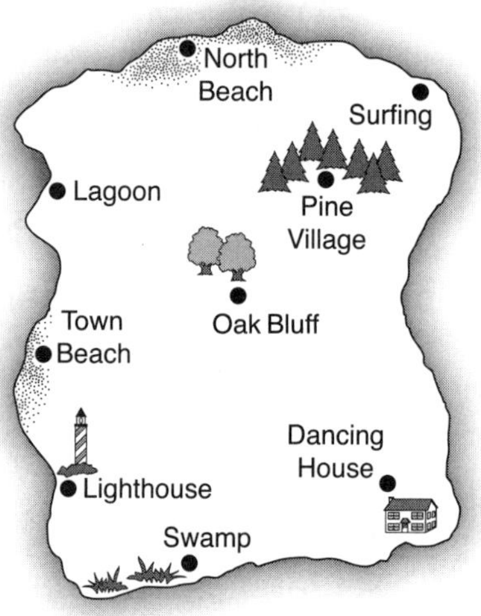

	To go from:	Scale Distance (cm)	Actual Distance (km)
1.	North Beach to Lagoon		
2.	Oak Bluff to Dancing House		
3.	Town Beach to North Beach		
4.	Pine Village to Town Beach		
5.	Lagoon to Surfing		
6.	Surfing to North Beach		
7.	Swamp to Lighthouse		

Use the scale drawing of the ladybug to answer each question.

8. What is the scale length of the ladybug's body? _______

9. What is the actual length of the ladybug's body? _______

10. What is the scale width of the ladybug's body? _______

11. What is the actual width of the ladybug's body? _______

Find the number of actual miles.
Scale: 1 in. = 15 mi

12. 4 in. = _______
13. 10 in. = _______
14. 20 in. = _______
15. 6 in. = _______

16. $5\frac{1}{3}$ in. = _______
17. $2\frac{1}{5}$ in. = _______
18. $3\frac{1}{2}$ in. = _______
19. $1\frac{3}{4}$ in. = _______

Find the number of actual feet.
Scale: 1 in. = 12 ft

20. 6 in. = _______
21. 5 in. = _______
22. 3 in. = _______
23. 10 in. = _______

24. $2\frac{1}{2}$ in. = _______
25. $13\frac{1}{4}$ in. = _______
26. $10\frac{3}{4}$ in. = _______
27. 25 in. = _______

Use with Lesson 11-9, pages 392–393 in the Student Book.
Then go to Lesson 11-10, pages 394–395 in the Student Book.

Relate Percents to Fractions

Name _______________________

Date _______________________

A **percent** is a ratio that compares a number to 100.

Rename 16% as a fraction.

- Drop the percent symbol. Then write the given percent as a fraction with a denominator of 100.

$$16\% \longrightarrow \frac{16}{100}$$

- Write the fraction in simplest form.

$$\frac{16}{100} = \frac{16 \div 4}{100 \div 4} = \frac{4}{25}$$

GCF = 4

So $16\% = \frac{4}{25}$.

Rename $\frac{7}{20}$ as a percent.

- Write a proportion, using $\frac{7}{20}$ and $\frac{d}{100}$ as the ratios.

$$\frac{7}{20} = \frac{d}{100}$$

- Use cross products to solve. Write the percent symbol next to the value of d.

$$\frac{7}{20} \times \frac{d}{100}$$

$$7 \times 100 = 20 \times d$$
$$700 \div 20 = 20d \div 20$$
$$35 = d$$

So $\frac{7}{20} = 35\%$.

Write each percent as a ratio and a fraction.

1. 70% _______________ **2.** 55% _______________ **3.** 40% _______________

4. 65% _______________ **5.** 24% _______________ **6.** 25% _______________

Write as a fraction in simplest form.

7. 80% _______ **8.** 20% _______ **9.** 11% _______ **10.** 32% _______

11. 2% _______ **12.** 88% _______ **13.** 90% _______ **14.** 74% _______

15. 43% _______ **16.** 66% _______ **17.** 7% _______ **18.** 15% _______

Write as a percent.

19. $\frac{19}{100}$ _______ **20.** $\frac{37}{100}$ _______ **21.** $\frac{3}{10}$ _______ **22.** $\frac{1}{10}$ _______

23. $\frac{2}{5}$ _______ **24.** $\frac{1}{2}$ _______ **25.** $\frac{9}{25}$ _______ **26.** $\frac{18}{20}$ _______

27. $\frac{38}{50}$ _______ **28.** $\frac{4}{5}$ _______ **29.** $\frac{7}{20}$ _______ **30.** $\frac{15}{75}$ _______

Draw a number line to show each percent. Write each percent as a fraction.

31. 45% _______ **32.** 60% _______

Relate Percents to Decimals

Name _______________________

Date _______________________

Rename 6% as a decimal.	Rename 0.12 as a percent.
Drop the percent (%) symbol. Then move the decimal point 2 places to the *left*.	Move the decimal point 2 places to the *right*. Then write the percent (%) symbol.
6% = 0 6. = 0.06	0.12 = 0.12 = 12%

Write as a decimal.

1. 26% _______   **2.** 54% _______   **3.** 14% _______   **4.** 50% _______

5. 7% _______   **6.** 2% _______   **7.** 5% _______   **8.** 9% _______

Write as a percent.

9. 0.1 _______   **10.** 0.86 _______   **11.** 0.51 _______   **12.** 0.8 _______

13. 0.04 _______   **14.** 0.03 _______   **15.** 0.01 _______   **16.** 0.08 _______

Find the percent, decimal, and fraction equivalents to complete each table. Then write the percents in each table in order from least to greatest.

	Percent	Decimal	Fraction
17.	30%		
18.	75%		
19.		0.2	
20.			$\frac{11}{20}$
21.			$\frac{3}{50}$

22. _______________________

	Percent	Decimal	Fraction
23.		0.05	
24.	38%		
25.		0.65	
26.	40%		
27.			$\frac{19}{20}$

28. _______________________

Problem Solving

29. In a survey of 100 people, 7 out of every 25 said that Abraham Lincoln was the greatest U.S. President. What percent of the people surveyed does this represent?

____

Use with Lesson 11-11, pages 396–397 in the Student Book.
Then go to Lesson 11-12, pages 398–399 in the Student Book.

Decimals, Fractions, and Percents

Name _______________________

Date _______________________

Rename $\frac{5}{8}$ as a percent.

- Divide the numerator by the denominator to the hundredths place. If necessary, write the remainder as a fraction.

$$\begin{array}{r} 0.62 \\ 8\overline{)5.00} \\ -4\,8 \\ \hline 20 \\ -16 \\ \hline 4 \end{array} \longrightarrow 0.62\frac{4}{8} = 0.62\frac{1}{2}$$

- Write the quotient as a percent.

$$0.62\frac{1}{2} \longrightarrow 62\frac{1}{2}\%$$

So $\frac{5}{8} = 62\frac{1}{2}\%$.

Order $\frac{9}{20}$, 40%, and 0.04 from least to greatest.

- Rename all the rational numbers as percents (or all fractions or all decimals).

$$\frac{9}{20} = \frac{9 \times 5}{20 \times 5} = \frac{45}{100} = 45\%$$

$$0.04 = \frac{4}{100} = 4\%$$

- Order the percents.

4%, 40%, 45%

From least to greatest, the order is

0.04, 40%, $\frac{9}{20}$.

Write as a decimal.

1. 16.3% _______
2. 41.2% _______
3. 56% _______
4. 28.9% _______
5. 3% _______
6. 12.54% _______
7. 1.1% _______
8. 70.5% _______

Write as a percent.

9. $\frac{6}{10}$ _______
10. $\frac{4}{5}$ _______
11. $\frac{3}{8}$ _______
12. $\frac{5}{16}$ _______
13. $\frac{3}{16}$ _______
14. $\frac{6}{40}$ _______
15. $\frac{9}{20}$ _______
16. $\frac{13}{20}$ _______

Write as a fractional percent.

17. $\frac{7}{9}$ _______
18. $\frac{2}{3}$ _______
19. $\frac{1}{8}$ _______
20. $\frac{5}{12}$ _______
21. $\frac{4}{9}$ _______
22. $\frac{4}{7}$ _______
23. $\frac{7}{12}$ _______
24. $\frac{1}{6}$ _______

Order each set from least to greatest on a number line. Show how you changed from fractions and decimals to percents.

25. 6%, 0.68, $\frac{2}{15}$ _______________
26. 0.126, 76%, $\frac{6}{25}$ _______________
27. $\frac{39}{50}$, 0.237, 53% _______________
28. 2.2%, 0.18, $\frac{21}{25}$ _______________

Problem Solving

29. Marion read $\frac{1}{3}$ of the book. What percent of the book did she read?

____

30. Harvey completed $\frac{7}{8}$ of his homework. What percent of his homework did he complete?

____

Percents Greater Than 100%

Rename 125% and 310% as equivalent decimals.

$$125\% = 1.25. = 1.25$$

$$310\% = 3.10. = 3.1$$

Rename 125% and 310% as equivalent mixed numbers.

$$125\% = \frac{125}{100} = 1\frac{25}{100} = 1\frac{1}{4}$$

$$310\% = \frac{310}{100} = 3\frac{10}{100} = 3\frac{1}{10}$$

Find the percent, decimal, and mixed number equivalents to complete each table. Write each mixed number in simplest form.

	Percent	Decimal	Fraction
1.	425%		
2.	112%		
3.	250%		
4.	300%		
5.	440%		

	Percent	Decimal	Fraction
6.	108%		
7.		1.1	
8.			$4\frac{1}{25}$
9.	932%		
10.	150%		

Explain the meaning of each statement.

11. Kristin's dinner has 150% of the protein in Ed's dinner.

12. The crowd at today's game was 200% of yesterday's crowd.

13. Emily's bowling score is 135% of Kate's score.

14. This year's donations were 175% of last year's donations.

Problem Solving

15. The number 18 is $1\frac{1}{2}$ times 12. Write $1\frac{1}{2}$ as a percent. _______________

16. The cost of living is 230% of what it was 10 years ago. What mixed number is this? _______________

17. The rainfall this month is 180% of last month's rainfall. What decimal is this? _______________

18. This year the cost of a pair of tennis shoes is 35% higher than it was last year. What percent of last year's price is this year's price? _______________

Use with Lesson 11-13, pages 400–401 in the Student Book.
Then go to Lesson 11-14, pages 402–403 in the Student Book.

Percents Less than 1%

Name _______________________

Date _______________________

<table>
<tr><td>

Write 0.24% as an equivalent fraction.

• Write the percent as a decimal.

$0.24\% = 0.24 \div 100 = 0.0024$

• Write the decimal as a fraction. Simplify.

$0.0024 = \dfrac{24}{10{,}000} = \dfrac{3}{1250}$

So $0.24\% = \dfrac{3}{1250}$.

</td><td>

Write $\frac{1}{5}$% as an equivalent decimal.

• Write the percent as a fraction.

$\dfrac{1}{5}\% = \dfrac{\frac{1}{5}}{100} = \dfrac{1}{5} \div 100 = \dfrac{1}{5} \times \dfrac{1}{100} = \dfrac{1}{500}$

• Divide the numerator by the denominator.

$$500\overline{)1.000}\quad 0.002$$

So $\frac{1}{5}\% = 0.002$.

</td></tr>
</table>

Express each as an equivalent percent.

1. 0.0017

2. 0.004

3. $\dfrac{3}{1000}$

4. $\dfrac{45}{10{,}000}$

5. 0.00084

6. $\dfrac{7}{800}$

7. $\dfrac{31}{5000}$

8. 0.00009

Express each as an equivalent decimal.

9. 0.2% _______

10. 0.96% _______

11. $\dfrac{8}{25}\%$ _______

12. 0.06% _______

13. $\dfrac{1}{20}\%$ _______

14. $\dfrac{3}{25}\%$ _______

15. 0.014% _______

16. $\dfrac{7}{50}\%$ _______

Express each as an equivalent fraction.

17. $\dfrac{9}{20}\%$ _______

18. 0.54% _______

19. 0.75% _______

20. $\dfrac{5}{8}\%$ _______

21. 0.95% _______

22. $\dfrac{1}{16}\%$ _______

23. $\dfrac{4}{5}\%$ _______

24. 0.37% _______

Write in order from least to greatest.

25. $0.008,\ 0.3\%,\ \dfrac{1}{500},\ \dfrac{7}{10}\%,\ \dfrac{1}{200}$

26. $0.009,\ \dfrac{3}{500},\ 0.005,\ \dfrac{1}{250},\ \dfrac{1}{100}\%$

Problem Solving

27. A total of 250 people bought raffle tickets. Of those people, 1 won a prize. What percent of the people who bought raffle tickets won a prize?

28. Sonja has 1000 coins. Of those coins, 0.8% are silver dollars. How many silver dollars does Sonja have?

Problem-Solving Strategy: Combine Strategies

The Johnsons built a rectangular brick patio behind their new home. It is 3 times as long as it is wide. To build the patio, the Johnsons needed enough bricks to cover 675 square feet. What are the dimensions of the patio?

Use the formula for the area of a rectangle:

$A = \ell \times w$

The problem tells you that the length is 3 times the width.

Make a table and *guess and test* to solve the problem.

The patio is 15 feet wide and 45 feet long.

	Guess 1	Guess 2	Guess 3	Guess 4
Width	10 ft	20 ft	12 ft	15 ft
Length	30 ft	60 ft	36 ft	45 ft
Area	300 ft²	1200 ft²	432 ft²	675 ft²

Solve. Do your work on a separate sheet of paper.

1. Liane collected seashells. She gave $\frac{1}{4}$ of the shells to her cousin. The next day she gave 5 shells to her aunt. Then she had 55 shells left. How many shells did Liane start with?

2. Gina worked part-time after school. One day she addressed 50 letters and postcards. Gina noticed that she addressed 1 postcard for every 4 letters. How many postcards did Gina address?

3. Hamid worked 2 hours each day from Monday through Friday. He worked 6 hours on Saturday and did not work on Sunday. At the end of the week, he was paid $76.80. How much per hour did Hamid earn?

4. Elena is making a rectangular dog pen. The dimensions are 20 ft by 16 ft. There is a fence post at each corner and every 4 ft in between. If posts cost $7.95 each, how much will they cost in all?

5. The 15 members of Herb's scout troop are on a weekend camp-out. Herb takes 3 dozen eggs from the ice chest and cooks 2 eggs for each member of the troop. If he returns the unused eggs to the ice chest, how many eggs does he return?

6. There are 56 members of the Golden Age Travel Group. One-fourth of them are 75 years or older. Fifty percent are between 65 and 74 years old. If $\frac{1}{2}$ of the remaining members are women, how many men in the group are less than 65 years old?

Use with Lesson 11-15, pages 404–405 in the Student Book.
Then go to Lesson 11-16, pages 406–407 in the Student Book.

Problem-Solving Applications: Mixed Review

Name ___________________

Date ___________________

Solve each problem and explain the method you used. If needed, do all your work on a separate sheet of paper.

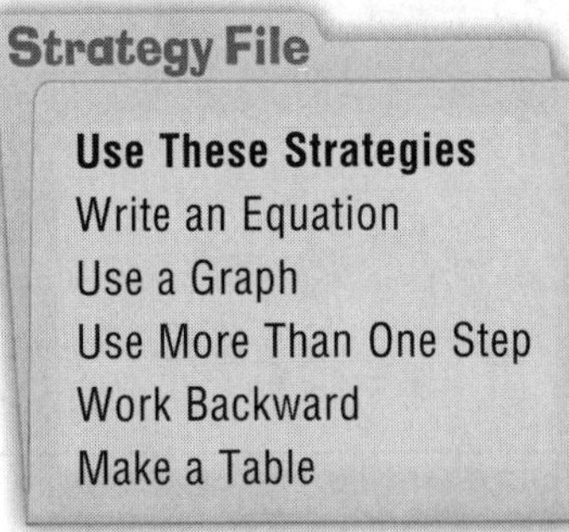

1. At the mall parking lot there are 4 red cars for every 10 black cars. At the grocery store parking lot, there are 15 black cars for every 6 red cars. Is the ratio of red to black cars the same at both parking lots?

2. For every 2 ounces of baby formula, Mrs. Lindberg uses 1 scoop of powder and 2 ounces of water. How much powder and water does she use to prepare six 4-ounce bottles of formula?

3. Mr. Lynch buys four 5-pound boxes of pretzels. He divides these into 8-ounce bags to hand out at the field hockey game. How many bags of pretzels can Mr. Lynch hand out?

4. The skate park awards 2 snack coupons and 3 drink coupons for every 75 skaters. Last weekend the park awarded a total of 20 snack and drink coupons. How many skaters were at the skate park last weekend?

5. At the last stop, there were 21 people on the train. At the second-to-last stop, 25% of the people on the train got off. At the stop before that, 5 people got on. How many people were on the train before the 5 people got on?

Use the circle graph for problems 6–9.

6. What fractional part of the animals is cats?

7. What is the ratio of rabbits to hamsters?

8. If there are 40 animals at Adoption Day, how many are rabbits?

9. Now suppose that, in addition to the 40 animals mentioned above, there were also 10 monkeys. What percent of the new total would cats represent?

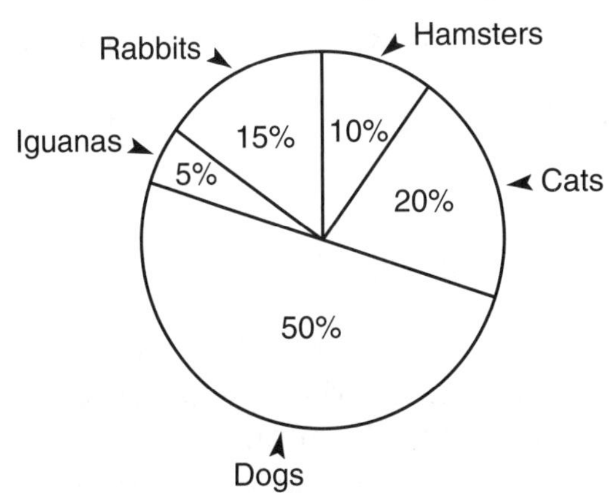

Use with Lesson 11-16, pages 406–407 in the Student Book.

Mental Math: Percent

Name _______________________

Date _______________________

Use common fractions to find a percent of a number mentally.

60% of 35 = __?__   30% of 90 = __?__ $87\frac{1}{2}$% of 56 = __?__

Think: 60% = $\frac{3}{5}$ Think: 30% = $\frac{3}{10}$ Think: $87\frac{1}{2}$% = $\frac{7}{8}$

$\frac{3}{5}$ of 35 = 21 $\frac{3}{10}$ of 90 = 27 $\frac{7}{8}$ of 56 = 49

So 60% of 35 = 21.   So 30% of 90 = 27.   So $87\frac{1}{2}$% of 56 = 49.

Complete. Compute mentally.

1. $\frac{1}{10}$ of 40 = 4, so 10% of 40 = _____.   **2.** $\frac{2}{10}$ of 40 = 8, so 20% of 40 = _____.

3. $\frac{2}{5}$ of 40 = 16, so 40% of 40 = _____.   **4.** $\frac{3}{5}$ of 40 = _____, so 60% of 40 = _____.

5. $\frac{1}{8}$ of 64 = 8, so $12\frac{1}{2}$% of 64 = _____.   **6.** $\frac{1}{4}$ of 64 = 16, so 25% of 64 = _____.

7. $\frac{3}{8}$ of 64 = 24, so $37\frac{1}{2}$% of 64 = _____.   **8.** $\frac{1}{2}$ of 64 = _____, so 50% of 64 = _____.

9. $\frac{1}{6}$ of 54 = _____, so $16\frac{2}{3}$% of 54 = _____.   **10.** $\frac{1}{3}$ of 54 = _____, so $33\frac{1}{3}$% of 54 = _____.

Find the percent of the number. Compute mentally.

11. 20% of 10 _____   **12.** 50% of 22 _____   **13.** 30% of 40 _____

14. 60% of 70 _____   **15.** 25% of 16 _____   **16.** 75% of 24 _____

17. 40% of 55 _____   **18.** 10% of 80 _____   **19.** $12\frac{1}{2}$% of 64 _____

20. $33\frac{1}{3}$% of 21 _____   **21.** $16\frac{2}{3}$% of 42 _____   **22.** 80% of 40 _____

23. $37\frac{1}{2}$% of 32 _____   **24.** $83\frac{1}{3}$% of 36 _____   **25.** $87\frac{1}{2}$% of 80 _____

26. $83\frac{1}{3}$% of 60 _____   **27.** $62\frac{1}{2}$% of 88 _____   **28.** 75% of 56 _____

Problem Solving

29. Four fifths of the 30 students in Ms. Asai's class watched a special on television last night. What percent of the students watched the special? How many students is this?

____

Use with Lesson 12-1, pages 414–415 in the Student Book.
Then go to Lesson 12-2, pages 416–417 in the Student Book.

Percent Sense

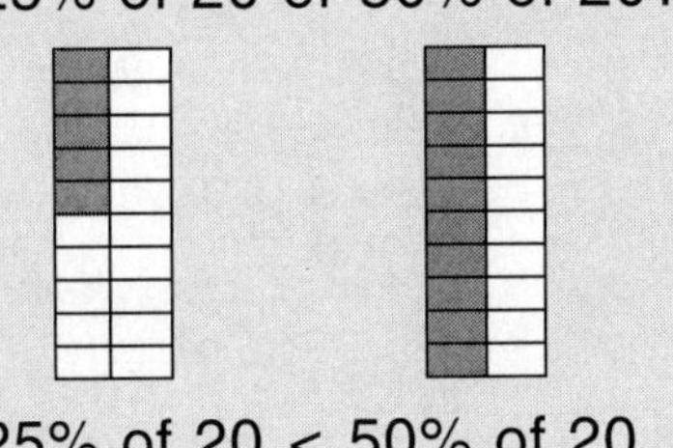

Which is less:

25% of 20 or 50% of 20?

25% of 20 < 50% of 20

Is $\frac{16}{40}$ less than 25%?

$25\% = \frac{1}{4}$

$\frac{1}{4}$ of 40 = 10

10 is less than 16

So $\frac{16}{40}$ is *not* less than 25%.

Compare. Write < or >.

1. 25% of 44 _______ 25% of 64

2. 30% of 50 _______ 30% of 20

3. 4% of 12 _______ 4% of 15

4. 5% of 20 _______ 50% of 20

5. 18% of 45 _______ 30% of 45

6. 85% of 64 _______ 20% of 6

7. $12\frac{1}{2}$% of 80 _______ 19% of 20

8. $83\frac{1}{3}$% of 48 _______ $66\frac{2}{3}$% of 45

9. $\frac{1}{8}$ of 24 _______ $37\frac{1}{2}$% of 24

10. $\frac{5}{6}$ of 18 _______ 75% of 18

11. $16\frac{2}{3}$% of 42 _______ $\frac{1}{3}$ of 42

12. $\frac{1}{4}$ of 24 _______ 20% of 24

Write *true* or *false* for each situation. Explain your answer.
Draw a picture to help you.

Lola has one hour to finish her homework. She studies history for 25 minutes.

13. Lola studies history for exactly $33\frac{1}{3}$% of the hour. _______

14. Lola studies history for less than $33\frac{1}{3}$% of the hour. _______

15. Lola studies history for more than $33\frac{1}{3}$% of the hour. _______

There are 110 entries in the city-wide art competition.
Twenty-five of the entries are acrylic paintings.

16. Fewer than 25% of the entries are acrylic paintings. _______

17. Fewer than 15% of the entries are acrylic paintings. _______

18. More than 30% of the entries are acrylic paintings. _______

Forty out of 60 students received a passing grade on a math test.

19. Fewer than 30% of the students did *not* pass the test. _______

20. More than 80% of the students passed the test. _______

21. Exactly $66\frac{2}{3}$% of the students passed the test. _______

Percentage of a Number

Name ___________________________

Date ___________________________

Find: 27% of $320
Estimate: 25% of $320 or $\frac{1}{4}$ of $320 = $80

rate (r) × base (b) = percentage (p)

Use a decimal.

$r \quad \times \quad b \quad = p$
27% of $320 = p$

$0.27 \times $320 = p$

$86.40 = p$

Use a fraction.

$r \quad \times \quad b \quad = p$
27% of $320 = p$

$\frac{27}{100} \times \frac{\overset{16}{\cancel{$320}}}{1} = p$
$\qquad \underset{5}{} \quad $86.40 = p$

Use a proportion.

$\frac{p}{$320} \quad \diagdown \quad \frac{27}{100}$

$p \times 100 = 320×27
$100p \div 100 = $8640 \div 100$
$p = 86.40

Use the formula and decimals to find the percentage of the number.

1. 50% of 42

2. 75% of 52

3. 5% of $14

4. 8% of $112

5. 60% of 120

6. 90% of 140

Use the formula and fractions to find the percentage of the number.

7. 40% of 25

8. 78% of 400

9. 75% of 168

10. 25% of $60

11. 14% of $250

12. 70% of $420

Use a proportion to find the percentage of the number.

13. 80% of 30

14. 15% of 120

15. 25% of 36

16. 12% of $550

17. 76% of 250

18. 24% of $125

Problem Solving

19. The distance between two cities is 150 miles. What is 60% of this distance? ___________________________

20. In a basketball game, 37.5% of the 40 foul shots were missed. How many were missed? ___________________________

C Use with Lesson 12-3, pages 418–419 in the Student Book.
C Then go to Lesson 12-4, pages 420–421 in the Student Book.

Find the Rate

> What percent (or rate) of 80 is 32?
>
> **Use the formula.** $r \times b = p$ **Use a proportion.**
>
> $\frac{32}{80} = r$ $\frac{p}{b} = r$
>
> $80\overline{)32.00}$ with 0.40
>
> $40\% = r$
>
> So 32 is 40% of 80.
>
> $\frac{\text{part}}{\text{whole}} \longrightarrow \frac{32}{80} \quad \frac{n}{100} \longleftarrow \frac{\text{part}}{\text{whole}}$
>
> $32 \times 100 = 80 \times n$
>
> $3200 \div 80 = 80n \div 80$
>
> $40 = n$
>
> $\frac{n}{100} = \frac{40}{100} = 40\%$

Find the percent or rate. Estimate first.

1. What percent of 90 is 27? _______

2. 80 is what percent of 240? _______

3. What percent of 100 is 13? _______

4. What percent of 50 is 50? _______

5. 3.2 is what percent of 80? _______

6. 7 is what percent of 28? _______

7. What percent of 27 is 18? _______

8. 18 is what percent of 90? _______

9. 48 is what percent of 120? _______

10. 2.2 is what percent of 40? _______

11. What percent of 25 is 12? _______

12. 2.4 is what percent of 25? _______

13. 180 is what percent of 60? _______

14. 48 is what percent of 64? _______

Problem Solving

15. First Street School won 12 out of 30 awards in the team competition. What percent of the awards did the school win? _______

16. From a group of 280 children, 14 made the swim team. What percent of the children is this? _______

17. Mari had $2. She spent 50¢ to buy fruit for lunch. What percent of her money did she spend? _______

18. Sometimes the doors of Marguerite's train do not open. Of 24 doors on Marguerite's train, 3 doors did not open. What percent of the doors did not open? _______

Find the Original Number

Name _______________

Date _______________

Find: 50% of *n* is 19.

Use the formula. Write an equation.

$$r \times b = p$$

50% of *n* = 19
0.50*n* = 19
0.50*n* ÷ 0.50 = 19 ÷ 0.50
n = 38

So 50% of 38 is 19.

Use a proportion.

$$\frac{\text{part}}{\text{whole}} \longrightarrow \frac{50}{100} \times \frac{19}{n} \longleftarrow \frac{\text{part}}{\text{whole}}$$

50 × *n* = 100 × 19
50*n* ÷ 50 = 1900 ÷ 50
n = 38

Find the original number. Explain the method you used.

1. 80% of *a* is 100

2. 45% of *s* is 18

3. 23% of *j* is 92

4. 65% of *t* is $97.50

5. 35% of *u* is $26.25

6. 10.4% of *r* is 312

7. 3% of *i* is 90

8. $10\frac{1}{2}$% of *y* is 63

9. $19\frac{1}{2}$% of *p* is 39

10. 38% of *n* is $1710

11. 37% of *z* is 72.15

12. 19% of *f* is $855

Compare. Write <, =, or >.

13. 14% of *v* is 112.28

12% of *w* is 113.75

v _______ *w*

14. 23.9% of *g* is 21.51

82.7% of *h* is 74.43

g _______ *h*

15. $37\frac{1}{2}$% of *k* is 240

$16\frac{2}{3}$% of *n* is 110

k _______ *n*

Problem Solving

16. Of the paper clips in the box, 25% are gold and the rest are silver. If there are 37 gold paper clips, how many paper clips are in the box?

17. The sixth-grade classes have collected $69.80 toward their class trip to the state capital. This is 34.9% of the total amount they need. What is the total cost of the trip to the state capital?

Use with Lesson 12-5, pages 422–423 in the Student Book.
Then go to Lesson 12-6, pages 424–425 in the Student Book.

Percent Problems

Name _______________________

Date _______________________

Find a percentage of a number.	**Find a percent of a number.**

Find a percentage of a number.

$$82\% \text{ of } \$41 = n \qquad \boxed{r \times b = p}$$

$$0.82 \times \$41 = n$$

$$\$33.62 = n$$

So 82% of $41 = $33.62.

Find a percent of a number.

$$\$12 \text{ out of } \$80 = n \qquad \boxed{\frac{p}{b} = r}$$

$$\frac{\$12}{\$80} = n$$

$$\$80\overline{)\$12.00}^{0.15} \longrightarrow 15\% = n$$

So $12 out of $80 = 15%.

Problem Solving

1. What is 35% of 120? _________

2. $200 is what percent of $50? _________

3. Four thousand runners began the marathon. Eighty-nine percent of them completed the run. What percentage of the runners finished the marathon? _________

4. In a spelling test of 50 words, Joan spelled 43 words correctly. What percent of the words did Joan *not* spell correctly? _________

5. Mr. Butler sells apples. Of the 400 bushels of apples he sells weekly, 85% are Red Delicious. How many bushels of Red Delicious does Mr. Butler sell weekly? _________

6. On Saturday, $87\frac{1}{2}\%$ of the students attended the championship game. If there are 728 students in all, how many attended the game? _________

7. Frank had 55 marbles. After a few games, he had 120% of his original number. How many marbles does he have now? _________

8. Jerry earned $950 last week. He spent $247 on a stereo. What percent of his earnings did he spend? _________

9. The goal for the book drive for the school library was 120 books. The book drive brought in 175% of the goal. How many books were received in the drive? _________

10. Jonathan had $180.00 in the bank. He spent $62\frac{1}{2}\%$ of it on a bicycle. How much did the bicycle cost? _________

11. Cole has 400 paperback books, of which 112 are mysteries. What percent of the books are mysteries? _________

Discount and Sale Price

Name _______________________

Date _______________________

A book that costs $26.00 is being sold at a 30% rate of discount.
What is the discount? What is the sale price?

| Discount = Rate of Discount × List Price |

$D = 30\%$ of $26.00
$D = 0.30 \times \$26.00$
$D = \$7.80$

The discount on the book is $7.80.

| Sale Price = List Price − Discount |

$SP = \$26.00 - \$7.80$
$SP = \$18.20$

The sale price of the book is $18.20.

Find the discount and sale price.

	Item	List Price	Rate of Discount	Discount	Sale Price
1.	Sweater	$80	25%		
2.	CD	$14	20%		
3.	Poster	$33	15%		
4.	Jacket	$120	12%		
5.	Computer	$1800	8%		

6.

List Price: $52
Rate of Discount: 10%

Discount = _____________

Sale Price = _____________

7.

List Price: $45
Rate of Discount: 20%

Discount = _____________

Sale Price = _____________

8.

List Price: $170
Rate of Discount: 8%

Discount = _____________

Sale Price = _____________

9.

List Price: $258
Rate of Discount: 5%

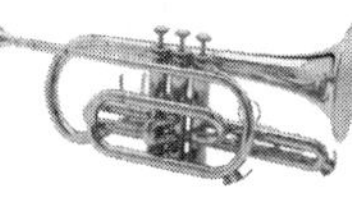

Discount = _____________

Sale Price = _____________

Problem Solving

10. Ronald bought a notebook. The regular price was $4.50.
It was discounted 20%. How much did Ronald pay? _______________

11. The price of a table is $478. It is on sale at 40% off.
What is the discount? What is the sale price? _______________

12. The rate of discount on a motorcycle is 10%. If the list
price is $6299, what is the sale price? _______________

Use with Lesson 12-7, pages 426–427 in the Student Book.
Then go to Lesson 12-8, pages 428–429 in the Student Book.

Sales Tax and Total Cost

Name _______________________

Date _______________________

A shirt costs $38.95 plus 6% sales tax. What is the total cost?

| Sales Tax | = | Rate of Sales Tax | × | Marked Price |

| Total Cost | = | Marked Price | + | Sales Tax |

$T = 6\%$ of $38.95
$T = 0.06 \times \$38.95$
$T = 2.337 \approx \$2.34.$

$TC = \$38.95 + \$2.34$
$TC = \$41.29$

The sales tax is $2.34.

The total cost of the shirt is $41.29.

Find the sales tax and the total cost.

	Item	Marked Price	Rate of Sales Tax	Sales Tax	Total Cost
1.	Softball	$7.98	4%		
2.	Glove	$45.25	6%		
3.	Wooden Bat	$23.50	2%		
4.	Thermos	$18	5%		
5.	Jersey	$59.95	7%		

6. Price: $128.50
Rate of Sales Tax: 4%

Sales Tax = _______________

Total Cost = _______________

7. Price: $140.98
Rate of Sales Tax: 7%

Sales Tax = _______________

Total Cost = _______________

8. Price: $230
Rate of Sales Tax: 3%

Sales Tax = _______________

Total Cost = _______________

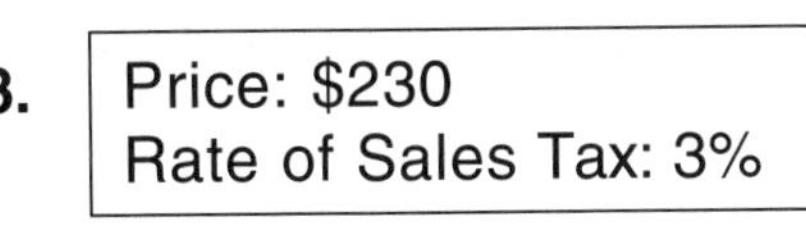

9. Price: $24,750
Rate of Sales Tax: 5%

Sales Tax = _______________

Total Cost = _______________

Problem Solving

10. A video game costs $82.25 plus 6% sales tax. Find the sales tax. _______________

11. A video cassette recorder costs $143.75 plus 8% sales tax. Find the sales tax and the total cost. _______________

12. A rug cost $296 plus $6\frac{1}{2}\%$ sales tax. What is the total cost for the rug? _______________

Better Buy

Name ___________________________

Date ___________________________

Pens cost 4 for $4.41 or 6 for $6.03. Which is the better buy?

$$\frac{4}{\$4.41} = \frac{1}{n} \qquad\qquad \frac{6}{\$6.03} = \frac{1}{m}$$

$$4 \times n = \$4.41 \times 1 \qquad 6 \times m = \$6.03 \times 1$$

$$4n \div 4 = \$4.41 \div 4 \qquad 6m \div 6 = \$6.03 \div 6$$

$$n = \$1.1025 \qquad\qquad m = \$1.005$$

$$n \approx \$1.10 \qquad\qquad m \approx \$1.01$$

$$\$1.01 < \$1.10$$

So 6 pens for $6.03 is a better buy.

To decide which is the better buy, find each unit cost. Then compare them.

Which is the better buy? Explain.

1. 3 apples for $.75
9 apples for $2.00

2. 4 cans of juice for $3.20
A 6-pack for $4.45

3. 1 pair of socks for $1.35
3 pairs for $4.69

4. 1 dozen roses for $15.25
$1.25 per rose

5. 8-oz can for 48¢
6-oz can for 42¢

6. 2-lb box for $1.84
5-lb box for $4.50

Estimate using compatible numbers to find the better buy.

7. 1 pair of socks for $2.50
3 pairs for $9.65

8. 1 can of juice for $.85
6 cans of juice for $4.75

9. 1 dozen rolls for $3.58
Rolls: 35¢ each

10. 1 orange for $.35
Bag of 6 oranges for $2.50

11. 1 dozen pencils for $3.56
36¢ for 1 pencil

12. 10-oz box of cereal for $3.10
15-oz box of cereal for $2.99

Problem Solving Tell which is the better buy for each.

13. A pair of jeans at Fine Fitters costs $19.95. The same jeans sell at Custom Clothes for 2 pairs for $38.95.

14. Soap sells for $2.15 a bar, or one box of 5 bars for $10.95.

15. An 8-oz can of mixed fruit costs $.83. A 14-oz can costs $1.38.

16. A package of 4 glasses costs $2.98. A package of 6 of the same glasses costs $4.68.

Use with Lesson 12-9, pages 430–431 in the Student Book.
Then go to Lesson 12-10, pages 432–433 in the Student Book.

Commission

Name ______________________

Date ______________________

The rate of commission is 4%, the salary is $420, and the amount sold is $4280. Find the commission and the total earnings.

Commission = Rate of Commission × Total Sales

$$C = R \times TS$$
$$C = 4\% \text{ of } \$4280$$
$$C = 0.04 \times \$4280$$
$$C = \$171.20$$

Total Earnings = Salary + Commission

$$TE = S + C$$
$$TE = \$420 + \$171.20$$
$$TE = \$591.20$$

So the commission is $171.20 and the total earnings are $591.20.

Find the commission and the total earnings.

1. Salary = $250

   Amount sold = $950

   Rate of Commission = 3%

   Commission = ______________

   Total Earnings = ______________

2. Salary = $170

   Amount sold = $1000

   Rate of Commission = 5.5%

   Commission = ______________

   Total Earnings = ______________

3. Salary = $520

   Amount sold = $450

   Rate of Commission = 5%

   Commission = ______________

   Total Earnings = ______________

4. Salary = $300

   Amount sold = $800

   Rate of Commission = 15%

   Commission = ______________

   Total Earnings = ______________

5. Salary = $380

   Amount sold = $690

   Rate of Commission = 6.5%

   Commission = ______________

   Total Earnings = ______________

6. Salary = $600

   Amount sold = $4500

   Rate of Commission = 2.75%

   Commission = ______________

   Total Earnings = ______________

Problem Solving

7. Mr. Bouchard sells television sets and VCRs at a $6\frac{1}{2}\%$ rate of commission. What is his commission on sales totaling $5245? ______________

8. Ms. Sumner sold $2578 worth of clothes last month. Her rate of commission was 5%. If her salary was $2500, what were her total earnings? ______________

Simple Interest

Name ___________________________

Date ___________________________

> | Manuel deposits $900 at a simple interest rate of 2.5% for 5 years in a savings account. Find the interest he will earn. | $I = prt$
 $I = \$900 \times 0.025 \times 5$
 $I = \$112.50$ | I: amount of simple interest
 p: principal
 r: rate of interest
 t: time in years |
> | --- | --- | --- |
>
> Manuel will earn $112.50 interest at the end of 5 years.

Find the simple interest, *I*, for each loan.

1. $1000 at 4% for 3 years   **2.** $450 at 5% for 7 years   **3.** $9900 at 4.5% for 10 years

_______________   _______________   _______________

4. $1380 at $6\frac{1}{4}$% for 2 years   **5.** $2480 at 3.9% for 5 years   **6.** $8100 at 6.7% for 9.5 years

_______________   _______________   _______________

Find the simple interest earned for each number of years.
Round to the nearest cent when necessary.

	Principal	Rate	3 years	5 years	$7\frac{1}{2}$ years	10 years
7.	$275	1.6%				
8.	$7340	12.9%				
9.	$8005	3.2%				
10.	$5500	$5\frac{1}{4}$%				
11.	$7780	6.4%				

Problem Solving

12. Cecilia borrows $2810 at a simple interest rate of 5.4% for 4 years. At the end of the loan, how much principal and interest will she have paid back? _______________

13. Hunter deposits $490 in a new savings account, and earns a simple interest rate of 2.9%. If he never makes any deposits or withdrawals, how much money will be in his account at the end of 5 years? _______________

14. Ethan borrows $1402 at a simple interest rate of 4.3% for 5 years. Amy borrows $1684 at a simple interest rate of 3.8% for 5 years. At the end of 5 years, who will have paid more interest? how much more? _______________

Use with Lesson 12-11, pages 434–435 in the Student Book.
Then go to Lesson 12-12, pages 436–437 in the Student Book.

Make Circle Graphs

Name _______________________

Date _______________________

Cedric has 8 apples and 12 pears. What percent of his fruit is apples?
Find the number of degrees (d) that 8 apples represents in the circle graph.

Percent of Total	Angle Measure	Fruit Sold

Percent of Total

$$\frac{8}{20} = \frac{n}{100}$$

$$8 \times 100 = 20n$$

$$800 \div 20 = 20n \div 20$$

$$40 = n$$

$$\frac{n}{100} = \frac{40}{100} = 40\%$$

Angle Measure

$$40\% \text{ of } 360° = d$$

$$40\% = \frac{40}{100} = \frac{2}{5}$$

$$\frac{2}{5} \times 360° = d$$

$$144° = d$$

Fruit Sold

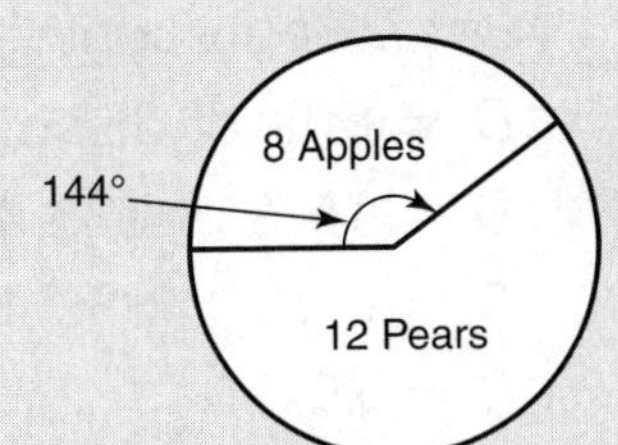

Use the circle graph at the right to answer exercises 1–3.

Family Budget

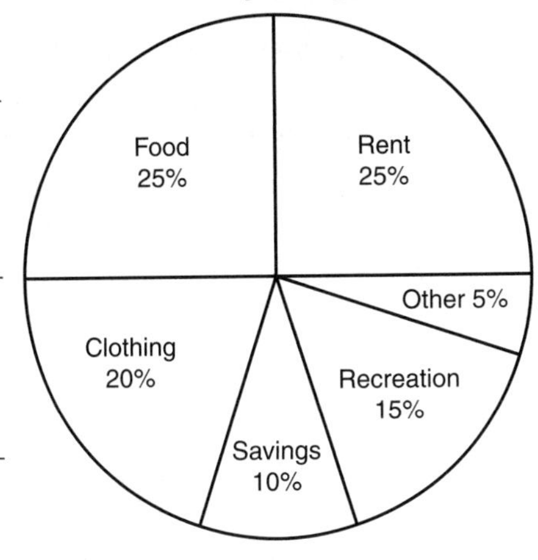

1. What percent of the budget is *not* food? _______________________

2. If the budget is $600 per week, how much money is set aside for savings? for rent? _______________________

3. If the budget is $600, how much more money is spent on clothing than on recreation? _______________________

Complete the table showing Ron's vacation expenses.

	Item	Amount Spent	Percent of Total	Angle Measure
4.	Hotel	$65.10		
5.	Gas	$18.60		
6.	Meals	$46.50		
7.	Clothes	$37.20		
8.	Other	$18.60		
9.	Totals			

**Draw a circle graph showing the sale of fruit.
Label your graph and include a title.**

	Fruit	Plums	Apples	Pears	Peaches	Oranges
10.	Number Sold	150	210	30	60	150

Use with Lesson 12-12, pages 436–437 in the Student Book.
Then go to Lesson 12-13, pages 438–439 in the Student Book.

Problem-Solving Strategy: Write an Equation

Name _______________

Date _______________

Taylor's Department Store is offering a 15% discount on all merchandise.
The list price of a sweater is $35.40. How much is the discount?
What is the sale price?

Let D represent the discount.

D = rate of discount × list price

D = 15% of $35.40

D = 0.15 × $35.40

D = $5.31

The discount is $5.31.

Let SP represent the sale price.

SP = list price − discount

SP = $35.40 − $5.31

SP = $30.09

The sale price is $30.09.

Write and solve an equation. If needed, do your work on a separate sheet of paper.

1. In a survey, 480 people were asked if they were in favor of developing the town park. The results showed that 65% of the people surveyed were in favor. How many people were in favor of developing the town park?

2. Ms. Juliano sold 4 computer packages for the following amounts: $1525, $1250, $2050, and $3075. If her rate of commission on these 4 sales was 3%, what was her total commission for all 4 sales?

3. Of the 1566 people at the ball game, $66\frac{2}{3}$% sat on the home-team side. How many people sat on the visiting-team side?

4. Anita bought a car that cost $19,950 plus 8% sales tax. Find the sales tax and total cost of the car.

5. There are 40 animals in the Perky Pet Store. Of these animals, 30% are dogs. How many of the animals are dogs?

6. A camera that costs $250 is on sale for $220. What is the rate of discount on the camera?

7. Blue Ribbon Supplies had a 20% sale on all horse items. Karen bought a hay net that had a list price of $6.80. How much was the discount? What was the sale price?

8. The house that Shawna lives in is on a 15,000 square foot lot. If the house occupies 8% of the lot, how many square feet does the house occupy?

Use with Lesson 12-13, pages 438–439 in the Student Book.
Then go to Lesson 12-14, pages 440–441 in the Student Book.

Problem-Solving Applications: Mixed Review

Name _______________

Date _______________

Solve each problem and explain the method you used. If needed, do all your work on a separate sheet of paper.

Strategy File

Use These Strategies
Write an Equation
Use More Than One Step
Work Backward
Use a Graph

1. A spinner with 8 equal sections has 5 sections with a star. Are the chances of the spinner landing on a section with a star better than 65%?

   ____

2. Alexa sold $9280 of stereo equipment last month. Her rate of commission is $4\frac{1}{2}$%. If her salary for the month was $2500, what were her total earnings for the month?

   ____

3. Andy borrows $2850 at a simple interest rate of 7% for 6 years. Ryan borrows $2600 at a simple interest rate of $8\frac{1}{4}$% for 6 years. Who will have paid more interest at the end of his loan? how much more?

   ____

4. Of the 25 children at Dawn's Daycare, 4 are infants. What percent of the children are infants?

   ____

5. Before noon today, 75% of the ducks at the pond flew away. After noon, 20% of the remaining ducks flew away. There are now 28 ducks at the pond. How many ducks were there to begin with?

6. Penelope bought a pair of shoes that cost $20.80. She paid 7.2% sales tax on the shoes. How much did Penelope spend in all on the shoes?

   ____

Use the bar graph for problems 7–9.

7. What percent of the people in the Fox family chose Thanksgiving?

   ____

8. Which holiday did 30% of the people in the Woods family choose?

   ____

9. How many more people chose Halloween than 4th of July?

   ____

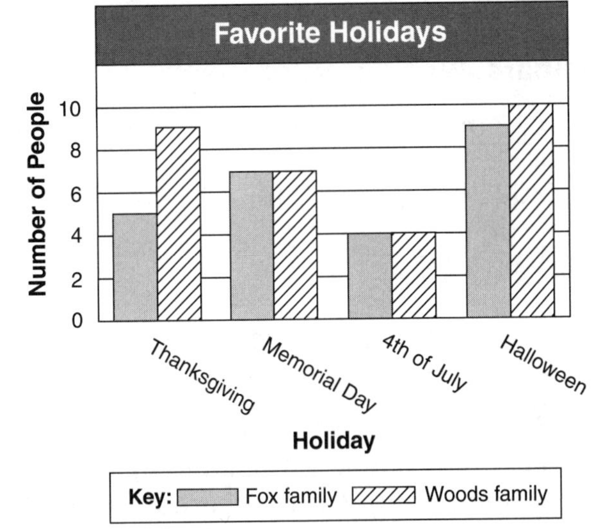

Use with Lesson 12-14, pages 440–441 in the Student Book.

Measure Metric Length

Name ___________________________

Date ___________________________

thousands	hundreds	tens	ones	tenths	hundredths	thousandths
1000	100	10	1	0.1	0.01	0.001
kilometer (km)	hectometer (hm)	dekameter (dam)	meter (m)	decimeter (dm)	centimeter (cm)	millimeter (mm)

Multiply by a power of 10 to rename larger units as smaller units.
Divide by a power of 10 to rename smaller units as larger units.

Measure each line segment to the nearest centimeter and to the nearest millimeter.

1.

2.

3.

4.

5.

Draw each quadrilateral described. Then draw and measure its diagonals.

6. square *ABCD* with *AB* = 19 mm

7. parallelogram *EFGH* with *EF* = 2.7 cm and *EH* = 1.3 cm

Rename each unit of measure. Use the table above to help you.

8. 17 m = _______ cm

9. 35 cm = _______ mm

10. 120 cm = _______ m

11. 3.5 km = _______ m

12. 775 m = _______ km

13. 150 mm = _______ cm

Compare. Write <, =, or >.

14. 0.73 m _______ 73 cm

15. 31.4 m _______ 314 cm

16. 80 km _______ 8000 m

17. 0.003 km _______ 3 m

18. 95 cm _______ 9.5 m

19. 43 dm _______ 0.43 m

Problem Solving

20. How many 1-cm pieces of metal can be cut from a rod that is 2.3 m long?

21. Ribbon A and ribbon B are the same length. Tom says that one is 24.6 cm long and the other is 246 mm long. Can he be correct? Explain.

C Use with Lesson 13-1, pages 448–449 in the Student Book.
C Then go to Lesson 13-2, pages 450–451 in the Student Book.

Measure Metric Capacity and Mass

Name _______________

Date _______________

kiloliter (kL)	hectoliter (hL)	dekaliter (daL)	liter (L)	deciliter (dL)	centiliter (cL)	milliliter (mL)
1000 L	100 L	10 L	1 L	0.1 L	0.01 L	0.001 L

kilogram (kg)	hectogram (hg)	dekagram (dag)	gram (g)	decigram (dg)	centigram (cg)	milligram (mg)
1000 g	100 g	10 g	1 g	0.1 g	0.01 g	0.001 g

Rename each unit of measure. Use the table above to help you.

1. 2800 g = _______ kg

2. 7.8 mL = _______ L

3. 630 hg = _______ g

4. 1.7 hL = _______ L

5. 350 dg = _______ g

6. 16 000 mL = _______ L

7. 72.695 L = _______ mL

8. 85 mg = _______ cg

9. 62 100 cg = _______ kg

Compare. Write <, =, or >.

10. 800 L _______ 8 dL

11. 2000 kg _______ 2 g

12. 4.5 L _______ 4500 mL

13. 26 g _______ 0.26 dg

14. 6.7 L _______ 67 cL

15. 5300 g _______ 5.3 kg

16. 9000 mL _______ 90 L

17. 850 mg _______ 8.5 g

18. 7650 cL _______ 7.65 L

Problem Solving

19. Alonzo needs 1.65 L of distilled water for an experiment. How many 550 mL containers of water will he need for the experiment?

20. Mr. Wong has a box that contains 1 kg of salt. Is there enough salt in the box for him to give 42 g to each of his 25 science students?

21. A bottle holds 750 mL of liquid. How many liters of liquid do 8 bottles hold?

22. A dictionary has a mass of 5.85 kg. A large telephone directory has a mass of 5625 g. Which has the greater mass?

C Use with Lesson 13-2, pages 450–451 in the Student Book.
C Then go to Lesson 13-3, pages 452–453 in the Student Book.

Measure Customary Length

> *Multiply* to rename larger units as smaller units.
> *Divide* to rename smaller units as larger units.
>
> | 12 inches (in.) = 1 foot (ft) |
> | 3 feet = 1 yard (yd) |
> | 5280 ft or 1760 yd = 1 mile (mi) |
>
> $8\frac{1}{3}$ yd = _?_ ft
>
> $8\frac{1}{3}$ yd = $(8\frac{1}{3} \times 3)$ ft
>
> $= \frac{25}{3} \times \frac{3}{1}$ ft = 25 ft
>
> 100 in. = _?_ ft
>
> 100 in. = $(100 \div 12)$ ft
>
> = 8 ft 4 in. $\frac{4}{12}$ or $\frac{1}{3}$ ft
>
> = $8\frac{1}{3}$ ft

Find the missing value to complete each proportion.

1. 6 feet (ft) : 72 inches (in.) = 9 ft : _____ in.

2. 9 ft : 3 yards (yd) = 21 ft : _____ yd.

3. _____ in. : 5 ft = 12 in. : 1 ft

4. 2 yd : 6 ft = 4 yd _____ in.

Rename each unit of measure. Use the table above to help you.

5. 3 ft = _____ in.

6. 24 yd = _____ ft

7. $3\frac{1}{4}$ mi = _____ ft

8. 80 ft = _____ yd

9. 10,560 ft = _____ mi

10. $6\frac{1}{4}$ ft = _____ in.

11. 25 ft = _____ yd

12. $2\frac{1}{2}$ mi = _____ ft

13. 3 mi = _____ yd

14. 100 in. = _____ yd

15. 90 in. = _____ ft

16. 2 mi = _____ yd

Compare. Write <, =, or >.

17. 52 ft _____ 18 yd

18. 224 in. _____ 18 ft 8 in.

19. 74 in. _____ 6 ft

20. 16 yd _____ 500 in.

21. 1 mi _____ 63,360 in.

22. 15,840 ft _____ 3 mi

Use a ruler to measure each segment to the nearest in., $\frac{1}{2}$ in., $\frac{1}{4}$ in., $\frac{1}{8}$ in., and $\frac{1}{16}$ in.

23. •————————————•

24. •————————————•

25. •————————————————•

Problem Solving

26. A length of clothesline is $75\frac{1}{2}$ ft long. How would you report its length in inches? in yards? _____

Use with Lesson 13-3, pages 452–453 in the Student Book.
Then go to Lesson 13-4, pages 454–455 in the Student Book.

Measure Customary Capacity and Weight

Name ___________________

Date ___________________

Multiply to rename larger units as smaller units.
Divide to rename smaller units as larger units.

| 1 c = 8 fl oz |
| 1 pt = 2 c |
| 1 qt = 2 pt |
| 1 gal = 4 qt |

| 1 lb = 16 oz |
| 1 T = 2000 lb |

$3\frac{1}{2}$ c = __?__ fl oz

$3\frac{1}{2}$ c = $(3\frac{1}{2} \times 8)$ fl oz

$= \frac{7}{2} \times \frac{8}{1}$ fl oz

$= 28$ fl oz

54 oz = __?__ lb

54 oz = $(54 \div 16)$ lb

$= 3$ lb 6 oz

$\frac{6}{16}$ or $\frac{3}{8}$ lb

$= 3\frac{3}{8}$ lb

Find the missing value to complete each proportion.

1. 3 quarts (qt) : 12 cups (c) = 4 qt : _____ c

2. 1 pound (lb) : _____ ounces (oz) = 4 lb : 64 oz

3. 128 fluid ounces (fl oz) : 1 gallon (gal) = _____ fl oz : 5 gal

Rename each unit of measure. Use the table above to help you.

4. 2 qt = _____ fl oz

5. 12 pt = _____ qt

6. 5 qt = _____ pt

7. 16 qt = _____ gal

8. 7 pt = _____ c

9. $1\frac{1}{2}$ gal = _____ qt

10. $4\frac{1}{2}$ lb = _____ oz

11. 4 lb 15 oz = _____ oz

12. 4.5 T = _____ lb

13. 52 oz = _____ lb

14. 8 oz = _____ lb

15. $6\frac{1}{8}$ pt = _____ fl oz

16. 3000 lb = _____ T

17. $4\frac{3}{4}$ lb = _____ oz

18. 2400 lb = _____ T _____ lb

Compare. Write <, =, or >.

19. 36 lb _____ 524 oz

20. 4 c 7 fl oz _____ 40 fl oz

21. 256 oz _____ 15 lb 4 oz

22. 5 gal 2 qt _____ 24 qt

23. 12 T 850 lb _____ 25,000 lb

24. 6 c 3 fl oz _____ 51 fl oz

25. 75 lb 10 oz _____ 1210 oz

26. 100 qt _____ 25 gal

27. 2 gal 1 c _____ 140 fl oz

Problem Solving

28. How many pints are equal to $3\frac{3}{4}$ gallons? ___________________

29. At \$3.52 per pound, what is the cost of 12 ounces of ground beef? ___________________

Use with Lesson 13-4, pages 454–455 in the Student Book.
Then go to Lesson 13-5, pages 456–457 in the Student Book.

Compute
Customary Units

Name ___________________________

Date ___________________________

2 ft 9 in. + 3 ft 8 in. 5 ft 17 in. = 6 ft 5 in. → 1 ft 5 in.	$\overset{4}{\cancel{5}}$ gal $\overset{5}{\cancel{1}}$ qt ⟶ 4 gal 5 qt − 3 gal 3 qt − 3 gal 3 qt 1 gal 2 qt
3 ft 7 in. × 3 9 ft 21 in. = 10 ft 9 in. → 1 ft 9 in.	4 lb 6 oz ÷ 2 = ? ↓ 64 oz + 6 oz ÷ 2 = ? ↓ 70 oz ÷ 2 = 35 oz = 2 lb 3 oz

Add.

1.   8 ft 9 in.   **2.**   3 gal 2 qt   **3.**   10 yd 1 ft   **4.**   5 pt 2 c
     + 2 ft 6 in.   + 2 gal 3 qt   + 8 yd 2 ft   + 8 pt 3 c

Subtract.

5.   7 ft 9 in.   **6.**   8 yd 4 in.   **7.**   6 gal 1 qt   **8.**   12 pt 1 c
     − 3 ft 10 in.   − 5 yd 8 in.   − 3 gal 3 qt   − 8 pt 2 c

Multiply.

9.   4 ft 3 in.   **10.**   7 yd 4 ft   **11.**   3 mi 26 yd   **12.**   6 qt 1 pt
     ×   3   ×   6   ×   8   ×   5

Divide.

13. 3 gal 3 qt ÷ 5   **14.** 6 yd 2 ft ÷ 4   **15.** 3 lb 6 oz ÷ 3   **16.** 2 mi 500 ft ÷ 4

Problem Solving

17. Find the combined length of two sticks that are 4 yd 2 ft and 6 yd 2 ft long. _______________

18. David's fishing pole is 7 ft 4 in. long. Paul's is 9 ft 2 in. long. How much longer is Paul's fishing pole? _______________

C Use with Lesson 13-5, pages 456–457 in the Student Book.
Then go to Lesson 13-6, pages 458–459 in the Student Book.

Compute with Time

Name _______________________

Date _______________________

Find the elapsed time from 2:48 P.M.
until 5:05 P.M.

	4:65	$\overset{515}{4:\cancel{65}}$
5:05	$\cancel{5:05}$	$\cancel{5:05}$
− 2:48	− 2:48	− 2:48
		2:17

The elapsed time is 2 h 17 min.

60 seconds (s) = 1 minute (min)
60 minutes = 1 hour (h)
24 hours = 1 day (d)
7 days = 1 week (wk)
12 months (mo) = 1 year (y)
365 days = 1 year
100 years = 1 century (c)

13 h 45 min	4 y 9 mo	5 wk 1 d ÷ 4
+ 5 h 30 min	× 5	36 d ÷ 4 = 9 d
18 h 75 min = 19 h 15 min	20 y 45 mo = 23 y 9 mo	9 d = 1 wk 2 d

Find the elapsed time.

1. from 4:15 A.M. to 9:30 A.M. ___________

2. from 1:45 P.M. to 11:00 P.M. ___________

3. from 11:18 A.M. to 3:20 P.M. ___________

4. from 7:12 A.M. to 1:30 P.M. ___________

5. from 9:30 A.M. to 4:10 P.M. ___________

6. from 8:44 A.M. to 2:35 P.M. ___________

Rename each unit of time. Use the table above to help you.

7. 2 y = _____ mo

8. 120 min = _____ h

9. 21 d = _____ wk

10. 240 s = _____ min

11. 30 mo = _____ y

12. 3 y = _____ d

13. $3\frac{1}{4}$ h = _____ min

14. 425 y = _____ c

15. 192 h = _____ d

16. 128 h = _____ d _____ h

17. 90 d = _____ wk _____ d

18. 525 min = _____ h _____ min

Compute.

19.
8 h 25 min
+ 4 h 15 min

20.
12 h 38 min
− 8 h 15 min

21.
6 h 45 min
+ 7 h 35 min

22.
10 wk 2 d
− 2 wk 5 d

23.
4 d 9 h
× 2

24.
3 d 8 h
× 7

25. 18 wk 6 d ÷ 3 _______

26. 9 c 24 y ÷ 4 _______

27. 25 min 4 s ÷ 8 _______

Problem Solving

28. Ohura left for Dodge City at 8:35 A.M. She arrived
in Dodge City at 2:10 P.M. How long was her trip? _______________

Use with Lesson 13-6, pages 458–459 in the Student Book.
Then go to Lesson 13-7, pages 460–461 in the Student Book.

Relate Customary and Metric Units

Name _______________________

Date _______________________

Customary and Metric Unit Equivalents		
Length	**Capacity**	**Weight/Mass**
1 in. = 2.54 cm	1 fl oz ≈ 30 mL	1 oz ≈ 28.35 g
1 m ≈ 39.37 in.	1 L ≈ 1.06 qt	1 kg ≈ 2.2 lb
1 mi ≈ 1.61 km	1 gal ≈ 3.79 L	1 metric ton (t) ≈ 1.102 T

Find the missing value to complete each proportion.

1. **a.** 1 in. : 2.54 cm = 5 in. : _______ cm   **b.** 30 mL : 1 fl oz = 45 mL : _______ fl oz

   c. 1 kg : 2.2 lb = _______ kg : 15.4 lb   **d.** 2 mi : 3.22 km = _______ mi : 9.982 km

Rename each unit of measure. Round to the nearest hundredth. Use the table above to help you.

2. 6 in. = _______ cm

3. 9 fl oz ≈ _______ mL

4. 19 lb ≈ _______ kg

5. 45 in. ≈ _______ m

6. 5 qt ≈ _______ L

7. 47 oz ≈ _______ g

8. 31 cm ≈ _______ in.

9. 3.5 gal ≈ _______ L

10. 5 T ≈ _______ t

11. 20 km ≈ _______ mi

12. 10 L ≈ _______ gal

13. 7 kg ≈ _______ lb

Compare. Write <, =, or >.

14. 7 m _______ 264 in.

15. 12 qt _______ 11 L

16. 10 gal _______ 37.9 L

17. 100 g _______ 4 oz

18. 9 L _______ 2 gal

19. 100 in. _______ 2.5 m

20. 50 oz _______ 1 kg

21. 5 yd _______ 5 m

22. 3 ft _______ 91 cm

Problem Solving

23. The Corns drive 351 miles from their house to their cousins' house. About how many kilometers do they drive? Round to the nearest tenth of a kilometer.

24. Mrs. Jacey weighs 57 kilograms. About how many pounds does Mrs. Jacey weigh?

25. Which holds more, a 5-gallon jug or a 20-liter jug? About how much more does it hold?

Use with Lesson 13-7, pages 460–461 in the Student Book.
Then go to Lesson 13-7A, pages 247–248 in this Workbook.

Perimeter

To find the perimeter of a complex figure, break it down into simpler figures. Then add the lengths of its actual sides.

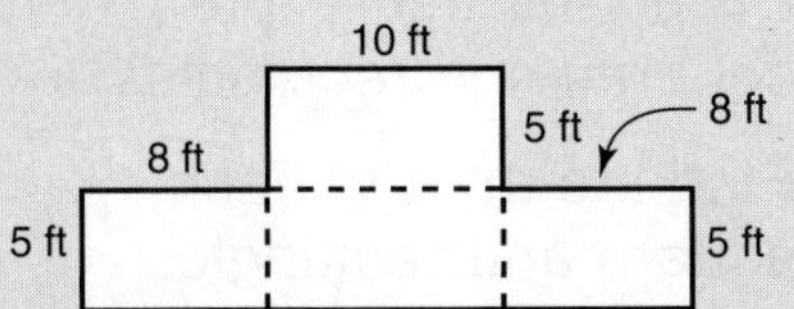

$$P = 5 + 8 + \underline{?} + 10 + 5 + 8 + 5 + \underline{?}$$
$$= 5 + 8 + 5 + 10 + 5 + 8 + 5 + (8 + 10 + 8)$$
$$= 72 \text{ ft}$$

Rectangle $P = 2\ell + 2w$, where ℓ = length and w = width

Regular Polygon $P = ns$, where n = number of congruent sides and s = length of one side

Find the perimeter of each polygon.

1. Regular hexagon
$s = 18$ cm

____

2. Rhombus
$s = 12$ in.

____

3. Rectangle
$\ell = 4\frac{1}{3}$ ft
$w = 2\frac{2}{3}$ ft

____

4. 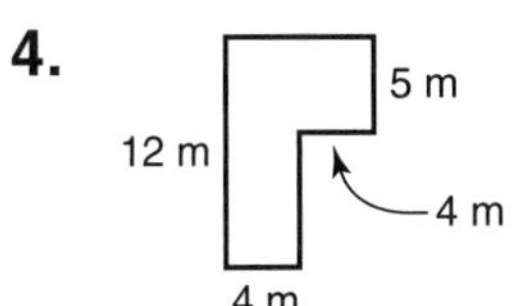

5. 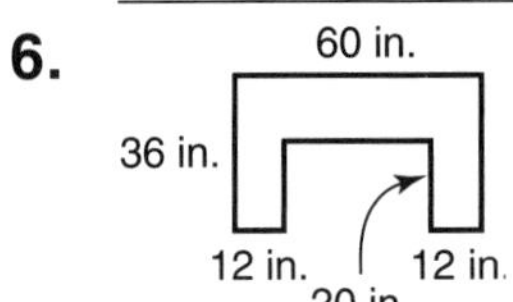

6. 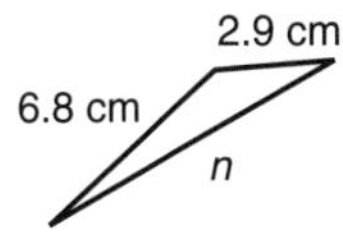

7.

Find the length of each unknown side.

8. 

$P = 19.9$ cm

9. 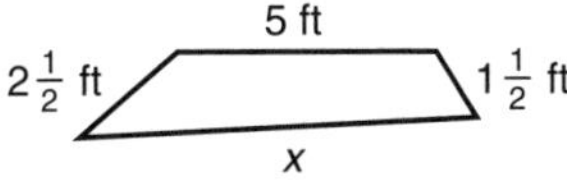

$P = 16\frac{1}{2}$ ft

10. 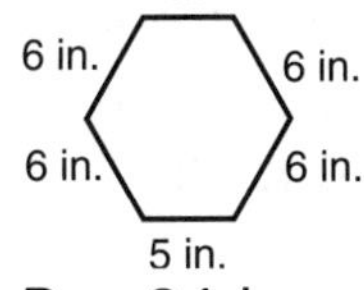

$P = 34$ in.

Problem Solving

11. What is the perimeter of a quadrilateral with sides that measure $14\frac{1}{3}$ ft, $12\frac{3}{4}$ ft, 9 ft, and 10 ft?

12. How many feet of wallpaper border are needed to go around the walls of a rectangular room that measures $3\frac{1}{2}$ yd by 4 yd?

Area of Rectangles and Squares

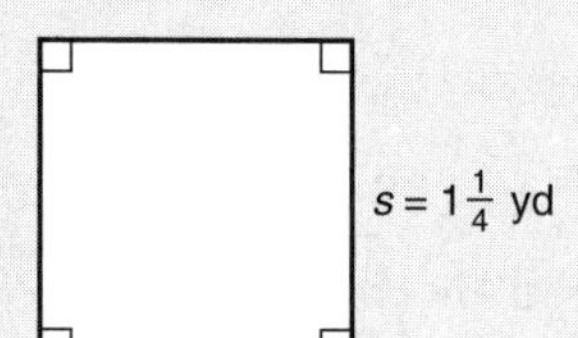

$A = s \times s$ or $A = s^2$

$A = 1\frac{1}{4}$ yd $\times 1\frac{1}{4}$ yd

$A = 1\frac{9}{16}$ yd^2

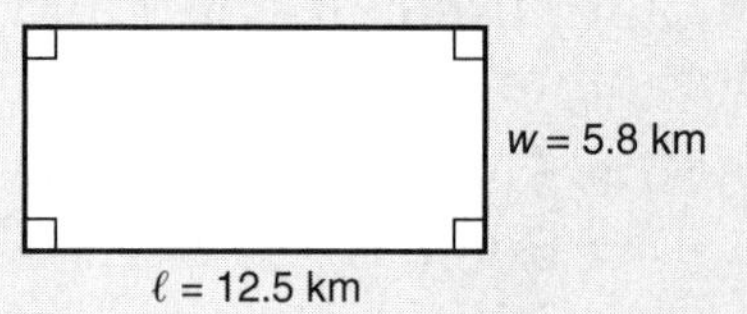

$A = \ell \times w$

$A = 12.5$ km $\times 5.8$ km

$A = 72.5$ km^2

Area of a complex figure:

- Divide the figure into squares and rectangles.
- Find the area of each square and rectangle.
- Add to find the area of the entire figure.

Use formulas to find the areas. Estimate to help you.

1. 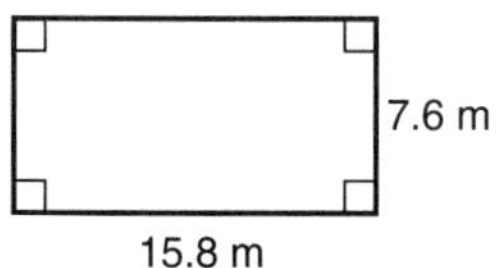

____

2. 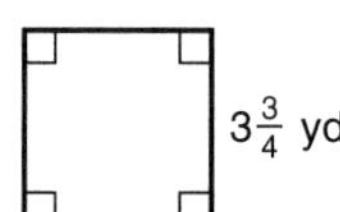

____

3. 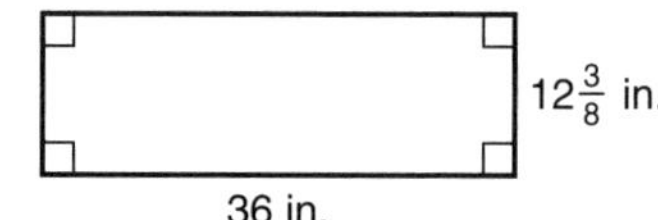

____

4. 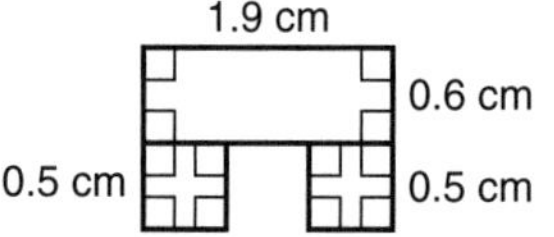

____

5. 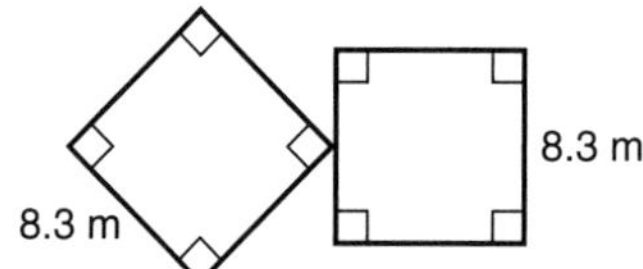

____

6. 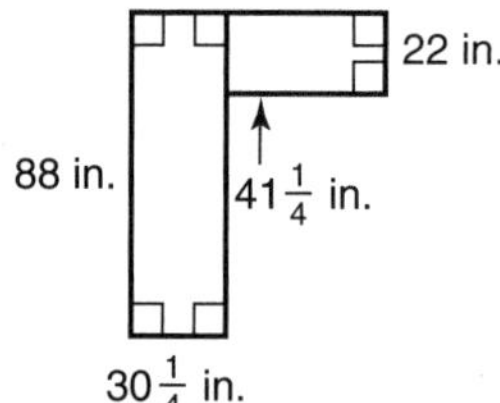

____

Problem Solving Use a formula to solve each problem.

7. A baseball diamond is really a square that measures 90 feet along each base path. What is the area of a baseball diamond?

____

8. A tennis court is a rectangle that is 23.4 m long and 8.1 m wide. What is the area of a tennis court?

____

9. How many square yards of carpeting are needed to cover the floor of a rectangular room that is 21 ft long and 12 ft wide?

____

10. Floor tile is sold in 12-in. squares. How many tiles would you buy to cover the floor of a rectangular hallway that is 3 yd long and $1\frac{1}{3}$ yd wide?

____

Use with Lesson 13-9, pages 464–465 in the Student Book.
Then go to Lesson 13-10, pages 466–467 in the Student Book.

Area of Triangles and Parallelograms

Name _______________________

Date _______________________

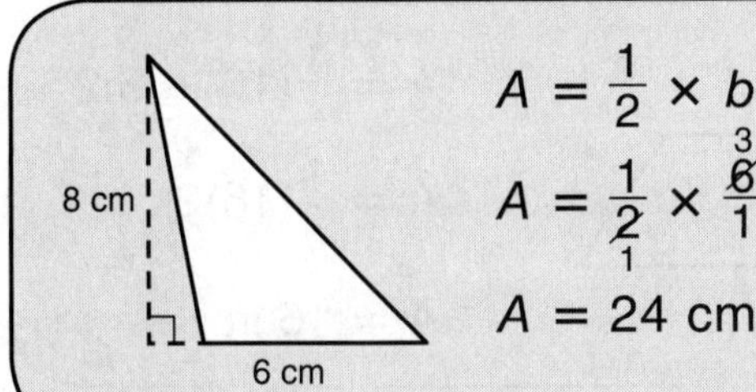

$$A = \frac{1}{2} \times b \times h$$

$$A = \frac{1}{2} \times \overset{3}{\underset{1}{\cancel{\frac{6}{1}}}} \text{ cm} \times \frac{8}{1} \text{ cm}$$

$$A = 24 \text{ cm}^2$$

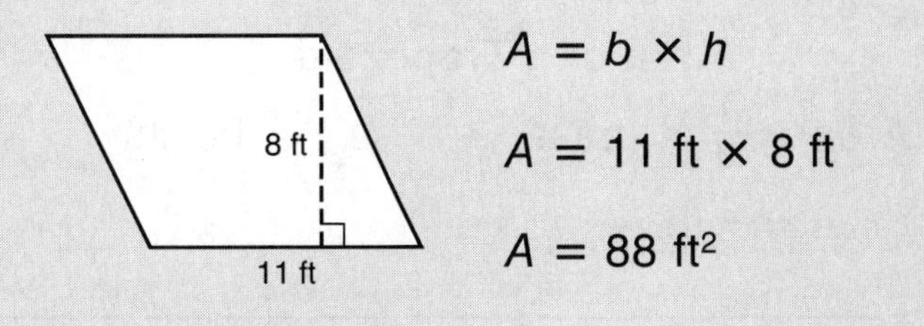

$$A = b \times h$$

$$A = 11 \text{ ft} \times 8 \text{ ft}$$

$$A = 88 \text{ ft}^2$$

Find the area of each triangle.

1.
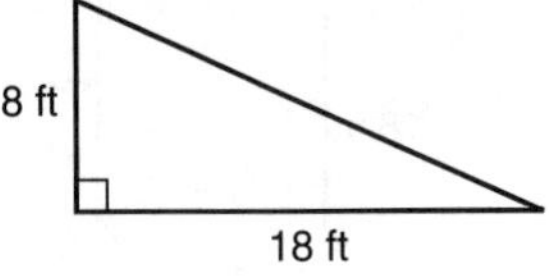

2.
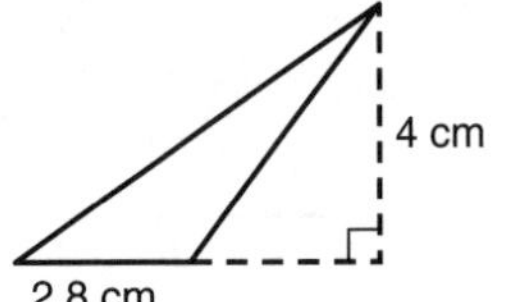

3.
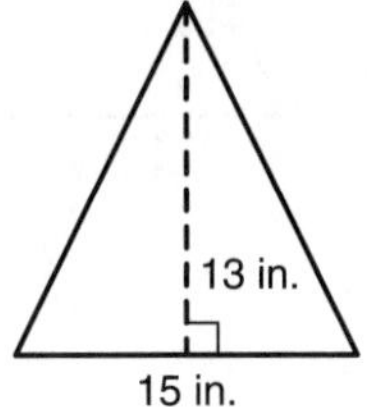

_______________________   _______________________   _______________________

Find the area of each parallelogram.

4.
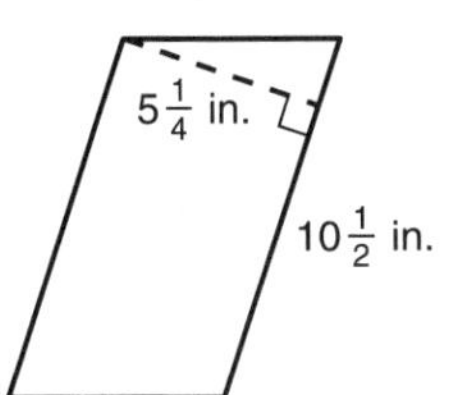

5.
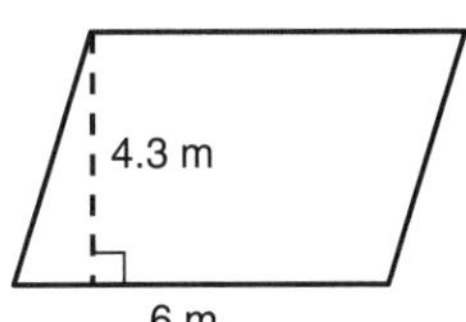

6.
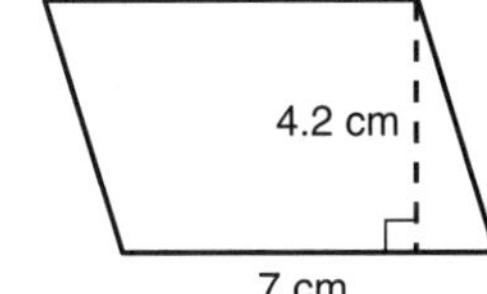

_______________________   _______________________   _______________________

Find the area of each triangle and each parallelogram to complete each table.

Area of Triangle		
Base	**Height**	**Area**
7. 30 yd	9 yd	
8. 3 m	1.2 m	
9. 8 ft	$5\frac{1}{4}$ ft	

Area of Parallelogram		
Base	**Height**	**Area**
10. 6.3 km	2.1 km	
11. $4\frac{1}{2}$ ft	$2\frac{1}{4}$ ft	
12. $9\frac{1}{2}$ yd	2 yd	

Problem Solving

13. Find the area of this triangle: base–15 ft, height–$\frac{3}{4}$ ft. _______________________

Area of Trapezoids

Name _______________________

Date _______________________

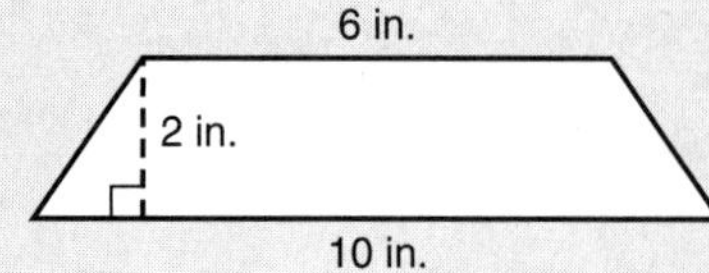

Area of a Trapezoid

Area = $\frac{1}{2}$ × (base$_1$ + base$_2$) × height

$A = \frac{1}{2}(b_1 + b_2)h$

$A = \frac{1}{2}(10 + 6)2$

$A = \frac{1}{2}(16)\overset{1}{\cancel{2}}$

$A = 16$ in.^{2}

Find the area of each trapezoid.

1.

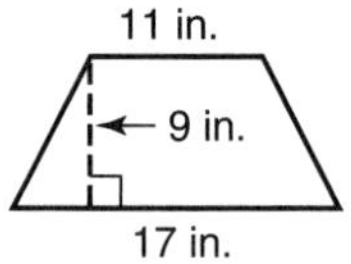

2.

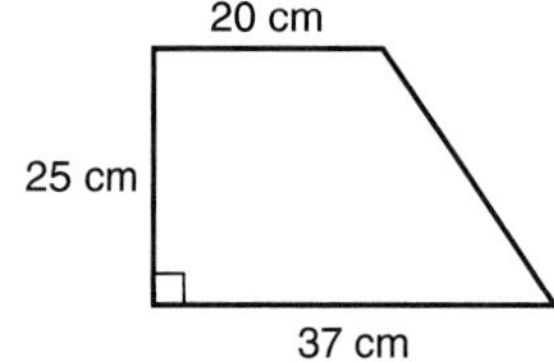

3.

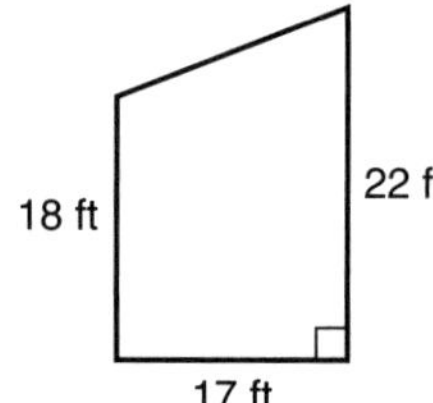

____

4.

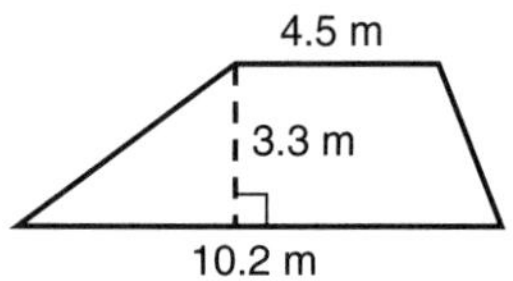

5.

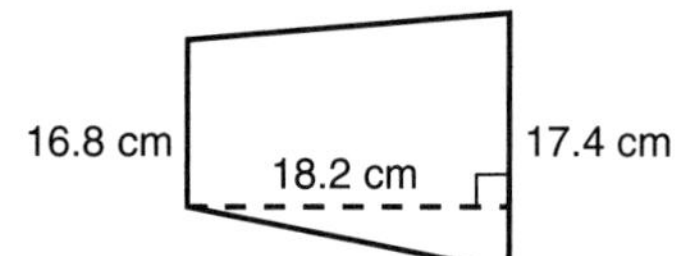

6.

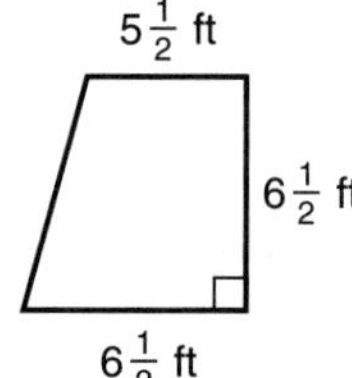

____

7.

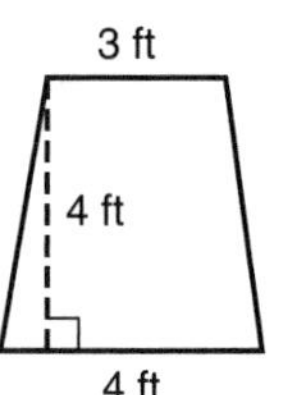

8.

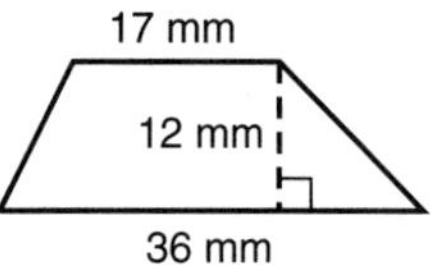

9.

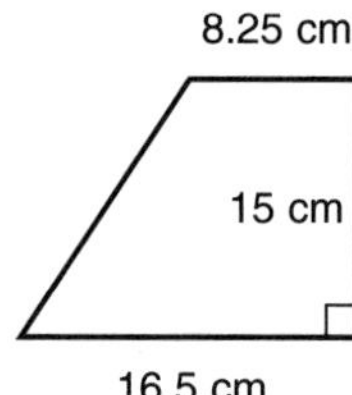

____

Problem Solving

10. A trapezoid has a longer base that is 24 mm long and a shorter base that is 19 mm long. The area of the trapezoid is 301 mm. What is the height of the trapezoid?

____

11. Dan makes a mosaic-tile trapezoid. Its parallel bases are 34 and 17 cm long. Its height is 26 cm. Dan buys mosaic tiles for $0.04 per square cm. How much does he spend?

____

12. A trapezoid has one base that is 3 times the length of the other base. Its height is twice the length of the longer base. Its shorter base is 3.5 in. What is the area of the trapezoid?

____

C Use with Lesson 13-11, pages 468–469 in the Student Book.
C Then go to Lesson 13-11A, pages 249–250 in this Workbook.

Circumference

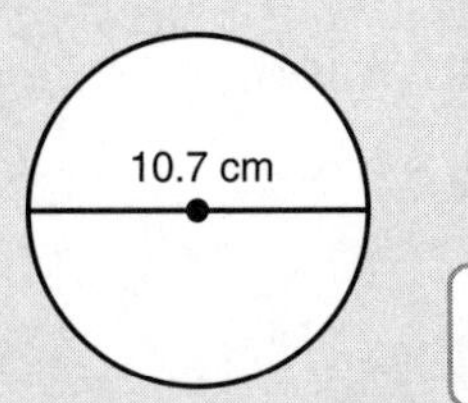

$\pi \approx 3.14$

$C = \pi \times d$

$C \approx 3.14 \times 10.7$

$C \approx 33.598$ cm

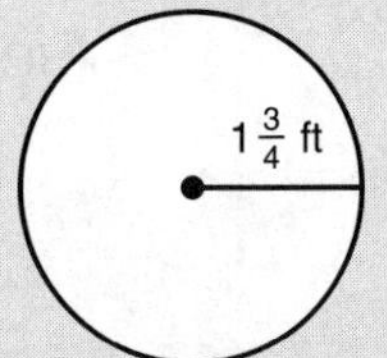

$\frac{22}{7} \approx 3.14$

$C = 2 \times \pi \times r$

$1\frac{3}{4}$ ft $= \frac{7}{4}$ ft

$C \approx \overset{1}{2} \times \dfrac{\overset{11}{22}}{\underset{1}{7}} \times \dfrac{\overset{1}{7}}{\underset{\underset{1}{2}}{4}}$

$C \approx 11$ ft

Use $\pi = 3$ to estimate the circumference. Then use 3.14 for π to find the circumference of each circle.

1. 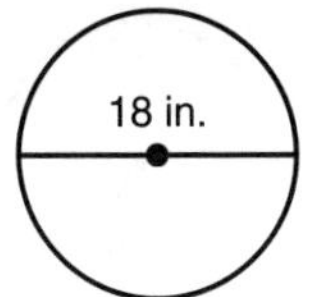
18 in.

____

2. 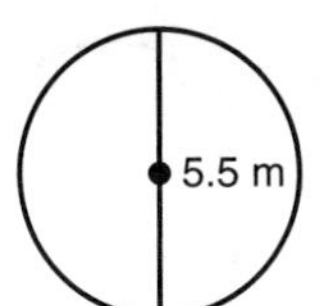
5.5 m

____

3. 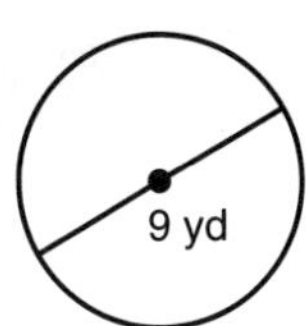
9 yd

____

4. 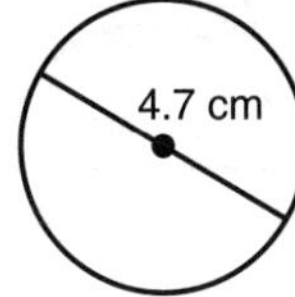
4.7 cm

____

5. 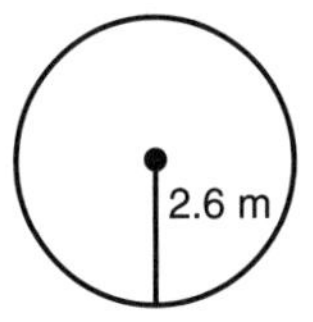
2.6 m

____

6. 
7.5 in.

____

7. 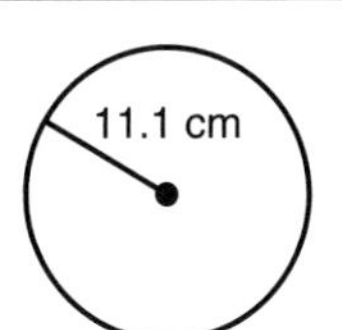
11.1 cm

____

8. 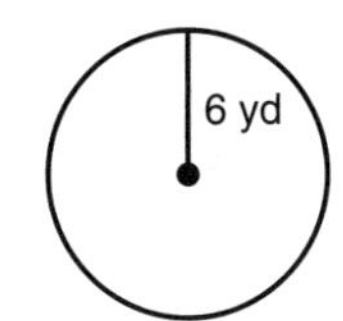
6 yd

____

Find the circumference. Use $\frac{22}{7}$ for π.

9. $d = 4$ cm

10. $r = 1\frac{3}{4}$ mi

11. $d = 15$ ft

12. $r = 2\frac{1}{2}$ m

13. $r = 1\frac{1}{6}$ in.

14. $d = 10.5$ m

15. $r = 8\frac{3}{4}$ cm

16. $r = 14$ dm

17. $d = 3\frac{1}{2}$ ft

18. $r = 2\frac{1}{3}$ mi

19. $d = 21$ yd

20. $d = 42$ mm

Problem Solving

21. The diameter of Mercury is 3031 mi. What is its circumference?

____

22. What is the circumference of Jupiter if its equatorial radius is 44,000 mi?

____

C Use with Lesson 13-12, pages 470–471 in the Student Book.
C Then go to Lesson 13-13, pages 472–473 in the Student Book.

Area of a Circle

Name ___________________________

Date ___________________________

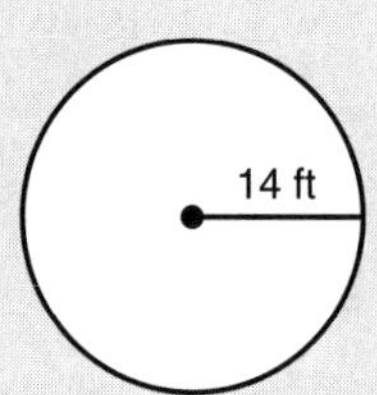

$A = \pi \times r^2$

$A \approx \dfrac{22}{7} \times (14 \text{ ft})^2$

$A \approx 616 \text{ ft}^2$

Find the area of the shaded region.

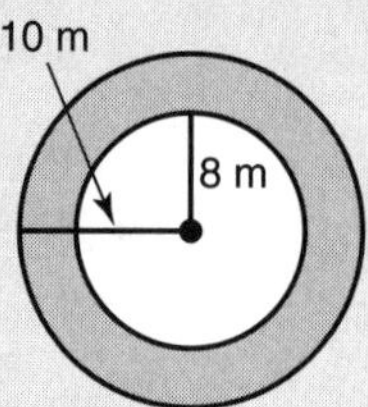

$A =$ area of big circle $-$ area of small circle

$A \approx 3.14 \times (10 \text{ m})^2 \quad - 3.14 \times (8\text{m})^2$

$A \approx 314 \text{ m}^2 \qquad\qquad - 200.96 \text{ m}^2$

$A \approx 113.04 \text{ m}^2$

Find the area of each circle. Use 3.14 or $\dfrac{22}{7}$ for π. Estimate to help.

1. 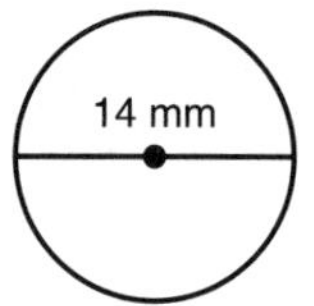

2. 

3. 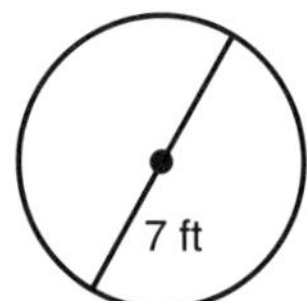

4. 

_______________   _______________   _______________   _______________

5. $d = 10$ cm   **6.** $r = 4$ in.   **7.** $r = 5.5$ mm   **8.** $d = 56$ in.

_______________   _______________   _______________   _______________

9. $r = 17$ in.   **10.** $d = 45$ ft   **11.** $r = 10.3$ km   **12.** $d = 27$ cm

_______________   _______________   _______________   _______________

Find the area of the shaded region.

13. 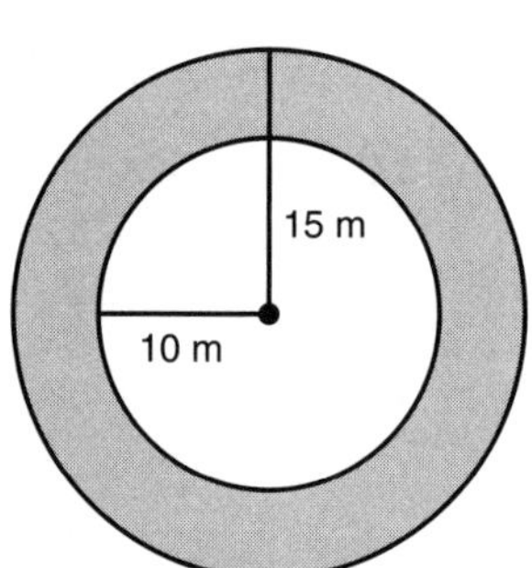

14. 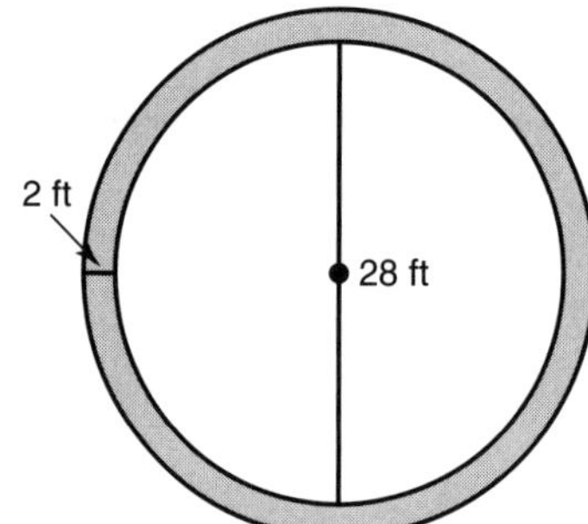

15. 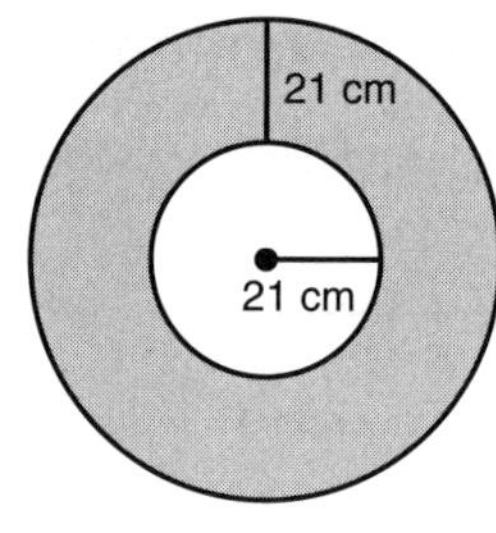

_______________   _______________   _______________

Problem Solving

16. Earl opened his compass to 4 cm to draw a circle. What is the area of the circle he drew? _______________

17. What is the area of a circular garden with a diameter of 4 ft? _______________

Use with Lesson 13-13, pages 472–473 in the Student Book.
Then go to Lesson 13-13A, pages 251–252 in this Workbook.

Surface Area of Cubes, Rectangular Prisms, and Cylinders

Name _______________________

Date _______________________

Cube	Rectangular Prism	Cylinder
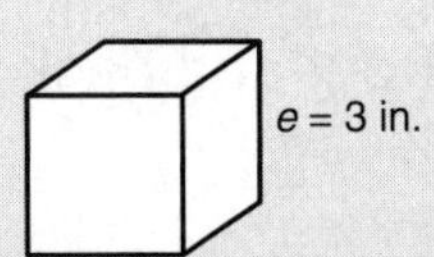	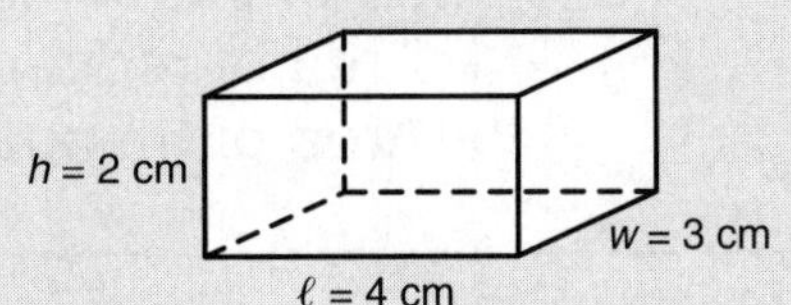	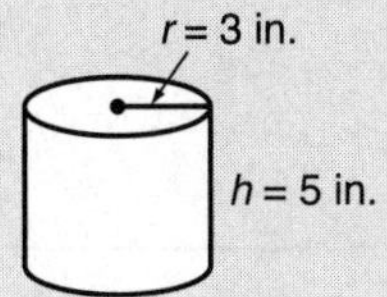
$S = 6e^2$ $S = 6 \times 3^2$ $S = 54$ in.^{2}	$S = 2\ell w + 2wh + 2\ell h$ $S = 2(4 \times 3) + 2(3 \times 2) + 2(4 \times 2)$ $S = 52$ cm^2	$S = 2\pi r^2 + 2\pi rh$ $S = 150.72$ in.^{2}

Find the surface area of each cube.

1. 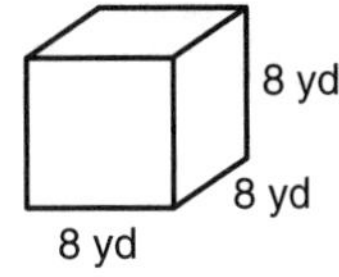

____

2. 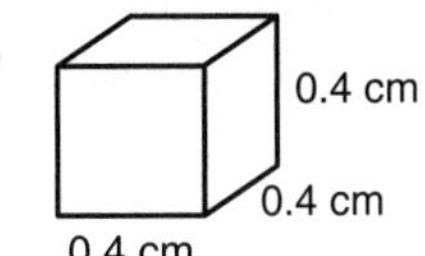

____

3. 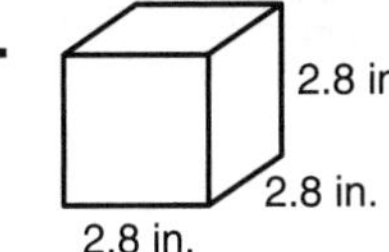

____

4. $e = 3.2$ m

____

5. $e = 38$ mm

____

6. $e = 0.8$ ft

____

7. $e = 0.5$ dm

____

Find the surface area of each rectangular prism.

8. 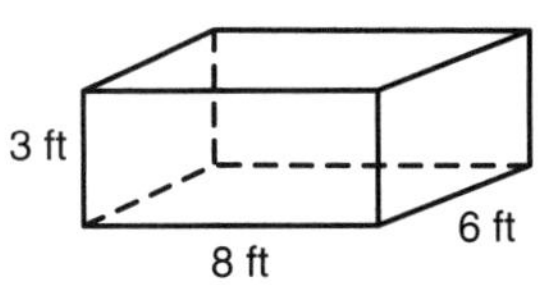

____

9. 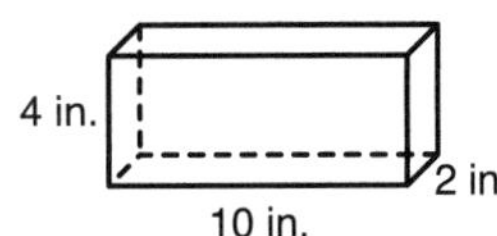

____

10. 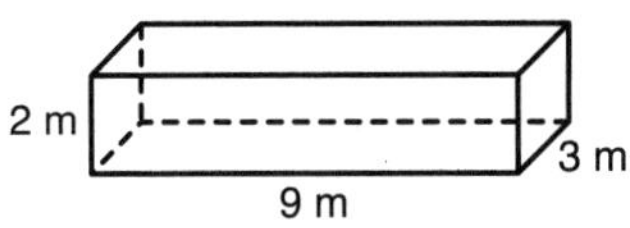

____

11. $\ell = 12$ dm
 $w = 4$ dm
 $h = 5$ dm

____

12. $\ell = 7.1$ m
 $w = 4$ m
 $h = 2.3$ m

____

13. $\ell = 5$ ft
 $w = 2\frac{1}{2}$ ft
 $h = 4$ ft

____

14. $\ell = 6$ yd
 $w = 3\frac{1}{3}$ yd
 $h = 2\frac{1}{2}$ yd

____

Find the surface area of each cylinder. Use 3.14 for π.

15. 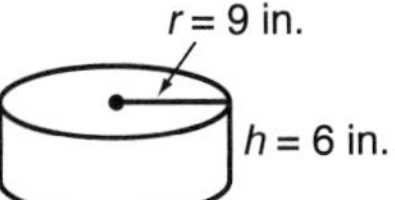

____

16. 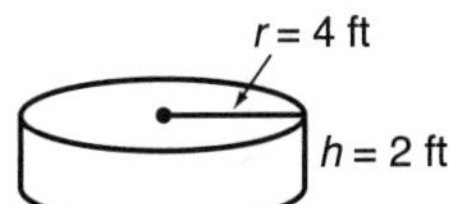

____

17. 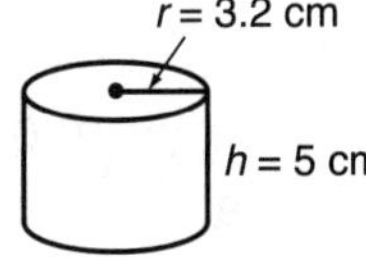

____

Use with Lesson 13-14, pages 474–475 in the Student Book.
Then go to Lesson 13-15, pages 476–477 in the Student Book.

Surface Area of Pyramids and Triangular Prisms

Name _______________________

Date _______________________

Square Pyramid	Triangular Prism
$S = 4(A_{triangle}) + A_{square}$	$S =$ Area of bottom face + Area of rectangular front and back faces + Area of triangular bases

Find the surface area of each figure.

1.

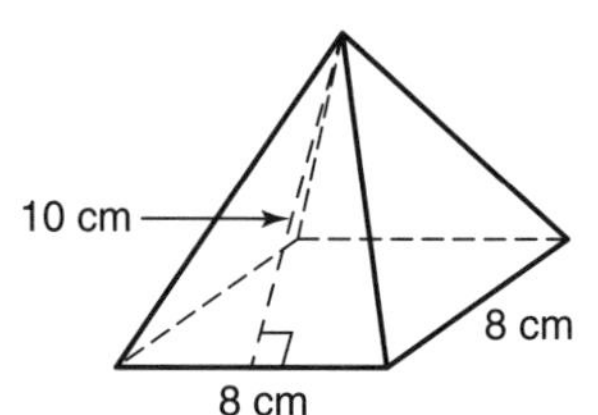

____

2.

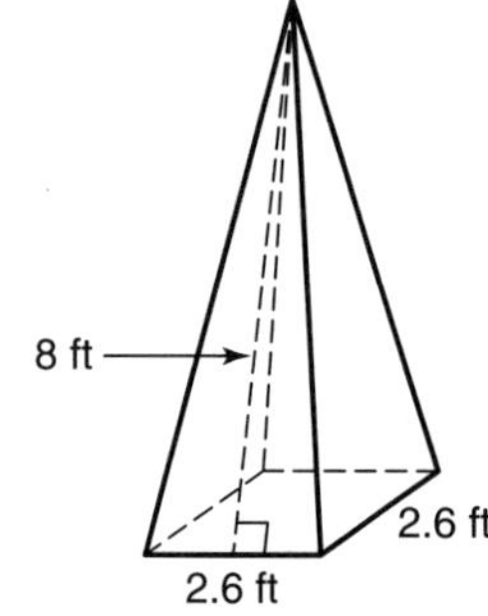

____

3.

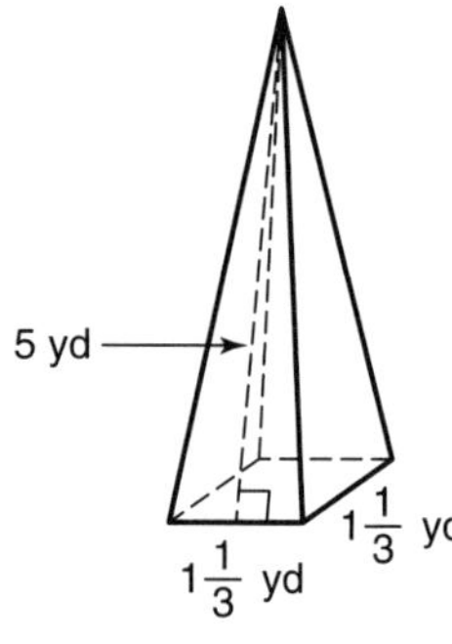

____

4.

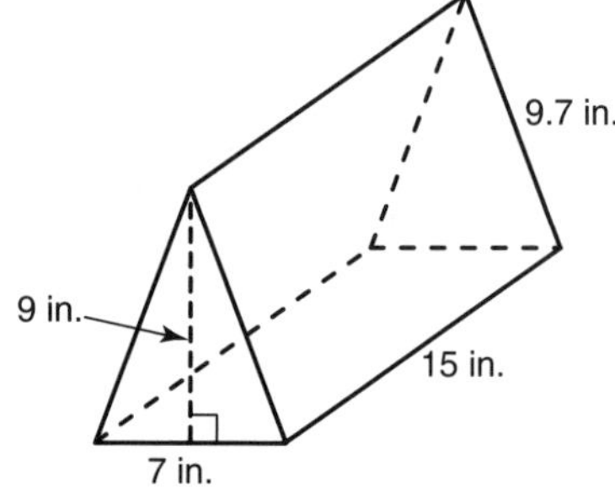

____

5.

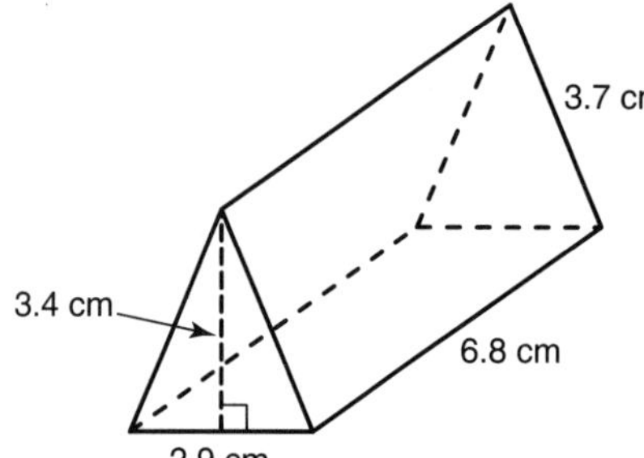

____

6.

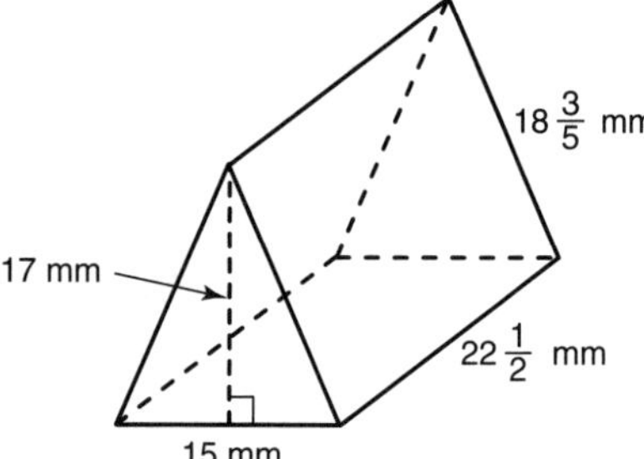

____

Problem Solving

7. Denise makes a pyramid with a 3.5-cm square base. Each triangular face has a height of 2.8 cm. Gus makes a pyramid with a 2.4-cm square base. Each triangular face has a height of 4.7 cm. Whose pyramid has the greater surface area? by how many square centimeters?

____

186

Use with Lesson 13-15, pages 476–477 in the Student Book.
Then go to Lesson 13-16, pages 478–479 in the Student Book.

Volume of Prisms

Name _______________________

Date _______________________

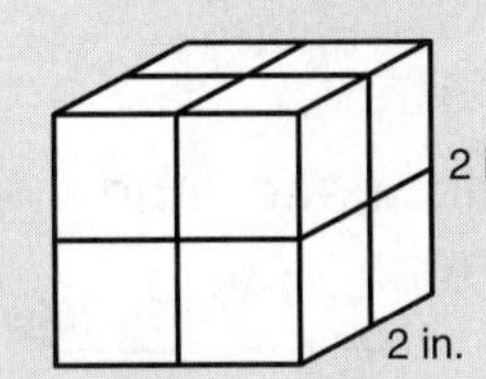

Volume of a Cube

$$V = e^3$$
$$V = 2^3 \text{ or } 2 \times 2 \times 2$$
$$V = 8 \text{ in.}^3$$

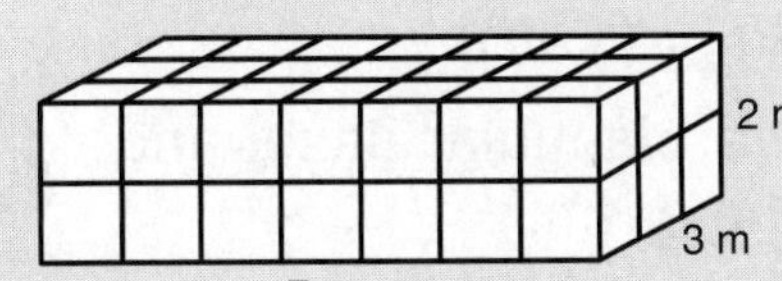

Volume of a Rectangular Prism

$$V = \ell \times w \times h$$
$$V = 7 \times 3 \times 2$$
$$V = 42 \text{ m}^3$$

Find the volume of each cube.

1. 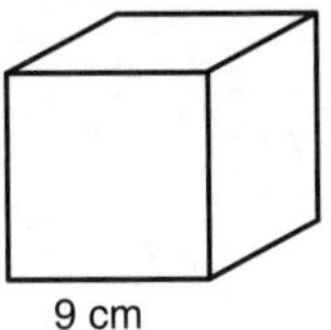
9 cm

____

2. 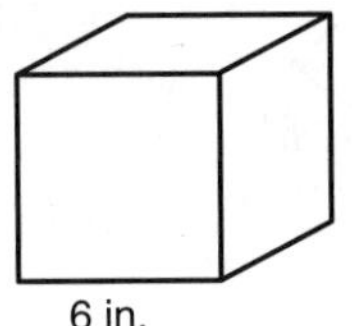
6 in.

____

3. 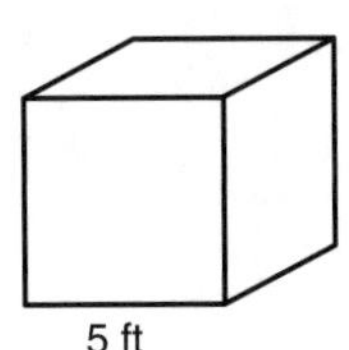
5 ft

____

4. 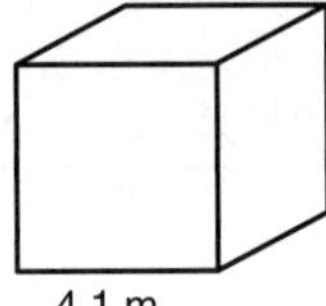
4.1 m

____

5. $e = 7\frac{1}{2}$ ft

____

6. $e = 1.2$ cm

____

7. $e = 6.1$ mm

____

Find the volume of each rectangular prism.

8. 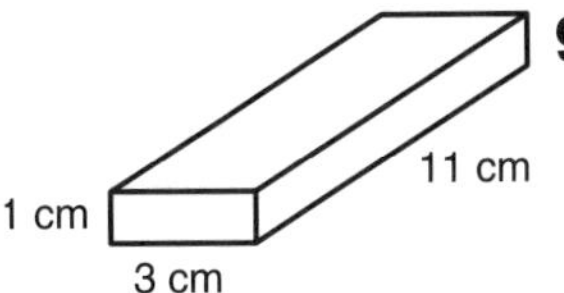
1 cm, 3 cm, 11 cm

____

9. 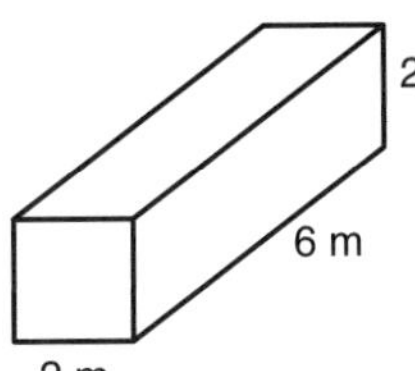
2 m, 6 m, 2 m

____

10. 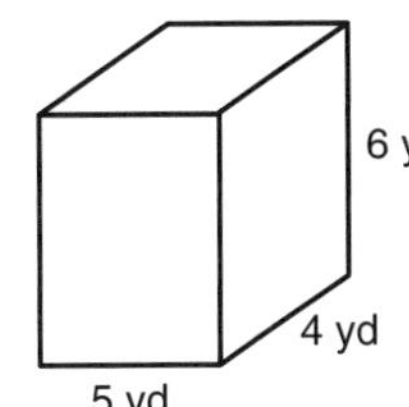
6 yd, 4 yd, 5 yd

____

11. 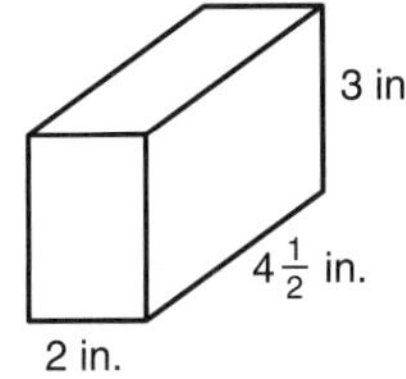
3 in., $4\frac{1}{2}$ in., 2 in.

____

12. $\ell = 4$ cm
$w = 1.2$ cm
$h = 3.1$ cm

____

13. $\ell = 3$ ft
$w = 1\frac{1}{4}$ ft
$h = 2\frac{1}{3}$ ft

____

14. $\ell = 10$ m
$w = 8.4$ m
$h = 5$ m

____

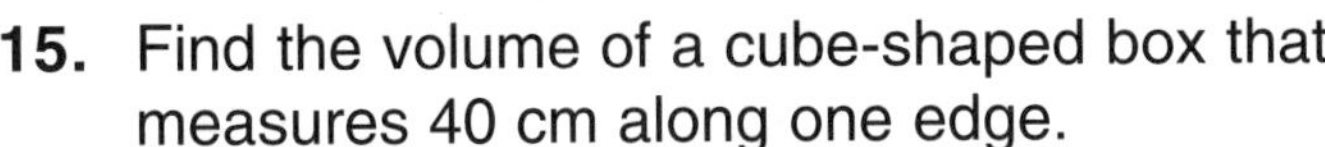 **Problem Solving**

15. Find the volume of a cube-shaped box that measures 40 cm along one edge.

____

16. A box is 10 in. long, 8 in. wide, and 2 in. high. How many cubes that measure 1 in. on each edge will fit inside the box?

____

17. Find the volume of a swimming pool that is 24 ft long, 15 ft wide, and 5 ft deep.

____

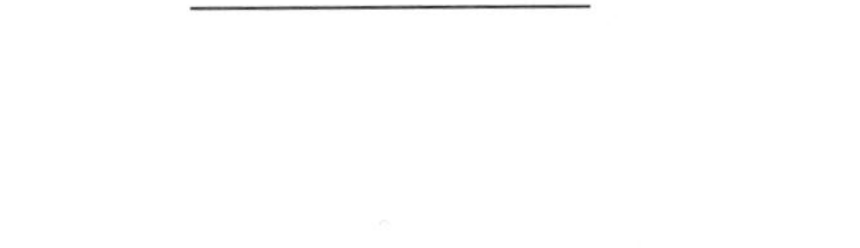 Use with Lesson 13-16, pages 478–479 in the Student Book.
Then go to Lessons 13-16A and 13-16B, pages 253–256 in this Workbook.

Volume of Triangular Prisms and Cylinders

Name _______________

Date _______________

Volume of a Triangular Prism	**Volume of a Cylinder**
$V = Bh = (\frac{1}{2}bh)h$	$V = Bh = (\pi r^2)h$
B is the area of the triangular base, and h is the height of the prism.	B is the area of the circular base, and h is the height of the cylinder.

Find the volume of each triangular prism.

1.

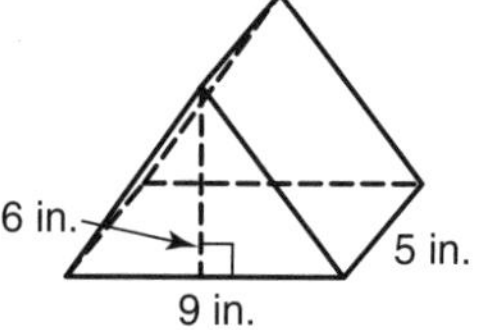

____

2.

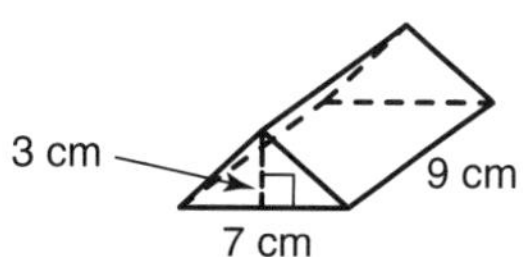

____

3.

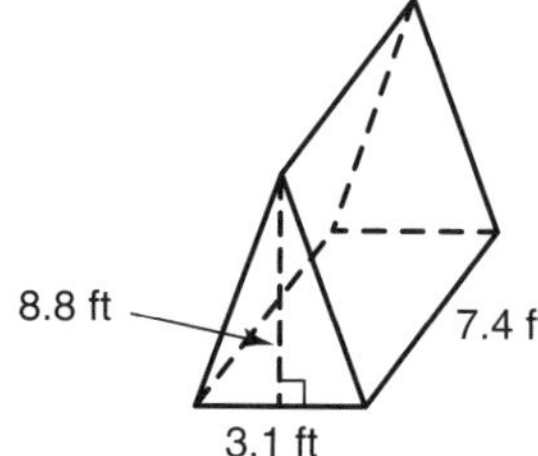

____

4.

____

5.

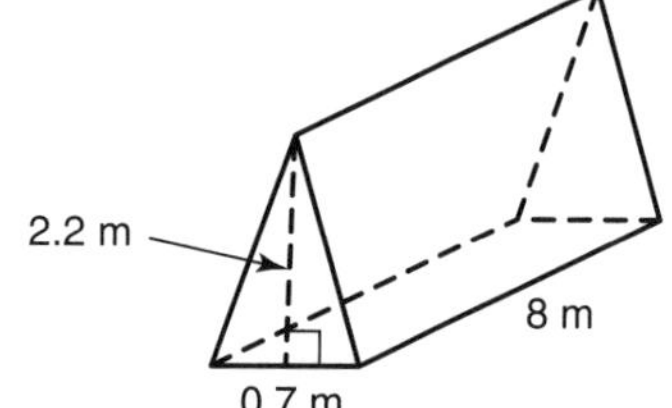

____

6.

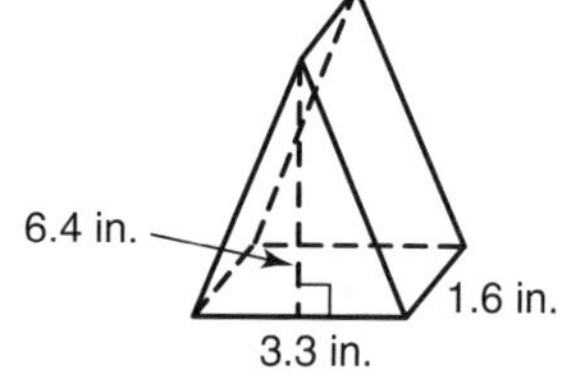

____

Find the volume of each cylinder, to the nearest tenth.

7.

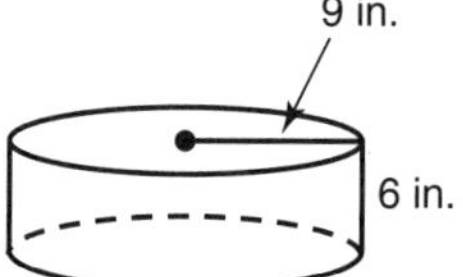

____

8.

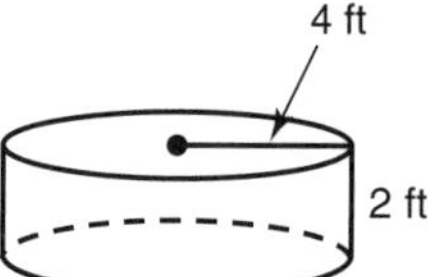

____

9.

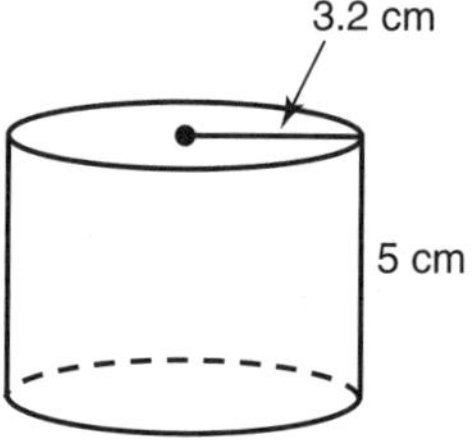

____

10. $r = 7$ m
$h = 2$ m _______________

11. $r = 6$ yd
$h = 4$ yd _______________

12. $d = 12$ mm
$h = 9$ mm _______________

Problem Solving

13. The volume of a cylinder is about 251.2 in.^{3}. The radius of the cylinder is 4 in. About what is the height of the cylinder?

____

Use with Lesson 13-17, pages 480–481 in the Student Book.
Then go to Lesson 13-18, pages 482–483 in the Student Book.

Volume of Pyramids

Name _______________________

Date _______________________

The volume of a pyramid is equal to one-third the product of the area of the base and the height of the pyramid.

Volume of a Pyramid

$$V = \frac{1}{3}Bh$$

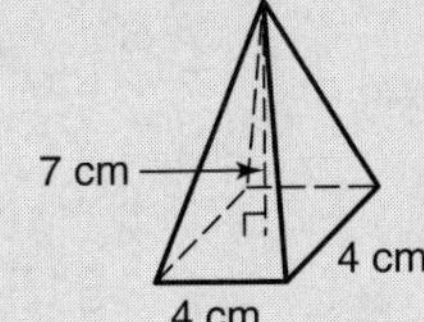

$$V = \frac{1}{3} Bh$$
$$V = \frac{1}{3} (4 \times 4) \, 7$$
$$V = \frac{1}{3} \times 16 \times 7 = 37\frac{1}{3} \text{ cm}^3$$

Find the volume of each pyramid.

1.

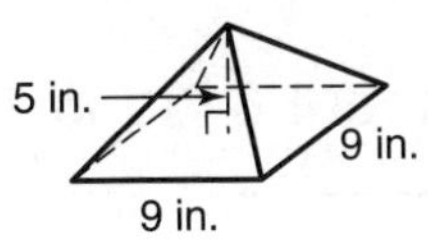

____

2.

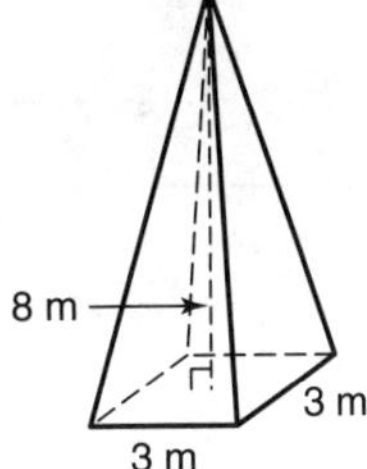

____

3.

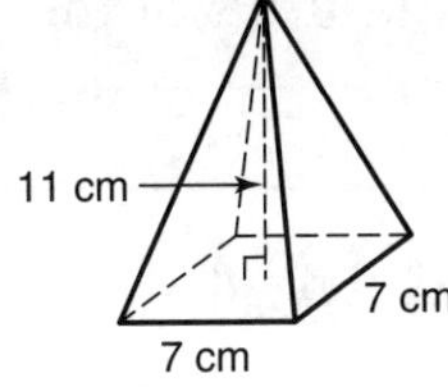

____

4.

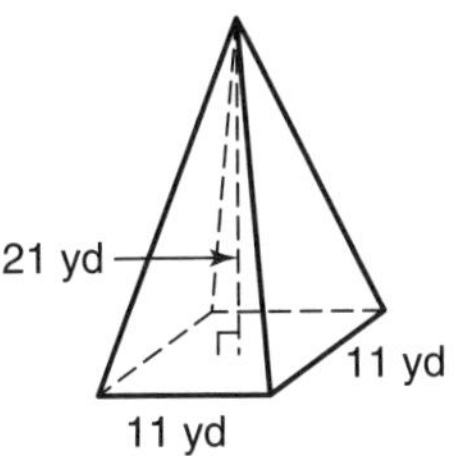

____

5.

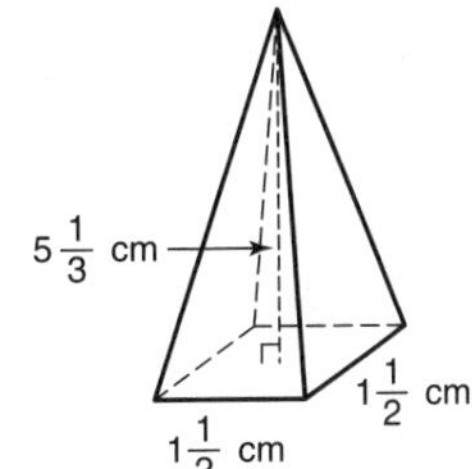

____

6.

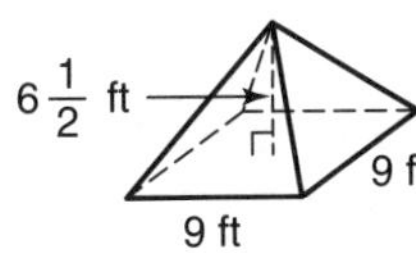

____

7.

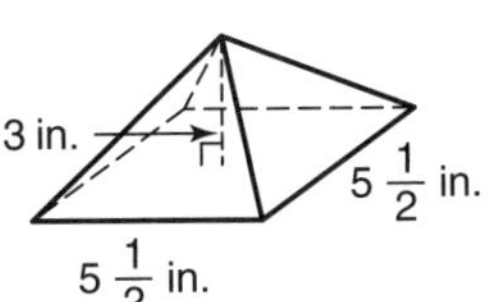

____

8.

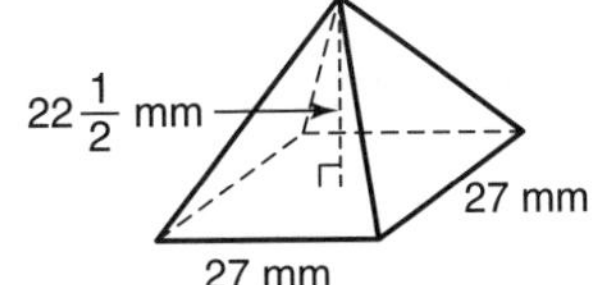

____

9.

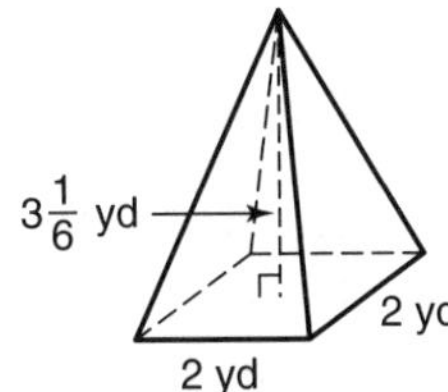

____

Problem Solving

10. A paperweight shaped like a pyramid has a $2\frac{1}{2}$-in. square base. The height of the pyramid is 3 in. What is the volume of the pyramid?

____

11. A square pyramid with a volume of 100 cm³ has a height of 12 cm. How long is each edge of the pyramid's base?

____

Use Formulas to Solve Problems

To find the area of the figure below:

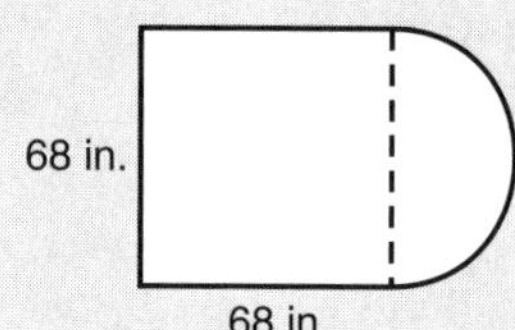

- find the area of the square
- find the area of the semicircle
- find the sum of the two areas

$A_{square} = s^2$
$= (68 \text{ in.})^2 = 4624 \text{ in.}^2$

$A_{semicircle} = \frac{1}{2}(\pi r^2)$

$\approx \frac{1}{2} \times 3.14 \times (34 \text{ in.})^2$

$\approx 1815 \text{ in.}^2 \longleftarrow$ Round to the nearest whole number.

$A_{figure} = 4624 \text{ in.}^2 + 1815 \text{ in.}^2$
$= 6439 \text{ in.}^2$

So, the area of the figure is about 6439 in.^{2}.

Problem Solving

Use the figure above for problems 1–2.

1. Carl wants to glue yarn along the outside border of the figure. How much yarn will he need? (Round to the nearest whole number.)

2. Suppose another semicircle with a diameter of 68 in. is attached to the other side of the figure. What will the area of the new figure be? (Round to the nearest whole number.)

Use the diagram of the garden for problems 3–4.

3. Shelly wants to place mulch as a border around the garden. About what is the area of the border that Shelly wants to mulch?

4. Reed wants to run a hose along the inside border of the mulched area. How long does the hose need to be, to the nearest meter, if the garden is shaped like a rhombus?

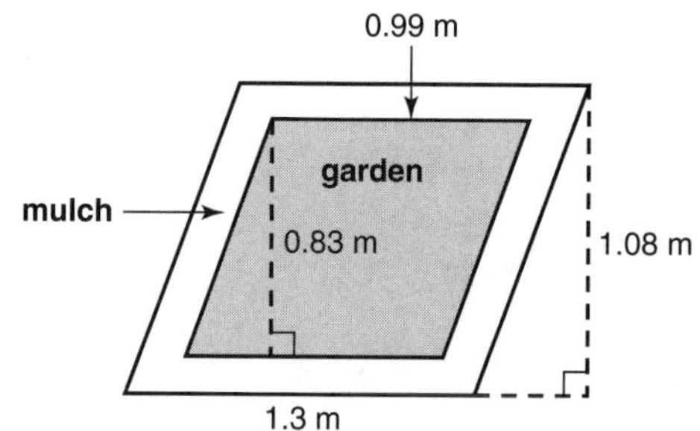

Use with Lesson 13-19, pages 484–485 in the Student Book.
Then go to Lesson 13-20, pages 486–487 in the Student Book.

Problem-Solving Strategy: Use Drawings/Formulas

Name ___________________

Date ___________________

A swimming pool is 60 ft long and 30 ft wide.
A 10-foot wide paved walkway surrounds the pool.
What is the perimeter of the outside edge of the walkway?

Use a picture and a formula to solve the problem.

The length is 10 + 60 + 10 or 80 feet.

The width is 10 + 30 + 10 or 50 feet.

The formula is $P = 2 \times \ell + 2 \times w$.

The perimeter is (2 × 80) + (2 × 50) or 260 feet.

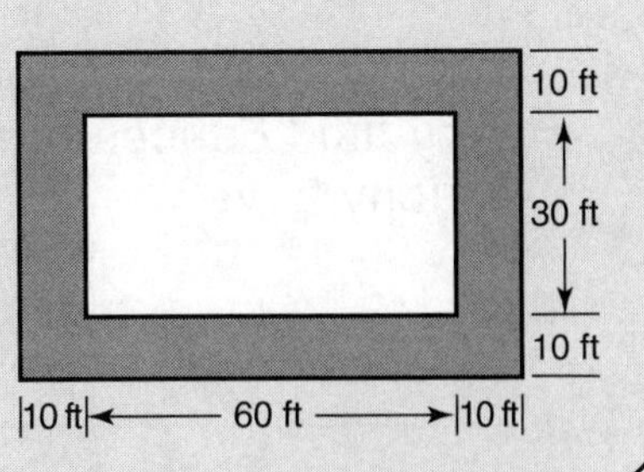

Solve. Do your work on a separate sheet of paper.

1. Four sticks of butter are packed in a box that is 12.2 cm long, 6.8 cm wide, and 6.8 cm high. To the nearest hundredth, what is the volume of each stick of butter?

2. A shed shaped like a rectangular prism is 10 ft long, 5 ft wide, and 7 ft high. If you cover the four outside walls with cedar shingles, how many square feet will be covered?

3. Jon's rectangular garden is 12 ft long and 8 ft wide. There is a stone walk on all four sides of the garden. The stones are 2 feet square. What is the distance around the outer edge of the walk?

4. The diameter of Philip's circular fish pond is 2.4 m. A concrete border around the pond is 0.3 m wide. What is the area of the fish pond? To the nearest hundredth, what is the area of the border around the fish pond?

5. What is the area of the garden described in problem 3? What is the area of the stone walk around the garden?

6. What is the circumference of the border around the fish pond described in Problem 4?

7. Each side of a square park measures 12 yd. Along one side is a triangular playground. Its height is the side of the square, and its base is 6 yd long. What is the combined area of the park and the playground?

8. Sherman pasted 6 square photos on a rectangular sheet of posterboard that is 12 in. long and 8 in. wide. One side of each photo measures 3 in. What area of the posterboard is left showing?

Use with Lesson 13-20, pages 486–487 in the Student Book.
Then go to Lesson 13-21, pages 488–489 in the Student Book.

Problem-Solving Applications: Mixed Review

Name _______________________

Date _______________________

Solve each problem and explain the method you used. If needed, do all your work on a separate sheet of paper.

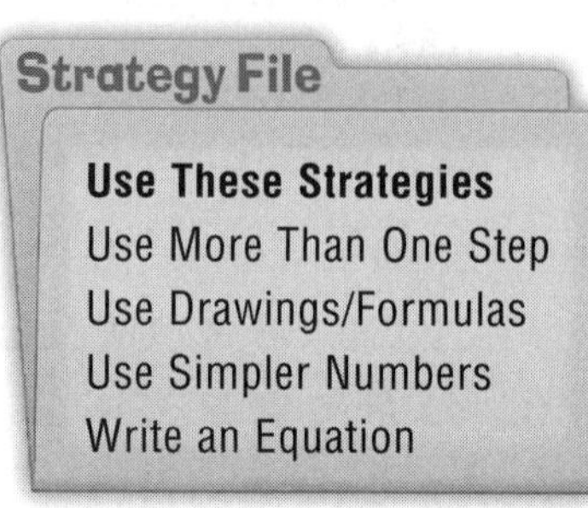

1. Anthony has $\frac{1}{4}$ gal of milk left. How many fluid ounces of milk does Anthony have?

____

2. Gerri uses $\frac{3}{8}$ package of sprinkles for cookies and $\frac{1}{3}$ of the same package of sprinkles for cupcakes. How much of the package of sprinkles is left?

____

3. Judy has a glass shaped like a cylinder. The diameter of the base of the glass is 7.5 cm, and the glass is 15.5 cm tall. What is the volume of the glass? Round to the nearest tenth.

____

4. LaTeisha has 3 packed suitcases that each weigh 21 lb 13 oz. She is allowed to bring a total of 75 lb on her flight. How much can her fourth packed suitcase weigh?

____

5. The courtyard at school is a 43-ft by 29-ft rectangle. Leonard estimates the area of the courtyard to be about 120 ft². Is his estimate reasonable? Explain.

____

6. Franklin has a circular desk with a circumference of about 4.71 m. What is the approximate diameter of Franklin's desk?

Use the drawings for problems 7–9.

7. Eduardo drew a parallelogram. What is its area?

____

8. Is the area of the figure Mimi drew greater than 4000 mm²? Explain.

____

9. Whose drawing has a greater perimeter? by how many millimeters?

____

Eduardo's Drawing

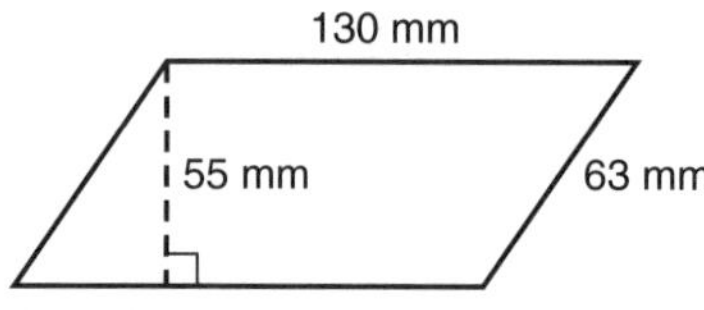

Mimi's Drawing

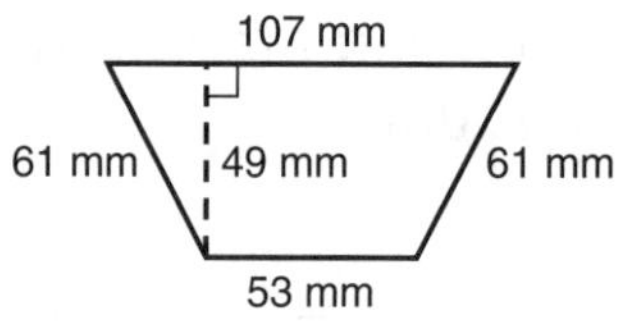

Use with Lesson 13-21, pages 488–489 in the Student Book.

Two-Step Equations

Name _______________

Date _______________

Solve: $\frac{w}{9} + 7.7 = 14.5$

$\frac{w}{9} + 7.7 - 7.7 = 14.5 - 7.7$

$\frac{w}{9} = 6.8$ Check: $\frac{61.2}{9} + 7.7 \overset{?}{=} 14.5$

$\frac{w}{9} \cdot 9 = 6.8 \cdot 9$ $6.8 + 7.7 \overset{?}{=} 14.5$

$w = 61.2$ $14.5 = 14.5$ True

Solve and check.

1. $5u + 8 = 43$ _______

2. $7p - 3 = 74$ _______

3. $25 + 3h = 574$ _______

4. $3.6k - 33 = 93$ _______

5. $83.3 = 6.3x + 14$ _______

6. $0.3n - 21 = 42.105$ _______

7. $\frac{a}{6} + 16 = 93$ _______

8. $\frac{t}{9} - 19 = 62$ _______

9. $\frac{c}{18} + 35 = 68$ _______

10. $\frac{135}{z} - 7 = 8$ _______

11. $12 = \frac{5d}{6} + 7$ _______

12. $\frac{3}{g} + 14 = 43$ _______

13. $\frac{5r}{12} - 8 = 44$ _______

14. $\frac{5e}{8} + 6.5 = 9.4$ _______

15. $2.9 = 8.2 + 4b - 9.7$ _______

Problem Solving Write an equation, then solve.

16. Eight dollars more than one-third the price of a medium pizza is \$13. What is the price of the pizza? _______

17. In the card shop, there is a shelf with 25 cards in each row. There is a display rack with 45 cards. There are 220 cards altogether. How many rows are on the shelf? _______

18. Eight tenths less than 6 times a certain number is equal to 0.4. What is the number? _______

19. Yesterday's high temperature was 5° less than twice the low temperature. The high temperature was 55°F. What was the low temperature? _______

20. Twenty-nine subtracted from 17 times a number is equal to 158. What is the number? _______

Use with Lesson 14-1, pages 496–497 in the Student Book.
Then go to Lesson 14-2, pages 498–499 in the Student Book.

Addition and Subtraction Equations with Integers

Name _______________

Date _______________

Solve: $f - {}^+21 = {}^-85$

$f - {}^+21 + {}^+21 = {}^-85 + {}^+21$

$f = {}^-64$

Check: ${}^-64 - {}^+21 \stackrel{?}{=} {}^-85$

${}^-85 = {}^-85$ True

Complete each step to solve and check each equation.

1. $h + {}^+34 = {}^+78$

$h + {}^+34 - \underline{\quad} = {}^+78 - \underline{\quad}$

$h = \underline{\quad}$

Check: $\underline{\quad} + {}^+34 \stackrel{?}{=} {}^+78$

$\underline{\quad} = {}^+78$

2. $m - {}^+12 = {}^-7$

$m - {}^+12 + \underline{\quad} = {}^-7 + \underline{\quad}$

$m = \underline{\quad}$

Check: $\underline{\quad} - {}^+12 \stackrel{?}{=} {}^-7$

$\underline{\quad} = {}^-7$

Solve and check.

3. $h + {}^-5 = {}^-17$

4. $q - {}^+59 = {}^-76$

5. $w + {}^+76 = {}^-32$

6. $u - {}^-93 = {}^+96$

7. $l + {}^-19 = {}^-73$

8. ${}^+65 = s - {}^-27$

9. ${}^-42 = x - {}^+91$

10. ${}^+28 = a + {}^-82$

11. $y + {}^+39 + {}^+22 = {}^-75$

12. ${}^-26 + e - {}^-19 = {}^+48$

13. $k - ({}^+27 + {}^+8) = {}^-59$

14. ${}^-52 = b - ({}^-73 + {}^+90)$

Problem Solving **Write an equation and then solve.**

15. Seventeen more than a number is ${}^-61$. Find the number. _______________

16. Twenty less than a number is ${}^-67$. Find the number. _______________

17. A number decreased by ${}^-4$ is ${}^-73$. Find the number. _______________

18. From 5:00 A.M. to 11:00 A.M., the temperature rose 7°C. The temperature at 11:00 A.M. was ${}^+2$°C. What was the temperature at 5:00 A.M.? _______________

194

Use with Lesson 14-2, pages 498–499 in the Student Book.
Then go to Lesson 14-3, pages 500–501 in the Student Book.

Multiplication and Division Equations with Integers

Name _______________

Date _______________

Solve: $^-6x = {}^+114$

$^-6x \div {}^-6 = {}^+114 \div {}^-6$

$x = {}^-19$

Check: $^-6(^-19) \overset{?}{=} {}^+114$

$^+114 = {}^+114$ True

Solve: $\dfrac{n}{^+12} = {}^-9$

$\dfrac{n}{^+12} \cdot {}^+12 = {}^-9 \cdot {}^+12$

$n = {}^-108$

Check: $\dfrac{^-108}{^+12} \overset{?}{=} {}^-9$

$^-9 = {}^-9$ True

Complete each step to solve and check each equation.

1.

$^-8b = {}^+232$

$^-8b \div \underline{\quad} = {}^+232 \div \underline{\quad}$

$b = \underline{\quad}$

Check: $^-8 \cdot \underline{\quad} \overset{?}{=} {}^+232$

$\underline{\quad} = {}^+232$

2.

$x \div {}^-7 = {}^-28$

$x \div {}^-7 \cdot \underline{\quad} = {}^-28 \cdot \underline{\quad}$

$x = \underline{\quad}$

Check: $\underline{\quad} \div {}^-7 \overset{?}{=} {}^-28$

$\underline{\quad} = {}^-28$

Solve and check.

3. $^-6y = {}^-54$

4. $^+18n = {}^-144$

5. $a \div {}^+23 = {}^-9$

6. $f \div {}^-12 = {}^-7$

7. $^-24e = {}^+96$

8. $z \div {}^+31 = {}^+4$

9. $^-33m = {}^-231$

10. $^-13h + {}^-38 = {}^+27$

11. $^+6r - {}^-62 = {}^+26$

12. $^-25b - {}^+92 = {}^+133$

13. $\dfrac{i}{^+7} - {}^+32 = {}^-46$

14. $^-37 = \dfrac{s}{^-12} + {}^-66$

15. $^+5 = k \div {}^+51 + {}^-82$

16. $^+7 = {}^-104 + {}^+3u$

17. $^-159 = {}^-18v - {}^-21$

Problem Solving Write an equation and then solve.

18. When a number is divided by $^-6$, the result is $^-13$. What is the number? _______________

19. When a number is multiplied by $^+26$, the result is $^-286$. What is the number? _______________

20. Nine more than $^-8$ times a certain number is $^+273$. What is the number? _______________

Use with Lesson 14-3, pages 500–501 in the Student Book.
Then go to Lesson 14-4, pages 502–503 in the Student Book.

Functions and Ordered Pairs

Name ________________________

Date ________________________

A function is a set of ordered pairs (x, y) in which there is only one y-value for each x-value.

Rule: $y = x + {}^+4$		
x	**y**	**Ordered Pair**
${}^+4$	${}^+4 + {}^+4 = {}^+8$	$({}^+4, {}^+8)$
${}^+2$	${}^+2 + {}^+4 = {}^+6$	$({}^+2, {}^+6)$
0	$0 + {}^+4 = {}^+4$	$(0, {}^+4)$

Use the function rule to find the value of y in each ordered pair.

	Function Rule	Ordered Pairs		
1.	$y = x - {}^+2$	$({}^+9, \underline{\ \ })$	$({}^+6, \underline{\ \ })$	$({}^+4, \underline{\ \ })$
2.	$y = x + {}^+10$	$(0, \underline{\ \ })$	$({}^+4, \underline{\ \ })$	$({}^-10, \underline{\ \ })$
3.	$y = {}^+2x$	$({}^+5, \underline{\ \ })$	$({}^+8, \underline{\ \ })$	$(0, \underline{\ \ })$
4.	$y = x \div {}^+3$	$({}^-27, \underline{\ \ })$	$({}^+12, \underline{\ \ })$	$({}^+18, \underline{\ \ })$

Use the function rule to complete each function table.

Rule: $y = x + {}^+3$		
x	**y**	**Ordered Pair**
5. ${}^+8$		
6. ${}^-2$		
7. ${}^+6$		
8. ${}^+12$		
9. ${}^-10$		

Rule: $y = x - {}^+5$		
x	**y**	**Ordered Pair**
10. ${}^+7$		
11. ${}^+10$		
12. ${}^+3$		
13. ${}^-4$		
14. ${}^+6$		

Complete the function table. Then write a rule relating x and y.

15.

x	${}^+5$	${}^+8$	${}^-10$	${}^+1$	${}^-4$	${}^+12$	${}^+6$
y		${}^+24$	${}^-30$				
(x, y)	$({}^+5, {}^+15)$						

16. Rule: ________________________

C Use with Lesson 14-4, pages 502–503 in the Student Book.
C Then go to Lesson 14-4A, pages 257–258 in this Workbook.

Graph Ordered Pairs

Name _______________________

Date _______________________

An ordered pair (x, y) locates a point on a coordinate plane. The numbers, x and y, are called coordinates.

($^+$1, $^-$3) locates point B.

($^+$4, $^+$2) locates point A.

right 4   up 2

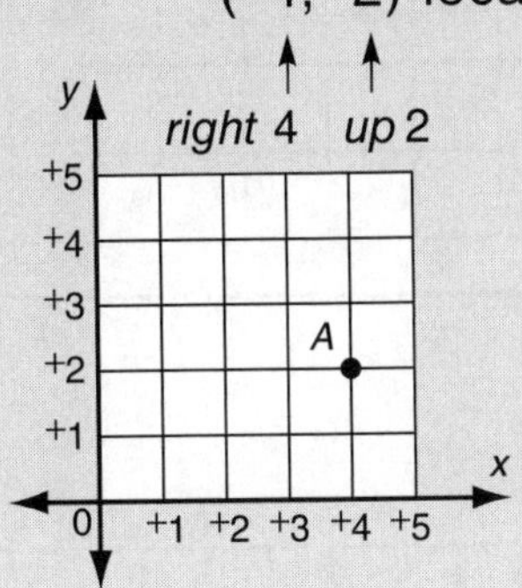

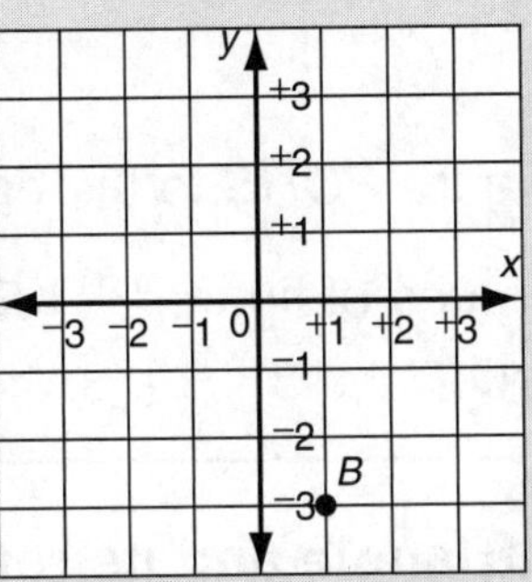

**Use the coordinate plane at the right for exercises 1–12.
Name the ordered pair for each point.**

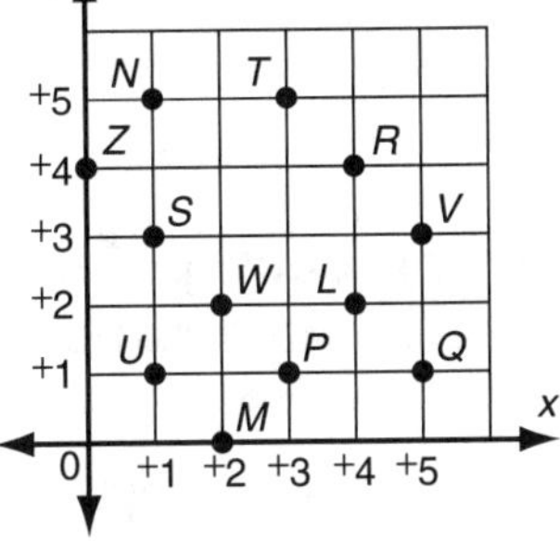

1. L _______

2. Z _______

3. U _______

4. R _______

5. N _______

6. V _______

Name the point for each ordered pair

7. ($^+$2, $^+$2) _______

8. ($^+$3, $^+$1) _______

9. ($^+$5, $^+$1) _______

10. ($^+$1, $^+$3) _______

11. ($^+$2, 0) _______

12. ($^+$3, $^+$5) _______

**Use the coordinate plane at the right for exercises 13–30.
Name the ordered pair for each point.**

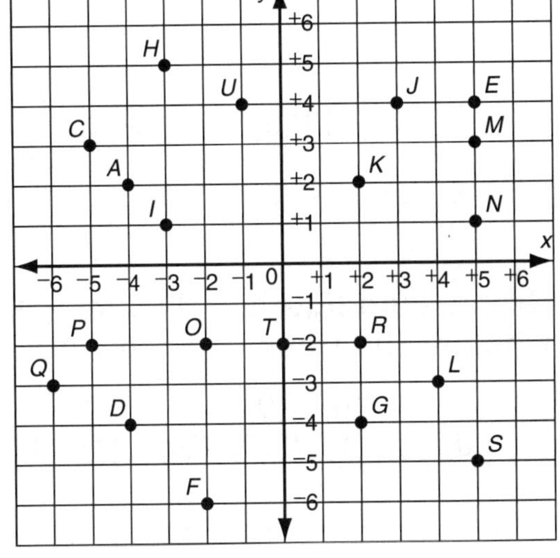

13. A _______

14. M _______

15. J _______

16. Q _______

17. E _______

18. H _______

19. F _______

20. S _______

21. D _______

22. P _______

23. K _______

24. U _______

Name the point for each ordered pair.

25. ($^-$5, $^+$3) _______

26. ($^-$2, $^-$6) _______

27. (0, $^-$2) _______

28. ($^+$4, $^-$3) _______

29. ($^-$2, $^-$2) _______

30. ($^+$2, $^-$4) _______

C Use with Lesson 14-5, pages 504–505 in the Student Book.
C Then go to Lessons 14-5A and 14-5B, pages 259–262 in this Workbook.

197

Graph Reflections and Translations

Name ___________________

Date ___________________

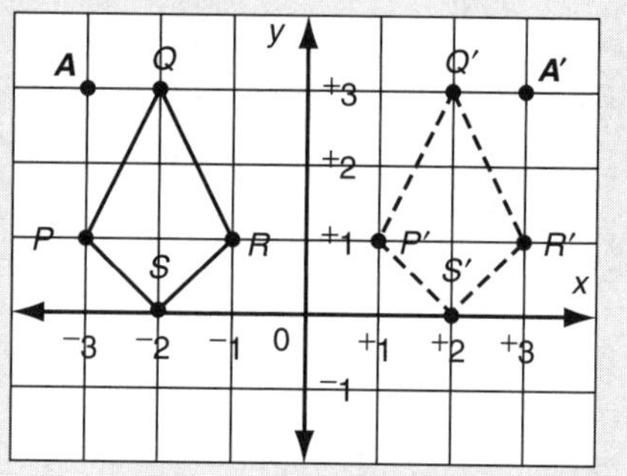

Graph *A* (⁻3, ⁺3) and its reflection across the *y*-axis.

The coordinates of point *A'* are (⁺3, ⁺3).

Translate figure *PQRS* to the right 4 units.

The coordinates of figure *P'Q'R'S'* are
P'(⁺1, ⁺1), *Q'*(⁺2, ⁺3), *R'*(⁺3, ⁺1), *S'*(⁺2, 0)

**Graph each triangle and its reflection across the indicated axis.
Use prime notation to write the coordinates of its reflection.**

1. *P*(⁻1, ⁺1), *Q*(⁻2, ⁺5), *R*(⁻5, ⁺1); *y*-axis

____

2. *X*(⁺1, ⁻4), *Y*(0, 0), *Z*(⁺5, ⁻4); *x*-axis

____

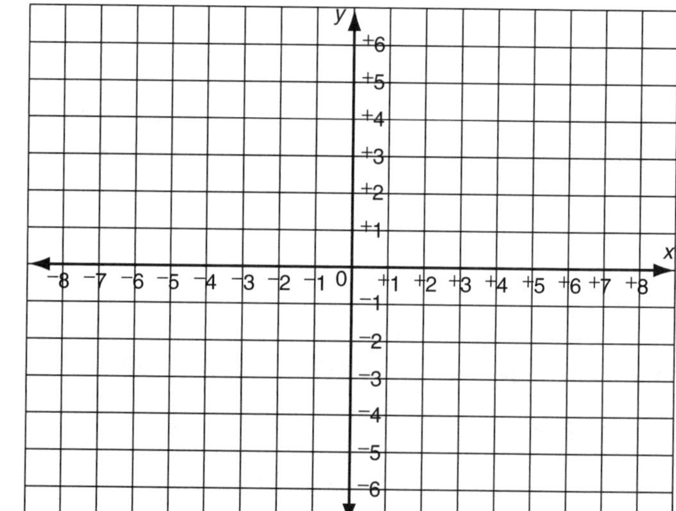

**Graph each point and its translation.
Use prime notation to write the coordinates
of its translation.**

3. *A*(⁻6, ⁻5) left 1 unit, up 3 units

____

4. *B*(⁺5, ⁻1) right 2 units, up 3 units

____

5. *C*(⁺6, ⁻2) left 1 unit, down 4 units

____

6. *D*(⁻3, ⁺2) right 2 units, up 4 units

____

7. *E*(⁺3, ⁺1) left 5 units, down 1 unit

____

**Graph each figure and its image on the same coordinate plane. Then tell
whether the transformation is a *reflection* or a *translation*.**

8. *J*(⁺1, ⁻6), *K*(0, 0), *L*(⁺5, ⁻5)
   J'(⁺1, ⁻1), *K'*(0, ⁺5), *L'*(⁺5, 0)

____

9. *F*(⁺5, ⁻5), *G*(⁺8, ⁻6), *H*(⁺6, ⁻3)
   F'(⁻5, ⁻5), *G'*(⁻8, ⁻6), *H'*(⁻6, ⁻3)

____

Use with Lesson 14-6, pages 506–507 in the Student Book.
Then go to Lesson 14-7, pages 508–509 in the Student Book.

Graph Rotations

Name

Date

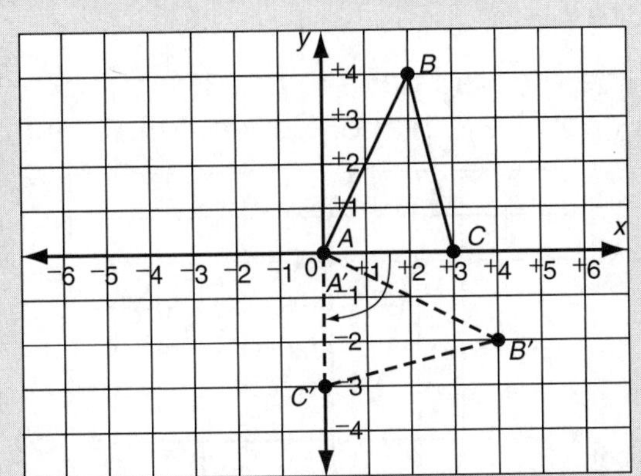

Rotate △ABC 90° clockwise about the origin.

A rotation is a transformation that turns a figure about a point in either a clockwise or in a counterclockwise direction.

- A rotation of 90° is a quarter turn.
- A rotation of 180° is a half turn.
- A rotation of 270° is a three-quarter turn.

△ABC is: A(0, 0), B($^+$2, $^+$4), C($^+$3, 0)

The rotation image △A′B′C′ is: A′(0, 0), B′($^+$4, $^-$2), C′(0, $^-$3).

On a separate sheet of paper, rotate each point counterclockwise about the origin on a coordinate plane. Use prime notation to write the coordinates of its rotation.

1. M($^+$4, $^-$3), 90° _______

2. L($^-$5, $^-$8), 270° _______

3. X($^+$1, $^-$8), 180° _______

4. F(0, $^+$4), 180° _______

5. C($^-$11, $^-$6), 90° _______

6. H($^-$6, 0), 270° _______

Use the given graph for exercises 7–9.

7. Give the coordinates of the vertices of triangle ABC.

____

8. Give the coordinates of the rotation image of triangle ABC.

____

9. Describe the rotation of triangle ABC.

____

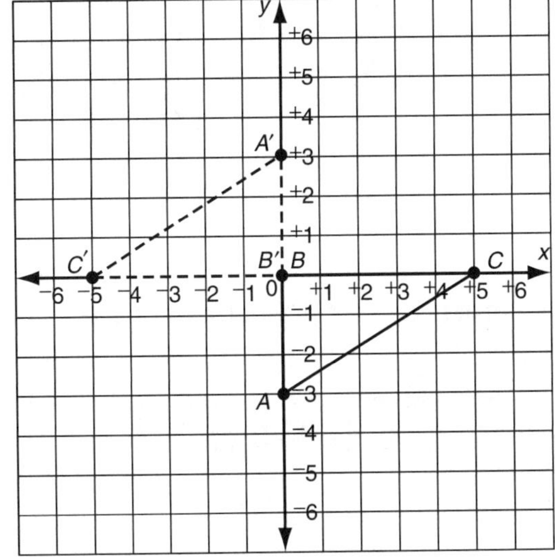

On a separate sheet of paper, graph each figure and its image on the same coordinate plane. Then describe its rotation.

10. S(0, 0), T($^+$1, $^+$4), U($^+$5, $^+$4), V($^+$6, 0)
S′(0, 0), T′($^-$1, $^-$4), U′($^-$5, $^-$4), V′($^-$6, 0)

11. F(0, 0), G($^-$3, $^+$1), H($^-$2, $^+$5)
F′(0, 0), G′($^-$1, $^-$3), H′($^-$5, $^-$2)

_______________   _______________

Use with Lesson 14-7, pages 508–509 in the Student Book.
Then go to Lesson 14-7A, pages 263–264 in this Workbook.

Graph Functions

For a linear function, the graphs of the ordered pairs are points that form a straight line. To graph the function $y = {}^-3x + {}^-2$ on a coordinate plane:

Make a function table.

x	$^-3x + {}^-2$	y
$^-2$	$^-3(^-2) + {}^-2 = {}^+6 + {}^-2 = {}^+4$	$^+4$
$^-1$	$^-3(^-1) + {}^-2 = {}^+3 + {}^-2 = {}^+1$	$^+1$
0	$^-3(0) + {}^-2 = 0 + {}^-2 = {}^-2$	$^-2$
$^+1$	$^-3(^+1) + {}^-2 = {}^-3 + {}^-2 = {}^-5$	$^-5$

Ordered pairs: $(^-2, {}^+4)$, $(^-1, {}^+1)$, $(0, {}^-2)$, $(^+1, {}^-5)$

These ordered pairs are solutions of $y = {}^-3x + {}^-2$ because when you substitute for x and y, you get true statements.

Use the ordered pairs to graph $y = {}^-3x + {}^-2$ on a coordinate plane. Connect the points.

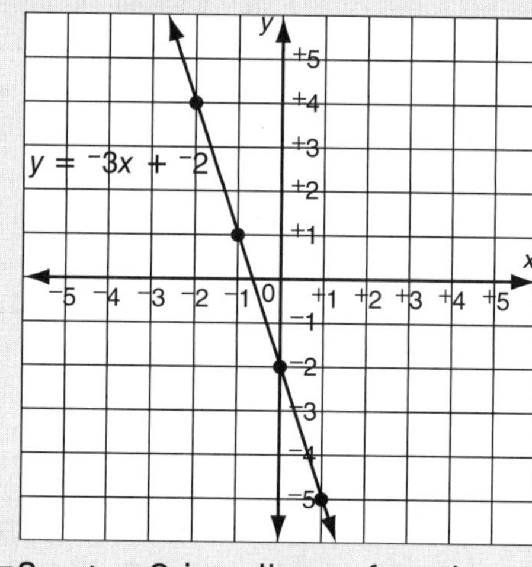

$y = {}^-3x + {}^-2$ is a linear function.

---

1. Complete the function table for $y = {}^-2x + {}^-4$. Then graph the ordered pairs on a coordinate plane. Is the function a linear function? ____

x	$y = {}^-2x + {}^-4$	(x, y)
$^-2$		
$^-1$		
0		

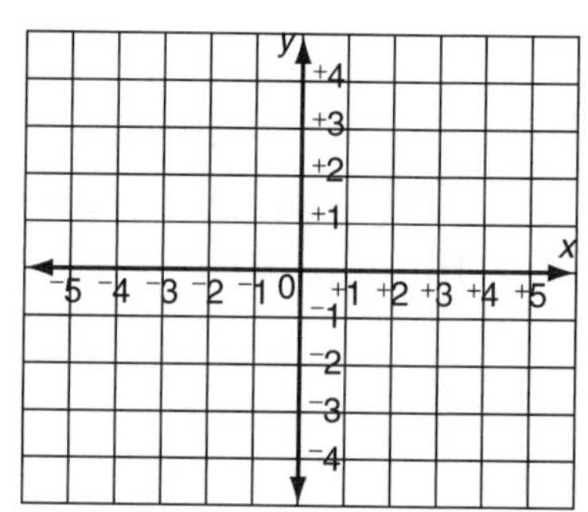

Complete each function table. Then graph each function on a coordinate plane.

2. $y = {}^-2x + {}^-1$

x	$y = {}^-2x + {}^-1$	(x, y)
$^+1$		
0		
$^-1$		
$^-2$		

3. $y = x + {}^-1$

x	$y = x + {}^-1$	(x, y)
$^+1$		
0		
$^-1$		
$^-2$		

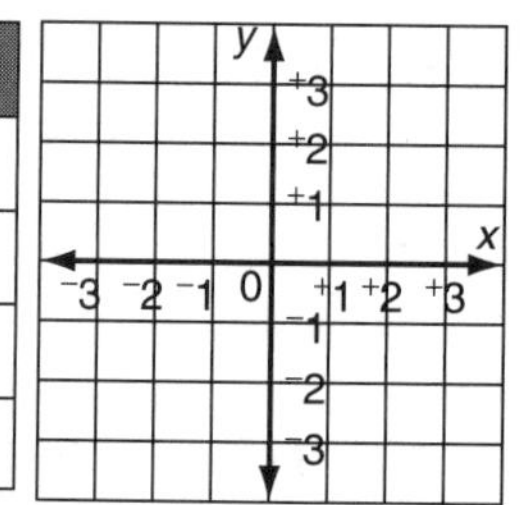

Problem Solving

4. A storm is following a linear path. Twice the horizontal distance (x) plus 2 miles is the vertical distance (y). Write a linear function for the path of the storm.

____

5. A car service charges a basic fee of $5 plus $8 per mile. Use x for the number of miles. Write a linear function for finding the cost of a ride (y).

____

Use with Lesson 14-8, pages 510–511 in the Student Book.
Then go to Lesson 14-8A, pages 265–266 in this Workbook.

Algebraic Patterns

Name _________________________

Date _________________________

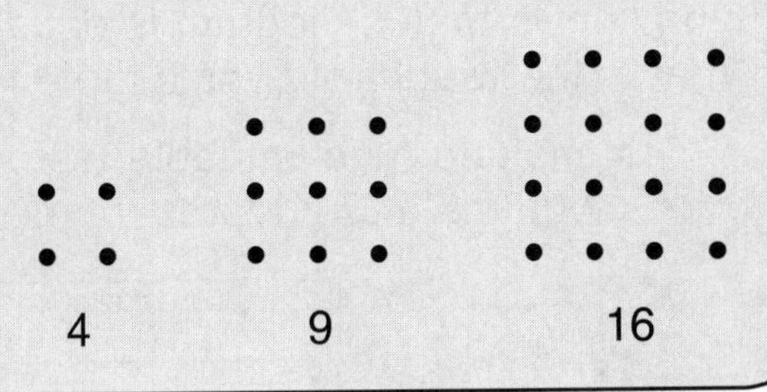

Triangular number sequence	Square number sequence
1 3 6 10	1 4 9 16

Find the next three terms in each sequence.
Describe the pattern.

1. 1, 2, 4, 5, 10, 11, 22, . . .

____

2. 1, 5, 13, 29, 61, 125, . . .

____

3. 1, ⁻3, 9, ⁻27, 81, ⁻243, . . .

____

4. 1, 3, 7, 13, 21, 31, . . .

____

Use the arrangement of dots at the top of the page to complete each table.
Look for a pattern.

5.

Triangular Numbers	
Number	**Number of Dots**
11th	
12th	
13th	
14th	

6.

Square Numbers	
Number	**Number of Dots**
11th	
12th	
13th	
14th	

Problem Solving

7. Julia reads one chapter of her book each day. She read 20 pages on the first day, 21 pages on the second day, 19 pages on the third day, and 20 pages on the fourth day. What conjecture would you make about the length of each chapter in Julia's book?

____

8. Phil started a savings plan with $75. For the past 6 weeks, he has saved $9.50 per week. How much has he saved? If he continues saving at this rate, how much will he have saved in another 10 weeks?

____

Use with Lesson 14-9, pages 512–513 in the Student Book.
Then go to Lesson 14-10, pages 514–515 in the Student Book.

Problem-Solving Strategy: Use More Than One Strategy

Lynn's pet turtle has a mass of no more than 5 kilograms.
Lynn knows that 1 kilogram is equal to about 2.2 pounds.
What is the weight of Lynn's turtle in pounds?

- First make a function table. Let x represent the number of kilograms and y represent the number of pounds.

Kilograms, x	1	2	3	4
Pounds, y	2.2	4.4	6.6	8.8

- Then **write an equation** or **make a graph.**

Each y-value is 2.2 times the corresponding x-value, so use the equation $y = 2.2x$ to solve.

When $x = 5$, $y = 2.2 \cdot 5 = 11$.

Graph the data in the table. Use the graph to find the value of y when $x = 5$.

When $x = 5$, $y = 11$.

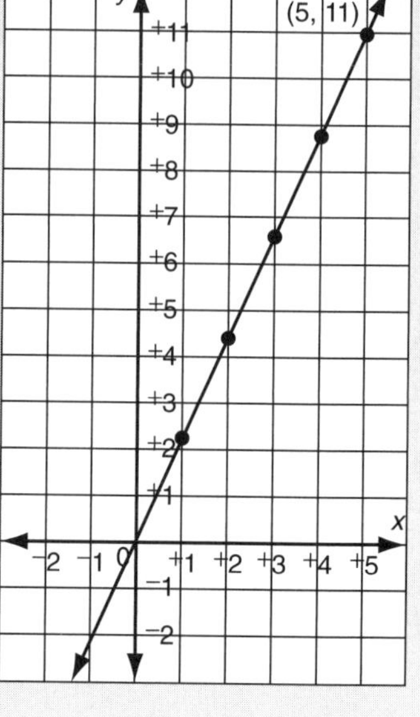

Five kilograms is about 11 pounds.
So Lynn's turtle weighs no more than 11 pounds.

1. Jason needs no less than 175 grams of sesame seeds. He has 4 ounces of sesame seeds already. He knows that 1 oz ≈ 28.35 g. If he buys another 2 ounces will he have enough?

2. Monica has a 15-kg dog. Jerome has a 28-lb dog. How many more pounds does Monica's dog weigh than Jerome's? Use 1 kg ≈ 2.2 lb.

3. The distance from Scott's house to the ski hill is no more than 12 km. Scott knows that 1 mi ≈ 1.61 km. How many miles from the ski hill does Scott live?

4. Haley's water bottle holds no more than 2 liters. How many fluid ounces does it hold? Use 1 L ≈ 33.8 fl oz.

5. Devon has a piece of climbing rope that is no longer than 15 meters. How many feet long is his rope? Use 1 m ≈ 3.28 ft.

6. Hannah completed 7 km in the walkathon. She earned a T-shirt if she walked more than 5 miles. Did Hannah earn the T-shirt? Explain. Use 1 mi ≈ 1.61 km.

Use with Lesson 14-10, pages 514–515 in the Student Book.
Then go to Lesson 14-11, pages 516–517 in the Student Book.

Problem-Solving Applications: Mixed Review

Solve each problem and explain the method you used. If needed, do all your work on a separate sheet of paper.

Read Plan Solve Check

Strategy File

Use These Strategies
Write an Equation
Guess and Test
More Than One Solution
Logical Reasoning
Use More Than One Step
Use More Than One Strategy
Make a Graph

1. Parker is thinking of a 2-digit number. The sum of the digits is 8. The difference between the digits is 4. What are two possibilities for Parker's number?

2. Nora thinks of a whole number. Reggie asks, "Is it greater than 15? Is it an odd number? Is it a multiple of 4? Is it less than 11?" Nora answers "no" to each of his questions. What number is she thinking of?

3. The red group has three times as many students as the green group. The green group has one-quarter the number of students as the blue group. The blue group has 12 students. How many students are in the red group?

4. Gino plotted point F on a coordinate plane at $(^+3, ^+5)$. From F, he went left 1 unit and down 3 units to plot G. From G he went left 6 units to plot H. From H he went right 1 unit and up 3 units to plot I. What are the coordinates of each point? Name the figure, and find the area.

5. The length of one side of a triangle is ℓ. The length of each remaining side is $2\ell + 4$. Write an equation to represent the perimeter of the triangle. Give two different values of ℓ, $2\ell + 4$, and the perimeter.

6. Ed wrote this riddle: "I am a number that is seven times the number of ounces in a pound. What number am I?"

7. Luz wrote this riddle: "I am a number that is 5.5 times the number of cups in a gallon. What number am I?"

8. Bev is twice as old as Lee. Flo is five years less than four times Lee's age. Bev's twin, Zoe, is 12. How old is Flo?

9. Ty inputs 118 words per minute. Lia inputs 59 words more than half of Ty's rate. How fast does Lia input?

Additional CCSS Lessons

Pages 207–266 of this workbook have additional lessons with content
based on the Common Core State Standards (CCSS). Each lesson has
teaching and practice exercises. These lessons can also be found online at
progressinmathematics.com. The bottom of the second page of every lesson
directs you to another workbook page of more practice of the math taught in the
lesson and also to the next *Progress in Mathematics* lesson.

Practice for Additional CCSS Lessons

Pages 268–297 have more practice of the math taught in the additional CCSS
lessons. Doing these practice exercises will help you master the work of each
additional CCSS lesson more quickly. The bottom of every practice page
identifies the lesson that is being reviewed by the workbook exercises, and also
identifies the next *Progress in Mathematics* lesson. Before starting a workbook
page, read the title. If you need to review the work in that lesson, turn to the
page in your workbook where it is taught.

Additional CCSS Lessons

Name ________________________

Objective: To identify parts of expressions using mathematical language

An expression represents a quantity and is made up of one or more **terms** connected by addition or subtraction signs. Numbers or variables with multiplication or division symbols are part of one term.

Expressions can be numerical or algebraic. Numerical expressions include only numbers and operation signs. Algebraic expressions also include variables.

- Numerical expressions: 4.2, $\frac{3}{4} + (7 \times 19)$

- Algebraic expressions: $2d$, a, $8(s - 3)$, $\frac{2y}{5}$, $10 - 4n + \frac{1}{2}y$

▶ To describe parts of an expression, use mathematical language you know. To find the number of terms, first name each term, then count the terms.

The algebraic expression $2d$ represents the product of the factors 2 and d. In the expression $2d$, 2 is the **coefficient** of d.

Expression	Description	First Term	Second Term	Third Term	Number of Terms
4.2	four and two tenths	4.2			1
$\frac{3}{4} + (7 \times 19)$	the sum of $\frac{3}{4}$ and the product of the factors 7 and 19	$\frac{3}{4}$	(7×19)		2
a	the variable a	a			1
$(s - 3)$	the difference of s and 3	s	3		2
$8(s - 3)$	the product of the factors 8 and $(s - 3)$	$8(s - 3)$			1
$\frac{2y}{5}$	the quotient of $2y$ and 5	$\frac{2y}{5}$			1
$10 - 4n + \frac{1}{2}y$	10 minus the product 4 times n, plus the product $\frac{1}{2}$ times y	10	$4n$	$\frac{1}{2}y$	3

Practice

Describe the underlined part of the expression.

1. $7 + \underline{(9 - 2)} \times 8$

2. $\underline{5y} + \frac{b}{7} - 7$

____

____

Name the terms in the expression. Then count the number of terms.

3. $16 \div (8 - 4) + 32$

Terms: _______________________

Number of terms: _______

4. $13z - \frac{2}{3} + 5q$

Terms: _______________________

Number of terms: _______

Discuss and Write

5. Why is $8(s - 3)$ considered a single term when $(s - 3)$ is the difference of two terms?

Name _______________________________

Practice

Describe the underlined part of the expression.

6. $42 \div 3 + 5$

____

7. $25t - 95$

____

8. $2a$

____

9. $\frac{2d}{3} + 19$

____

10. $9y + 27 - 72$

____

11. $\frac{5}{q} + 34x - 68$

____

Name the terms in the expression. Then count the number of terms.

12. $48 \times 6 + 36 \times 8$

Terms: _______________

Number of Terms: _______

13. $75 - (100 \div 4) + 10$

Terms: _______________

Number of Terms: _______

14. $(58 - 22) \div 3 + 5$

Terms: _______________

Number of Terms: _______

15. $3xy$

Terms: _______________

Number of Terms: _______

16. $3 + x + y$

Terms: _______________

Number of Terms: _______

17. $\frac{3}{x} + y$

Terms: _______________

Number of Terms: _______

18. $2q + 3r - 4s + 5t$

Terms: _______________

Number of Terms: _______

19. $(2q + 3r) \div (4s + 5t)$

Terms: _______________

Number of Terms: _______

20. $2q + (3r \div 4s) + 5t$

Terms: _______________

Number of Terms: _______

Problem Solving

Solve. Use a strategy that works best for you. Show your work.

21. A class of 20 students holds a canned food drive. Twelve students each bring in 4 cans. The others bring in 6 cans each. How many cans does the class collect?

____

22. Fifteen soccer players each give $20 for new uniforms. The coach gives $50. The uniforms cost $420. How much more money is needed?

____

23. Devin has $40 in cash. After he spends half his cash, he gets $50 from an ATM. How much cash does he have now?

____

24. Which is greater, the sum or the product of all the ten single-digit whole numbers? Explain your answer.

____

What's the Error?

25. Two numbers have a difference of 8. One of the numbers is 12. Matt says the other number must be 4. Why is he not correct?

C For additional Practice, go to page 268 in this Workbook.
C Then go to Lesson 4-2, pages 124–125 in the Student Book.

Name _______________________________

Objective: To write and evaluate numerical expressions involving exponents

Translate and evaluate the following expression.

the sum of six and four, to the third power, times two

1 Translate the word phrase into a numerical expression using numbers and symbols.

Look carefully for commas and *key words* that tell you to separate terms.

the sum of six and four, to the third power, *times* two

$(6 + 4)^3 \qquad \times \quad 2$

2 Evaluate. Use the Order of Operations.

$(6 + 4)^3 \times 2 = (10)^3 \qquad \times 2$ ← Simplify inside parentheses.

$= (10 \times 10 \times 10) \times 2$ ← Simplify numbers with exponents.

$= 1000 \qquad \times 2$ ← Multiply.

$= 2000$

So, the value of the expression is 2000.

Practice

Translate each word phrase into a numerical expression.
Then evaluate the expression.

1. nine to the second power

_______^{2}

_______ $\times$ _______

____

2. three to the fourth power, plus five

_______^{4} + _______

_______ + _______

____

3. two times six, plus four to the third power

$2 \times 6 +$ _______

$2 \times 6 +$ _______

_______ + _______

____

4. five times two to the third power, plus four times three to the third power

$5 \times$ _______ $+ 4 \times$ _______

$5 \times$ _______ $+ 4 \times$ _______

_______ + _______

____

Discuss and Write

5. Write the expressions $3(4 + 2)^2$ and $3 \times 4 + 2^2$ in words. Do they have different values? Why?

Practice

Translate each word phrase into a numerical expression.
Then evaluate the expression.

6. four times five to the second power

______ × ______^{2}

______ × ______

______

7. two to the fourth power, minus three to the second power

______^{4} − ______^{2}

______ − ______

______

8. two times four squared, minus two to the fifth power

______ × ______ − ______

______ × ______ − ______

______ − ______

______

9. five to the third power, minus the square of the difference of ten and two

______ − ______

______ − ______

______

Evaluate each expression.

10. $5^3 - 10^2 =$ ______

11. $2^5 + 1^8 =$ ______

12. $4 \times 3^2 + (5 - 3)^5 =$ ______

13. $2(3 + 1)^3 - 6^2 =$ ______

14. $6^3 - 2^4 =$ ______

15. $3^4 - (7 \times 3) =$ ______

Problem Solving

Write and evaluate an expression to solve the problem.

16. A club starts with five members. The number of members doubles every month. How many members does the club have after 3 months?

____

17. Jill has 4 baseball cards. Ryan has 3 more cards than Jill. Josh has twice as many cards as Ryan. How many baseball cards do they have altogether?

____

What's the Error?

18. Betty evaluated an expression as shown. Her teacher said that her answer is not correct. What error did Betty make? What is the correct value of the expression?

$6^2 + (9 - 2)^3$

$36 + (9 - 8)$

$36 + 1$

37

For additional Practice, go to page 269 in this Workbook.
Then go to Lesson 4-3, pages 126–127 in the Student Book.

Name _______________________________

Objective: To identify two equivalent algebraic expressions

Maria and James are making a model city. They have 4 kits that each have 1 small block and 1 large block. Each small block weighs 3 ounces. They are not sure what each large block weighs. To find the total weight of the blocks in the 4 kits, they each wrote an expression using x to represent the weight of a large block.

Maria's expression: $4(x + 3)$
James's expression: $4x + 12$

Are the expressions Maria and James wrote equivalent?

▶ To determine if two algebraic expressions are equivalent, substitute the same number for the variable in both expressions. Do this several times with different numbers. If the values of the expressions are always the same, the expressions are equivalent.

Substitute different values for x and evaluate both expressions.

The values of the expressions are the same for each substituted value of x, so $4(x + 3)$ and $4x + 12$ are equivalent expressions.

x	4(x + 3)	4x + 12	Same Value?
8	44	44	yes
5	32	32	yes
$4\frac{1}{2}$	30	30	yes

Practice

Substitute the given numbers for the variable to determine whether the expressions are equivalent.

1. $2(x + 5)$ and $2x + 10$

x	2(x + 5)	2x + 10
2	14	14
3	16	
4		

2. $x + 4$ and $2x$

x	x + 4	2x
4	8	8
5		10
6		

Discuss and Write

3. Explain why it is important to try more than one number for the variable to see if two expressions are equivalent. Use exercise 2 to help.

Name ___________________________

Practice

Evaluate each pair of expressions when $x = 1$ and $x = 3$.
Decide whether the expressions are equivalent.

4. $28 + 4x$ and $4(7 + x)$

5. $2(x + 3)$ and $2x + 3$

Tell whether the expressions are equivalent.

6. $5(x + 2)$ and $5x + 10$

7. $3(x - 4)$ and $3x + 12$

8. $3x$ and $x + 2$

9. $x(7 + 4)$ and $11x$

10. $7(x + 3)$ and $7x + 3$

11. $2(x - 4)$ and $2x - 8$

12. $3x + 2x + 4$ and $4 + 5x$

13. $9(2 + x)$ and $6 + 9x + 12$

Problem Solving

Use the given information to solve the problems. Use the strategy that
works best for you. Show your work.

Bob's Diner

Sandwich $5	Salad $4	Juice $2

14. A group of n friends each buy a sandwich
and juice for lunch. Jordan says the total
cost is $n(5 + 2)$. Ann says the total cost is
$5n + 2n$. Are they both correct? Explain.

15. Seven people each buy a salad and a
cup of soup that costs c dollars for lunch.
The total cost is $7(4 + c)$. Max says this is
equivalent to $4 + 7c$. Is he correct? Explain.

Explain Your Reasoning

16. If you substitute a number into two expressions and get different
values, do you need to try more numbers to check whether the
expressions are equivalent? Explain.

For additional Practice, go to page 270 in this Workbook.
Then go to Lesson 4-3B, pages 213–214 in this Workbook.

Name ___________________

Objective: To simplify first-degree expressions by combining like terms
and applying properties

Algebraic expressions often need to be rewritten or simplified in order to become easier to work with. By combining like terms you can write a compact equivalent expression.

> Terms that have the same variable parts are called **like terms**.

Simplify: $4x + 5y + 2y - 2x$.

▶ To combine like terms, you can use the
properties of operations.

❶ Use the Commutative Property to rewrite the expression so all like terms are next to each other. $4x - 2x + 5y + 2y$

❷ Use the Associative Property to group like terms with parentheses. $(4x - 2x) + (5y + 2y)$

❸ Use the Distributive Property to separate the variable parts of like terms from the number part. $(4 - 2)x + (5 + 2)y$

❹ Simplify the expressions in parentheses. $2x + 7y$

Since $2x$ and $7y$ do not have the same variable,
you cannot simplify the expression any further.
The simplified expression is $2x + 7y$.

So, $4x + 5y + 2y - 2x = 2x + 7y$.

Practice

Write the property that justifies each step in simplifying the expression.

1. $3(x + 4) + 2(2x - 3)$

$3x + 12 + 4x - 6$ _______________

$3x + 4x + 12 - 6$ _______________

$(3x + 4x) + 12 - 6$ _______________

$(3 + 4)x + 12 - 6$ _______________

$7x + 6$ _______________

2. $4x + 5 + x + 2y + 8$

$4x + x + 2y + 5 + 8$ _______________

$(4x + x) + 2y + 5 + 8$ _______________

$(4 + 1)x + 2y + 5 + 8$ _______________

$5x + 2y + 13$ _______________

Discuss and Write

3. Verify $7 + 5x - 3(x + y)$ and $6x + y + 4$ are equivalent.
Explain why or why not.

Practice

Complete each step in simplifying the expression.

4. Expression   Property Used   **5.** Expression   Property Used

$4n + 6m - 2m + 8n$ $x + 4y + 4(x + 4y)$

$4n + 8n + 6m - 2m$ __________   __________   Distributive

__________   Associative $x + 4x + 4y + 16y$ __________

$(4 + 8)n + (6 - 2)m$ __________   __________   __________

__________   __________   __________   __________

Simplify each expression.

6. $14y + 2y + 23x - 3x$ **7.** $4y + 20z + 9y - 3z$ **8.** $4(x + 2) + 3x + 2(x - y)$

Problem Solving

Solve. Use a strategy that works best for you. Show your work.

9. At a deli, all sandwiches cost x dollars. What is the total cost of 3 chicken sandwiches, 6 turkey sandwiches, and 5 roast beef sandwiches?

10. Children and senior citizens pay x dollars for movie tickets. Adults pay y dollars for movie tickets. What is the cost for movie tickets for a group of 8 children, 3 adults, and 2 senior citizens?

11. Each member of a drama club brings x dollars on a trip. Tickets to a play cost $8 per person, and lunch is $5 per person. How much money does each person have left after buying a ticket and lunch?

12. A rectangular garden is x feet wide. It is 3 times as long as it is wide. If someone walks around the garden 2 times, how far do they walk?

What's the Error?

13. Mario writes $5m - 2n + 3n$ as $5m - (2n + 3n)$. He simplifies this as $5m - 5n$. What is his error? What is the correct simplified expression?

For additional Practice, go to page 271 in this Workbook.
Then go to Lesson 4-4, pages 128–129 in the Student Book.

Name ______________________________

Objective: To translate word sentences into inequalities and graph the solution set

Zeke is thinking of a number less than 34.

▶ Zeke could be thinking of many numbers. To represent them, you can use an inequality or a number line diagram.

$x < 34$

| Use an open circle at 34 to show that 34 is not in the solution set. Then draw an arrow to the left to show all the numbers less than 34. |

Abby says that the number of stars in the sky is equal to or greater than 100.

▶ You can also describe this situation with an inequality or a number line diagram.

$s \geq 100$

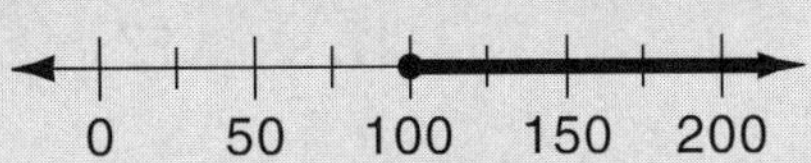

| Use a closed circle at 100 to show that 100 is in the solution set. Then draw an arrow to the right to show all the numbers greater than 100. |

Jake said that the number of stars he saw was 5 less than 129. Does $129 - 5$ make the inequality $s \geq 100$ true?

$$s \geq 100$$
$$129 - 5 \geq 100$$
$$124 \geq 100$$

So, the expression $(129 - 5)$ makes the inequality $s \geq 100$ true.

Practice

Make a number line diagram for the inequality. Then find a number that makes the inequality true.

1. $n \leq 345$

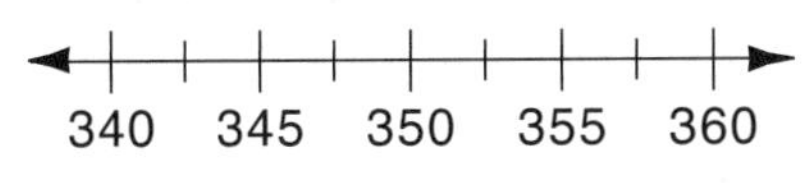

______ makes $n \leq 345$ true

2. $z > 40$

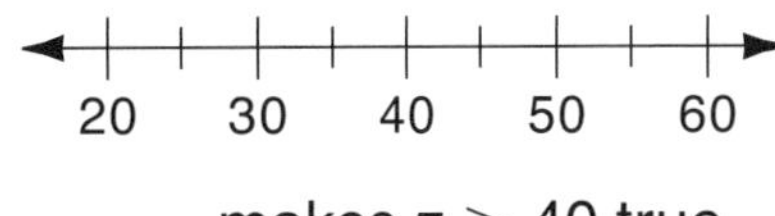

______ makes $z > 40$ true.

3. $m < 170$

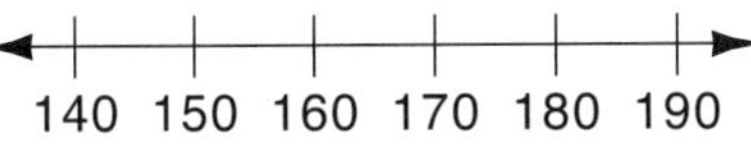

______ makes $m < 170$ true.

4. $x \geq 35$

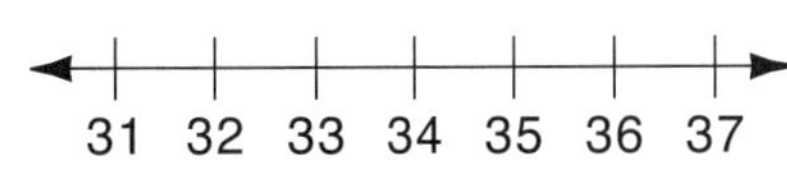

______ makes $x \geq 35$ true.

Discuss and Write

5. Why is $x = 43$ not in the solution set for the inequality $x < 34$?

Practice

Make a number line diagram for the inequality. Then find a number that makes the inequality true.

6. $x \leq 48$

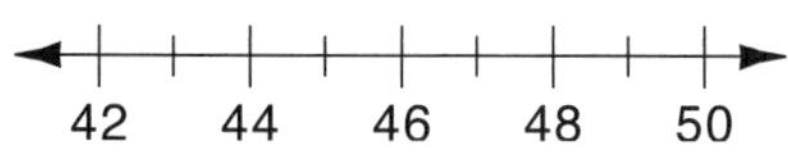

______

7. $n > 52$

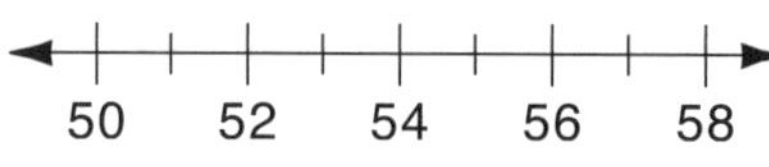

______

8. $s \geq 169$

______

9. $t < 73$

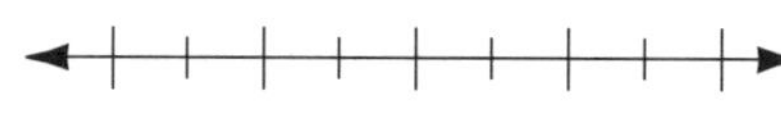

______

10. $p > 25$

______

11. $y \leq 17$

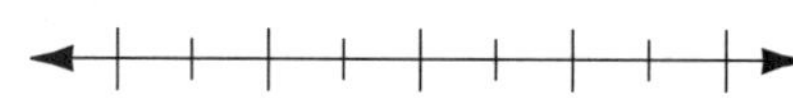

______

Tell whether the number makes the inequality $x \geq 27$ true.

12. 16

______

13. 27

______

14. 32

______

15. 26

______

Problem Solving

Write an inequality to describe the situation. Then answer the question.

16. Ariel exercises for at least forty-five minutes each day. Could she have exercised for fifteen minutes less than an hour on Tuesday?

____

17. Abe's family wants to buy a house less than 10 miles from his school. He currently lives 15 miles away from his school. Will his family consider a house 5 miles closer?

____

Critical Thinking

18. Graph the numbers that are solutions of both $x > 2$ and $x < 6$ on a number line. Describe the solution. Give an example of a number that is a solution to both and an example of a number that is not.

For additional Practice, go to page 272 in this Workbook.
Then go to Lesson 4-4B, pages 217–218 in this Workbook.

Name ______________________

Objective: To write an inequality to represent a constraint or condition in a real-world situation

You can use what you know about inequalities to model real-world situations.

Ms. Lawrence's truck cannot carry more than 1000 pounds safely. What weights can the truck safely carry?

▶ To find the weights that the truck can safely carry, write and graph an inequality.

❶ Let w represent the number of pounds the truck can safely carry. Write the inequality.

$w \leq 1000$

❷ Graph the solution set on the number line.

The truck cannot carry more than 1,000 pounds.

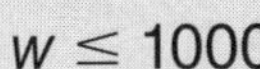

❸ Interpret the graph.

All weights *greater than or equal to* 0 pounds and *less than or equal to* 1000 pounds are part of the solution.

The graph of the inequality includes numbers less than 0, but it does not make sense for a truck to carry less than 0.

So, the truck can safely carry any weight less than or equal to 1000 pounds.

Practice

Graph the inequality. Then explain which part of the solution set makes sense for the given situation.

1. An elevator can safely carry at most 750 pounds. What weights can the elevator safely carry?

$y \leq 750$

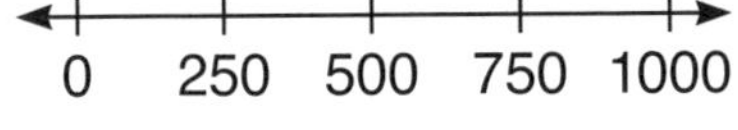

2. A contractor wants to mix more than 100 gallons of paint. What amounts of paint might be mixed?

$x > 100$

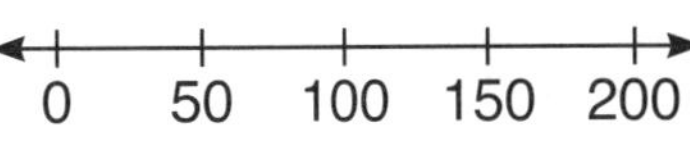

Discuss and Write

3. A van can hold up to 6 passengers. Explain why the graph shows all possible numbers of passengers, even though the inequality to represent the situation is $x \leq 6$.

Practice

Write an inequality. Then graph the inequality on a separate piece of paper. Explain which part of the solution set makes sense for the given situation.

4. The gas tank in Mr. Rock's car can hold 30 gallons. He is filling the tank. How many gallons of gas might he pump into the tank?

____

5. A submarine is 500 feet below the ocean surface and 1000 feet above the ocean floor. From that position, how many feet can the submarine rise?

____

6. Martha is packing toys. Each box can hold 20 toys. How many toys might she have packed into the last box?

____

7. A theater can hold up to 500 people. What are the possible numbers of people that could attend a performance at the theater?

____

Problem Solving

Solve. Use the strategy that works best for you. Justify your answer.

8. Andy has 5 boxes. Each box can hold no more than 12 light bulbs. What might be the total number of light bulbs that are in 3 boxes?

____

9. Each shelf can hold 15 snow globes. How many snow globes might be displayed on 5 shelves?

____

10. Marty's toy car can travel up to 88 meters per hour. Jenny's toy car can travel up to 76 meters per hour. If both cars are traveling side-by-side, how fast are they going?

____

11. A restaurant can hold 75 people. Wilma hosts a party for her grandmother at the restaurant. How many guests can she invite?

____

Critical Thinking

12. A bus runs every quarter hour. Andrew says the time he has to wait is represented by the inequality $t < 15$. What does t stand for? Is Andrew's inequality always true? Explain.

C For additional Practice, go to page 273 in this Workbook.
C Then go to Lesson 4-5, pages 130–131 in the Student Book.

Objective: To solve problems by writing and solving equations

▶ To solve some problems, you can write an equation. To solve equations, you can use properties of operations.

Use the Subtraction Property of Equality

One day, Tim rode 32 miles on his bike. He rode 8 miles before noon. How many miles did he ride after noon?

- Let d represent the number of miles Tim rode after noon.

- Write the equation.

  | total miles | = | miles before noon | + | miles after noon |

- Solve.

  $$32 = 8 + d$$

  $$32 - 8 = 8 + d - 8 \leftarrow$$

  $$24 = d$$

  Subtract 8 from both sides.

So, Tim rode 24 miles after noon.

Use the Division Property of Equality

One day, Tim rode 32 miles on his bike. His average speed was 8 miles per hour. How many hours did he ride?

- Let t represent the number of hours Tim biked.

- Write the equation.

  distance = speed × time

- Solve.

  $$32 = 8 \times t$$

  $$32 \div 8 = 8 \times t \div 8 \leftarrow$$

  $$4 = t$$

  Divide both sides by 8.

So, Tim rode for 4 hours.

Practice

Solve by writing an equation.

1. Becky and Andrew both collect baseball cards. Andrew has 250 cards. He has 12 more cards than Becky. How many baseball cards does Becky have?

   Andrew's = Becky's + 12

   _______ = b + _______

   _______ = b

2. Dana's bookcase has 6 shelves. Each shelf has the same number of books. There are a total of 126 books in the bookcase. How many books are on each shelf?

   total = shelves × books per shelf

   _______ = _______ × b

   _______ = b

Discuss and Write

3. Look back at the problems about Tim. Which words in each problem helped you decide the equation to write? Why?

Practice

Solve by writing an equation.

4. Michael is bagging walnuts for a food sale. He puts 64 walnuts in a bag. How many walnuts will he put in 6 bags?

total walnuts = bags × number in a bag

______ = ______ × ______

______ = ______

5. There are 395 students in sixth grade at Ali's school. That is 33 more students than are in seventh grade. How many seventh graders are there at Ali's school?

sixth graders = seventh graders + ______

______ = ______ + ______

______ = ______

Problem Solving

Solve. Use a strategy that works best for you. Show your work.

6. Billy's school is running a canned food drive. They collected 480 cans in the morning. They collected 70 more cans in the afternoon than in the morning. How many cans did Billy's school collect in all?

7. Roger bought 40 special forever stamps. They cost more than $20. He gave 8 stamps to his sister and 9 to his brother. How many forever stamps does he have now?

8. Martha uses 4 cups of flour to make a loaf of bread. She used 128 cups of flour in April. How many loaves of bread did she make?

9. The 25 students in Ms. Johnson's class each read an average of 60 hours each month. The 30 students in Mr. Ryan's class each read an average of 50 hours each month. Which class reads more? How much more?

What's the Error?

10. Lucy needs to know how many yards of tape are in a 45-ft roll of tape. She knows that 3 ft = 1 yard, so she lets y represent the number of yards. She writes and solves this equation.

$$y = 3 \times 45$$

$$y = 135 \text{ yards}$$

Find and correct Lucy's error.

For additional Practice, go to page 274 in this Workbook. Then go to Lesson 4-8, pages 136–137 in the Student Book.

Name _______________________

Objective: To graph and use integers and explain the meaning of 0 in real-world situations

▶ Quantities used in real-world situations can be described using integers, both positive and negative. All integers on a number line show the distance they are from zero.

Temperature and bank balances are examples of quantities that can be represented using both positive and negative values.

- A temperature of 5°C is warmer than 0°C. A temperature of −5°C is colder than 0°C. Both 5°C and −5°C are the same distance from 0°C.

- A bank balance of $200 is greater than $0. A bank balance of −$200 is less than $0. Both $200 and −$200 have the same absolute value, but −$200 shows how much someone owes, while $200 shows how much someone has.

▶ You can use number lines to represent situations involving integers.

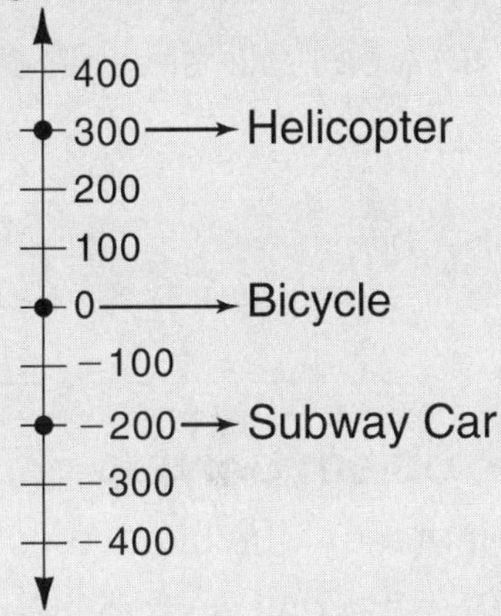

❶ A bicycle travels at ground level. The bicycle is neither above nor below the ground. It is at 0 feet. The point at 0 represents the bicycle.

❷ A helicopter flies three hundred feet above the ground. The helicopter is 300 feet above 0. The point at 300 represents the helicopter.

❸ A subway car travels two hundred feet underground. The subway car is 200 feet below 0. The point at −200 represents the subway car.

Practice

Plot the point that represents the situation. Then explain what 0 represents in the situation.

1. A football team loses 3 yards on a play.

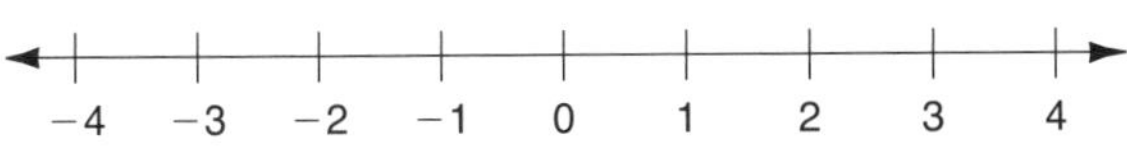

2. Marcy owes her sister $15.

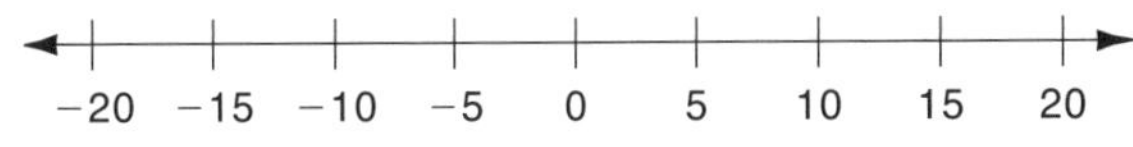

Discuss and Write

3. A scuba diver is swimming 20 feet below sea level. A mountain climber is on a cliff 20 feet above sea level. Explain how opposites can be used to describe their positions.

Practice

Plot the point that represents the situation. Then explain what 0 represents in the situation.

4. An elevator goes up five floors.

____

5. Sarah has $40 in her bank account.

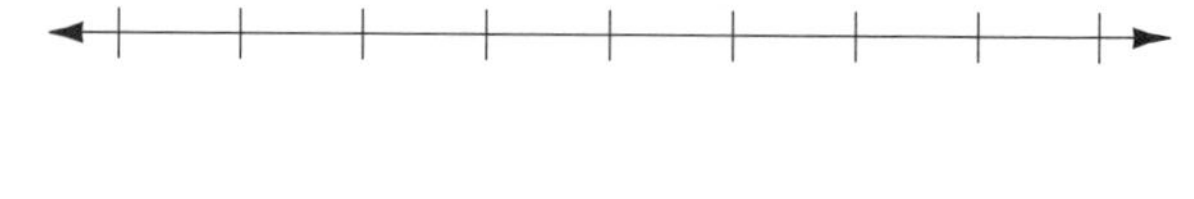

____

6. A diver is thirty-five feet below sea level.

____

7. Water freezes at 0°C. The temperature is eight degrees below the freezing point of water.

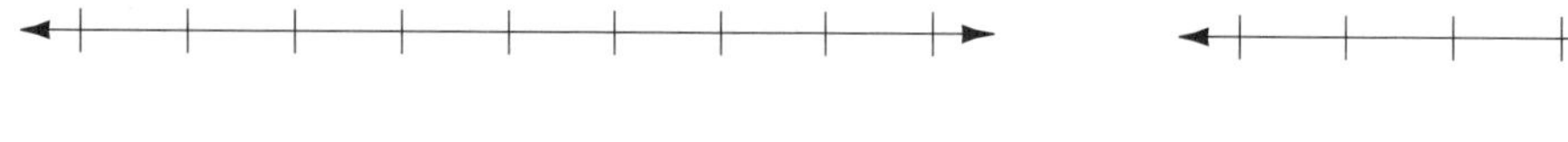

____

8. A ball rolls seven feet.

____

9. An airplane flies 1000 feet above the ground.

____

Problem Solving

Represent the situation on the number line. Then explain why the second statement is false.

10. One day, a shop spent $100 more on supplies than it earned. The shop made a profit of one hundred dollars that day.

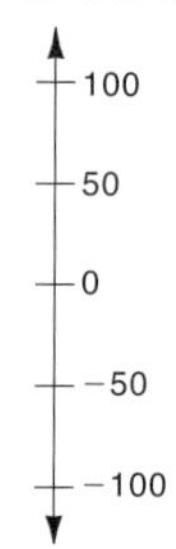

____

11. A football team lost 3 yards on a play. It advanced forward 3 yards on that play.

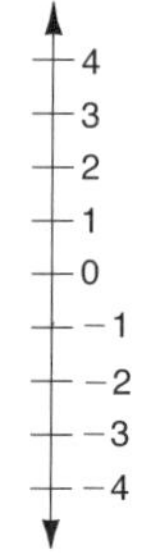

Critical Thinking

12. What is the opposite of the opposite of a number?
Give 3 examples to support your explanation.

C For additional Practice, go to page 275 in this Workbook.
C Then go to Lesson 5-2, pages 152–153 in the Student Book.

Name _______________________________

Objective: To compare rational numbers and their absolute values in context

When you compare numbers in real-world situations, you must decide whether to use their actual values or their absolute values. Absolute values represent the **magnitude**, or size, of numbers.

Bruce and Jean are at the foot of a cliff.
Jean explores a cave to a level of 85 feet below ground.
Bruce climbs to the top of the cliff at a level of 78 feet above ground.

▶ You can use integers to describe Bruce's and Jean's changes in level.

Jean went down 85 feet, so -85 describes her change.
Bruce went up 78 feet, so $+78$ describes his change.

To answer the following questions think about the meaning of the integers.

Who went to a greater level?
Compare the integers.

$$-85 < 78$$

Think
The value of -85 is less than the value of 78.

Bruce went to a greater level.

Who made a greater change in level?
Compare the absolute values.

$$|-85| > |78|$$

Think
The magnitude of -85 is greater than the magnitude of 78.

Jean made a greater change.

Practice

Write an inequality to represent the situation. Explain your reasoning.

1. A 15-yard penalty covers more distance than a 5-yard gain.

2. 3°F below 0 is colder than 5°F.

Discuss and Write

3. The absolute value of a number tells its magnitude, or size. Explain why the magnitudes of -3 and 3 are the same.

Name _______________________

Practice

Write an inequality to represent the situation.

4. A diver 20 feet underwater is closer to the surface than a glider 50 feet above the water.

____

5. A balance of −$15 is greater than a balance of −$40.

____

6. A temperature of −6°F is colder than a temperature of −1°F.

____

7. A person who gains 4 pounds is more pounds from his original weight than a person who loses 2 pounds.

____

8. The magnitude of a $100 charge is greater than a $50 credit.

____

9. The magnitude of a 5-yard gain and a 5-yard loss are the same.

____

Complete the statement by writing *more* or *less*.

10. Alan's credit card balance is less than −$156. Alan owes the credit card company _______ than $156.

11. The balloonist soared to a height greater than +156 feet. The balloon went _______ than 156 feet.

12. The temperature last night was below 68° F. The temperature was _______ than 68° F.

13. A diver went down to below −50 feet. She went _______ than 50 feet down.

Problem Solving

Describe a situation that the inequality could represent.

14. $|-10| < |-25|$

____

15. $|-20| = 20$

____

16. $-3 < -2$

____

17. $5 > -7$

____

Explain Your Reasoning

18. Melanie's account balance is less than −$50. Does she owe more or less than $50? Explain.

For additional Practice, go to page 276 in this Workbook. Then go to Lesson 5-3, pages 154–155 in the Student Book.

Name _______________________________________

Objective: To use the Distributive Property to rewrite addition expressions as multiplication expressions

Sometimes it can be helpful to rewrite an addition expression as a multiplication expression.

Rewrite $(36 + 16)$ as a multiple of a sum of two whole numbers with no common factor.

> **Distributive Property:** Multiplying a sum by a number is the same as multiplying each addend by that number and adding the products.
>
> Example: $2 \times (3 + 5) = (2 \times 3) + (2 \times 5)$

▶ You can use the Distributive Property to rewrite an expression as a product, if the expression has addends with a common factor.

  ❶ List all the factors of each number. Find the common factors and then choose the Greatest Common Factor (GCF) of the two addends.

    Factors of 36: **1, 2,** 3, **4,** 6, 9, 12, 18, 36
    Factors of 16: **1, 2, 4,** 8, 16
    Common factors: 1, 2, 4
    GCF: 4

  ❷ Write each addend as a multiple of the GCF.

    $36 = 4 \times 9$ $16 = 4 \times 4$

  ❸ Use the Distributive Property to rewrite the expression $(36 + 16)$.

    36   +   16
    ↓   ↓
    $(4 \times 9) + (4 \times 4)$
    $4 \times (9 + 4)$

So, $(36 + 16) = 4 \times (9 + 4)$.

Practice

Rewrite as a multiple of a sum of two whole numbers with no common factor.

1. $32 + 12$

    $4 \times ($ _____ $+$ _____ $)$

2. $48 + 6$

    $6 \times ($ _____ $+$ _____ $)$

3. $18 + 27$

    $9 \times ($ _____ $+$ _____ $)$

Discuss and Write

4. Julia and Ryan are measuring two rooms that are 15 feet wide. One room is 12 feet long and the other is 10 feet long. They need to find the total area. Julia finds the areas of both rooms and then adds them together. Ryan multiplies the width by the sum of the lengths of the rooms. Both are correct. Why?

The Distributive Property and Common Factors
Chapter 6, Lesson 5A

Practice

Rewrite as a multiple of a sum of two whole numbers with no common factor.

5. 15 + 35

6. 21 + 56

7. 18 + 66

_____ × (_____ + _____)   _____ × (_____ + _____)   _____ × (_____ + _____)

8. 12 + 27

9. 28 + 52

10. 14 + 40

11. 38 + 12

12. 55 + 10

13. 28 + 24

Rewrite each product as the sum of two numbers.

14. $3 \times (5 + 8)$

15. $7 \times (7 + 4)$

16. $6 \times (5 + 6)$

Problem Solving

Solve. Use a strategy that works best for you. Show your work.

17. Al has a bag of 18 snacks and a bag of 24 snacks. What is the greatest number of people who can share both kinds of snacks equally without any left over?

18. Denise wants to rewrite 37 + 39 as 3 times a sum of two whole numbers. Can she do this? Explain why or why not.

19. Rose rewrites a sum of two numbers as $3 \times (11 + 9)$. What sum did she start with? How do you know?

20. To find $(8 \times 28) + (8 \times 72)$, Edward rewrites the expression as 8×100. Does this makes sense? Explain why or why not.

Test Preparation

21. Ralph uses the Distributive Property to simplify an addition expression.

    a. The simplified expression is $17 \times (2 + 8)$. What is the addition expression?

    b. Why is the simplified expression easier to evaluate?

For additional Practice, go to page 277 in this Workbook.
Then go to Lesson 6-6, pages 188–189 in the Student Book.

Name ____

Objective: To solve problems involving division with fractions

Ms. Baker uses $\frac{3}{16}$ cup of honey to make one batch of muffins. She has $\frac{3}{4}$ cup of honey. How many batches of muffins can she make?

▶ To find the number of batches, divide $\frac{3}{4} \div \frac{3}{16}$.

You can use fraction models or the relationship between multiplication and division to divide.

Think
Multiplication and division are inverse operations.
If $a \times b = c$, then $c \div b = a$.
If $c \div b = a$, then $a \times b = c$.

Use a visual fraction model.

❶ Model $\frac{3}{4}$.

❷ Divide the same whole into sixteenths.

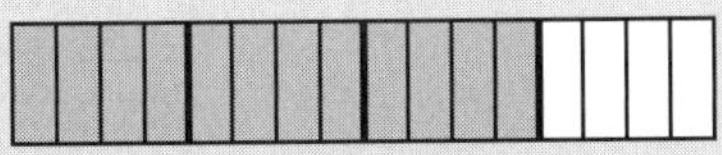

❸ Find how many $\frac{3}{16}$ are in $\frac{3}{4}$.

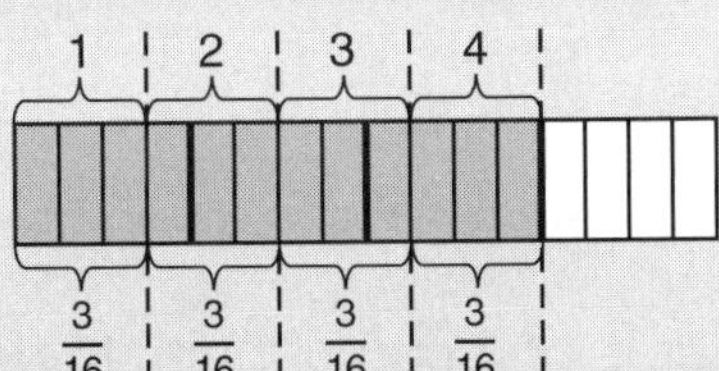

Ms. Baker can make 4 batches of muffins.

Use the relationship between multiplication and division.

❶ Rewrite $\frac{3}{4} \div \frac{3}{16} = n$ as a multiplication equation.

$$\frac{3}{4} = \frac{3}{16} \times n$$

❷ Use the Multiplication Property of Equality to multiply both fractions by 16.

$$16 \times \frac{3}{4} = 16 \times \frac{3}{16} \times n$$
$$12 = 3 \times n$$

❸ Use the Division Property of Equality to divide both sides by 3 to isolate n.

$$12 \div 3 = 3 \times n \div 3$$
$$4 = n$$

So, the number of $\frac{3}{16}$ in $\frac{3}{4}$ is 4.

Practice

Solve for n.

1. $\frac{2}{3} \div \frac{2}{6} = n$

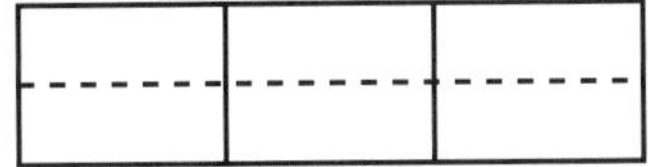

__________ = n

2. $\frac{2}{3} \div \frac{8}{9} = n$

Hint: $\frac{2}{3} = \frac{8}{9} \times n$

__________ = n

Discuss and Write

3. Why can you use multiplication to divide fractions?

Practice

Divide. Use fraction models.

4. $\frac{2}{3} \div \frac{1}{9}$

5. $\frac{2}{5} \div \frac{2}{10}$

6. $\frac{3}{4} \div \frac{3}{20}$

____

____

____

Solve for x.

7. $\frac{2}{7} \div \frac{2}{21} = x$

8. $\frac{5}{8} \div \frac{2}{16} = x$

9. $\frac{5}{6} \div \frac{3}{18} = x$

10. $\frac{6}{18} \div \frac{1}{9} = x$

_______ $= x$

_______ $= x$

_______ $= x$

_______ $= x$

11. $\frac{5}{8} \div \frac{1}{2} = x$

12. $\frac{2}{3} \div \frac{4}{5} = x$

13. $\frac{3}{18} \div \frac{9}{12} = x$

14. $\frac{4}{7} \div \frac{3}{28} = x$

_______ $= x$

_______ $= x$

_______ $= x$

_______ $= x$

15. $x = \frac{5}{4} \div \frac{2}{3}$

16. $x = \frac{5}{6} \div \frac{2}{3}$

17. $x = \frac{7}{8} \div \frac{3}{4}$

18. $x = \frac{14}{15} \div \frac{2}{5}$

$x =$ _______

$x =$ _______

$x =$ _______

$x =$ _______

Problem Solving

Solve. Use a strategy that works best for you. Show your work.

19. Murray is running at a constant rate of $\frac{2}{15}$ mile per minute. How long does it take him to run $\frac{1}{10}$ mile?

20. Anna uses $\frac{1}{9}$ of a can of paint to decorate one robot. If she has $\frac{2}{3}$ of a can of paint, how many robots can she decorate?

____

____

Test Preparation

21. When you multiply $\frac{2}{3} \times \frac{3}{4}$, the product is $\frac{1}{2}$.

   a. Write two related division equations for this multiplication.

   b. Write a problem for one of the two division equations you wrote in part a.

For additional Practice, go to page 278 in this Workbook.
Then go to Lesson 8-6, pages 260–261 in the Student Book.

Name _______________________

Objective: To understand numerical data displayed in a graph or table

Graphs and tables can tell you more than just the numerical values of data. You can count the data points to find the number of observations. You may learn what is being observed and how it was measured.

The bar graphs show the results of an experiment to find whether music helps plants grow taller.

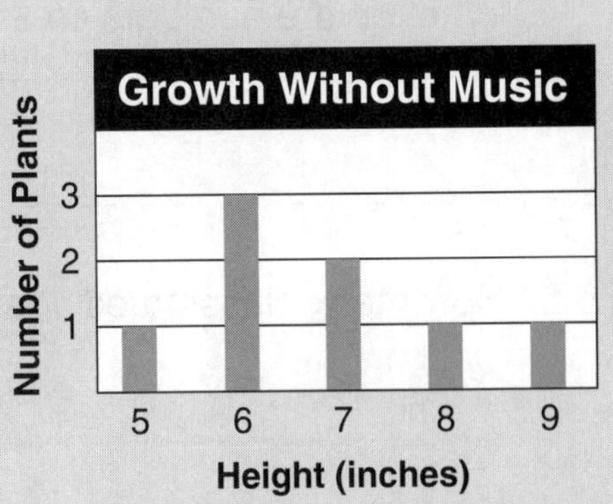

▶ What do you notice about the data?

- The bars show 8 plants grown without music and 8 plants grown with music.

- The data show that the heights of the plants were measured in inches.

- More of the plants grown with music reached 7 inches and 8 inches than for those grown without music.

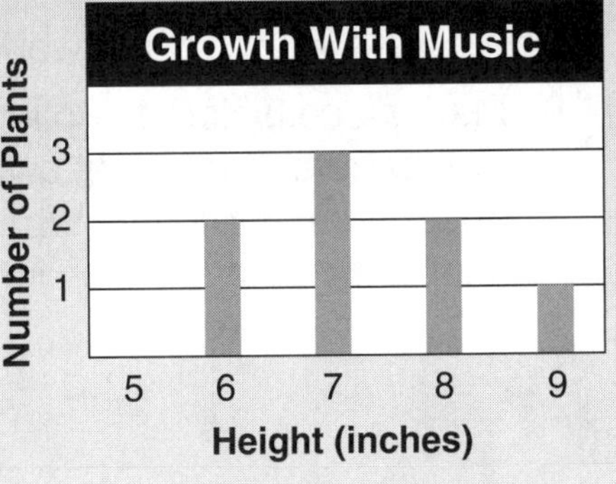

▶ What can you tell from the data?

- 16 plants were measured for the experiment.

- The measurements were probably made using a ruler.

- It seems that music may help plants grow taller.

Practice

Jeremy counts the number of birds he sees at his bird feeder each day. He records these results. Use the data to answer the questions.

Monday	Tuesday	Wednesday	Thursday	Friday	Saturday	Sunday
5	2	4	8	3	5	4

1. For how many days does Jeremy count birds? How do you know?

2. How many birds does Jeremy see during the week? How do you know?

Discuss and Write

3. Look at Jeremy's table. What other information might help you interpret the data?

Practice

Jodi surveys her classmates about their favorite type of music. Use the graph to answer the questions.

4. What do the numbers on the vertical axis show?

____

5. How many classmates does Jodi survey?

____

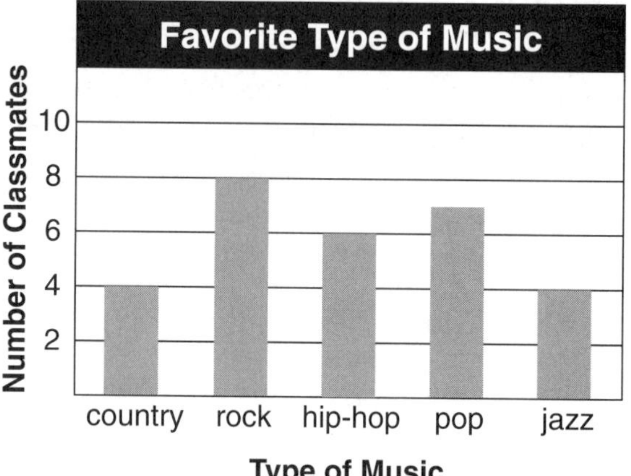

Problem Solving

Solve. Use a strategy that works best for you. Show your work.

6. Marissa collected the following data about the amount of food pet owners give their dogs at each feeding. What important information did Marissa forget to include in the data table?

____

Amount of Food				
0.5	1.25	2	0.75	1.5
2.75	3.5	1	3.25	2.25
2	2.25	1.75	2.5	1

7. The bar graph shows the heights of the players on the school's basketball team. How much taller is the tallest player than the shortest player?

____

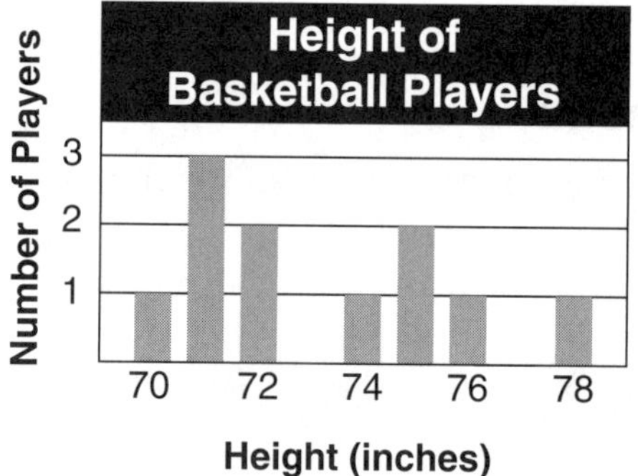

8. The pictograph shows the results of a survey about the number of brothers and sisters some students at the school have. Are more students in a family with 1 child or 2 children? Explain.

Number of Brothers and Sisters	
0	☺ ☺
1	☺ ☺ ☺ ☺
2	☺ ☺ ☺
3	☺

Key: Each ☺ = 5 students.

Explain Your Reasoning

9. Jacob says the pictograph above proves that most people in the world have at least 1 brother or sister. Do you agree? Why or why not?

For additional Practice, go to page 279 in this Workbook.
Then go to Lesson 9-4, pages 298–299 in the Student Book.

Name _______________

Objective: To identify and answer statistical questions

You can get a better understanding of statistical information that is visually displayed by answering **statistical questions**. Statistical questions are those that require investigation, analysis, comparison, or contrast of more than one data point.

Minutes on the Phone		
Day	**Jo**	**Dan**
Monday	40	50
Tuesday	60	0
Wednesday	5	45
Thursday	35	50
Friday	30	60
Saturday	40	55
Sunday	20	20

▶ Tell whether the questions are *statistical* or *not statistical* and why.

- How much time did Dan spend on the phone on Thursday?

  This is not a statistical question. Why? Only one piece of data is needed to answer it. Dan spent 50 minutes on the phone on Thursday.

- Who typically spent more time on the phone each day?

  This is a statistical question. Why? The times vary for each day. To answer it, you need to analyze and compare all the data at once. Here are two methods.

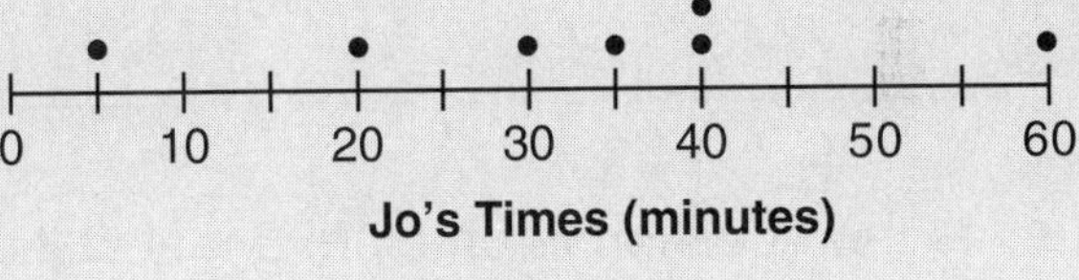

  Method 1 – Make and compare dot plots. These dot plots show the time Jo and Dan spent on the phone.

  Method 2 – Find and compare the means of both sets of data.

  Jo's mean = 32.9   Dan's mean = 40.0

So, both methods show that Dan typically spent more time on the phone each day.

Practice

Tell whether the question is *statistical* or *not statistical* and why.

1. How many email messages did you receive yesterday?

2. How long was a typical email message you received yesterday?

Discuss and Write

3. Consider these two questions:
   a. How far is it from your home to your school?
   b. How long does it take you to get to school in the morning?
   Which one is a statistical question? Which one is not statistical?
   Explain your reasoning.

Name ________________

Practice

Tell whether the question is *statistical* or *not statistical* and why.

4. Which brand of battery lasts longer?

____

5. How many classrooms are in your school?

____

6. How many siblings do students in your class have on average?

____

7. Did a class get better at doing sit-ups after a week of practice?

____

Problem Solving

Solve. Use a strategy that works best for you. Show your work.

Haley makes a table of the number of miles she jogs each day. Then she makes a dot plot of the data.

8. How many miles did Haley jog on Day 11?

____

9. Is the question in problem 8 a statistical question? How do you know?

____

10. How many miles does Haley jog on an average day? Justify your answer.

____

11. Is the question in problem 10 a statistical question? How do you know?

____

Miles Haley Jogs

Day	Miles	Day	Miles
1	3	9	3
2	10	10	2
3	3	11	7
4	6	12	6
5	4	13	1
6	8	14	1
7	3	15	0
8	5	16	2

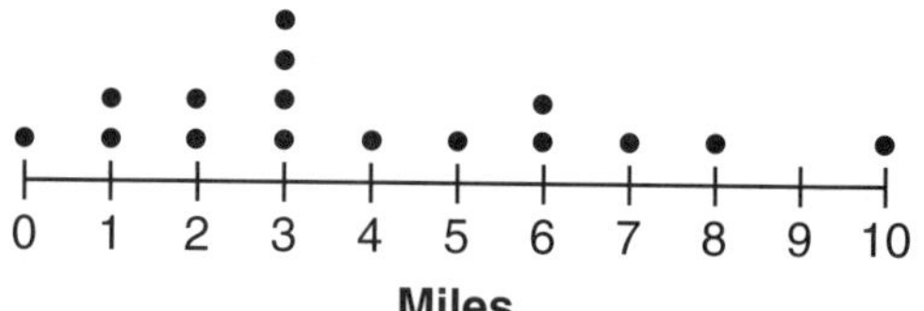

12. What is the greatest number of miles that Haley jogged in any single day? On which day did she jog that number of miles?

____

13. On how many days did Haley jog farther than the mean number of miles?

Critical Thinking

14. Noah says the question asked in problem 12 is *not statistical* because the answer is a single value from one day. Do you agree? Why or why not?

For additional Practice, go to page 280 in this Workbook.
Then go to Lesson 9-6B, pages 233–234 in this Workbook.

Name ______________________________

Objective: To choose the best measures of central tendency and spread to describe a set of data

Li collected data about salaries of 10 employees. She will use statistical measures to describe the distribution. The **measures of center** are the mean, median, and mode. The **measures of variability** are the **range, interquartile range,** and **mean absolute deviation.**

What are the measures of center and variability of the data?

Li knew how to find the measures of center and the range.
Mean: $36,500; Median: $29,000; Mode: $29,000; Range: $80,000

▶ The Interquartile Range (IQR) is the difference between the upper quartile and the lower quartile. It shows how close the middle half of the data is to the median.

❶ To find the IQR, start with the median, $29,000.

❷ Find the lower quartile, which is the median of the values in the lower half of the data. The lower quartile is $22,000.

❸ Find the upper quartile, which is the median of the values in the upper half of the data. The upper quartile is $43,000.

❹ Use the formula IQR = Upper Quartile − Lower Quartile.
$43,000 − $22,000 = $21,000

So, the IQR is $21,000.

Salaries of 10 Employees
$18,000
$20,000
$22,000
$23,000
$29,000
$29,000
$35,000
$43,000
$48,000
$98,000

▶ The **M**ean **A**bsolute **D**eviation (MAD) shows how much the values in the data set vary from the mean.

❶ To find the MAD, start with the mean, $36,500.

❷ Find how far each value is from the mean. This is the deviation of each value from the mean.

❸ Find the sum of the deviations. The sum of the deviations is $159,000.

❹ Divide the sum by the number of values.
$159,000 ÷ 10 = $15,900

So, the MAD is $15,900.

Value	Deviation from Mean
$18,000	$18,500
$20,000	$16,500
$22,000	$14,500
$23,000	$13,500
$29,000	$7,500
$29,000	$7,500
$35,000	$1,500
$43,000	$6,500
$48,000	$11,500
$98,000	$61,500
	Sum: $159,000

Discuss and Write

1. Look back at the teaching display. What might explain why the mean is greater than the median of the data set?

Practice

Find the statistical measures for the data set. Tell which measure(s) best describe the data.

2. 7 9 10 10 11 13 13 13 14 20

Mean: _____   Median: _____   Mode: _____

Range: _____   IQR: _____   MAD: _____

____

3. 27 28 29 29 29 29 30 38 42 49

Mean: _____   Median: _____   Mode: _____

Range: _____   IQR: _____   MAD: _____

____

4. 23 31 36 42 47 55 58 58 59 61

Mean: _____   Median: _____   Mode: _____

Range: _____   IQR: _____   MAD: _____

____

5. 18 41 41 41 43 43 43 43 43 44

Mean: _____   Median: _____   Mode: _____

Range: _____   IQR: _____   MAD: _____

____

6. 33 72 72 72 73 75 80 83 91 99

Mean: _____   Median: _____   Mode: _____

Range: _____   IQR: _____   MAD: _____

____

7. 87 100 104 106 107 109 110 111 111 125

Mean: _____   Median: _____   Mode: _____

Range: _____   IQR: _____   MAD: _____

____

Problem Solving

Use the data sets to answer the questions.

Shop A	5	5	7	4	6	7	8	5	8	5
Shop B	5	7	8	6	6	14	5	8	4	7

8. Two flower shops recorded the number of bouquets of roses sold over 10 days. Which shop stayed closest to the mean number of bouquets sold? Explain which measure you used to answer the question.

9. After the eleventh day's sales, both flower shops have the same mean number of bouquets sold. Shop B sold 7 bouquets that day. How many did Shop A sell?

Explain Your Reasoning

10. Why is it important to look at measures of center and variability of the data when you need to describe a data set?

For additional Practice, go to page 281 in this Workbook.
Then go to Lesson 9-7, pages 304–305 in the Student Book.

Name _______________________________

Objective: To choose the best measures of central tendency and spread to describe a set of data

Walter wants to find out how long it typically takes him to get to school. He keeps track for 10 days. On some days, he walks. On others, he gets driven.

▶ Measures of center and variability can help Walter find and describe the typical time it takes him to get to school. Graphs showing the distribution can add a visual to help him decide which measure best describes the data.

Here are three sets of data Walter might have collected. Each data set is shown in a dot plot and in a box-and-whisker plot.

I.

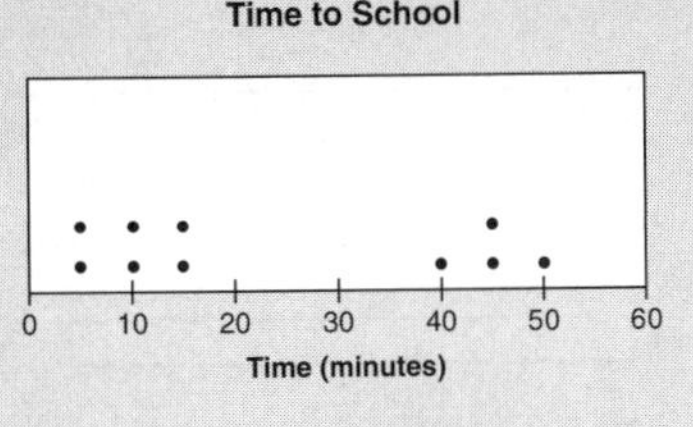

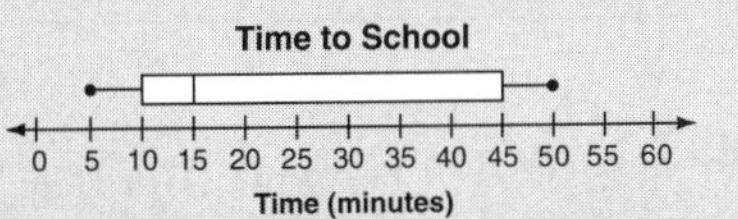

II.

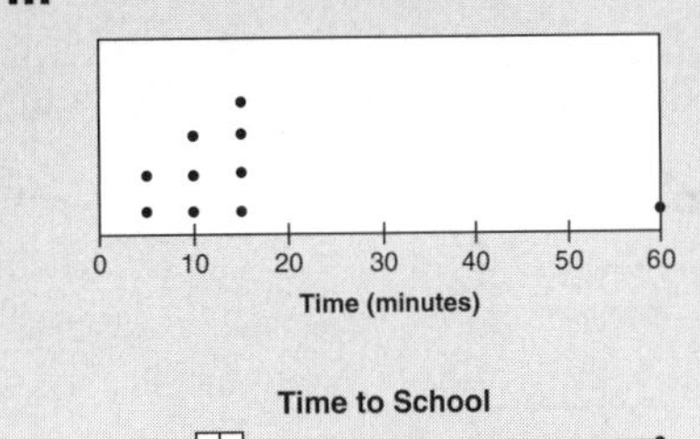

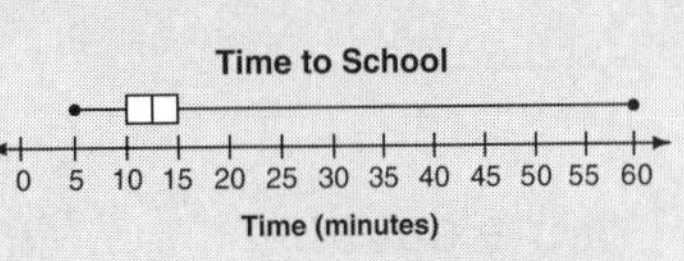

III.

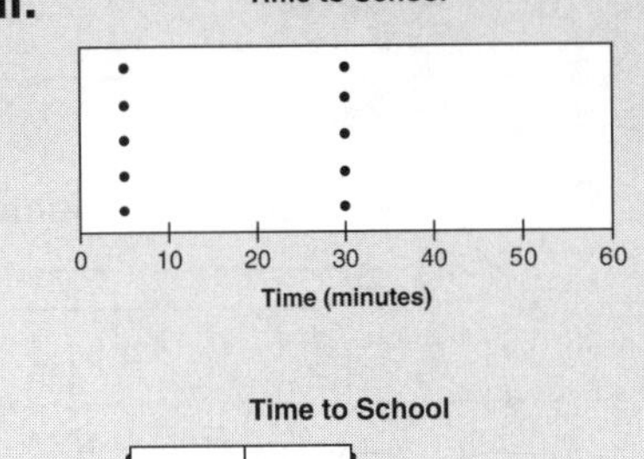

Either the mean or median can be used to describe data that are evenly spread. In this case, the mean, 24, is a *better measure* of the typical time than the median, 15.

The range of the times is 45. The interquartile range (IQR) is 35. The mean absolute deviation (MAD) is 16.8.

Use the median to describe data when there are outliers. The one long time has *less effect* on the median, 12.5, than on the mean, 16.

The IQR is 5. The MAD is 8.8. A *lesser* IQR shows the data are more closely centered around the median.

Sometimes the mode can be used to describe data when most have the *same value or values.*

The MAD is 12.5. The IQR is 25. A *lesser value* for the MAD shows that the data vary less from the mean.

Practice

Answer the questions.

1. Find the mean and median for data set III.

mean = _______   median = _______

2. Find the range for data sets II and III.

range II = _______   range III = _______

Discuss and Write

3. How does the shape of data in a dot plot help you decide which measures to use to describe the data?

Practice

Use the given data to answer each question.

4. Absences for 20 Students in Mr. Smith's Class

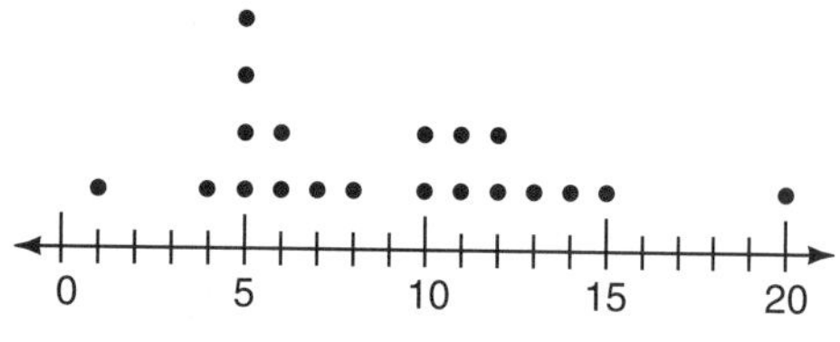

Number of Days Absent

What are the mean, median, mode, and range of the data?

5. Top 20 Rated Television Shows Last Week

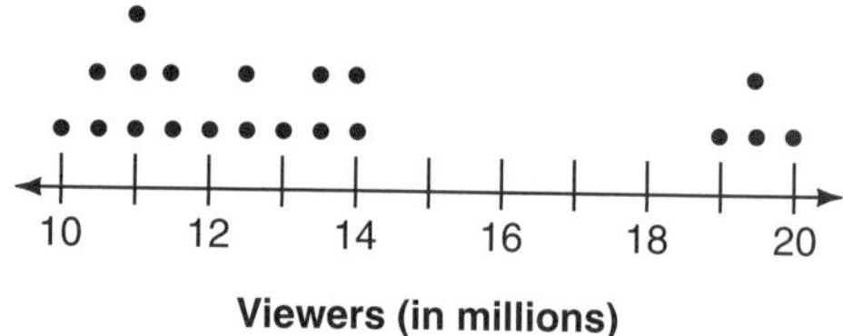

Viewers (in millions)

Which measure (mean, median, or mode) would be *least* useful for this data? Why?

6. Pages in Selected Books

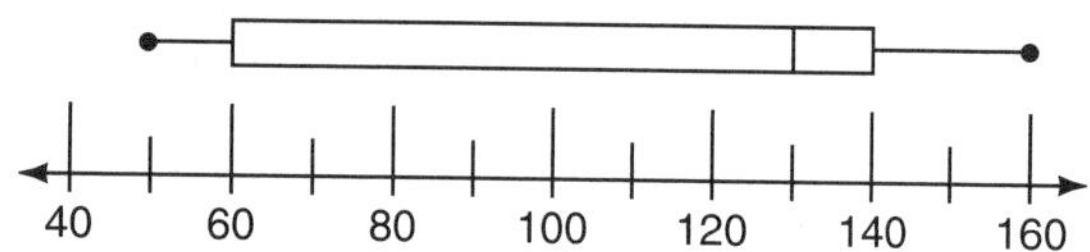

What are the range and IQR of the data?

7. Number of Raisins in Packs of Trail Mix

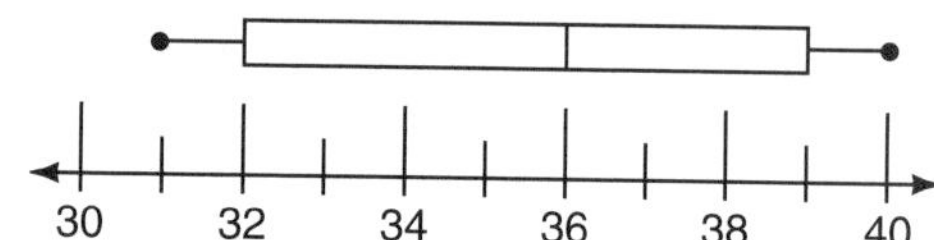

Why might the MAD be a more useful measure of variability to describe the box plot than the IQR?

Problem Solving

The dot plot shows the amounts of Pam's last 10 sales. Use the data to answer the questions.

Pam's Sales

400 450 500 550 600 650 700 750 800 850 900 950 1,000 1,050 1,100

dollars

8. Find the mean, median, and mode. Which measure might Pam want to use to describe her sales? Would this measure best represent the data? Explain.

9. Pam wants her mean sales to increase to $650. How much does her next sale need to be to do this?

Critical Thinking

10. The dot plot shows the favorite numbers of some students. Why would you not use the median or the mean to describe the data?

Favorite Numbers

1 2 3 4 5 6 7

For additional Practice, go to page 282 in this Workbook.
Then go to Lesson 9-8, pages 306–307 in the Student Book.

Name _______________________

Objective: To use tables of equivalent ratios to solve problems

For a class trip, 3 chaperones are needed for every 21 students. How many chaperones are needed for 126 students?

Students	Chaperones	
21	3	Ratio 21 : 3
42	6	21 × 2, 3 × 2
63	9	21 × 3, 3 × 3
84	12	21 × 4, 3 × 4
105	15	21 × 5, 3 × 5
126	18	21 × 6, 3 × 6

▶ To find how many chaperones are needed, write the ratio of students to chaperones, and then use this ratio to generate a table of equivalent student to chaperone ratios. Students to Chaperones ratio: 21 to 3.

All ratios are equivalent to $\frac{7}{1}$: $\frac{21}{3} = \frac{42}{6} = \frac{63}{9} = \frac{84}{12} = \frac{105}{15} = \frac{126}{18}$

So, 18 chaperones are needed for 126 students.

Given the table of equivalent ratios of Minutes Exercised to Calories Burned, find the missing values.

Minutes Exercised	Calories Burned
4	26
8	52
12	78
16	?
20	130
?	156

(+4 between Minutes Exercised rows; +26 between Calories Burned rows)

▶ To find the missing values in an equivalent ratio table, look for a pattern in each column. In the Minutes Exercised column, each value *increases by* 4.
Use the pattern to find 20 + 4 = 24.
In the Calories Burned column, each value *increases by* 26.
Use the pattern to find 78 + 26 = 104.
To check your values, use multiplication as repeated addition.
Multiply 4 and the row number of the missing value: 4 × 6 = 24.
Multiply 26 and the row number of the missing value: 26 × 4 = 104

So, the missing values are 24 and 104.

Practice

Use equivalent ratios.

1. There are 24 pencils in each box. Complete the table to show the number of pencils in 1 to 5 boxes.

Boxes	Pencils
1	24

2. What is the ratio of boxes to pencils? Ratio ________

3. How many boxes are there for 96 pencils? ________

4. How many pencils are needed to fill 5 boxes? ________

Discuss and Write

5. How did you use equivalent ratios to complete the table?

Practice

Use equivalent ratios.

6. Eighteen dollars is needed for every 2 tickets. Complete the table to show the costs of the tickets.

7. How many tickets can you get for $72? ______

8. What is the cost of 12 tickets? ______

9. What is the cost of 1 ticket? ______

10. What is the greatest number of tickets you can get if you have $100? ______

11. How much will it cost for you and 6 friends to get tickets? ______

Tickets	Price
2	$18
4	
6	$54
	$72
10	$90
12	

Problem Solving

The table shows Tommy's reading rate. Complete the table.

12. Tommy reads 10 pages for Language Arts class and 8 pages for History class. How long will it take him?

____

13. Tommy reads 16 pages for Math class and 4 pages for Science class. If he starts reading at 6:30 P.M. and takes a 5-minute break, at what time will he finish?

____

14. What is the greatest number of full pages Tommy can finish reading in 45 minutes?

____

Minutes	Pages
7	2
	4
21	6
	10
42	12
49	14

Critical Thinking

15. Explain two ways you can use the table to find the cost of 36 golf balls.

Golf Balls	Price
6	$8
12	$16
36	?

For additional Practice, go to page 283 in this Workbook.
Then go to Lesson 11-2B, pages 239–240 in this Workbook.

Objective: To understand and describe a ratio relationship and unit rates

▶ You can write a ratio to describe how two numbers are related. A ratio that compares two unlike quantities is called a **rate**.

A clothing store purchaser orders large shirts and medium shirts at a rate of 3 : 2. What does this ratio show?

The ratio, 3 to 2, shows the rate at which *the number of large shirts were ordered* to *the number of medium shirts.* This means that *for every* 3 large shirts ordered 2 medium shirts were also ordered.

▶ A ratio that is simplified to have a denominator of 1 unit is called a **unit rate**.

A car travels an average of 100 miles every 2 hours.

Find the unit rate of *distance traveled in miles* to the *time in hours*.

• The ratio or rate is 100 miles : 2 hours.

• Rewrite as a fraction. $\dfrac{100 \text{ miles}}{2 \text{ hours}}$ ⟵ distance traveled in miles ⟵ time in hours

• Simplify to get a denominator of 1.

$$\frac{100 \text{ miles}}{2 \text{ hours}} = \frac{50 \text{ miles}}{1 \text{ hour}}$$

Think
The car travels 50 miles every hour.

So, the unit rate is 50 miles per hour or $\dfrac{50 \text{ miles}}{1 \text{ hour}}$.

Practice

Write a ratio for the situation. Then find the unit rate.

1. A store charges $3 for every 12 oranges.

ratio: ____________

unit rate: ____________

2. A mixture has 2 parts oil to 1 part water.

ratio: ____________

unit rate: ____________

3. There are 120 students for every 4 classrooms.

ratio: ____________

unit rate: ____________

4. Jackie can type 182 words for every 4 minutes while writing a report.

ratio: ____________

unit rate: ____________

Discuss and Write

5. Use a ratio of oranges to dollars to describe the situation in exercise 1. What is the unit rate using this ratio? What does this unit rate mean?

Practice

Explain what the ratio means.

6. A trail mix recipe uses ounces of nuts and raisins in a ratio of 5 : 3.

____

7. Chaperones are needed for students on a field trip in a ratio of 2 : 12.

____

Write a ratio for the situation. Then find the unit rate.

8. Katie spends $12 for every 80 tiles.

ratio: ____________

unit rate: ____________

9. Luke travels 6 miles for every 45 minutes he runs.

ratio: ____________

unit rate: ____________

10. A drama club earns $375 for every 30 play tickets sold.

ratio: ____________

unit rate: ____________

11. A restaurant needs 30 pounds of fish for every 40 customers.

ratio: ____________

unit rate: ____________

Problem Solving

Find the unit rate. Then answer the question.

12. Jenna pays $12 for every 2 dozen bagels. How much would she pay for 8 bagels?

____

13. Jesse's car can travel 264 miles for every 12 gallons of gas. How far can the car travel using 5 gallons of gas?

____

14. Noel is making lemonade for a party. She uses 4 scoops of mix for every 2 quarts of water. The container of mix has 18 scoops. How much mix is left after making 5 quarts of lemonade?

____

15. A soccer league has 108 players for every 6 teams. The league has 3 fields to use for games. If each team has the same number of players, how many players are there in all on 9 teams?

____

Explain Your Reasoning

16. The ratios $\frac{\$15}{3 \text{ lunches}}$ and $\frac{3 \text{ lunches}}{\$15}$ both describe the relationship between the total cost and the number of friends who go to lunch. How can you use one of the ratios to find the cost of 8 lunches?

C For additional Practice, go to page 284 in this Workbook.
C Then go to Lesson 11-3, pages 380–381 in the Student Book.

Name ______________________

Objective: To use tables to compare ratios and solve problems

▶ You can make a table to compare two or more ratios. Use the table to generate and organize a list of equivalent ratios.

There are 8 girls for every 12 boys.

The ratio of girls to boys in Ms. Boylan's class is 2 : 3.
The ratio of girls to boys in Mr. Hall's class is 3 : 4.
Which class has the greater ratio of girls to boys?

Ms. Boylan's Class

Girls	2	4	6	8
Boys	3	6	9	12

❶ Make a table of equivalent ratios for each class.

Mr. Hall's Class

Girls	3	6	9	12
Boys	4	8	12	16

❷ Look for numbers you can compare. Try to find the numbers of boys that are the same in both classes.

Both tables have an entry for 12 boys.

There are 9 girls for every 12 boys.

$$\frac{9}{12} > \frac{8}{12}$$

So, Mr. Hall's class has the greater ratio of girls to boys.

Practice

Compare the ratios using a table. Then identify which ratio is greater.

1. a) 6 : 15   **b)** 9 : 20

6	12		
15			

9	18		
20			

2. a) 4 to 9   **b)** 5 to 12

4	8		
9			

5	10		
12			

3. a) $\frac{7}{30}$ **b)** 9 : 20

4. a) $\frac{19}{32}$ **b)** $\frac{14}{24}$

Discuss and Write

5. For one of the tables in the exercises, describe how to make a list of equivalent ratios. Explain why some of the tables do not need to be completely filled with terms.

Practice

Compare the ratios using a table. Then identify which ratio is greater.

6. a) 3 : 8   **b)** 5 : 12   **7. a)** 7 to 10   **b)** 11 to 15

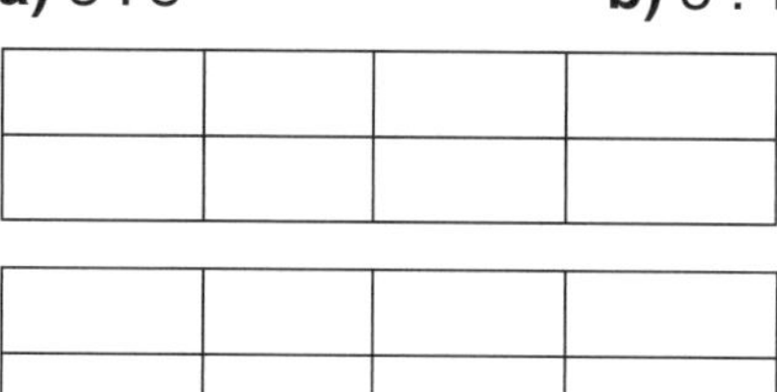

8. a) $\frac{8}{18}$ **b)** $\frac{10}{24}$ **9. a)** $\frac{5}{6}$ **b)** $\frac{6}{8}$

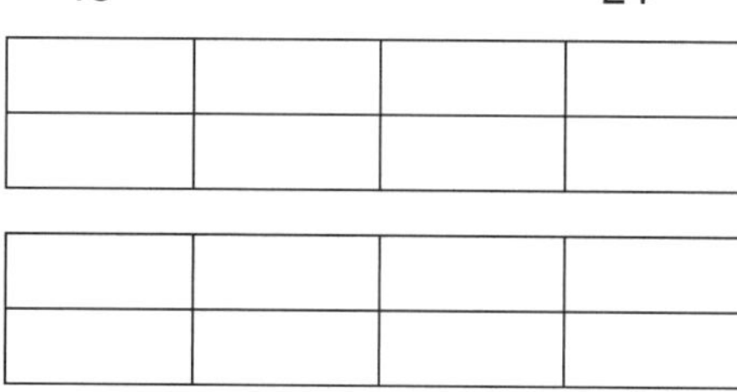

Problem Solving

Solve. Show your work and justify your answer.

10. Six cans of juice cost $2. Eight cans of the same juice cost $3. Each can is 8 ounces. Which is the better buy?

11. A bag of 10 oranges costs $4. A bag of 12 oranges costs $5. Which is the better buy?

12. Jan can ride her bike 32 miles in 5 hours. Hal can ride his bike 20 miles in 3 hours. Who would finish a 25-mile bike race first?

13. Quinn can type 275 words in 5 minutes. Rita can type 675 words in 15 minutes. Who can type 5,000 words faster?

Explain Your Reasoning

14. Roe is comparing the ratios 3 : 4 and 4 : 5. Is this the same as comparing the ratios 4 : 3 and 5 : 4? Use tables to justify your answer.

For additional Practice, go to page 285 in this Workbook.
Then go to Lesson 11-4, pages 382–383 in the Student Book.

Name ______________________

Objective: To use a double number-line diagram to model proportions and find equivalent ratios

The sixth grade is planning a field trip. Two adults are needed for every 9 students going on the trip. How many adults are needed for 54 students?

▶ To find the number of adults for 54 students, you can use a **double number-line** diagram to find equivalent ratios.

❶ Draw a double number-line diagram.

Use the *top line* for the number of adults and the *bottom line* for the number of students.

❷ Label the scales on each side.

Since the ratio of adults to students is 2 : 9, use intervals of 2 for adults and intervals of 9 for students.

❸ Use the double number-line diagram to find how many adults are needed.

Find the point for 54 students. Find the corresponding number of adults. The corresponding number is 12.

So, 12 adults are needed for 54 students.

A **double number-line diagram** has 2 number lines with different scales on each line. The intervals on the number lines are equal in size, but do not represent equal numbers. The intervals for each number line are different.

This double number line represents the ratio 2 adults : 9 students.

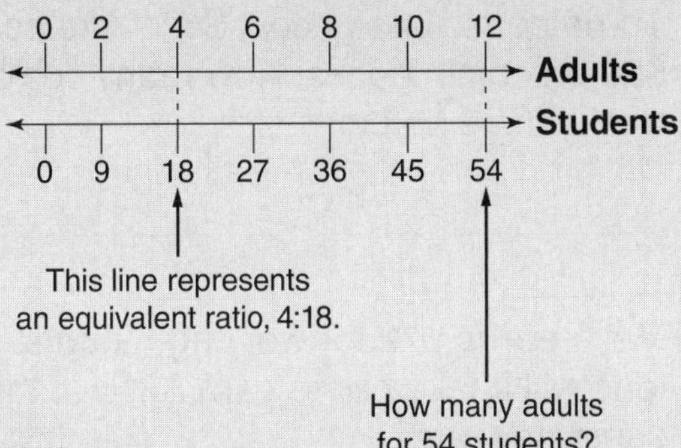

Practice

Complete the double number-line diagram to find 4 ratios equivalent to the given ratio.

1. Ratio 3 : 5

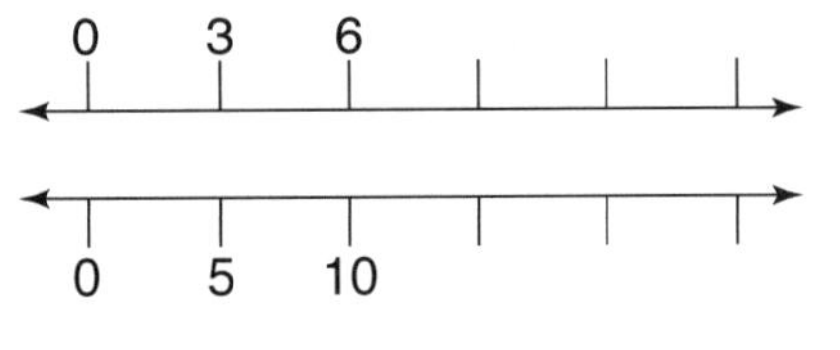

6 : 10; ____ : ____; ____ : ____; ____ : ____

2. Ratio 4 : 3

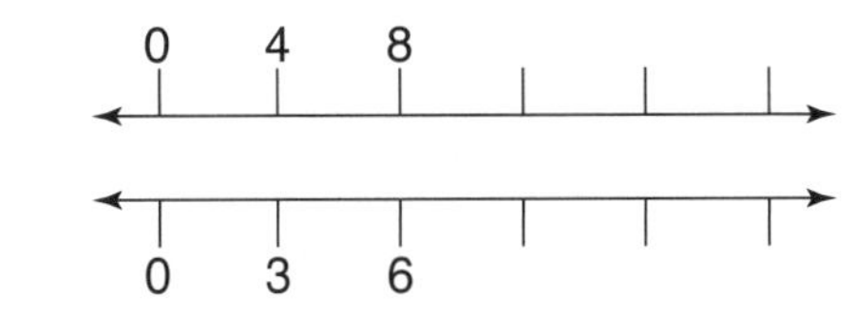

8 : 6; ____ : ____; ____ : ____; ____ : ____

Discuss and Write

3. Explain how to use the double number-line diagram from exercise 1 to find the cost of 20 apples if 5 apples cost $3.

Practice

Complete the double number-line diagram to find 4 ratios equivalent to the given ratio.

4. Ratio 7 : 10

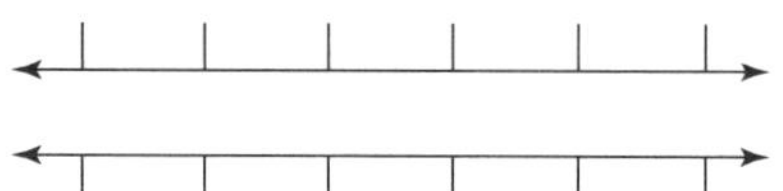

____

5. Ratio 15 : 4

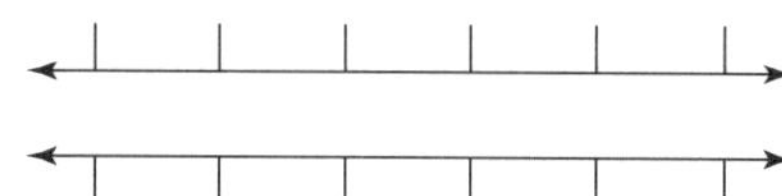

____

Problem Solving

Solve. Use a strategy that works best for you. Show your work.

6. Three comic books cost $12. Mike spends $20 on comic books. How many comic books does he buy?

7. Seven bananas weigh 2 pounds and are on sale for $1. How much does Lucy pay for 28 bananas on sale?

8. Maya earns $72 for working 5 hours. How long will it take her to earn $216 at the same pay rate?

9. Miguel runs $\frac{1}{4}$ mile in $2\frac{1}{2}$ minutes. How long does it take him to run $1\frac{1}{4}$ miles at the same rate?

10. Ben takes his pulse. He counts 18 beats in 15 seconds. How many beats per minute is that?

11. Amy has a photo 4 inches long and 3 inches wide. She enlarges it so that its length is 12 inches. How wide is the enlarged photo?

12. A recipe for 12 meatballs calls for 2 ounces of cheese. Ray is making 48 meatballs and has 3 ounces of cheese. How much more cheese does he need?

13. Amanda can buy 4 tubes of paint for $10. She uses 5 tubes of paint to make 3 paintings. How many paintings can she make from $50 worth of paint?

Critical Thinking

14. For a field trip there must be at least 3 adults for every 16 students. What is the least number of adults needed for 50 students? Explain your answer.

For additional Practice, go to page 286 in this Workbook.
Then go to Lesson 11-4B, pages 245–246 in this Workbook.

Objective: To use a tape diagram to find equal ratios

A **tape diagram** has strips divided into segments. Each segment represents the same quantity. You can use a tape diagram to find equivalent ratios.

A recipe for punch uses 2 cups of apple juice for every 3 cups of grape juice. How much grape juice is needed for 8 cups of apple juice?

▶ To find how much grape juice is needed, use a tape diagram.

Each segment on a tape diagram represents the same amount, so each segment must be the same size.

❶ Let one strip represent the apple juice and the other represent the grape juice.

Because the ratio is 2 : 3, the strip for apple juice should have 2 segments, and the strip for grape juice should have 3 segments.

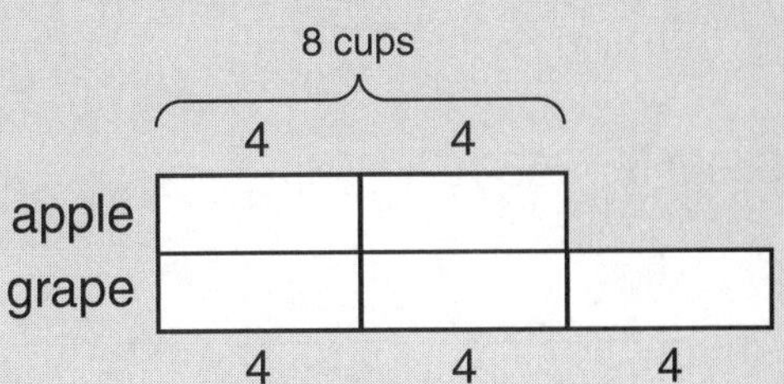

❷ Find the number that each segment represents.

There are 8 cups of apple juice and 2 segments. So, each segment represents 4 cups.

❸ Use the diagram to determine how much grape juice is needed.

The strip for grape juice has 3 segments.
3 segments × 4 cups per segment = 12 cups

The tape diagram shows that 2 : 3 and 8 : 12 are equivalent ratios.

So, 12 cups of grape juice are needed to go with 8 cups of apple juice.

Practice

Complete the tape diagram to find an equivalent ratio.

1. 4 : 5 = ______ : 35

2. 3 : 4 = 27 : ______

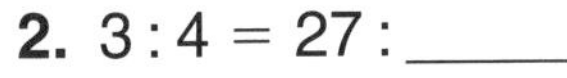

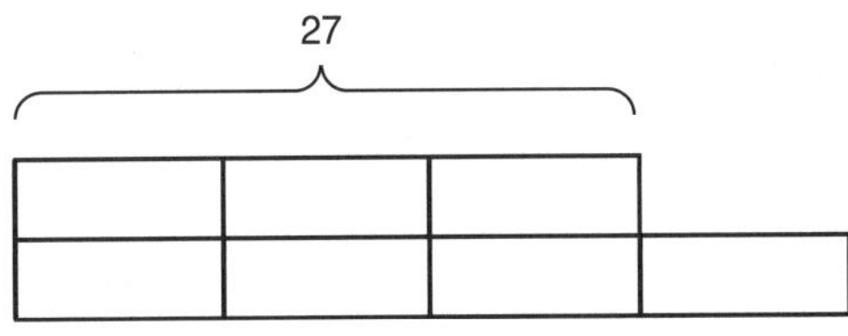

Discuss and Write

3. Look back at the teaching display. How can you use the tape diagram that shows the ratio 2 : 3 to find the number of cups of apple juice and grape juice needed to make 30 cups of punch?

Practice

Complete the tape diagram to find an equivalent ratio.

4. $1 : 4 =$ _______ $: 28$

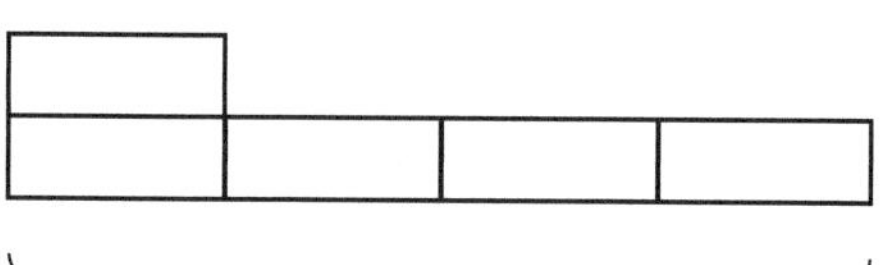

5. $5 : 4 = 90 :$ _______

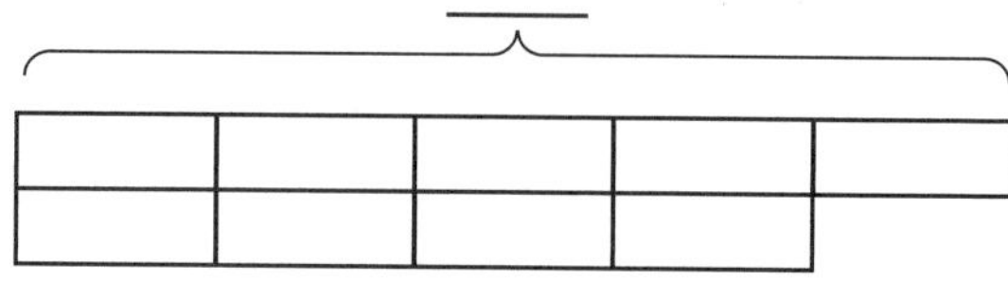

6. $4 : 3 = 56 :$ _______

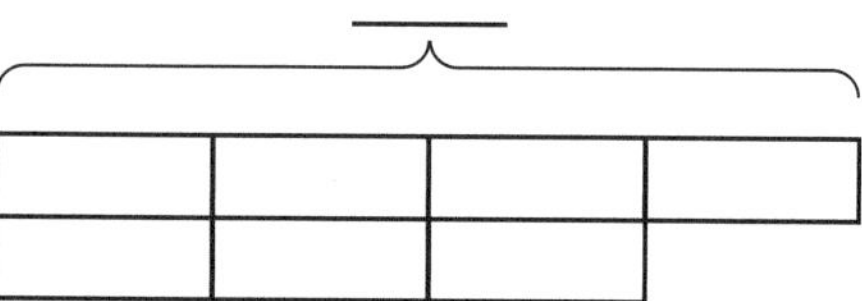

7. $2 : 5 =$ _______ $: 45$

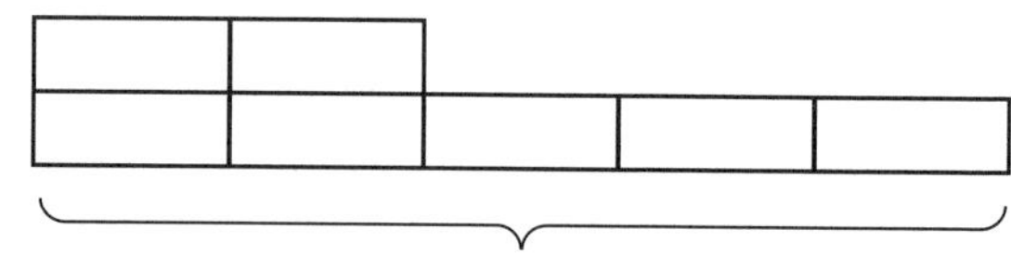

Problem Solving

Solve. Use a strategy that works best for you.

8. Rick enlarges a picture that is 6 inches long and 3 inches tall. The enlargement is 18 inches long. How tall is the enlargement?

9. Diana checks her pulse while she is exercising. She counts 5 beats in 2 seconds. At this rate, how many times will her heart beat in one minute?

10. Mandy spends 2 minutes stretching for every 9 minutes she spends running. If she spends a total of 55 minutes running and stretching, how long does she spend stretching?

11. A trail mix recipe calls for 3 cups of raisins and 2 cups of peanuts for every cup of chocolate. How much trail mix can you make with 12 cups of raisins, 3 cups of chocolate, and 12 cups of peanuts?

Explain Your Reasoning

12. Logan is making trail mix using 2 cups of dried fruit for every 3 cups of nuts. He has 12 cups of dried fruit and 15 cups of nuts. If he makes as much trail mix as he can, which ingredient will he run out of first? How much of the other ingredient will be left? Use a tape diagram to show why your answer is correct.

For additional Practice, go to page 287 in this Workbook.
Then go to Lesson 11-5, pages 384–385 in the Student Book.

Use Proportions to Convert Units
Chapter 13, Lesson 7A

Objective: To use a proportion to convert between units of measurement

You can convert from one measurement unit to another by writing and solving a proportion.

Mina has 3 gallons of juice. How many cups of juice does she have?

▶ To find how many cups of juice Mina has, use the relationship between cups and gallons.

❶ Write the ratio of cups to gallons.

$$16 \text{ cups} = 1 \text{ gallon} \longrightarrow \frac{16 \text{ cups}}{1 \text{ gallon}}$$

❷ Use a proportion to find how many cups are in 3 gallons.

$$\frac{16 \text{ cups}}{1 \text{ gallon}} = \frac{c \text{ cups}}{3 \text{ gallons}}$$

❸ Solve the proportion using the cross-products rule.

$$\frac{16}{1} = \frac{c}{3}$$
$$16 \times 3 = 1 \times c$$
$$48 = c$$

So, Mina has 48 cups of juice.

> Remember: A proportion is an equation that shows two ratios are equivalent. The ratios in a proportion compare similar things.

> Remember:
> Cross-Products Rule
> $$\frac{a}{b} \diagdown \frac{c}{d}$$
> $$a \times d = b \times c$$

Practice

Write and solve a proportion to convert between units of measure.

1. Jonathan has 5 yards of wire. How many inches of wire does he have?

36 inches = 1 yard

$$\frac{\text{inches}}{1 \text{ yard}} = \frac{n \text{ inches}}{\text{yards}}$$

$$\underline{\hspace{2em}} \times \underline{\hspace{2em}} = 1 \times n$$

$$\underline{\hspace{3em}} = n$$

He has ______ inches of wire.

2. Art and Trisha dance for 825 minutes. How many hours do they dance?

1 hour = 60 minutes

$$\frac{1 \text{ hour}}{\text{minutes}} = \frac{n \text{ hours}}{\text{minutes}}$$

$$1 \times \underline{\hspace{2em}} = \underline{\hspace{2em}} \times n$$

$$\underline{\hspace{3em}} = n$$

They dance for ______ hours.

Discuss and Write

3. Marc solved exercise 1 using the proportion $\frac{1 \text{ yard}}{36 \text{ inches}} = \frac{5 \text{ yards}}{n \text{ inches}}$.

Will this proportion lead to the correct answer? Explain.

Name ___________________________

Practice

Write and solve a proportion to convert between units of measure.

4. How many yards are in 3.5 miles?

1 mile = 1760 yards

5. How many quarts are in 64 cups?

1 quart = 4 cups

6. How many kilograms are in 8640 grams?

1 kilogram = 1000 grams

7. How many centimeters are in 60 inches?

1 inch = 2.54 centimeters

8. How many pounds are in 2.5 tons?

1 ton = 2000 pounds

9. How many inches are in 7 yards?

1 yard = 36 inches

10. How many gallons are in 20 liters? Round to the nearest tenth of a gallon.

1 gallon $\approx$ 3.79 liters

11. How many quarts are in 12 liters? Round to the nearest tenth of a quart.

1 liter $\approx$ 1.06 quarts

Problem Solving

Solve. Use a strategy that works best for you. Show your work.

12. Manny's heart rate is 75 beats per minute. How many times does his heart beat in 1 day?

13. Bags of gravel weigh 8.5 kilograms each. Bags of sand weigh 20 pounds each. Which kind of bag weighs more?

14. A carat is a unit of mass equal to 200 milligrams. What is the mass in grams of an 18-carat pearl?

15. Rosa rides her bike at a constant rate of 5 miles per hour. How many feet does she travel in 6 minutes?

What's the Error?

16. Diana used the proportion $\frac{8}{1} = \frac{3.5}{n}$ to find the number of pints in 3.5 gallons. What error did she make? (Hint: There are 8 pints in 1 gallon.)

For additional Practice, go to page 288 in this Workbook.
Then go to Lesson 13-8, pages 462–463 in the Student Book.

Name ________________________

Objective: To find the area of a complex figure by dividing the figure into simpler shapes

You can find the area of complex figures by decomposing or composing them into shapes whose areas you can find.

Janet is carpeting a floor. The shape of the floor is shown. How many square feet of carpet are needed?

► You can add or subtract areas to find the area of the floor.

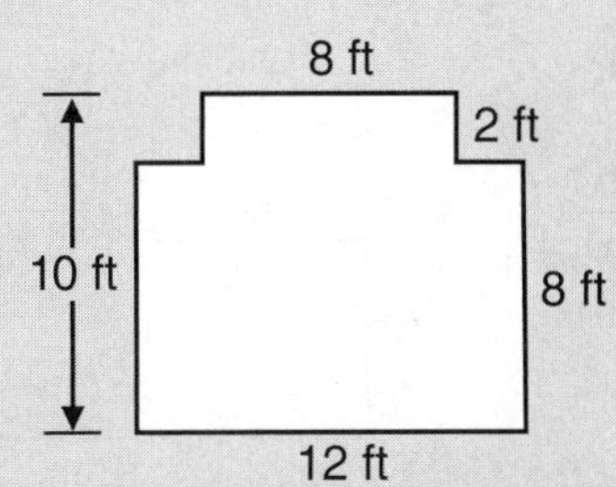

Method 1: Decompose and add areas.

❶ Look for simpler shapes that make up the floor. Divide the figure into two rectangles and label their dimensions.

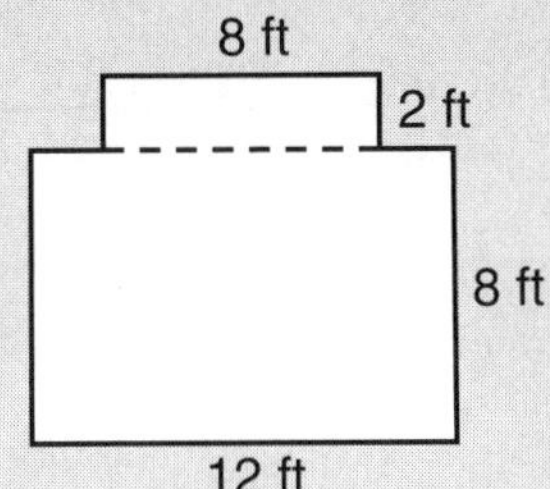

❷ Find the area of each part.

Area of large rectangle = length × width
96 ft² = 12 ft × 8 ft

Area of small rectangle = length × width
16 ft² = 8 ft × 2 ft

❸ *Add the areas* of the parts.
96 ft² + 16 ft² = 112 ft²

Method 2: Compose and subtract areas.

❶ The floor is a 12- by 10-foot rectangle with a pair of 2-foot squares cut out.

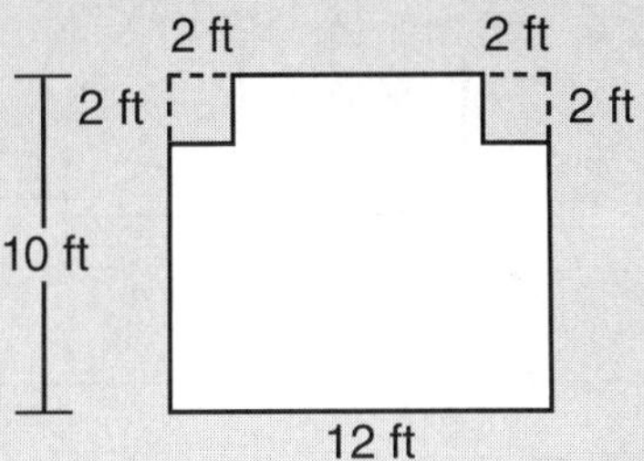

❷ Find the areas of the large rectangle and the small squares.

Area of large rectangle = length × width
120 ft² = 12 ft × 10 ft

Area of one small square = length × width
4 ft² = 2 ft × 2ft

❸ *Subtract the areas* of the squares.
120 ft² − 4 ft² − 4 ft² = 112 ft²

So, 112 square feet of carpet are needed for the floor.

Practice

Add the areas to find the area of the figure. Show your work.

1.

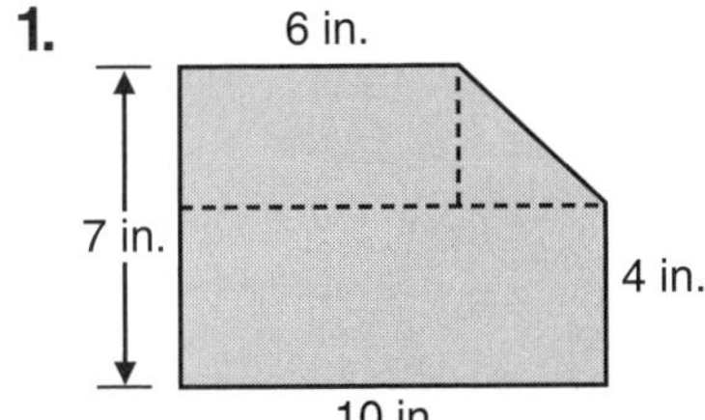

____

Discuss and Write

2. Explain another way to find the area of the figure in exercise 1.

Practice

Find the area of each figure by making simpler shapes.

3.

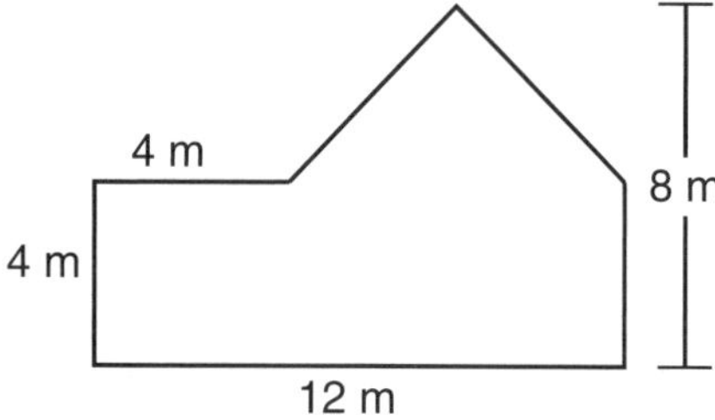

4.

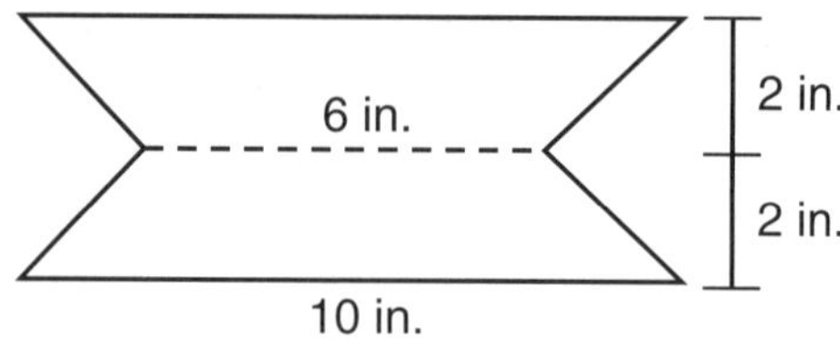

5.

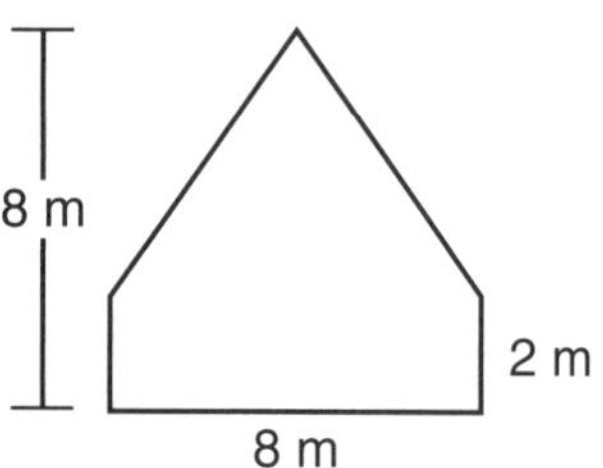

6.

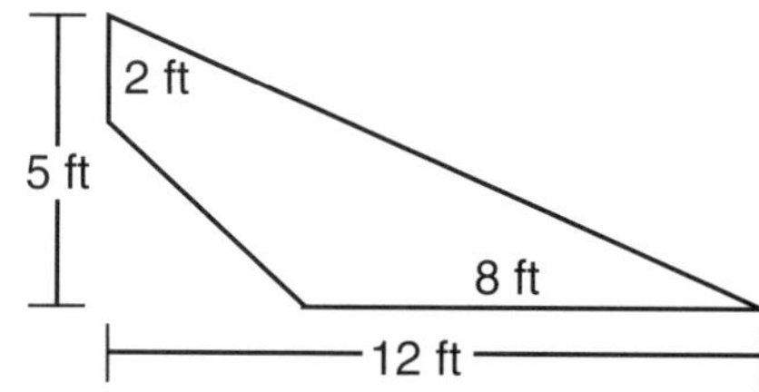

Problem Solving

Solve. Use a strategy that works best for you. Show your work.

7. Phil is spreading fertilizer over his entire garden, which has the shape shown. How many square feet must he cover?

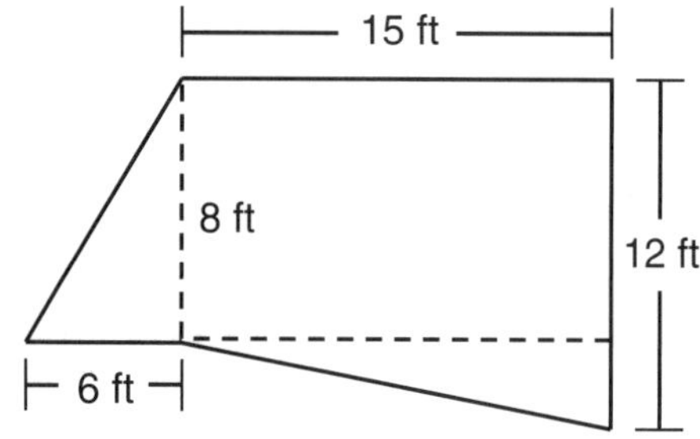

8. Cheryl is using wood to make the shaded part of the design shown. How many square centimeters of wood does she need?

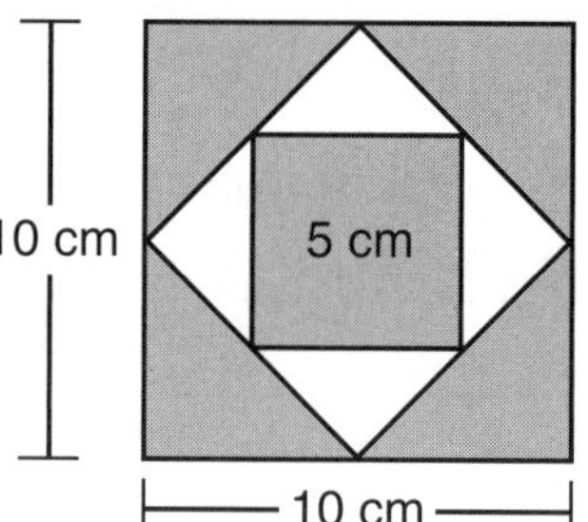

Explain Your Reasoning

9. Is the area of the shaded part of the first figure shown equal to the area of the second figure shown? Tell how you found the answer.

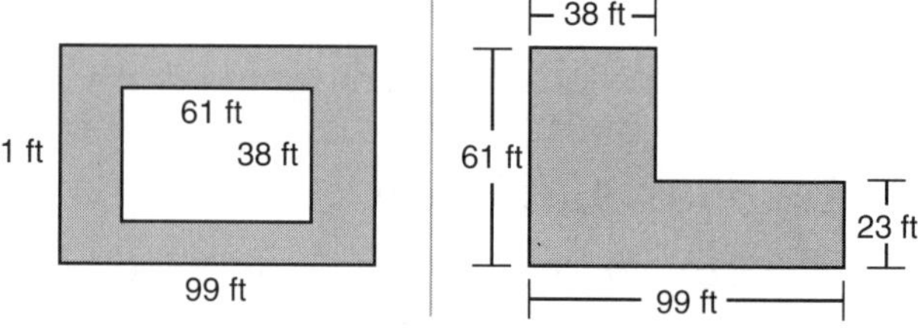

For additional Practice, go to page 289 in this Workbook.
Then go to Lesson 13-12, pages 470–471 in the Student Book.

Name _______________________________

Objective: To find the surface area of a solid figure by finding the area of its net

Surface area is the sum of the areas of all the faces of a solid figure. You can use the net of a solid figure to find its surface area. A **net** is a flat pattern that folds into a solid figure.

Miguel wants to wrap the box shown. How much surface area must he cover?

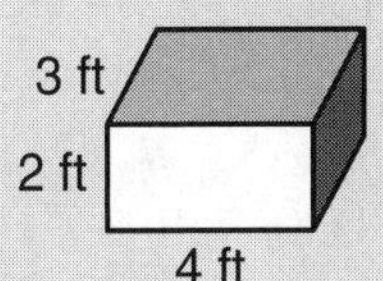

▶ Notice the box is a rectangular prism. To find the surface area of the box, follow the steps below.

❶ Draw a net of the prism. Draw the top, right, bottom, and left faces of the prism in a row to make one big rectangle.

Draw the front and back faces above and below the rectangle that represents the top.

❷ Find the area of *each shape* in the net.

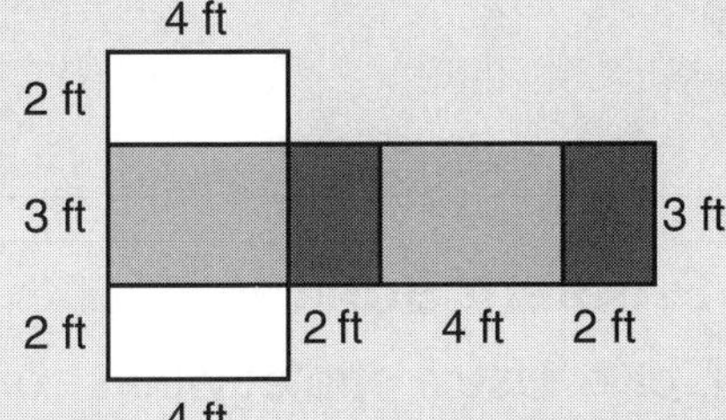

Area of one white face = 4 ft $\times$ 2 ft = 8 ft^2
Area of one grey face = 4 ft $\times$ 3 ft = 12 ft^2
Area of one black face = 3 ft $\times$ 2 ft = 6 ft^2

❸ Add the areas of each part of the net to find the surface area of the box.

8 ft^2 + 8 ft^2 + 12 ft^2 + 12 ft^2 + 6 ft^2 + 6 ft^2 = 52 ft^2

So, Miguel must cover 52 ft^2.

Practice

Use the net to find the surface area of the figure.

1.

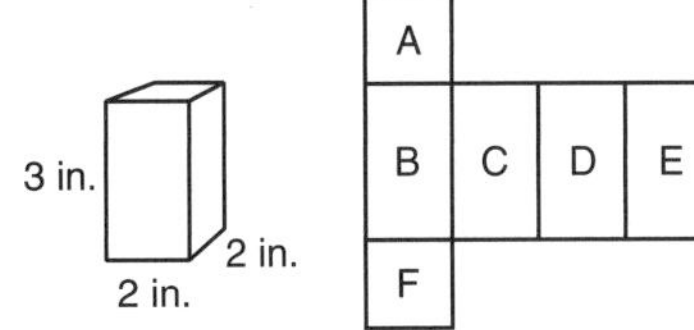

A: _______   B: _______   C: _______

D: _______   E: _______   F: _______

Surface Area = _______

2.

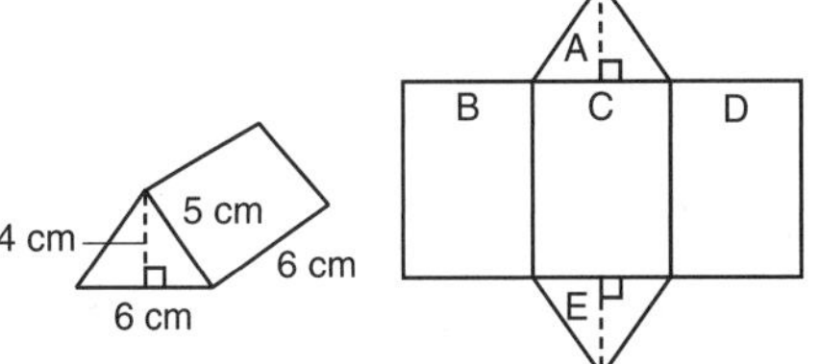

A: _______   B: _______   C: _______

D: _______   E: _______

Surface Area = _______

Discuss and Write

3. Why is using a net helpful for finding the surface area of a solid figure?

Name _______________________

Practice

Draw a net to find the surface area of the figure.

4.

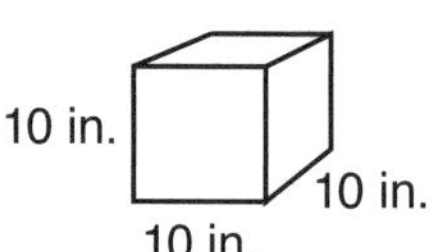

____

5.

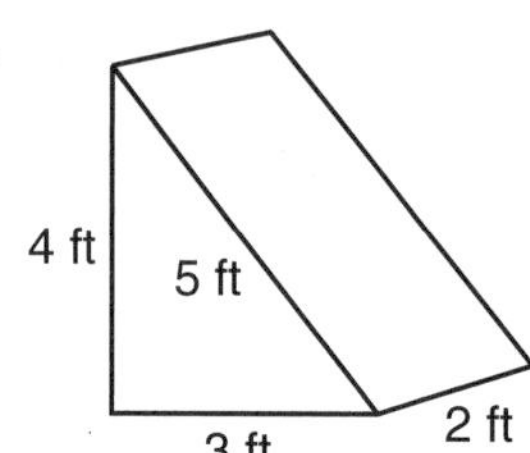

____

6.

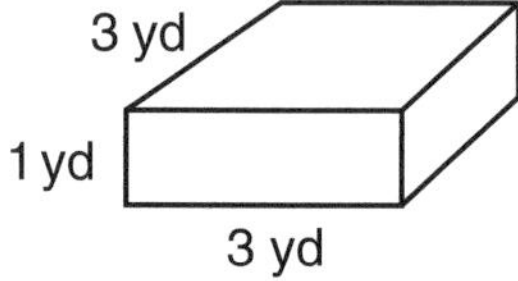

____

7.

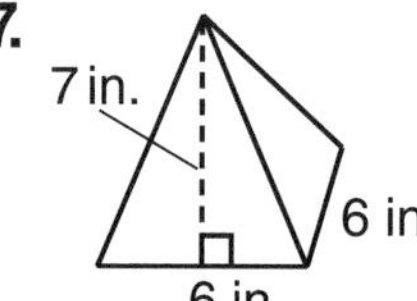

____

Problem Solving

Solve. Use a strategy that works best for you. Show your work.

8. Marjorie is wrapping a box that is shaped like a cube with sides that are $2\frac{1}{2}$ inches long. She has 36 square inches of paper. Is this enough to wrap the box? Explain.

9. Anthony is painting the four sides and top of a 4-foot tall platform shaped like a rectangular prism. The base of the prism is an 8-foot by 6-foot rectangle. Anthony has a can of paint that covers 175 square feet. Is this enough paint? Explain.

Test Preparation

10. Martin is designing a sculpture in the shape of a triangular prism. The triangles at the top and bottom are right triangles with sides of length 20 inches, 21 inches, and 29 inches. The height of the sculpture is 70 inches.

A. Draw a net of the prism.

B. What is the area of a piece of aluminum that covers the sculpture? Show your work.

C. If the aluminum costs 6 cents per square inch, how much will it cost to cover the sculpture in aluminum?

For additional Practice, go to page 290 in this Workbook.
Then go to Lesson 13-14, pages 474–475 in the Student Book.

Name ______________________________

Objective: To find the volume of a rectangular prism using unit cubes

A box has the dimensions shown. What is its volume?

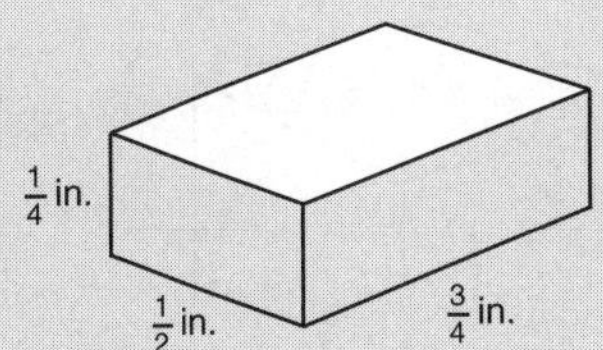

▶ You can model the volume of rectangular prisms using cubes with a **unit fraction** side length.

1 Rewrite the fractions with a common denominator.

The least common denominator of $\frac{1}{4}$, $\frac{1}{2}$, and $\frac{3}{4}$ is 4.

The equivalent fractions are $\frac{1}{4}$, $\frac{2}{4}$, and $\frac{3}{4}$.

The unit fraction with that denominator is $\frac{1}{4}$.

> Remember: A **unit fraction** has a numerator of 1.

2 Fill the rectangular prism with unit cubes with side lengths of $\frac{1}{4}$. Count the cubes.

There are 6 unit cubes with side lengths of $\frac{1}{4}$ in.

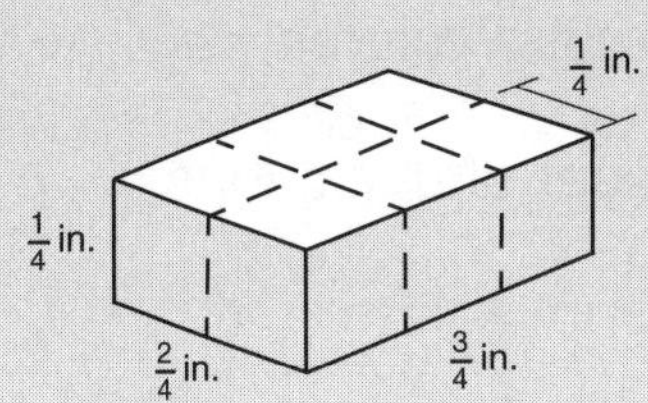

3 Multiply the number of unit cubes by the volume of each unit cube.

$6 \times \frac{1}{64}$ in.^{3} = $\frac{6}{64}$ in.^{3}, which simplifies to $\frac{3}{32}$ in.^{3}

So, the volume of the box is $\frac{3}{32}$ in.^{3}

Think

The volume of a unit cube with side lengths of $\frac{1}{4}$ is

$\frac{1}{4} \times \frac{1}{4} \times \frac{1}{4} = \frac{1}{64}$.

Practice

Find the volume of the prism by using cubes with a unit fraction side length.

1.

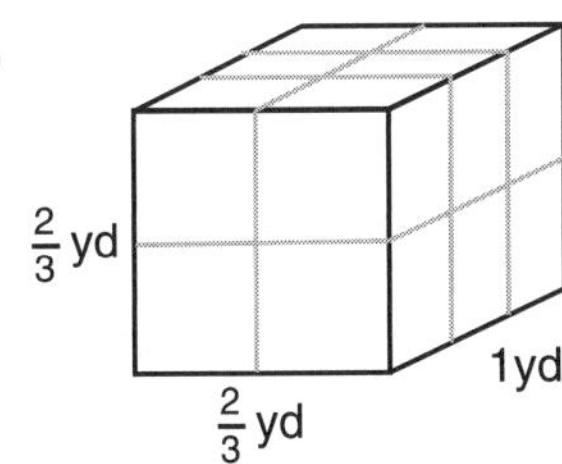

Unit cube side length = $\frac{1}{\_\_}$ yd

Unit cube volume = $\frac{1}{\_\_}$ yd^3

Number of unit cubes = ______

Volume = ______ yd^3

2.

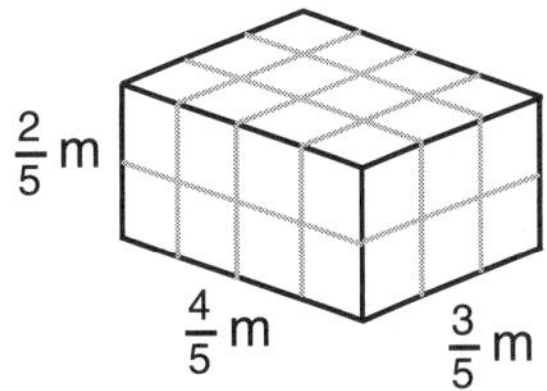

Unit cube side length = ______ m

Unit cube volume = ______ m^3

Number of unit cubes = ______

Volume = ______ m^3

Discuss and Write

3. How can you use cubes with unit fractions as side lengths to find the volume of a rectangular prism when one side length is a whole number?

Practice

Find the volume of the prism by using cubes with a unit fraction side length.

4.

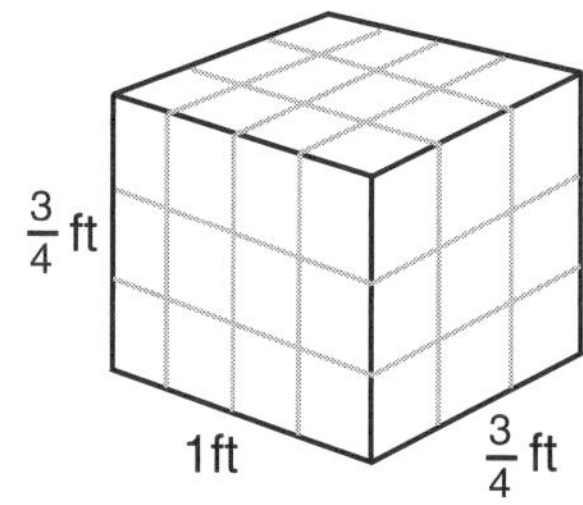

Unit cube side length = _______ ft

Unit cube volume = _______ ft³

Number of unit cubes = _______

Volume = _______ ft³

5.

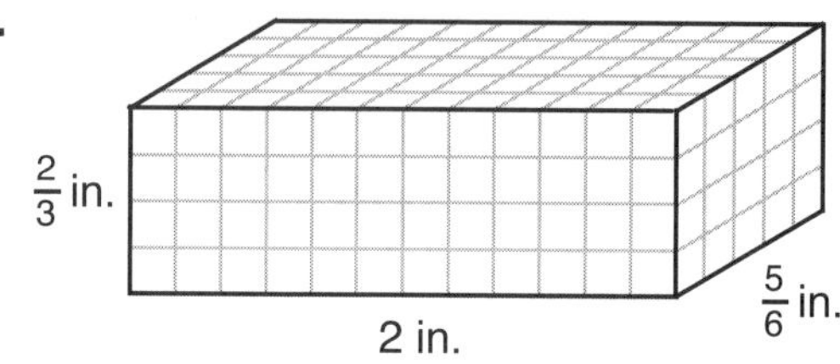

Unit cube side length = _______ in.

Unit cube volume = _______ in.³

Number of unit cubes = _______

Volume = _______ in.³

6.

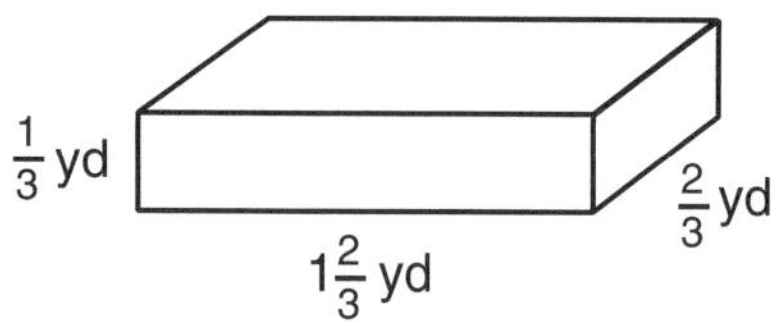

Volume = _______ yd³

7.

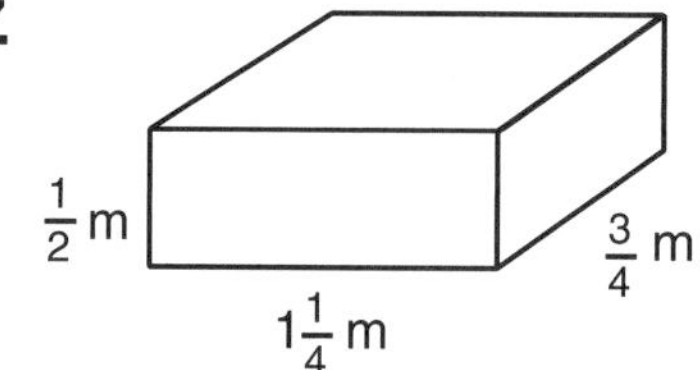

Volume = _______ m³

Problem Solving

Solve. Use a strategy that works best for you. Show your work.

8. A box is $\frac{1}{2}$ foot long, $\frac{2}{3}$ foot wide, and $\frac{5}{6}$ foot tall. Jackie has $\frac{1}{3}$ cubic foot of sand. Can the sand fit inside the box? Explain.

9. Ryan has a box shaped like a rectangular prism with a length and width of $\frac{7}{10}$ m. The volume of the box is $\frac{147}{500}$ m³. What is the height of the box?

Explain Your Reasoning

10. Decide which of the three rectangular prisms listed in the table has the greatest volume. Explain how you can use unit cubes to tell without finding the actual volumes.

Prism	Dimensions (in.)
A	$\frac{3}{8} \times \frac{3}{8} \times \frac{3}{8}$
B	$\frac{2}{8} \times \frac{3}{8} \times \frac{4}{8}$
C	$\frac{2}{8} \times \frac{2}{8} \times \frac{5}{8}$

For additional Practice, go to page 291 in this Workbook.
Then go to Lesson 13-16B, pages 255–256 in this Workbook.

Objective: To confirm that different ways of finding the volume of rectangular prisms give the same results

A storage locker has the shape of a rectangular prism. It is $2\frac{1}{2}$ feet wide, 3 feet deep, and $4\frac{1}{2}$ feet tall. What two methods can you use to find the volume of the storage locker? What is its volume?

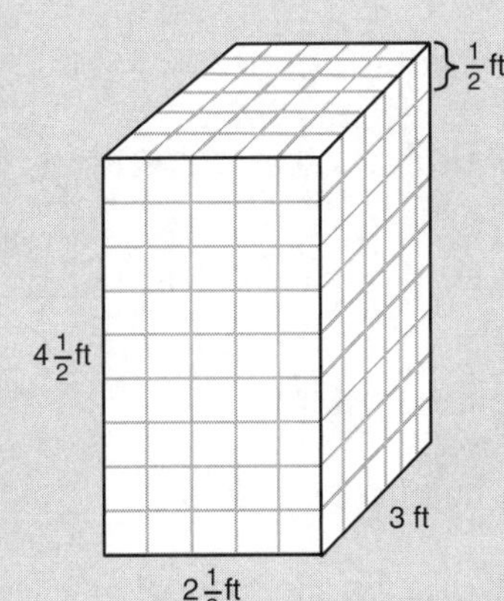

▶ To find the volume, you can model the prism using cubes with a unit fraction as a side length, or you can use a formula.

Method 1: Use unit fraction cubes.

❶ The least common denominator is 2, so use a cube with sides $\frac{1}{2}$ foot long.

❷ The volume of each cube is:

$$\frac{1}{2} \text{ ft} \times \frac{1}{2} \text{ ft} \times \frac{1}{2} \text{ ft} = \frac{1}{8} \text{ ft}^3$$

❸ There are 9 layers of 30 cubes.

$$30 \times 9 = 270$$
$$270 \times \frac{1}{8} \text{ ft}^3 = 33\frac{3}{4} \text{ ft}^3$$

Method 2: Use the volume formula.

$$V = \ell \times w \times h$$
$$V = 2\frac{1}{2} \text{ ft} \times 3 \text{ ft} \times 4\frac{1}{2} \text{ ft}$$
$$V = \frac{5}{2} \text{ ft} \times \frac{3}{1} \text{ ft} \times \frac{9}{2} \text{ ft}$$
$$V = 33\frac{3}{4} \text{ ft}^3$$

So, both methods show that the volume of the storage locker is $33\frac{3}{4}$ ft³.

Practice

A rectangular prism is $4\frac{1}{3}$ feet long, $3\frac{2}{3}$ feet wide, and 3 feet tall.
Find the volume of the prism two ways.

1. Use unit fraction cubes.

Volume of 1 unit fraction cube = _______ ft³

Number of cubes = _______

Volume of prism = _______ ft³

2. Use the volume formula.

$$V = \ell \times w \times h$$

$V = $ _______ ft $\times$ _______ ft $\times$ _______ ft

Volume of prism = _______ ft³

Discuss and Write

3. How is packing a prism with unit fraction cubes and counting to find the volume similar to using the volume formula?

Practice

Find the volume of the rectangular prism two ways.

4. $5\frac{1}{2}$ cm by $3\frac{1}{2}$ cm by 4 cm

   a) Use unit fraction cubes.

   Volume of 1 unit fraction cube = _______ cm³

   _______ cubes   Volume = _______ cm³

   b) Use the volume formula.

   $V =$ _______ cm $\times$ _______ cm $\times$ _______ cm

   Volume = _______ cm³

5. $6\frac{2}{3}$ in. by $2\frac{2}{3}$ in. by 3 in.

   a) Use unit fraction cubes.

   Volume of 1 unit fraction cube = _______ in.³

   _______ cubes   Volume = _______ in.³

   b) Use the volume formula.

   $V =$ _______ in. $\times$ _______ in. $\times$ _______ in.

   Volume = _______ in.³

Find the volume of the rectangular prism. Explain how you arrived at the answer.

6. $6\frac{1}{2}$ ft by $2\frac{1}{4}$ ft by $1\frac{1}{2}$ ft

7. $13\frac{1}{3}$ in. by $6\frac{2}{3}$ in. by 2 in.

8. $2\frac{1}{2}$ yd by $3\frac{1}{2}$ yd by $\frac{1}{2}$ yd

9. $1\frac{1}{4}$ in. by $2\frac{1}{3}$ in. by $\frac{1}{6}$ in.

Problem Solving

Solve. Use a strategy that works best for you. Show your work.

10. A rectangular pool is 24 feet long, $12\frac{1}{2}$ feet wide, and filled to a depth of $5\frac{1}{2}$ feet. One cubic foot holds 7.5 gallons of water. How many gallons of water are in the pool?

11. A block has a volume of 18 cm³. Its base is $2\frac{1}{2}$ cm long and $2\frac{4}{10}$ cm wide. What is the height of the block?

Explain Your Reasoning

12. Marty has 100 boxes that are cubes with sides $\frac{2}{3}$ foot long. He wants to arrange them in a storage bin that is 4 feet long, $3\frac{1}{3}$ feet wide, and 2 feet tall. Will he be able to arrange all the boxes in the storage bin? Explain.

For additional Practice, go to page 292 in this Workbook.
Then go to Lesson 13-17, pages 480–481 in the Student Book.

Name ______________________________________

Objective: To identify independent and dependent variables and write an equation from a table of values

Joan is buying music from a website. The table shows the cost for downloading different numbers of songs. What equation shows the relationship between the number of songs she buys and the cost of the songs?

Songs	1	2	3	4
Cost ($)	1.25	2.50	3.75	5.00

▶ To write the equation, express the cost in terms of the number of songs.

y = dependent variable or cost
x = independent variable or numbers of songs

❶ Since the cost *depends* on the number of songs that Joan buys, the cost is called the **dependent variable.** Use y to represent the cost.

❷ Since Joan can decide how many songs to buy, the number of songs is called the **independent variable.** Use x to represent the number of songs.

❸ Make a table. Look for a common difference *or* a common quotient between the two variables.

Think
Addition or subtraction equations will have a common difference. Multiplication or division equations will have a common quotient.

Cost (y)	Songs (x)	Difference	Quotient
1.25	1	$1.25 - 1 = 0.25$	$1.25 \div 1 = 1.25$
2.50	2	$2.50 - 2 = 0.50$	$2.50 \div 2 = 1.25$
3.75	3	$3.75 - 3 = 0.75$	$3.75 \div 3 = 1.25$
5.00	4	$5.00 - 4 = 1.00$	$5.00 \div 4 = 1.25$

❹ There is a common quotient of 1.25. The cost (y) is always equal to 1.25 times the number of songs (x).

So, the equation that shows this relationship is $y = 1.25x$.

Practice

Identify the independent and dependent variables. Then write an equation.

1.

Weight (lb)	1	2	3	5
Shipping Cost ($)	3	6	9	15

Independent (x): ______________________

Dependent (y): ______________________

Equation: ______________________

2.

Original Price($)	10	15	25	40
Sale Price ($)	5	10	20	35

Independent (x): ______________________

Dependent (y): ______________________

Equation: ______________________

Discuss and Write

3. For exercise 1, explain how you decided which variable is the dependent variable.

Practice

Identify the independent and dependent variable. Then write an equation.

4.

Hours (h)	2	2.5	3.5	6
Earnings ($)	21.60	27.00	37.80	64.80

Independent: _______________

Dependent: _______________

Equation: _______________

5.

Gift (oz)	4.6	5.1	7.0	8.8
Gift Wrapped (oz)	7.0	7.5	9.4	11.2

Independent: _______________

Dependent: _______________

Equation: _______________

6.

Cost ($)	9.50	12.00	16.50	20.00
Tax ($)	0.57	0.72	0.99	1.20

Independent: _______________

Dependent: _______________

Equation: _______________

7.

Usage ($)	14.95	17.60	22.25	28.20
Total ($)	27.45	30.10	34.75	40.70

Independent: _______________

Dependent: _______________

Equation: _______________

Problem Solving

Solve. Use a strategy that works best for you. Show your work.

8. Jamal currently owns 6 books. He buys 1 new book every month. Complete the table and write an equation relating the number of books Jamal owns to the number of months that pass. In how many months will Jamal own 15 books?

Months	0	1	2	5
Books				

9. At a sale, all items sell at half of their original price. Complete the table and write an equation relating the original cost of the merchandise to the sale price. What is the original price of a basket with a sale price of $18.50?

Original ($)	6.50	9.20	8.00	12.00
Sale ($)	3.25			

Critical Thinking

10. The table shows the ages of people and the prices they pay for movie tickets.

a. Is there a relationship between age and ticket price?

b. Let *a* represent the age of the person buying a ticket and *c* represent the cost of the ticket. Write an equation for the cost of one ticket.

Age (years)	Ticket Price ($)
17	8.50
25	8.50
33	8.50
55	8.50

For additional Practice, go to page 293 in this Workbook.
Then go to Lesson 14-5, pages 504–505 in the Student Book.

Name _________________________________

Objective: To use coordinates to find horizontal and vertical distances in the coordinate plane

To find the distance between two points on a coordinate plane joined by a vertical line or a horizontal line, you can use subtraction and absolute value.

Wilma uses a computer to control robots on a grid. She moves one robot from point $A(5, 4)$ to point $B(5, -3)$. How far does the robot move?

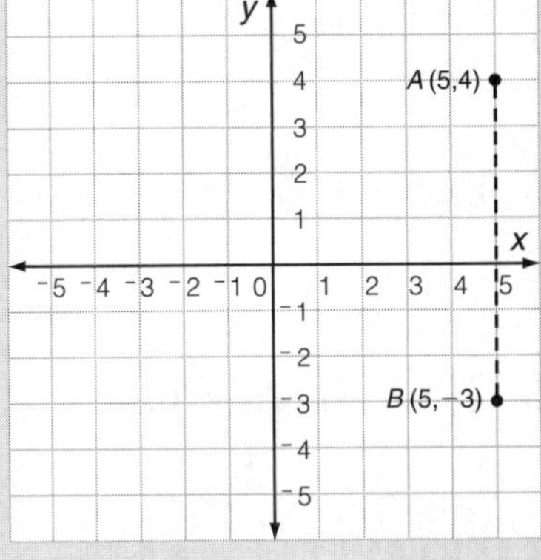

▶ To find the length of a vertical line segment, calculate the difference between the y-coordinates of its endpoints. Then take the absolute value of the difference.

❶ Subtract the y-coordinates.

$$(-3) - 4 = -7$$

❷ Find the absolute value of -7.

$$|-7| = 7$$

.Think.....................
You can check your answers by counting units on the coordinate plane.

So, the distance the robot moves between points A and B is 7 units.

Wilma moves another robot from point $P(-1, -3)$ to point $Q(-4, -3)$. How far does that robot move?

▶ To find the length of a horizontal line segment, calculate the difference between the x-coordinates of its endpoints. Then take the absolute value of the difference.

❶ Subtract the x-coordinates.

$$(-1) - (-4) = 3$$

❷ Find the absolute value of 3.

$$|3| = 3$$

So, the distance the robot moves between points P and Q is 3 units.

Practice

Find the distance between the points on a coordinate plane.

1. $D(1, 3)$ and $E(1, -4)$

$$|\text{\_\_\_\_\_} - 3| = \text{\_\_\_\_\_}$$

2. $P(-3, 0)$ and $Q(-7, 0)$

$$|\text{\_\_\_\_\_} - \text{\_\_\_\_\_}| = \text{\_\_\_\_\_}$$

Discuss and Write

3. Joseph finds the distance between the points $R(3, 5)$ and $S(-6, 5)$ using the expression $|(-6) - 3|$. Jackie finds the same distance using the expression $|3 - (-6)|$. Do they both get the correct answer? Explain.

Practice

Find the distance between the points on a coordinate grid.

4. $J(-3, 1)$ and $K(-3, -3)$

____

5. $K(-3, -3)$ and $L(2, -3)$

____

6. $M(-1, -2)$ and $N(-2, -2)$

____

7. $N(-2, -2)$ and $P(-2, 4)$

____

8. $Q(3, -4)$ and $R(3, -2)$

____

9. $S(-12, 0)$ and $T(-9, 0)$

____

10. $U(-5, 6)$ and $V(-12, 6)$

____

11. $X(9, 7)$ and $Y(9, -4)$

____

Problem Solving

Use the information below to solve problems 12–15. Show your work.

A map of Heather's town can be shown on a coordinate plane, where each unit represents 1 block. Heather's house is located at $(-4, 4)$. The coordinates of other places in Heather's town are given.

School: $(-2, -3)$　　　Town Hall: $(1, 1)$　　　Post Office: $(-4, -3)$
Grocery Store: $(5, 1)$　　　Theater: $(5, -3)$　　　Library: $(-2, 1)$

12. Heather walks from her house to the post office to drop off a letter. Then she walks to school. How many blocks does she walk in all?

____

13. From school, Heather walks to the theater. Then she walks to the grocery store. How far does she walk to get from school to the grocery store?

____

14. At the library, Heather realizes she left her book at school. She walks to school, then to the post office, then home. How far does she walk after leaving the library?

____

15. Heather walks from her house to the theater and passes all of the other places in town listed above. What is the shortest distance she could walk?

____

What's the Error?

16. Steve finds the distance from point $A(4, -6)$ to point $B(-4, 2)$ using the expression $|2 - (-6)| = 8$. Is this correct? Explain.

For additional Practice, go to page 294 in this Workbook.
Then go to Lesson 14-5B, pages 261–262 in this Workbook.

Name ________________

Objective: To solve problems by plotting the vertices of polygons on a coordinate plane

You can draw a polygon on a coordinate plane by plotting its vertices and connecting the points. The sides of polygons are made by joining vertices with line segments.

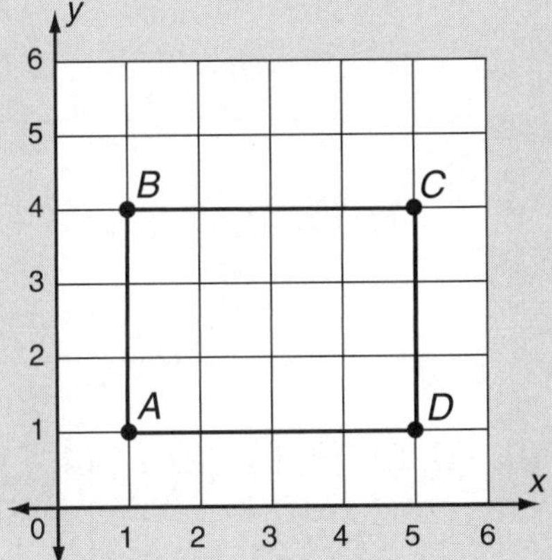

▶ What is the name for a polygon that has vertices at points $A(1, 1)$, $B(1, 4)$, $C(5, 4)$, and $D(5, 1)$?

❶ Graph the points on a coordinate plane and connect them with line segments.

❷ Examine the polygon that is created.

- The polygon has four sides.
- This polygon has four right angles.
- It has two pairs of congruent sides.
- It has two pairs of parallel sides.

Think
Find the distances between vertices to check if the sides are congruent.

❸ Name the polygon. Use the *most specific name* that describes it.

So, the polygon with vertices at coordinates $(1, 1)$, $(1, 4)$, $(5, 4)$, and $(5, 1)$ is a rectangle.

Practice

Graph the points. Draw the polygon. Then give the most specific name for it.

1. $A(0, 2)$, $B(4, 2)$, $C(5, 4)$, $D(-1, 4)$

____

2. $E(-3, -2)$, $F(0, -2)$, $G(0, 1)$, $H(-3, 1)$

____

3. $I(2, -4)$, $J(5, -1)$, $K(2, -1)$

____

4. $L(-2, -4)$, $M(1, -3)$, $N(-3, -3)$

____

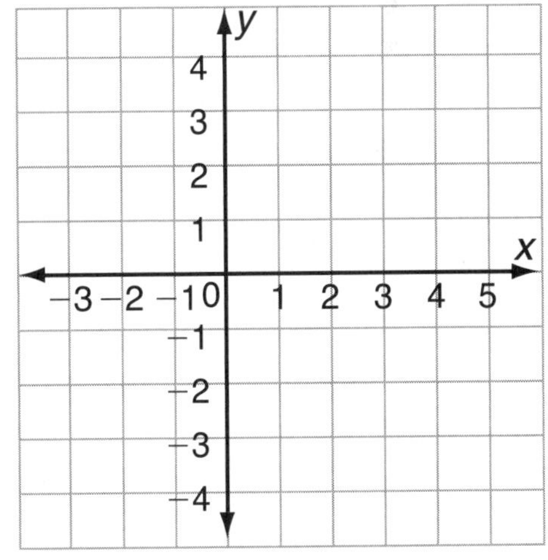

Discuss and Write

5. Gus says the shape formed in exercise 2 is a rectangle. Is he correct? Is this the best answer? Explain.

Practice

Graph the points. Draw the polygon. Then give the most specific name for it.

6. $(4, 1), (2, -2), (-3, -2), (-1, 1)$

7. $(5, 2), (0, -2), (0, 2), (5, -2)$

8. $(1, 1), (6, 1), (3, 4), (6, 4)$

9. $(-2, -2), (2, 1), (2, -2), (-1, 2)$

10. $(0, 0), (3, 0), (2, 4), (4, 2)$

11. $(-1, 2), (-2, -1), (1, -2), (2, 1)$

12. $(0, 0), (4, 0), (2, 6)$

13. $(1, 1), (3, 2), (-3, 2)$

14. $(-4, 1), (4, 1), (0, -3)$

15. $(-3, 1), (1, -4), (-3, -4)$

Problem Solving

June is in charge of planning the formation of the marching band when it performs. She uses a coordinate plane to plot the locations of band members.

16. Tuba players are marked at $(-5, -4)$, $(-5, 3), (5, 3),$ and $(5, -4)$. What kind of polygon do they form?

17. Trombone players are marked at $(-4, -3), (4, -3),$ and $(0, 0)$. What kind of triangle do they form?

18. June wants the drummers to be in a square formation. Three drummers will be at $(-3, -2), (2, -2),$ and $(2, 3)$. Where should the fourth drummer be?

19. June adds a fourth trombone player to the arrangement in problem 17. She wants them to form a parallelogram. Where could the fourth trombone player be?

Critical Thinking

20. Two vertices of an isosceles right triangle are at $(2, 0)$ and $(0, 2)$. Give three different possible coordinates for the third vertex.

For additional Practice, go to page 295 in this Workbook.
Then go to Lesson 14-6, pages 506–507 in the Student Book.

Name ___________________________

Objective: To use graphs to model and interpret rates

You know how to use ratios to compare two quantities. You can also use ratios to make a graph to solve problems.

▶ Inga is bicycling at a rate of 15 miles per hour. Make a graph to show the relationship between how long Inga rides and how far she travels. How far can Inga ride in 2.5 hours?

❶ Make a table using the information in the problem.

Inga rides 15 miles every hour. This means that she rides 30 miles in 2 hours, 45 miles in 3 hours, and so on.

❷ Use the table to write ordered pairs (hours, miles). Plot the ordered pairs on the graph.

Plot (1, 15), (2, 30), (3, 45), and (4, 60).

❸ Draw a line through the points to show the relationship between time and distance.

❹ Find the point on the line that corresponds to 2.5 hours.

The point (2.5, 37.5) is on the line.

So, Inga can ride 37.5 miles in 2.5 hours.

Inga's Bicycle Ride

Hours	1	2	3	4
Miles	15	30	45	60

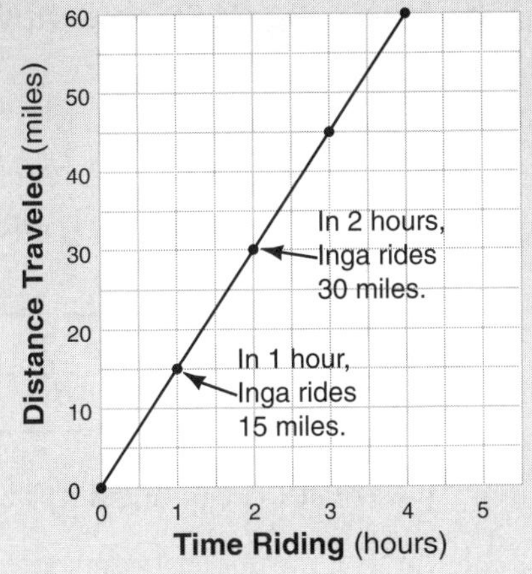

Practice

Use the following information.

Every 2 ounces of cereal have 1 gram of fat.

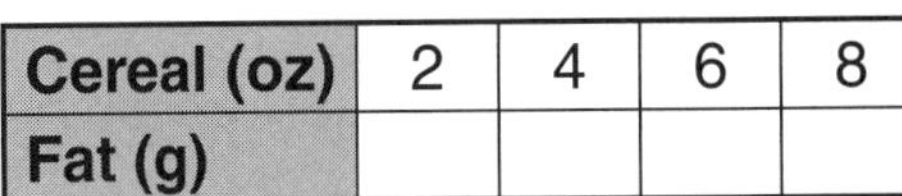

Cereal (oz)	2	4	6	8
Fat (g)				

1. Complete the table to show the relationship between the amount of fat in different amounts of cereal.

2. Use the table to make a graph.

3. How many grams of fat are in 8 ounces of cereal?

____

4. How many ounces of cereal contain exactly 3 grams of fat? _______________________

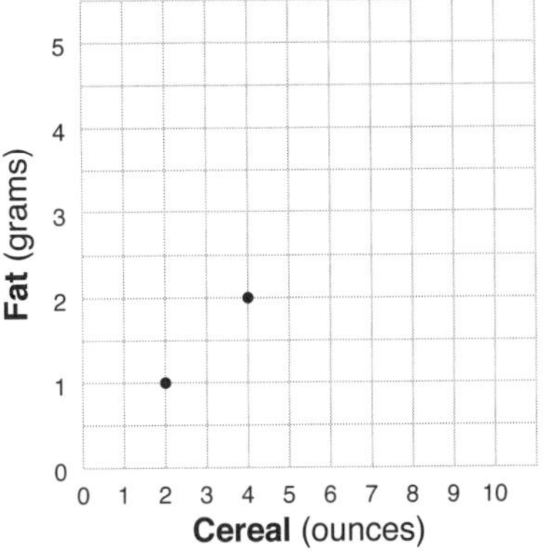

Discuss and Write

5. How can you use the graph to find the amount of fat in 5 ounces of cereal?

Name _______________________

Practice

Kate earns $8 per hour at work. Graph the relationship. Then use the graph to answer the questions.

Hours			
Pay			

6. How much does Kate earn in three hours?

____

7. Does Kate earn more or less than $18 in $2\frac{1}{2}$ hours? _______________________

8. How long does Kate have to work to earn $10?

____

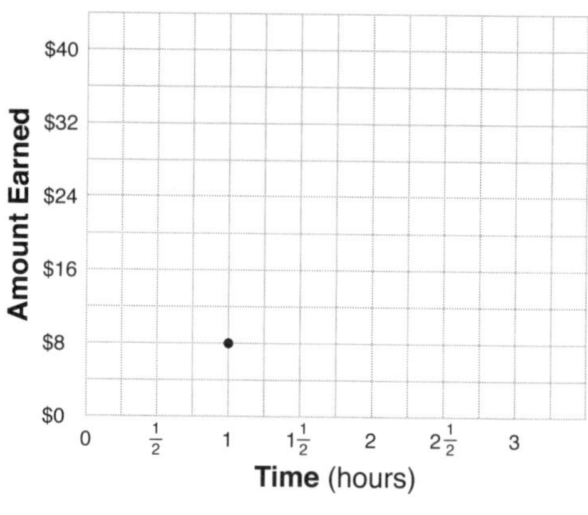

There are 12 grams of protein in 3 ounces of granola. Graph the relationship. Then use the graph to answer the questions.

Granola (oz)				
Protein (g)				

9. How much protein is in 5 ounces of granola?

____

10. How much granola would you need to eat to get 30 grams of protein? _______________________

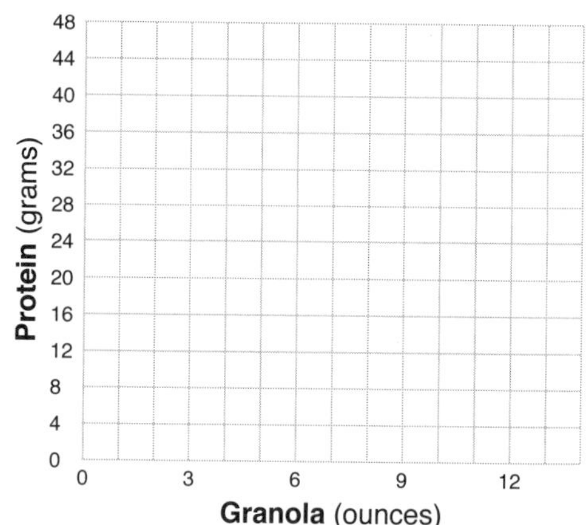

Problem Solving

Solve. Use a strategy that works best for you. Show your work.

11. On Saturday, John rides his bike for 2 hours. On Sunday, he rides his bike and travels 25 miles. Suppose John bikes at a constant rate of 6 miles every 20 minutes. How many miles does John travel in all over both days?

12. A recipe for 2 quarts of soup calls for 6 tomatoes. Jonas wants to make 5 quarts of soup. He has 13 tomatoes. Is this enough to make the soup? Explain.

Explain Your Reasoning

13. Kim bikes 10 miles in 30 minutes. George bikes 12 miles in 40 minutes. Is Kim's speed greater than or less than George's? Explain.

For additional Practice, go to page 296 in this Workbook.
Then go to Lesson 14-8, pages 510–511 in the Student Book.

Name _______________

Objective: To use tables, graphs, and equations to represent the relationship between quantities

To show how two quantities are related, you can use graphs, tables, and equations.

▶ The cost for x cups of smoothies at a juice stand is represented by the equation $y = 4.25x$, where y stands for the cost in dollars.

❶ Use the equation to make a table. List values for the number of cups, x. Then multiply by $4.25 to find the cost in dollars, y.

x (Cups)	$4.25 (x)	y (Dollars)
1	$4.25 (1)	$4.25
2	$4.25(2)	$8.50
3	$4.25(3)	$12.75
4	$4.25(4)	$17.00

Think
independent variable = number of cups
dependent variable = cost in dollars

❷ Use the values in the table to write ordered pairs.

(1, 4.25), (2, 8.5), (3, 12.75), (4, 17)

❸ Graph each ordered pair and connect the points.

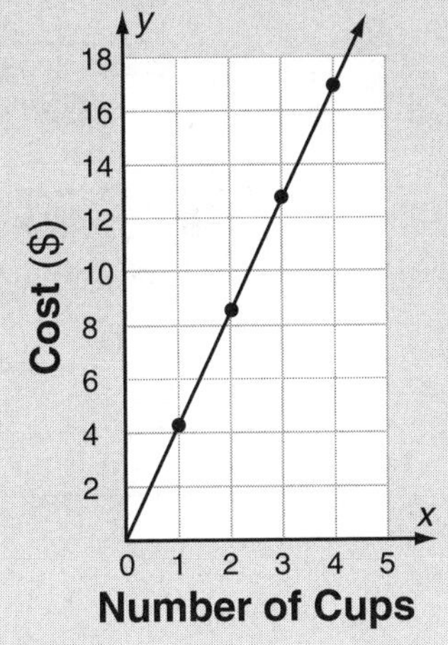

Note that the equation, the table, and the graph are different ways to represent the cost of buying cups of smoothies.

Practice

Delia earns 15 dollars per hour. Use this information to show the relationship.

1. Write an equation for Delia's earnings. Use d for the dollars she earns and h for the number of hours she works. _______________

2. Complete the table.

Hours	Earnings
1	
2	
3	
4	

3. Make a graph.

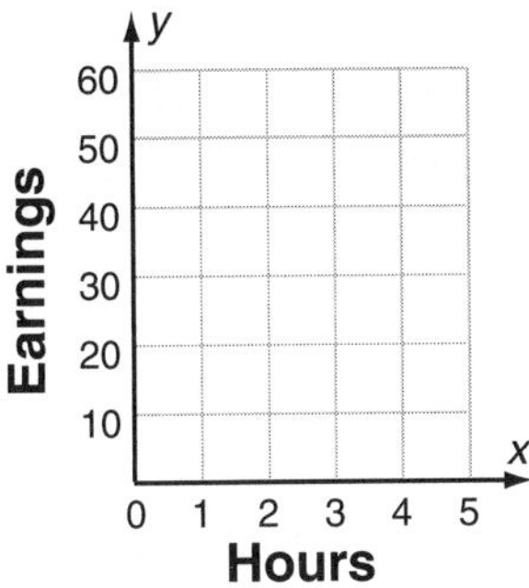

Discuss and Write

4. Explain when you would use the equation, table, and graph in the teaching display to show the relationship between cups and cost.

Name _______________________

Practice

Use the information to show the relationship two ways.

5. The graph shows the relationship between Gary's age and his sister's age. Complete the table. Then write an equation.

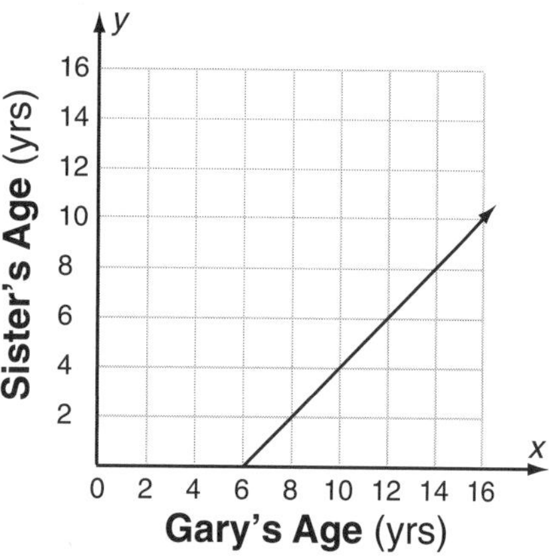

Gary's Age (years)	Sister's Age (years)
10	
13	
	10

6. The table relates the time it takes to hear thunder after a lightning strike with the distance of the lightning. Make a graph. Then write an equation.

Time (seconds)	Approx. Distance (miles)
4	0.8
7	1.4
10	2

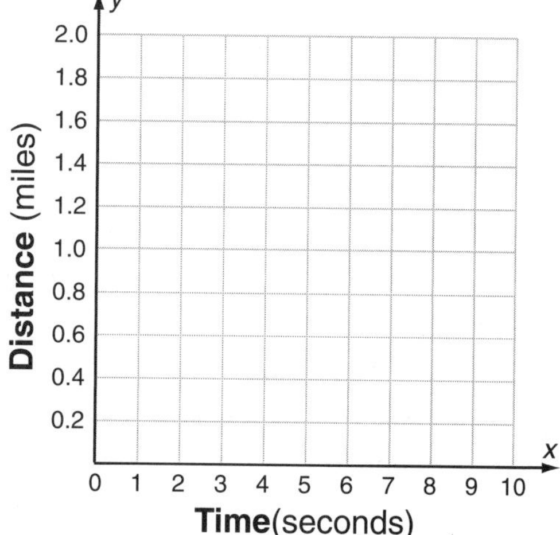

Problem Solving

Solve. Use a strategy that works best for you. Show your work.

7. Evan wants to buy a guitar that costs $150. He has saved $50 so far. Each week, he saves an additional $20. How long will it take Evan to save enough for the guitar?

8. Kris uses beads to make necklaces. She spends $120 for beads. Then she sells the necklaces for $15 each. How many necklaces must Kris sell to have a profit of $120?

Explain Your Reasoning

9. Look back at exercise 8. Suppose Kris wants to know how much profit she would make from selling 50 necklaces. Would a table, a graph, or an equation be most useful for this?

For additional Practice, go to page 297 in this Workbook.
Then go to Lesson 14-9, pages 512–513 in the Student Book.

Practice for Additional CCSS Lessons

Expressions

Translate the word phrase into a numerical expression.
Then state the number of terms in the expression.

Think

Terms are separated by + and − signs.

Numbers in parentheses count as 1 term.

The sum of 9 and 7 divided by 4 times 2

$(9 + 7) \qquad \div \quad 4 \times 2$

There is 1 term in the expression.

State the number of terms in each expression.

1. $6 \times (4 + 3 - 1)$ _______

2. $12 - (4 + 10 - 1) \times 6 \div (3 + 2) + 5$ _______

3. $3 + 5 (8 \times 2) \div 4$ _______

4. $10 - 5(2 + 6) - 2 + 4 \times (4 + 1)$ _______

Write each expression as a word phrase.

5. $7 \times (8 - 1) + 4$ _______________________________

6. $(40 \div 4) + (3 + 16)$ _______________________________

7. $90 - (5 \times 3) \div 2$ _______________________________

Write each word phrase as an expression.

8. the sum of twenty and ten divided by the product of two and nine _______________________________

9. fifty minus six plus five times the quotient of thirty and two _______________________________

10. the quotient of the sum of nine and forty and the difference of six and two _______________________________

Problem Solving

11. Lila bought 15 books. Six of the books each cost $7. Four of the books each cost $5. The rest of the books each cost $3. How much do the books cost in all?

____

12. Ellie has 74 marbles. She divides the marbles evenly between herself and her brother. Then she gives 15 of her marbles to her best friend. How many marbles does Ellie have left?

____

C Use with Lesson 4-1A, pages 207–208 in this Workbook.
C Then go to Lesson 4-2, pages 124–125 in the Student Book.

Expressions Involving Exponents

Name ___________________________

Translate and then evaluate.

the difference of 5 and 2, to the fourth power, plus eight

$(5 - 2)^4$ $+$ 8

- Use the Order of Operations to evaluate the expression.

$(5 - 2)^4 + 8 = (3)^4 \quad\quad + 8$ ⟵ Simplify inside parentheses.

$= (3 \times 3 \times 3 \times 3) + 8$ ⟵ Simplify numbers with exponents.

$= 81 \quad\quad + 8$ ⟵ Add.

$= 89$

So, the value of the expression is 89.

**Translate each word phrase into a numerical expression.
Then evaluate the expression.**

1. three to the fourth power, divided by 9

_______$^4 \div$ _______

_______ $\div$ _______

____

2. two to the third power, plus five squared

_______$^3 +$ _______^{2}

_______ $+$ _______

____

3. the sum of one and four, to the third power, minus five times twenty

_______$^3 -$ _______ $\times$ _______

_______$^3 -$ _______ $\times$ _______

_______ $-$ _______

____

4. the square of the sum of four and two, plus the difference of seven and three

_______$^2 +$ _______

_______$^2 +$ _______

_______ $+$ _______

____

Evaluate each expression.

5. $8^2 \div (5 - 1) =$ _______

6. $3^4 + 5^2 =$ _______

Problem Solving

7. Sherrie sells 15 raffle tickets. Jorge sells 3 fewer tickets than Sherrie. Aiden sells twice as many tickets as Jorge. How many raffle tickets do they sell in all?

____

8. Olivia deposits $3.00 into her savings account. The money in that account doubles every month. How much money is in her account after 4 months?

____

Use with Lesson 4-2A, pages 209–210 in this Workbook.
Then go to Lesson 4-3, pages 126–127 in the Student Book.

Equivalent Expressions

Name ___________________________

Determine whether the expressions are equivalent.

$$3(2x - 4) \text{ and } 6x - 12$$

- Substitute different values of x and evaluate both expressions.

The values of the expressions are the same for each substituted value of x, so $3(2x - 4)$ and $6x - 12$ are equivalent expressions.

x	$3(2x - 4)$	$6x - 12$	Same Value?
3	6	6	yes
4	12	12	yes
5	18	18	yes

Evaluate each pair of expressions when $x = 2$ and $x = 4$. Decide whether the expressions are equivalent.

1. $10x + 5$ and $10(x + 5)$

2. $6(x + 2x)$ and $18x$

Tell whether the expressions are equivalent.

3. $4(x + 9)$ and $4 + x + 13$

4. $6(x - 5)$ and $6x - 1$

5. $x(8 + 3)$ and $3x + 8x$

6. $7(5x + x)$ and $42x$

7. $4x + 3 - 2x$ and $5x$

8. $4(x + 5)$ and $x + 20 + 3x$

Problem Solving

Class Log

Day 1: 4 miles	Day 2: 6 miles	Day 3: 3 miles

9. There are n students on the cross country team. They all run the Day 1 and Day 2 miles. Michael says the total number of miles run by the group is $4n + 6n$. Willis says the total number of miles is $n(4 + 6)$. Who is correct? Explain.

10. The same group of students runs all three days. The total number of miles run can be expressed as $n(4 + 6 + 3)$. Which of the following is another way to express the total number of miles run: $13n$ or $4n + 6n + 3n$? Explain.

270

Use with Lesson 4-3A, pages 211–212 in this Workbook.
Then go to Lesson 4-3B, pages 213–214 in this Workbook.

Simplify Expressions

Name _______________________

Simplify: $7n + 2m - 4n + 6m$.

- Use the Properties of Operations.

$$7n - 4n + 2m + 6m \quad \longleftarrow \text{ Use the Commutative Property.}$$

$$(7n - 4n) + (2m + 6m) \quad \longleftarrow \text{ Use the Associative Property.}$$

$$(7 - 4)n + (2 + 6)m \quad \longleftarrow \text{ Use the Distributive Property.}$$

$$3n + 8m \quad \longleftarrow \text{ Simplify. This is the equivalent simplified expression.}$$

So, $7n + 2m - 4n + 6m = 3n + 8m$.

Complete each step in simplifying the expression.

1. Expression	Property Used
$8x + 5y + 2y - 3x$	
$8x - 3x + 5y + 2y$	__________
__________	Associative
$(8 - 3)x + (5 + 2)y$	__________
__________	__________

2. Expression	Property Used
$2(a + 3b) + 5(3a - b)$	
__________	Distributive
$2a + 15a + 6b - 5b$	__________
__________	__________
__________	__________
__________	__________

Simplify each expression.

3. $6y + 15x - 8x - 2y$

4. $5p + 9q + 2p - 4q$

5. $10r + 3(r - 4) + 7(2r - 3s)$

6. $3a + 3b - 2a + 5b$

7. $13c - 7d - 6c + 9d$

8. $2(4w + 3) - 4z + 5(w + 2z)$

Problem Solving

9. A rectangle has a length of x meters. The width of the rectangle is 5 meters more than the length. What is the perimeter of the rectangle?

10. At a school store, erasers cost x cents, pencils cost y cents, and pens cost z cents. Sam buys 5 of each. What is the total cost?

Inequalities

Name ______________________________

Marc is thinking of a number greater than 15.

- Write the solution set as an inequality.
  $x > 15$
- Represent the solution set on a number line.
  $x > 15$

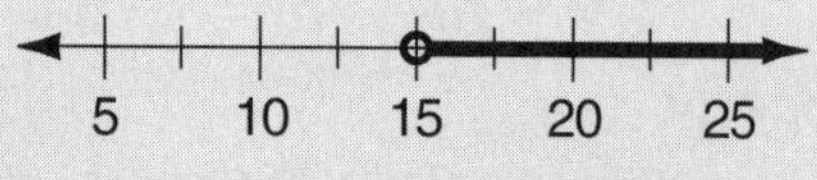

Use an open circle at 15 and shade to the right.

- Does $25 - 4$ make the inequality $x > 15$ true?
  $x > 15$
  $25 - 4 > 15$
  $21 > 15$ True

So, the expression $25 - 4$ makes the inequality true.

Make a number line diagram for the inequality. Then find a number that makes the inequality true.

1. $n > 16$

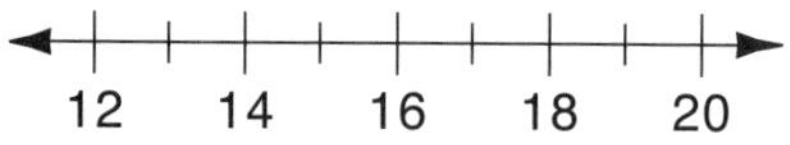

______

2. $y \leq 200$

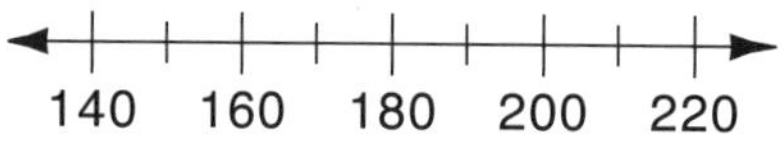

______

3. $s < 45$

______

4. $m \geq 12$

______

Tell whether the number makes the inequality $x < 19$ true.

5. 16 ______

6. 25 ______

7. 19 ______

8. 10 ______

Problem Solving

Write an inequality to describe the situation. Then answer the question.

9. Devin's score on his last math quiz was 82. He wants to score at least 8 points higher on his next quiz. Will he meet his goal if he scores an 89 on his next quiz?

____

10. Tito is making a model car. The glue has been drying for 25 minutes. It must dry for at least one hour before it is painted. Can Tito begin painting in 35 minutes?

____

Use with Lesson 4-4A, pages 215–216 in this Workbook.
Then go to Lesson 4-4B, pages 217–218 in this Workbook.

Write Inequalities

To ride a roller coaster, a person must be at least 48 inches tall. What heights can a passenger on the roller coaster be?

$h \geq 48$

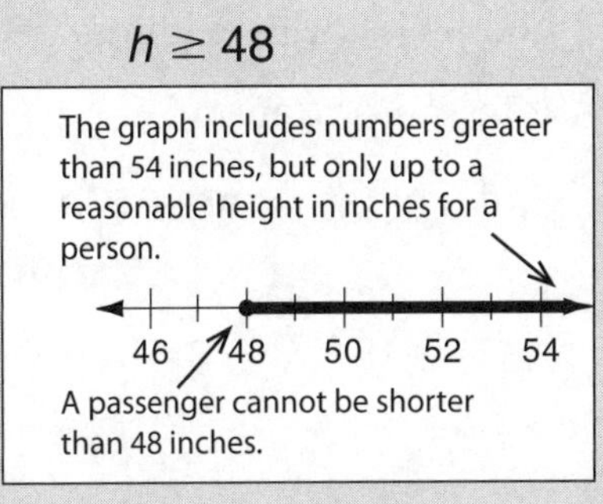

- Let h be the height of a person that is allowed to ride the roller coaster. Write an inequality.

- Graph the solution set on the number line.

- Interpret the graph.

So, a passenger can be 48 inches or taller.

Write an inequality. Then graph the inequality on a separate piece of paper. Explain which part of the solution set makes sense for the given situation.

1. A pickup truck can carry no more than 1940 pounds. How many pounds can the truck carry?

2. A basketball team must have 5 or more players. What are the possible numbers of players on a team?

3. Jan is building a box that must be more than 12 inches wide. How wide can the box be?

4. According to the Federal Aviation Administration, a hang glider must fly lower than 18,000 feet. How high can a hang glider fly?

Problem Solving

5. Mary has $48 to spend at the county fair. She pays $12 to enter the fair. How much money can she spend on food, games, and rides at the fair?

6. Eli found 3 boxes of nails in the garage. If they were full, each box would contain 100 nails, but Eli knows that some nails have been used. How many nails might be in the 3 boxes?

Use with Lesson 4-4B, pages 217–218 in this Workbook.
Then go to Lesson 4-5, pages 130–131 in the Student Book.

Write an Equation

Name ______________________________

> Three sacks of potatoes weigh 48 pounds. How much does one sack of potatoes weigh?
>
> - Let w represent the weight in pounds of one sack of potatoes.
> - Write the equation.
>
>   total weight = three $\times$ weight of one sack
>
> $$48 = 3 \times w$$
>
> - Solve.
>
> $$48 = 3 \times w$$
> $$48 \div 3 = 3 \times w \div 3 \quad \longleftarrow$$
> $$16 = w$$
>
>   Use the Division Property of Equality.
>
> So, one sack of potatoes weighs 16 pounds.

Solve by writing an equation.

1. There are 29 open spaces on the first floor of a parking garage. This is 12 more open spaces than on the second floor. How many spaces are open on the second floor?

   first floor = second floor + ______

   ______ = ______ + ______

   ______ = ______

   ____

2. Twelve tickets to the state football championship game cost \$72. How much does one ticket to the game cost?

   total cost = ______ $\times$ dollar amount for one ticket

   ______ = ______ $\times$ ______

   ______ = ______

   ____

Problem Solving

3. Lilly charges \$12 per hour for babysitting. In March, she earned \$264 for babysitting. How many hours did Lilly babysit in March?

   ____

4. Anna bought 12 red pens. She bought 8 more blue pens than red pens. How many pens did she buy in all?

   ____

5. A jeep used for sightseeing trips has 19 gallons of fuel in its tank. It uses 6 gallons of fuel on its first trip. After its second trip it has 5 gallons of fuel left in the tank. How many gallons of fuel does the jeep use on its second trip?

   ____

6. Mrs. Truman is buying 5 notebooks. Each notebook costs \$1.50. How much does she spend in all for the notebooks?

   ____

Use with Lesson 4-7A, pages 219–220 in this Workbook.
Then go to Lesson 4-8, pages 136–137 in the Student Book.

Integers in the Real World

Name _______________________________

A scuba diver is swimming 30 meters below the surface of the water. A boat is waiting for him at the surface. Use a number line to represent this situation. What does 0 mean on the number line?

- The diver is 30 meters below the surface of the water. The integer is −30.

- The boat is neither above nor below the surface of the water. The integer is 0.

So, 0 represents the surface of the water in this situation.

Plot the point that represents the situation. Then explain what 0 represents in the situation.

1. Angela opens a savings account with an initial deposit of $100.

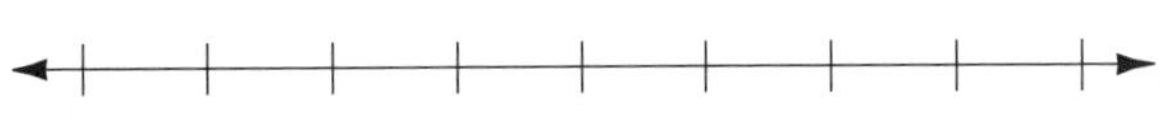

____

2. Arthur digs a hole 2 feet deep.

____

3. A submarine travels 500 feet below the surface of the ocean.

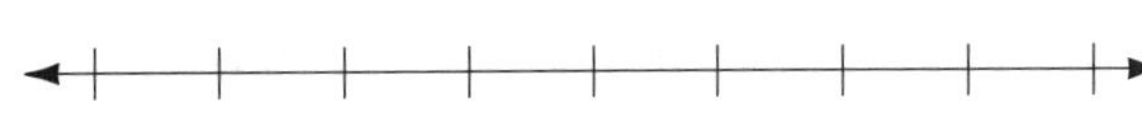

____

4. A bird flies 50 feet above the ground.

____

Problem Solving

Represent the situation on the number line. Then explain why the second statement is false.

5. Marge builds a 4-foot tower of blocks on a table. The top of the tower is 4 feet below the top of the table.

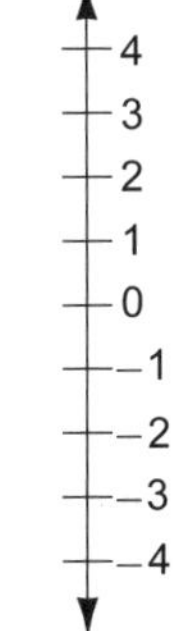

____

6. Johan moves down 15 meters from the top of a ladder. He is now 15 meters above the ground.

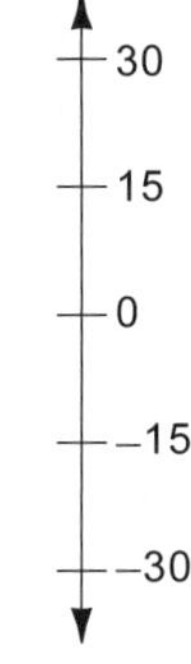

____

C Use with Lesson 5-1A, pages 221–222 in this Workbook.
C Then go to Lesson 5-2, pages 152–153 in the Student Book.

Using Reasoning to Compare and Order Rational Numbers

Name _______________________

Leslie and Jarmal both have $200 in their accounts.

Leslie deposits $60 and Jarmal withdraws $80.

- Who has the greater balance? Compare the integers.

  $-80 < 60$

  Think
  The value of -80 is less than the value of 60.

  Leslie has the greater balance.

- Whose balance had the greater change? Compare the absolute values.

  $|-80| > |60|$

  Think
  The magnitude of -80 is greater than the magnitude of 60.

  Jarmal's balance had the greater change.

Write an inequality to represent the situation.

1. A person who earns $125 gets more money than a person who earns $120.

2. A flock of seagulls flying 10 feet above a lake is closer to the surface of the water than a school of fish swimming 15 feet below the surface.

3. The magnitude of a $90 increase in stocks and a $90 decrease in stocks is the same.

4. On a number line, the integer -10 has a greater distance from 0 than the integer 8.

Complete the statement by writing *more* or *less*.

5. An airplane ascended to a height greater than 5000 feet. The airplane flew _______ than 5000 feet.

6. A whale is swimming at a depth above -20 meters. The whale is _______ than 20 meters from the ocean's surface.

Problem Solving

Describe a situation that the inequality could represent.

7. $-5 < 0$

8. $|-30| > |-25|$

Use with Lesson 5-2A, pages 223–224 in this Workbook.
Then go to Lesson 5-3, pages 154–155 in the Student Book.

The Distributive Property and Common Factors

Name _______________________

Rewrite $(24 + 40)$ as a multiple of a sum of two whole numbers with no common factor.

- List all the factors of each number. Find the Greatest Common Factor (GCF).

  Factors of 24: **1, 2**, 3, **4**, 6, **8**, 12, 24
  Factors of 40: **1, 2, 4**, 5, **8**, 10, 20, 40
  Common factors: 1, 2, 4, **8**. GCF: **8**

- Write each addend as a multiple of the GCF.

  $24 = \mathbf{8} \times 3$ $40 = \mathbf{8} \times 5$

- Use the Distributive Property to rewrite the expression.

  $$24 \quad + \quad 40$$
  $$(\mathbf{8} \times 3) + (\mathbf{8} \times 5)$$
  $$\mathbf{8} \times (3 + 5)$$

So, $(24 + 40) = 8 \times (3 + 5)$.

Rewrite as a multiple of a sum of two whole numbers with no common factor.

1. $20 + 48$

___ $\times$ (___ + ___)

2. $64 + 40$

___ $\times$ (___ + ___)

3. $28 + 35$

___ $\times$ (___ + ___)

4. $12 + 18$

___ $\times$ (___ + ___)

5. $45 + 25$

___ $\times$ (___ + ___)

6. $14 + 8$

___ $\times$ (___ + ___)

Rewrite each product as the sum of two numbers.

7. $4 \times (9 + 5)$

____

8. $2 \times (5 + 8)$

____

9. $6 \times (3 + 7)$

____

10. $7 \times (3 + 9)$

____

11. $3 \times (8 + 5)$

____

12. $9 \times (6 + 8)$

____

Problem Solving

13. Mr. Owens has 16 green pens and 24 red pens. How many students can share both color pens equally without any left over?

____

14. To find $(9 \times 36) + (9 \times 14)$, Denise rewrites the expression as 9×50. Does this make sense? Explain why or why not.

____

Dividing with Fractions

Name ______________________

Mr. Lambert needs to clean the floor using $\frac{1}{8}$ cup of bleach per bucket of water. He has $\frac{3}{4}$ cup of bleach. How many buckets of the mixture can he make?

Divide: $\frac{3}{4} \div \frac{1}{8}$

Use a visual fraction model.

- Model $\frac{3}{4}$.

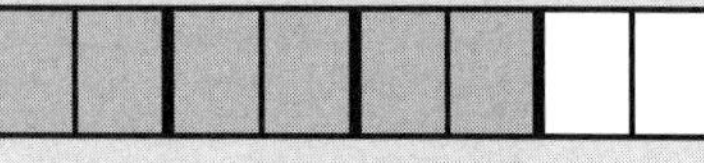

- Divide the same whole into eighths.

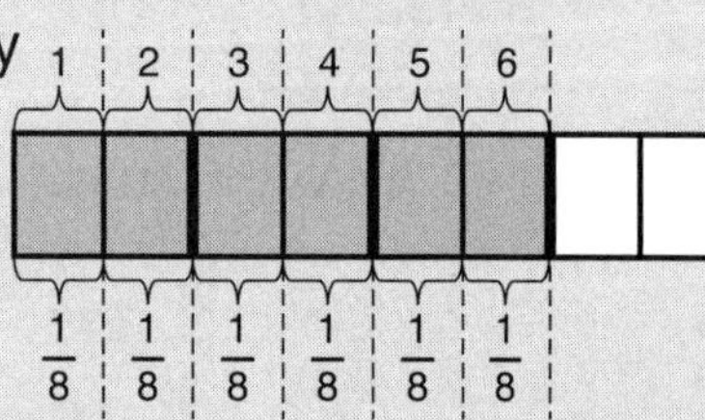

- Find how many $\frac{1}{8}$ are in $\frac{3}{4}$.

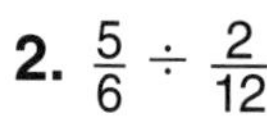

Use the relationship between multiplication and division.

- Rewrite as a multiplication equation.

$$\frac{3}{4} = \frac{1}{8} \times n$$

- Use the Division Property of Equality.

$$\frac{3}{4} \div \frac{1}{8} = \frac{1}{8} \div \frac{1}{8} \times n$$

$$6 = n$$

The number of $\frac{1}{8}$ in $\frac{3}{4}$ is 6.

So, Mr. Lambert can make 6 buckets of the bleach mixture.

Divide. Use fraction models.

1. $\frac{2}{4} \div \frac{3}{12}$

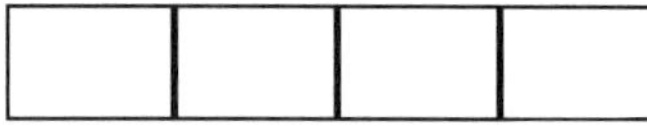

____

2. $\frac{5}{6} \div \frac{2}{12}$

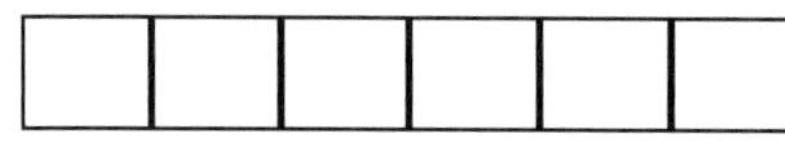

____

3. $\frac{4}{5} \div \frac{6}{15}$

____

Solve for x.

4. $\frac{5}{8} \div \frac{2}{16} = x$

________ $= x$

5. $\frac{3}{5} \div \frac{6}{10} = x$

________ $= x$

6. $\frac{1}{7} \div \frac{5}{14} = x$

________ $= x$

7. $x = \frac{15}{16} \div \frac{3}{4}$

$x =$ ________

Problem Solving

8. Josh uses $\frac{1}{8}$ cup of oil to make one batch of clay. He has $\frac{3}{4}$ cup of oil. How many batches of clay can he make?

____

Use with Lesson 8-5A, pages 227–228 in this Workbook.
Then go to Lesson 8-6, pages 260–261 in the Student Book.

Summarize the Data

Name _______________________

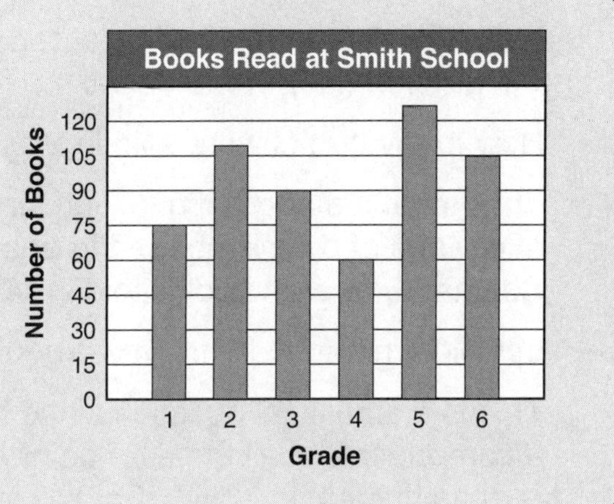

The bar graph shows the number of books read by all the students at the Smith School. What can you tell from the graph?

- Smith School consists of Grades 1 through 6.

- The 5th grade class read more books than any other grade.

- In all, the students at Smith School read approximately 567 books.

Todd surveys high school students about their favorite sport.

Use the graph to answer the questions.

1. What do the numbers on the vertical axis show?

   ____

2. How many students did Todd survey?

   ____

3. How many more students preferred basketball over swimming? How do you know?

   ____

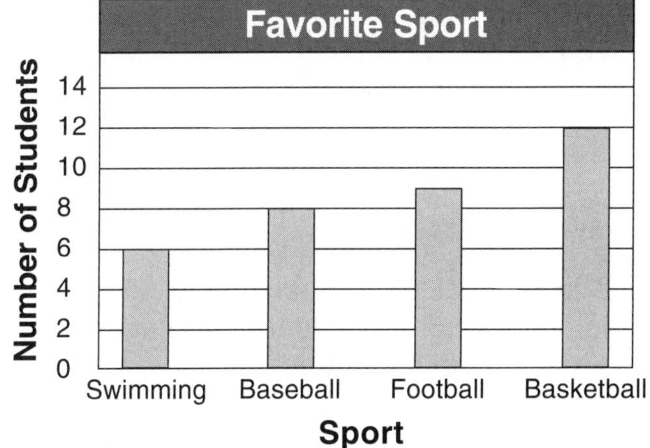

Problem Solving

4. The Shoe Shack recorded the number of pairs of shoes they sold each day during the week. How many pairs of shoes were sold on Wednesday and Thursday?

   ____

5. How many more pairs of shoes did they sell on their highest sale day than on their lowest sale day?

   ____

Shoe Shack	
Day	**Pairs Sold**
Mon.	16
Tue.	32
Wed.	22
Thu.	28
Fri.	12

C Use with Lesson 9-3A, pages 229–230 in this Workbook.
C Then go to Lesson 9-4, pages 298–299 in the Student Book.

Statistical Characteristics of a Data Set

Name ___________________________

Tell whether each question is *statistical* or *not statistical* and why. Then answer the question.

- How many books were sold in May?

  This is not a statistical question since only one piece of data is needed to answer it. So, the number of books sold in May was 40.

- In which month were the most books sold?

  This is a statistical question since it involves a comparison of all the data points. The line plot is at its highest in March. So, the month in which the most books were sold was March.

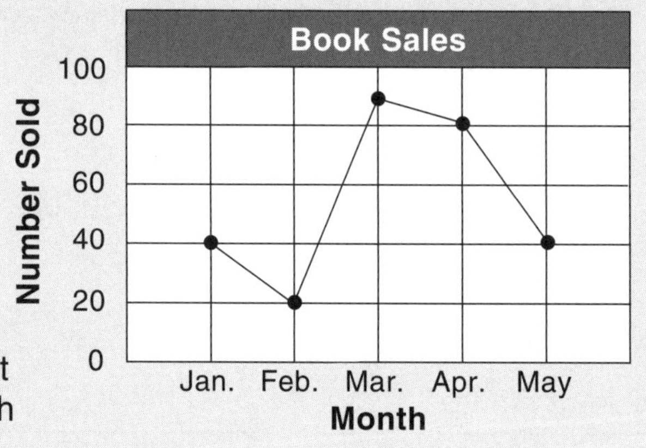

Tell whether the question is *statistical* or *not statistical* and why.

1. How many rivers run through Arizona?

2. What is the average price of a tablet computer?

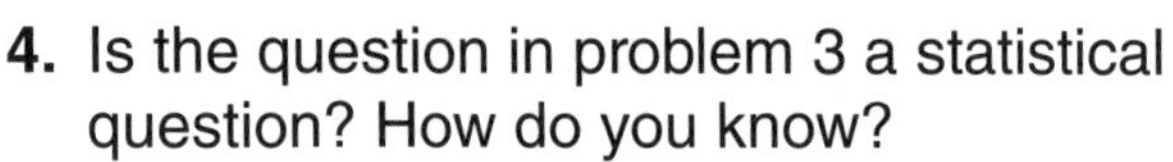

The national tourism bureau has contracted a lumber company to clear a trail through a forest. Their progress is recorded in the bar graph.

3. On an average day, how many feet of trail does the lumber company clear?

4. Is the question in problem 3 a statistical question? How do you know?

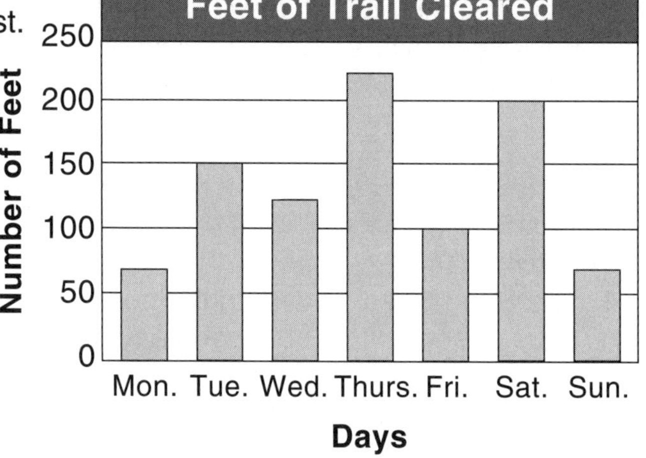

5. On how many days did the lumber company clear more than the mean number of feet of trail?

6. Is the question in problem 5 a statistical question? How do you know?

Use with Lesson 9-6A, pages 231–232 in this Workbook.
Then go to Lesson 9-6B, pages 233–234 in this Workbook.

Choosing the Best Measures to Describe Data

Name _______________________

Find the statistical measures for the data set.

| 12 | 13 | 14 | 15 | 15 |
| 16 | 17 | 18 | 21 | 69 |

Mean: 21; Median: 15.5; Mode: 15; Range: 57

• Find the Interquartile Range (IQR).

Upper Quartile = 18
Lower Quartile = 14
Upper Quartile − Lower Quartile = 18 − 14 = 4

So, the IQR is 4.

• Find the Mean Absolute Deviation (MAD).

$(9 + 8 + 7 + 6 + 6 + 5 + 4 + 3 + 0 + 48) \div 10 = 96 \div 10 = 9.6$

So, the MAD is 9.6.

Find the statistical measures for the data set. Tell which measure(s) best describe the data.

1. 25 48 48 48 50 50 50 50 50 51

Mean: _____ Median: _____ Mode: _____

Range: _____ IQR: _____ MAD: _____

____

2. 32 33 35 35 36 38 38 38 39 46

Mean: _____ Median: _____ Mode: _____

Range: _____ IQR: _____ MAD: _____

____

3. 50 51 52 52 52 52 53 61 65 72

Mean: _____ Median: _____ Mode: _____

Range: _____ IQR: _____ MAD: _____

____

4. 92 105 110 111 112 114 115 116 116 129

Mean: _____ Median: _____ Mode: _____

Range: _____ IQR: _____ MAD: _____

____

Problem Solving

	M	T	W	Th	F	M	T	W	Th	F
Food Bank	2	6	10	6	8	3	5	11	5	14
Animal Shelter	5	8	7	10	14	4	5	6	8	13

5. The chart represents the number of students who volunteered after school at the local food bank and animal shelter over the course of two weeks. On the average, which organization had more students per day?

6. Which organization's number of volunteers stayed closest to the mean? Explain which measure you used to answer the question.

____

Describe Data

Name ___________________________

The dot plot shows the number of students in 10 middle schools.

Which measure of central tendency best describes the data?

Number of Middle School Students

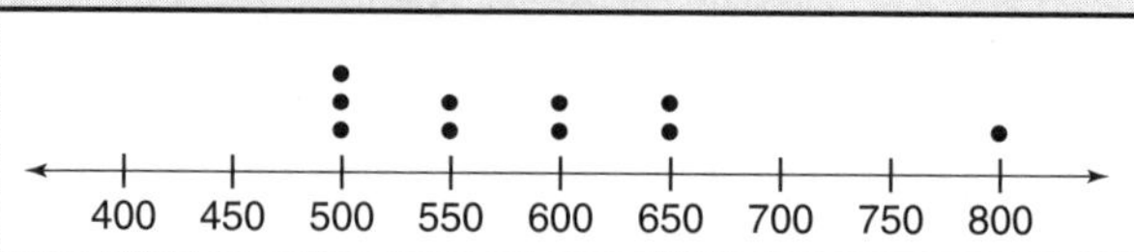

The mode is 500, which is also the lowest data value. So, the mode is not a good measure.

The median, 575, and the mean, 590, are fairly close. So, examine the spread of the data.

Number of Middle School Students

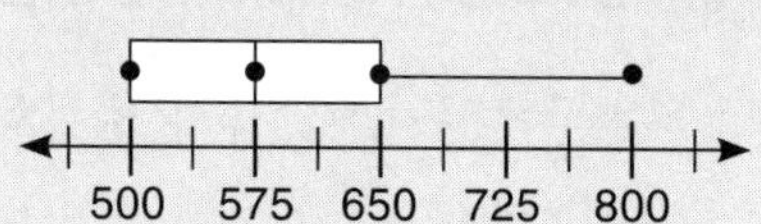

The IQR is 150, and the MAD is 70. A *lesser value* for the MAD shows that the data vary less from the mean.

So, the mean, 590, best describes the data.

Use the given data to answer each question.

1. Numbers of Times Eating Out Last Month

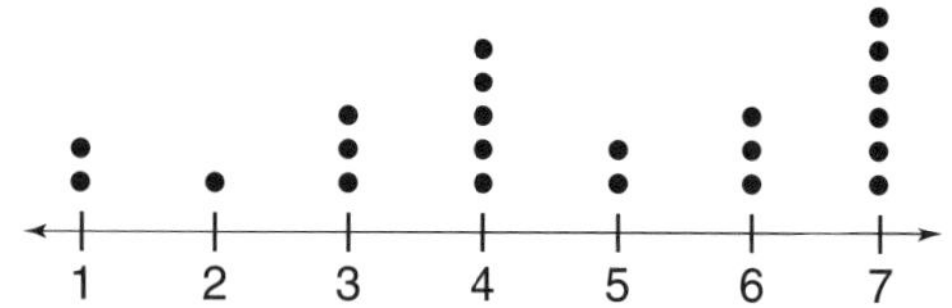

Which measure (mean, median, or mode) would be least useful for this data? Why?

2. Workshop Attendance

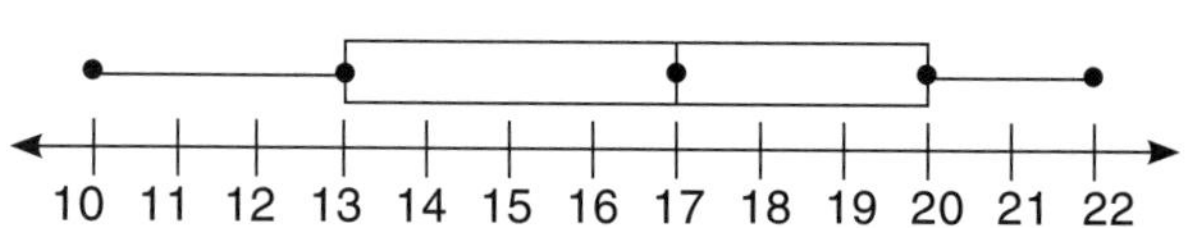

What are the range, median, and IQR of the data?

Problem Solving

The dot plot shows the prices of 25 audiobooks. Use the data to answer the questions.

3. Find the mean, median, and mode of the data.

Audiobook Prices

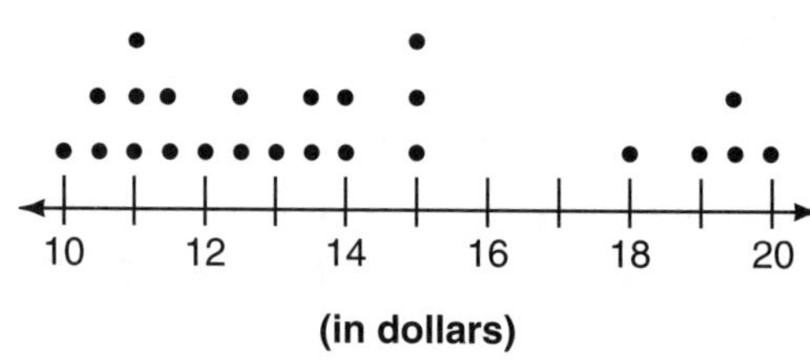

4. Which measure best represents the data? Explain.

Use with Lesson 9-7A, pages 235–236 in this Workbook.
Then go to Lesson 9-8, pages 306–307 in the Student Book.

Ratio and Rate Tables

Name _______________________

For every $15 Jasmine earns, she deposits $6 into her savings account. How much money does Jasmine put into her savings account if she earns $105?

- Write the ratio of dollars earned to dollars saved. Then use the ratio to generate a table of equivalent ratios.

$$\frac{15}{6} = \frac{30}{12} = \frac{45}{18} = \frac{60}{24} = \frac{75}{30} = \frac{90}{36} = \frac{105}{42}$$

$ Earned	$ Saved	
15	6	Ratio 15 : 6
30	12	$15 \times 2, 6 \times 2$
45	18	$15 \times 3, 6 \times 3$
60	24	$15 \times 4, 6 \times 4$
75	30	$15 \times 5, 6 \times 5$
90	36	$15 \times 6, 6 \times 6$
105	42	$15 \times 7, 6 \times 7$

So, if Jasmine earns $105, she puts $42 into her savings account.

Use equivalent ratios.

1. A recycling company pays 25 cents for every 5 aluminum cans. Complete the table.

2. How much are 12 cans worth? _______

3. How many cans are worth $1.00? _______

4. How much are 2 cans worth? _______

5. How many cans are worth $1.40? _______

Cans	Value
4	20¢
8	
12	60¢
	80¢
20	$1.00
24	

Problem Solving

The table shows Dustin's average gas mileage. Complete the table.

6. Dustin travels 138 miles, stops for lunch, and then travels 230 miles more. How many gallons of gas does Dustin use?

____

7. After dinner, Dustin fills his gas tank. He drives for several hours and then stops to get gas again. It takes 13 gallons to fill his tank this time. About how far did Dustin travel after dinner?

Gallons	Miles
2	46
	92
6	138
	230
12	
	322

Ratios and Unit Rates

Name _______________________

> The office assistant answered 21 calls in 7 minutes. Find the unit rate of the number of calls to time in minutes.
>
> - The ratio or rate is 21 calls : 7 minutes.
> - Rewrite as a fraction: $\frac{21 \text{ calls}}{7 \text{ minutes}}$.
> - Simplify to get a denominator of 1: $\frac{21 \text{ calls}}{7 \text{ minutes}} = \frac{3 \text{ calls}}{1 \text{ minute}}$.
>
> So, the unit rate is 3 calls per minute or $\frac{3 \text{ calls}}{1 \text{ minute}}$.

Explain what the ratio means.

1. A school has a student-teacher ratio of 15 : 1.

2. The ratio of hydrogen atoms to oxygen in a molecule of water is 2 : 1.

Write a ratio for the situation. Then find the unit rate.

3. Rachel pays $5.40 for a 12-pound bag of plant food.

ratio: _______________

unit rate: _______________________

4. On a map, 400 miles is represented by 5 inches.

ratio: _______________

unit rate: _______________________

5. Jason burns 132 calories for every 12 minutes he runs on a treadmill.

ratio: _______________

unit rate: _______________________

6. A hotel charges $575 for a 5-night stay.

ratio: _______________

unit rate: _______________________

Problem Solving

7. Erika sews a 16-inch table runner and uses 2 yards of fabric. How many yards of fabric will it take to make a 4-foot or 48-inch long table runner?

8. A brunch at a restaurant costs $1100 for 50 guests. How much will the brunch cost if there are 80 guests?

Use with Lesson 11-2B, pages 239–240 in this Workbook.
Then go to Lesson 11-3, pages 380–381 in the Student Book.

Compare Ratios

> Brand A trail mix has a ratio of 10 almonds : 3 cranberries.
> The ratio for Brand B is 15 almonds : 4 cranberries.
> Which brand of trail mix has the greater ratio of almonds
> to cranberries?
>
> - Make a table of equivalent ratios
>   for each brand.
>
> - Both tables have an entry
>   for 12 cranberries.
>   Compare the entries. $\frac{45}{12} > \frac{40}{12}$
>
> **Brand A**
>
> | Almonds | 10 | 20 | 30 | 40 |
> |---|---|---|---|---|
> | Cranberries | 3 | 6 | 9 | 12 |
>
> **Brand B**
>
> | Almonds | 15 | 30 | 45 | 60 |
> |---|---|---|---|---|
> | Cranberries | 4 | 8 | 12 | 16 |
>
> So, Brand B has the greater ratio of almonds to cranberries.

Compare the ratios using a table. Then identify which ratio is greater.

1. a) 3 : 14   **b)** 5 : 21

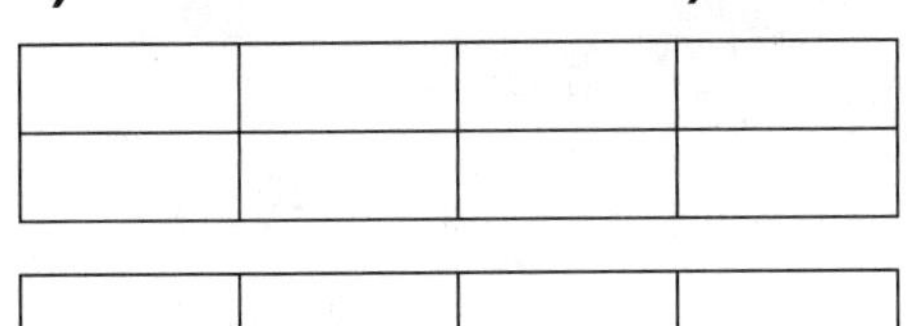

2. a) 9 : 16   **b)** 13 : 24

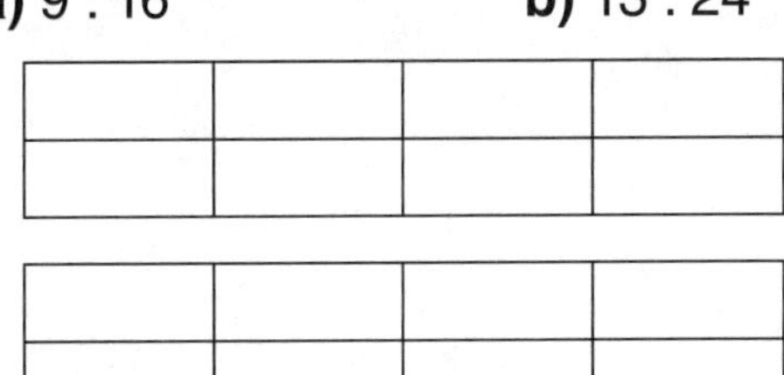

3. a) $\frac{5}{12}$ **b)** $\frac{6}{16}$

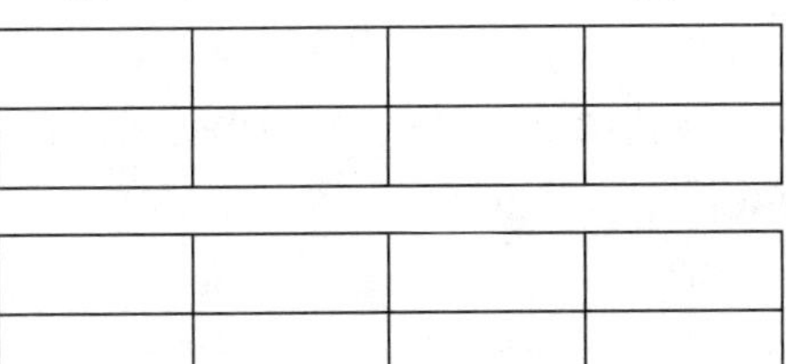

4. a) $\frac{7}{15}$ **b)** $\frac{13}{20}$

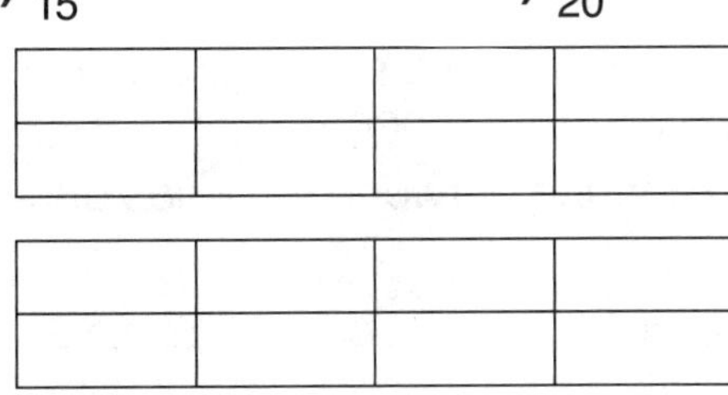

Problem Solving

5. Roxanne can jump rope 70 times in
2 minutes. Deanne can jump rope 90 times
in 3 minutes. Who can jump rope faster?

6. A 4-pound bag of organic birdseed costs
$14. A 25-pound bag costs $70. Which is
the better buy?

Model Proportions with Double Number Lines

Name _________________________

An art teacher plans to buy 2 boxes of fine point markers for every 5 students in his class. How many boxes should he buy if he has 25 students?

- Draw a double number-line diagram.

- Label the scales on each side.

- Find the point for 25 students. Find the corresponding number of boxes. The corresponding number is 10.

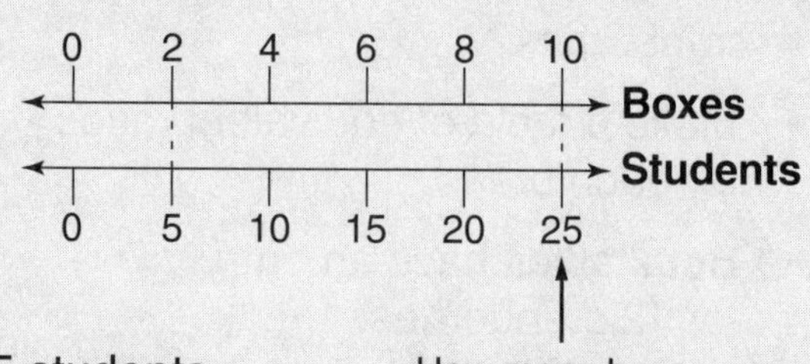

So, he should buy 10 boxes of fine point markers for 25 students.

Complete the double number-line diagram to find 4 ratios equivalent to the given ratio.

1. Ratio 6 : 7

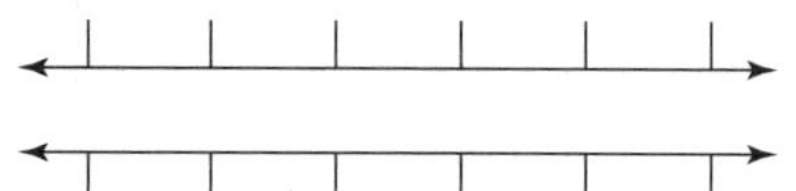

____

2. Ratio 11 : 4

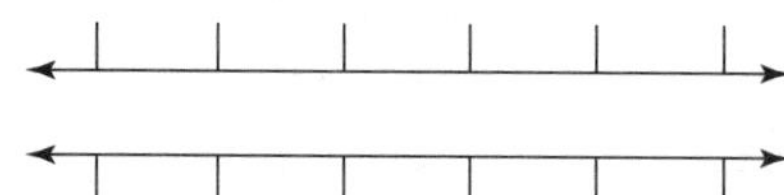

____

Problem Solving

3. Three inches on a map represent 500 miles. If two cities are 2000 miles apart, what is the distance between the cities on the map?

____

4. Clarisse can make 3 friendship bracelets in $2\frac{1}{2}$ hours. How many bracelets can she make in 15 hours?

____

5. A professional baseball team uses 8 new baseballs in 3 innings. At this rate, how many new baseballs will they use in 9 innings?

____

6. Four baby elephants eat about 1000 pounds of food each day. At this rate, about how much food is needed to feed 10 baby elephants for 7 days?

____

Use with Lesson 11-4A, pages 243–244 in this Workbook.
Then go to Lesson 11-4B, pages 245–246 in this Workbook.

Model Proportions with Tape Diagrams

Name _______________________

Use a tape diagram to find an equivalent ratio.

- Draw a tape diagram. Since the ratio is 3 : 4, the top strip has 3 segments and the bottom strip has 4 segments.

- Find the number that each segment represents. Since the first term in the second ratio is 18, each segment represents $18 \div 3 = 6$.

- Use the tape diagram to find the second term in the second ratio: $4 \times 6 = 24$.

So, the ratio 18 : 24 is equivalent to 3 : 4.

$$3 : 4 = 18 : \rule{2cm}{0.4pt}$$

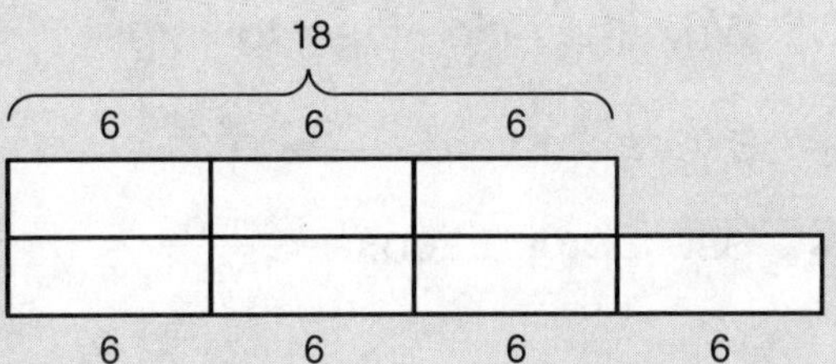

Complete the tape diagram to find an equivalent ratio.

1. $2 : 3 = \rule{1cm}{0.4pt} : 75$

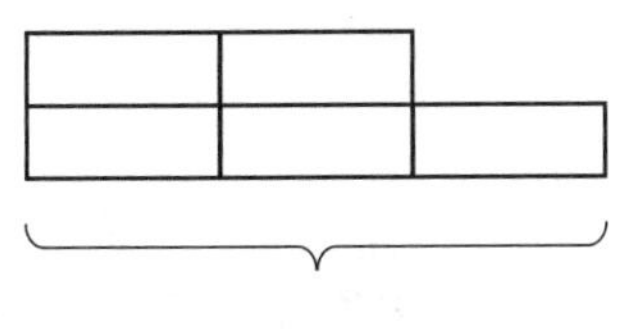

2. $5 : 3 = 35 : \rule{1cm}{0.4pt}$

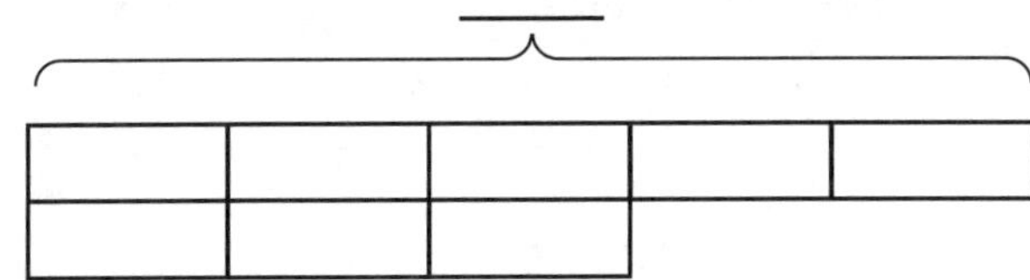

3. $4 : 5 = 48 : \rule{1cm}{0.4pt}$

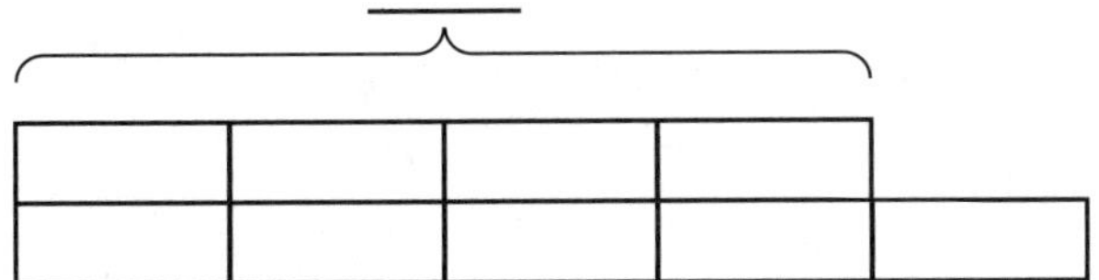

4. $1 : 3 = \rule{1cm}{0.4pt} : 45$

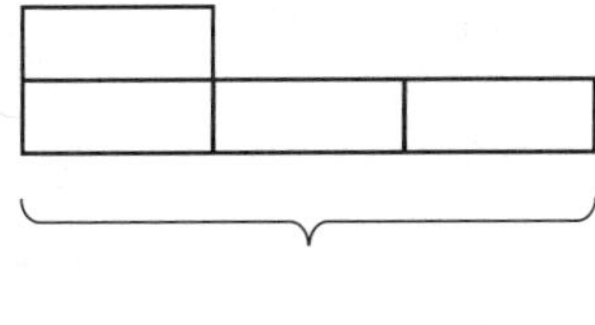

Problem Solving

5. The driver of a delivery truck can deliver to 11 locations in 2 days. How long will it take him to deliver to 44 locations?

____

6. Mr. Petersen grades 50 papers in a half hour. How long will it take him to grade 300 papers?

____

Use Proportions to Convert Units

Name _______________________

How many feet are in 45 yards?

- Write the ratio of feet to yards.

  3 feet = 1 yard $\longrightarrow \dfrac{3 \text{ feet}}{1 \text{ yard}}$

- Use a proportion. $\dfrac{3 \text{ feet}}{1 \text{ yard}} = \dfrac{f \text{ feet}}{45 \text{ yard}}$

  $$\dfrac{3}{1} = \dfrac{f}{45}$$

- Solve the proportion. $3 \times 45 = 1 \times f$

  $$135 = f$$

So, there are 135 feet in 45 yards.

Remember:
Cross-Products Rule

$$\dfrac{a}{b} \diagdown \dfrac{c}{d}$$

$$a \times d = b \times c$$

Write and solve a proportion to convert between units of measure.

1. How many pints are in 22 gallons?
1 gallon = 8 pints

2. How many yards are in 378 inches?
1 yard = 36 inches

3. How many meters are in 23 kilometers?
1 kilometer = 1000 meters

4. How many liters are in 6 gallons?
1 gallon $\approx$ 3.79 liters

5. How many minutes are in 14 hours?
1 hour = 60 minutes

6. How many inches are in
76.2 centimeters?
1 inch = 2.54 centimeters

7. How many pounds are in 56 ounces?
1 pound = 16 ounces

8. How many milligrams are in
8 centigrams?
1 centigram = 10 milligrams

Problem Solving

9. A weather satellite checks the air pressure 3 times per hour. How many times per week does the satellite check the air pressure?

10. Marion walks at a constant rate of 176 feet per minute. How many miles does she walk in 1 hour?
(1 mile = 5280 feet)

Use with Lesson 13-7A, pages 247–248 in this Workbook.
Then go to Lesson 13-8, pages 462–463 in the Student Book.

Plane Figures and Area

Name ______________________

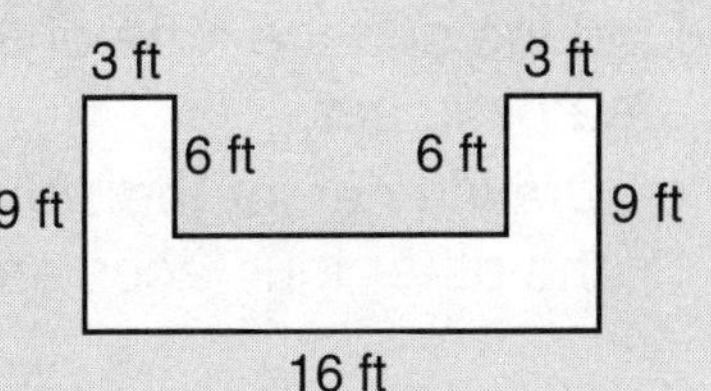

Find the area of the figure.

- Divide the figure into three rectangles. Label their dimensions.

- Find the area of each part.

  Area of one vertical rectangle = length × width
  $$18 \text{ ft}^2 = 3 \text{ ft} \times 6 \text{ ft}$$
  Area of horizontal rectangle = length × width
  $$48 \text{ ft}^2 = 16 \text{ ft} \times 3 \text{ ft}$$

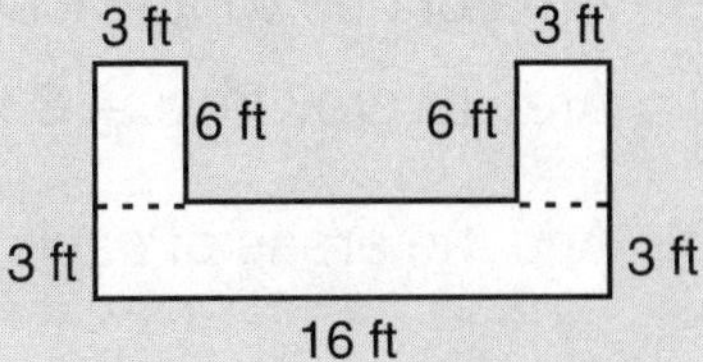

- Add the areas of the parts. Be sure to include the area of both vertical rectangles.

$$18 \text{ ft}^2 + 18 \text{ ft}^2 + 48 \text{ ft}^2 = 84 \text{ ft}^2$$

So, the area of the figure is 84 ft².

Find the area of each figure by making simpler shapes.

1.

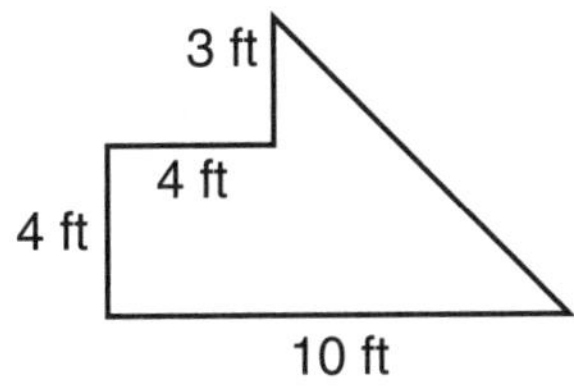

____

2.

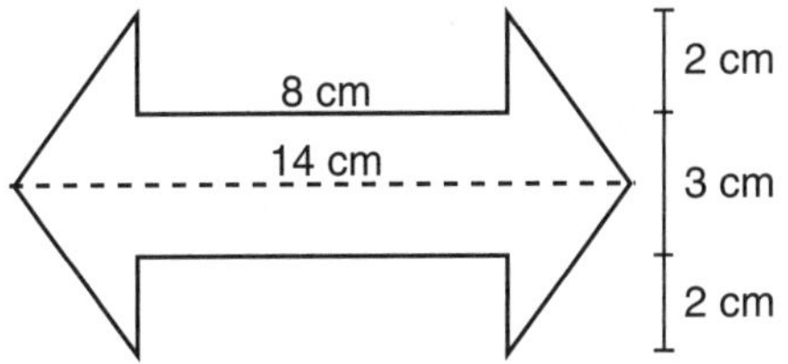

____

Problem Solving

3. Carrie is covering her entire patio, which has the shape shown, with new tile. How many square meters of tile does she need?

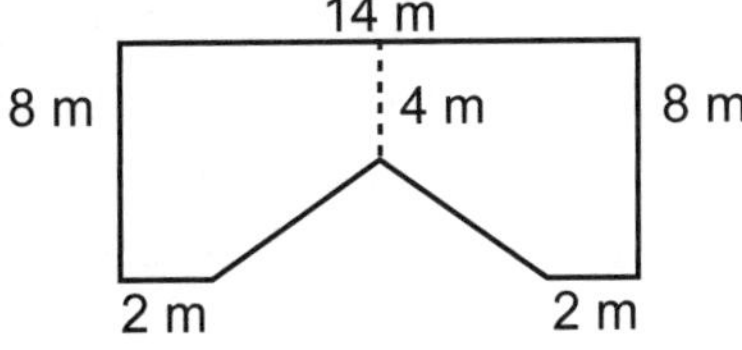

4. Tyler makes an E by cutting two small rectangles out of a large rectangular piece of wood that is 10 inches by 6 inches. If the small rectangles measure 2 inches by 4 inches, what is the area of the E?

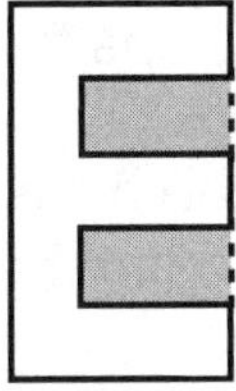

____

Use Nets to Find Surface Area

Name _______________________

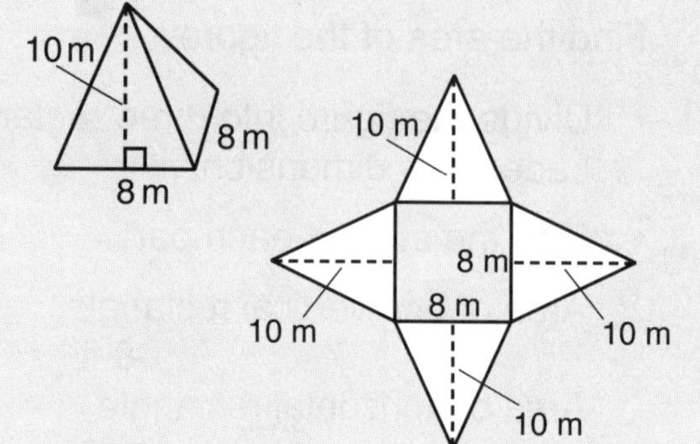

Find the surface area of the solid by finding the area of its net.

- Draw a net for the solid. One face is a square and the other four faces are triangles.

- Find the area of *each shape* in the net.

  Area of one white face = $\frac{1}{2}(8 \times 10) = 40$ m²

  Area of grey face = $8 \times 8 = 64$ m²

- Add the areas of each part. 64 m² + 40 m² + 40 m² + 40 m² + 40 m² = 224 m²

So, the surface area of the solid is 224 m².

Draw a net to find the surface area of the figure.

1.

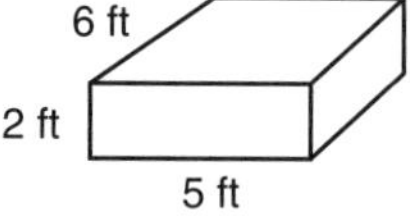

____

2.

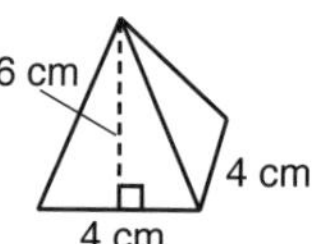

____

3.

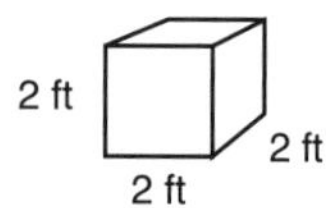

____

4.

____

Problem Solving

5. Tina is decorating a box that is shaped like a cube by gluing small 1-inch by 1-inch color strips to it. She has 200 color strips. The box has sides that are 6 inches long. Does she have enough color strips to cover the entire box? Explain.

6. Mr. Hardy is painting the four sides and floor of a pool. The pool is 4 feet deep, 18 feet long, and 12 feet wide. One can of paint covers 124 square feet. How many cans of paint does he need?

Use with Lesson 13-13A, pages 251–252 in this Workbook.
Then go to Lesson 13-14, pages 474–475 in the Student Book.

Use Partial Cubes to Find Volume

Name ___________________________

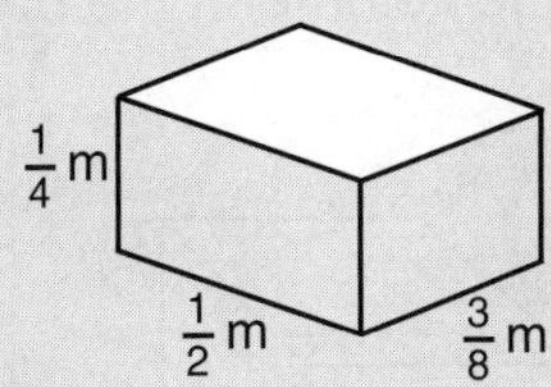

A box has the dimensions shown. What is its volume?

- Rewrite the dimensions with a common denominator. The least common denominator is 8. Equivalent fractions are $\frac{2}{8}$, $\frac{3}{8}$, and $\frac{4}{8}$. The unit fraction is $\frac{1}{8}$.

- There are 2 rows of 12 cubes.

  There are 24 unit cubes with sides of length $\frac{1}{8}$ m.

- Multiply the number of unit cubes by the volume of one unit cube.

  $24 \times \frac{1}{512}$ m³, $\frac{24}{512}$ m³, which simplifies to $\frac{3}{64}$ m³.

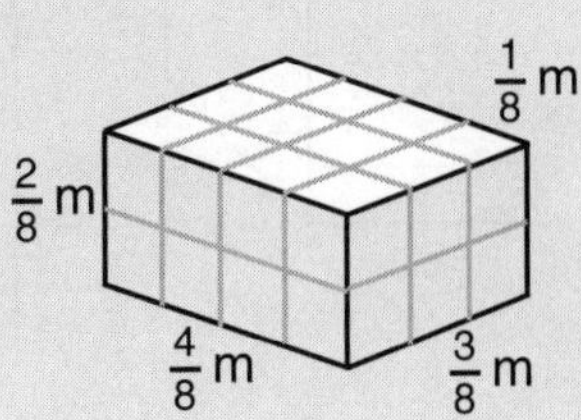

So, the volume of the box is $\frac{3}{64}$ m³.

Find the volume of the prism by using cubes with a unit fraction side length.

1.

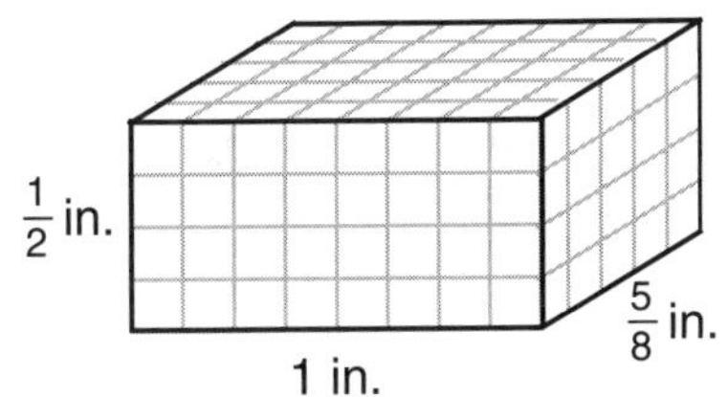

Unit cube side length = _______ in.

Unit cube volume = _______ in.³

Number of unit cubes = _______

Volume = _______ in.³

2.

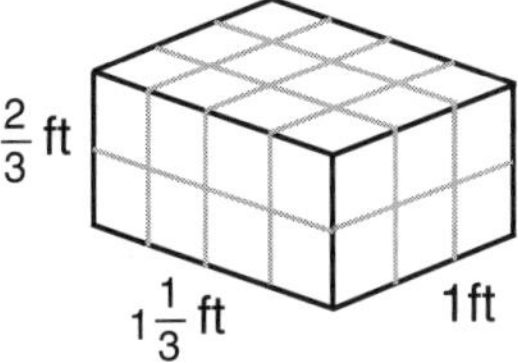

Unit cube side length = _______ ft

Unit cube volume = _______ ft³

Number of unit cubes = _______

Volume = _______ ft³

Problem Solving

3. A plastic container is in the shape of a rectangular prism that is $\frac{3}{4}$ inch long, $\frac{3}{4}$ inch wide, and 3 inches tall. Will 2 cubic inches of a liquid fit inside the container? Explain.

4. Levi fills a cube with sand. It takes $3\frac{3}{8}$ cubic feet of sand to fill the box. What is the length of the box? (Hint: Write the volume as a fraction greater than 1.)

Volume of a Prism

Name ______________________

Find the volume of the prism two ways.

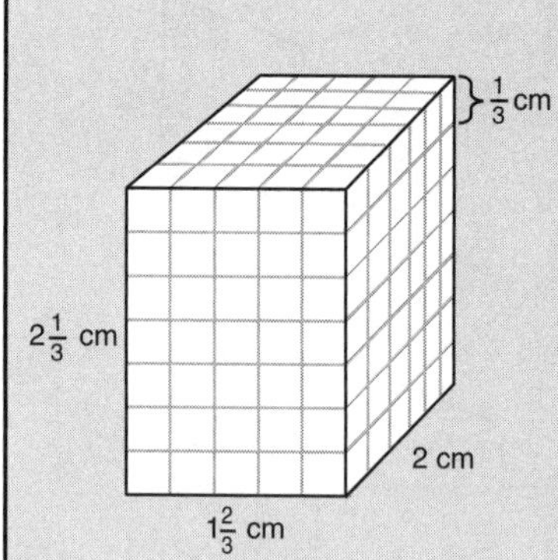

$2\frac{1}{3}$ cm

$1\frac{2}{3}$ cm

2 cm

$\frac{1}{3}$ cm

Method 1: Use unit fraction cubes.

- Use a unit cube with sides $\frac{1}{3}$ cm.
- The volume of each unit cube is:

$$\frac{1}{3}\text{ cm} \times \frac{1}{3}\text{ cm} \times \frac{1}{3}\text{ cm} = \frac{1}{27}\text{ cm}^3$$

- There are 7 layers of 30 cubes.

$$30 \times 7 = 210$$

$$210 \times \frac{1}{27}\text{ cm}^3 = 7\frac{7}{9}\text{ cm}^3$$

Method 2: Use the volume formula.

$$V = \ell \times w \times h$$

$$V = 1\frac{2}{3}\text{ cm} \times 2\text{ cm} \times 2\frac{1}{3}\text{ cm}$$

$$V = \frac{5}{3}\text{ cm} \times \frac{2}{1}\text{ cm} \times \frac{7}{3}\text{ cm}$$

$$V = 7\frac{7}{9}\text{ cm}^3$$

So, both methods show that the volume of the prism is $7\frac{7}{9}$ cm³.

Find the volume of the rectangular prism two ways.

1. $2\frac{1}{3}$ ft by $4\frac{2}{3}$ ft by 9 ft

a) Use unit fraction cubes.

Volume of 1 unit fraction cube = ______ft³

______cubes

Volume = ______ft³

b.) Use the volume formula.

$V =$ ______ ft $\times$ ______ ft $\times$ ______ ft

$V =$ ______ ft³

Find the volume of the rectangular prism. Explain how you arrived at the answer.

2. $3\frac{1}{2}$ m by $4\frac{3}{4}$ m by 2 m

3. $5\frac{1}{3}$ in. by $3\frac{1}{2}$ in. by $1\frac{2}{3}$ in.

Problem Solving

4. Toy blocks come in a container shaped like a cube. The length of a side of the cube is 8 inches. Each block is a 1 in. by 1 in. by 1 in. cube. The container is exactly half full. How many blocks are in the container?

5. The trailer of Mike's transfer truck is a rectangular prism that is $9\frac{1}{2}$ feet tall and $8\frac{1}{2}$ feet wide. If the volume of the trailer is 1615 cubic feet, how long is the trailer?

Use with Lesson 13-16B, pages 255–256 in this Workbook.
Then go to Lesson 13-17, pages 480–481 in the Student Book.

Independent and Dependent Variables

Name _______________________

Write an equation that shows the relationship between the American Dollar and the British Pound in 2013.

British Pound	7.85	15.70	23.55	31.40
American Dollar	5	10	15	20

- Dependent variable (y): value of the American Dollar.
- Independent variable (x): value of the British Pound.
- Make a table.
- There is a common quotient. The value of the American Dollar (y) is always equal to the value of the British Pound (x) divided by 1.57.

American Dollar (y)	British Pound (x)	Difference	Quotient
5	7.85	2.85	1.57
10	15.70	5.70	1.57
15	23.55	8.55	1.57
20	31.40	11.40	1.57

So, the equation that shows this relationship is $y = x \div 1.57$.

Identify the independent and dependent variables. Then write an equation.

1.

Items Sold	3	4	6	7
Commission	7.5	10	15	17.5

Independent: _______________________

Dependent: _______________________

Equation: _______________________

2.

Cereal (cal)	125	140	160	190
With Milk (cal)	195	210	230	260

Independent: _______________________

Dependent: _______________________

Equation: _______________________

3.

Months (m)	2	3	6	10
Balance ($)	150	225	450	750

Independent: _______________________

Dependent: _______________________

Equation: _______________________

4.

Retail Price ($)	85	90	120	135
Sale Price ($)	70	75	105	120

Independent: _______________________

Dependent: _______________________

Equation: _______________________

Problem Solving

5. Latoya buys a pack of 18 bottles of a sport drink. She drinks 1 bottle every day. Complete the table and write an equation relating the number of days that pass and the number of bottles remaining. After how many days does Latoya have one-third of the bottles left?

Days	0	1	2	5
Bottles	18			

6. Dean hikes up a mountain at a rate of 2.25 kilometers per hour. Complete the table and write an equation to show the relationship between how long Dean hikes and how far he travels. How long does it take him to hike 15.75 kilometers?

Hours	1	2	3	4
Kilometers				

Use with Lesson 14-4A, pages 257–258 in this Workbook.
Then go to Lesson 14-5, pages 504–505 in the Student Book.

Distances and the Coordinate Plane

Name _______________________

Find the distance between the points on a coordinate plane.

Horizontal Distance

$M(-2, 1)$ and $N(4, 1)$

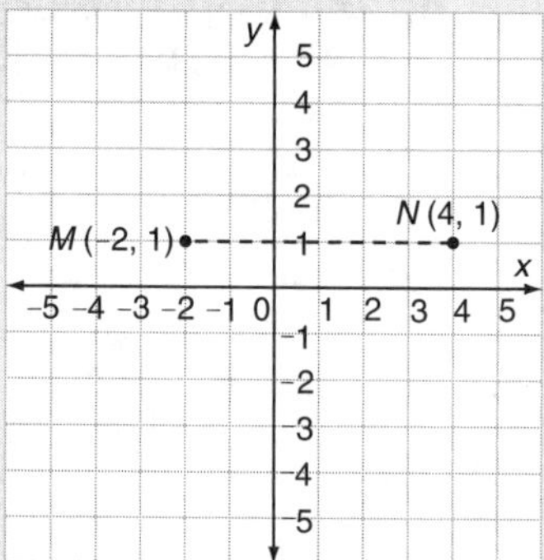

- Subtract the x-coordinates.
  $(-2) - 4 = -6$
- Find the absolute value of -6.
  $|-6| = 6$

So, the horizontal distance is 6 units.

Vertical Distance

$C(2, 2)$ and $D(2, -3)$

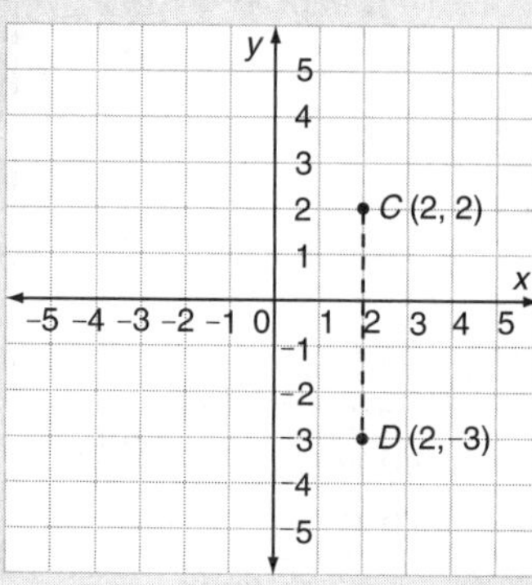

- Subtract the y-coordinates.
  $2 - (-3) = 5$
- Find the absolute value of 5.
  $|5| = 5$

So, the vertical distance is 5 units.

Find the distance between the points on a coordinate plane.

1. $A(5, 4)$ and $B(-1, 4)$

____

2. $C(-7, 1)$ and $D(-7, 9)$

____

3. $E(2, -3)$ and $F(2, 7)$

____

4. $G(-2, -1)$ and $H(-6, -1)$

____

5. $J(-1, 0)$ and $K(1, 0)$

____

6. $L(-5, -9)$ and $M(0, -9)$

____

Problem Solving

Four children are playing a board game that involves moving a piece horizontally and vertically. The locations of their game pieces can be shown on a coordinate plane, where each unit represents 1 space on the board. The coordinates of their game pieces are given.

Abel: $(5, -2)$ Sara: $(-3, 7)$ Joe: $(1, -2)$ Kim: $(-3, -6)$

7. Kim moves her piece vertically and lands on the space where Sara's piece is located. How many spaces does Kim move?

8. There is a prize space at $(-3, -2)$. Which two players are closest to the prize? Explain.

_______________________   _______________________

Use with Lesson 14-5A, pages 259–260 in this Workbook.
Use with Lesson 14-5B, pages 261–262 in this Workbook.

Graphing Polygons

Name _______________________

What is the name for a polygon that has vertices at points $A(1, 5)$, $B(5, 5)$, and $C(5, 2)$?

- Graph the points and connect them.

- Examine the polygon that is created.

  The polygon has three sides.
  None of the sides has the same length.
  The polygon has a right angle.

- Name the polygon using the *most specific name* that describes it.

So, the polygon with vertices at (1, 5), (5, 5), and (5, 2) is a scalene right triangle.

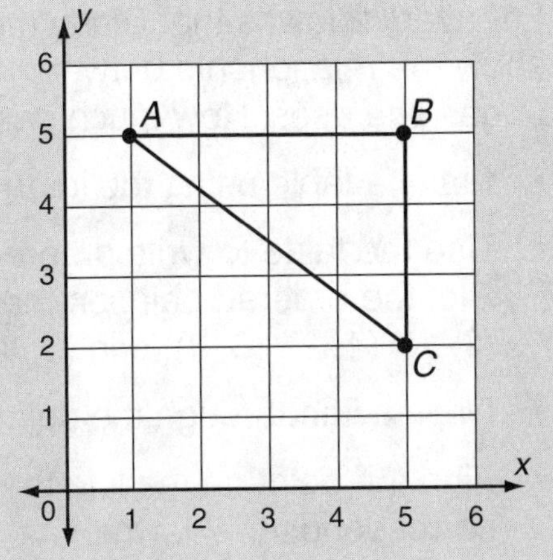

Graph the points. Draw the polygon. Then give the most specific name for it.

1. (−2, 2), (0, 5), (3, 3), (1, 0)

____

2. (−5, 1), (7, 3), (2, −4)

____

3. (−2, 4), (4, 2), (4, −1), (−4, −3)

____

4. (−5, 3), (−3, 6), (5, 0), (−1, 0)

____

5. (−6, −1), (−4, 1), (0, −3), (−2, −5)

____

6. (−5, 7), (5, −1), (−1, −2)

____

Problem Solving

Stephan is directing this year's play, "Creatures of the Forest."
He uses a coordinate plane to plot the locations of the students in the play.

7. Students playing raccoons are marked at (−3, −2), (0, 5), and (3, −2). What kind of polygon do they form?

____

8. Students playing squirrels are marked at (−4, 5), (3, 2), (6, −5), and (−1, −2). What kind of polygon do they form?

____

Use with Lesson 14-5B, pages 261–262 in this Workbook.
Then go to Lesson 14-6, pages 506–507 in the Student Book.

Model Rates

For every 2 lawns that Cindy mows, she uses 1 gallon of gas. Make a graph to show the relationship between the number of lawns Cindy mows and the amount of gas she uses. How much gas does she use if she mows 7 lawns?

- Make a table using the information given.

- Use the table to write ordered pairs. Plot the ordered pairs on the graph. (2, 1), (4, 2), (6, 3), and (8, 4).

- Draw a line through the points.

- Find the point on the line that corresponds to 7 lawns.

So, Cindy uses 3.5 gallons of gas to mow 7 lawns.

Lawns	2	4	6	8
Gas (gal)	1	2	3	4

A tutoring center can accommodate 8 students for every 2 instructors. Graph the relationship. Then use the graph to answer the questions.

Instructors			
Students			

1. How many students can the tutoring center accommodate if they have 6 instructors?

____

2. How many instructors are needed to accommodate 36 students?

____

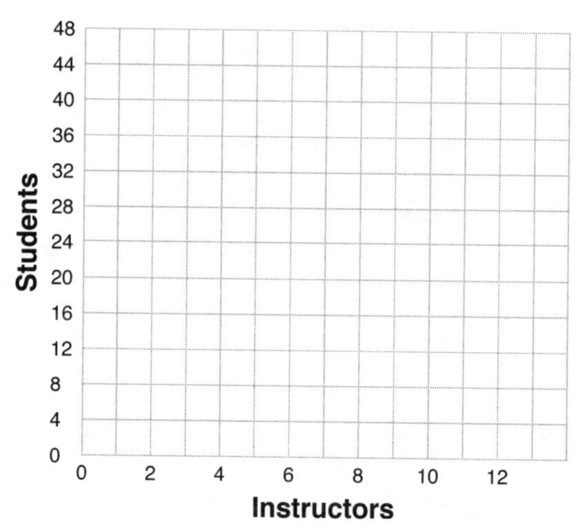

Problem Solving

3. Before lunch, Abby paints 5 walls. After lunch, she paints for 3 more hours. If she can paint 1 wall in 30 minutes, how many walls did she paint in all that day?

____

4. Rafael needs 3 boards to make 12 birdhouses. He has 7 boards. Does he have enough boards to make 26 birdhouses? Explain.

____

Use with Lesson 14-7A, pages 263–264 in this Workbook.
Then go to Lesson 14-8, pages 510–511 in the Student Book.

Related Variables

A grocery store pays $10 per hour to restock shelves. Earnings can be represented by the equation $y = 10x$, where y stands for earnings in dollars.

- Use the equation to make a table.

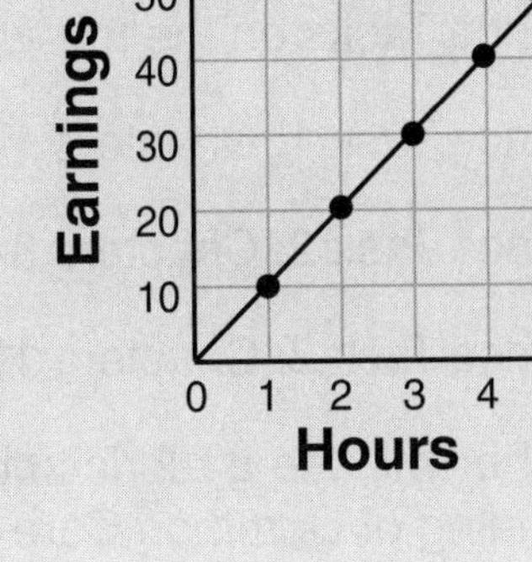

x (Hours)	$10 (x)	y (dollars)
1	$10(1)	$10
2	$10(2)	$20
3	$10(3)	$30
4	$10(4)	$40

- Use the values in the table to write ordered pairs.
  (1, 10), (2, 20), (3, 30), (4, 40)

- Graph the ordered pairs and connect the points.

Note that the equation, the table, and the graph are different ways to represent the earnings per hour.

Use the information to show the relationship two ways.

1. The graph shows the relationship between the amount of money Sue spent at the store and the amount she was left with. Complete the table. Then write an equation.

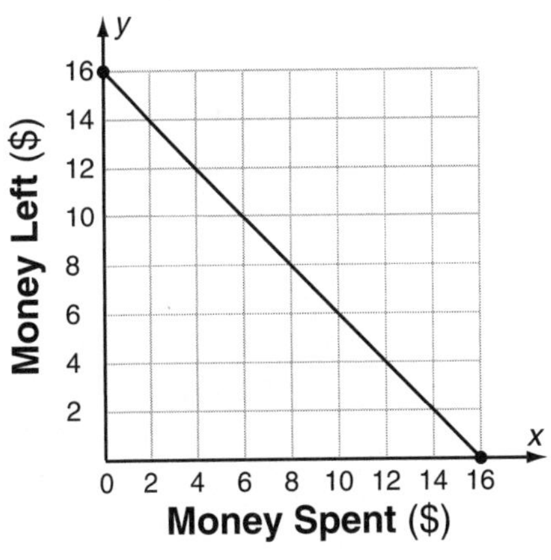

Money Spent ($)	Money Left ($)
2	
6	
	4

____

Problem Solving

2. Paula has 120 baseball cards. She gives her brother 30 baseball cards. Then she gives one of her friends 20 cards each week. After how many weeks will Paula have only 10 baseball cards left?

3. Rob owes his father $20. He earns $12 each week raking leaves. How long will it take Rob to earn enough money to buy a $76 technology item and pay his father back?

___________________________   ___________________________

Dear Student,

Pages 300–314 of this workbook have Performance Tasks that let you show your understanding of the Common Core math taught in *Progress in Mathematics.*

Each performance task has five parts. The content of each part meets the Common Core State Standards (CCSS) for *Progress in Mathematics* lessons. The goal of each performance task is for you to apply critical thinking skills and various problem-solving strategies to the math content learned in the chapters. The Performance Tasks are useful tools for evaluating your understanding of Grade 6 math and the Common Core State Standards. You will find the Performance Tasks on the following pages.

Performance Task 1: Chapters 1–4   pages 300–304

Performance Task 2: Chapters 5–9   pages 305–309

Performance Task 3: Chapters 11–14   pages 310–314

Your teacher will use a rubric in the Teacher's Edition of this workbook to record your understanding of Common Core State Standards.

Performance Task Contents

Name ___________________________

1 Lena works at Spice Emporium, a store that sells spices from all over the world. Today she is preparing a mixture of spices for Turkish dishes. She uses 3.58 ounces of salt, 2.4 ounces of cumin, 1.25 ounces of black pepper, 1.1 ounces of oregano, 0.74 ounce of paprika, and 0.5 ounce of cayenne pepper.

A. Ms. McDonald wants to buy 9.25 ounces of the spice mix for her Turkish recipes. How much spice mix will Lena have left?

Another customer wants to buy 6.5 ounces of thyme. The canister of thyme has t ounces. Lena measures out the customer's order and puts the canister back. Later, she replenishes the thyme in the canister with 10.75 ounces.

B. Write an expression for the amount of thyme in the canister now. If the canister started with 8.1 ounces of thyme, how much is in the canister now?

Ⓒ Performance Task 1
Duplicating Spices

2 Malik also works at Spice Emporium. His manager asks him to put 1.35 ounces of salt, 0.8 ounce of pepper, and 0.09 ounce of saffron in each of 100 bags.

A. How much salt does Malik need? How much pepper? How much saffron?

Malik is making 36 small packs of chili spices and 15 large packs of chili spices. A small pack contains 2.35 ounces of spices. A large pack contains 10.8 ounces of spices.

B. How many ounces of chili spices should Malik make?

The jar of oregano contains 9.6 ounces of this most popular spice. Ms. Asher buys 3.75 ounces of the oregano. Then Mr. King buys 0.6 as much oregano as Ms. Asher bought.

C. How much oregano is left in the jar?

Name _______________________

3 Lena mixed 12.5 ounces of basil, 8.42 ounces of rosemary, 7.6 ounces of tarragon, and 20.25 ounces of a black pepper and sea salt mixture. She wants to separate the mixture equally into 100 bags.

A. Can Lena use bags that can hold 0.4 ounce of spices or bags that can hold 0.5 ounce?

Spice Emporium received a shipment of 41.92 pounds of curry powder. Lena stored half the curry powder in the basement. Then she separated the other half equally into 4 boxes.

B. How much curry powder did Lena put in each box?

A jar contained p ounces of paprika. Malik separated the paprika equally into packets. Each packet had 0.8 ounce of paprika.

C. Write an expression for the number of packets Malik filled with paprika. If the jar contained 116.8 ounces of paprika, how many packets did Malik prepare?

Name _______________________

4 Spice Emporium has a mailing list of customers. The mailing list started with 7 customers four months ago. The number of customers has doubled each month. Malik needs to mail a letter to the customers on the list.

A. Write and evaluate an expression for the number of copies of the letter Malik will mail.

Today n customers each bought a 0.5-ounce packet of saffron. Half that number of customers bought 3-ounce packets of saffron.

B. Suppose 12 customers bought 0.5-ounce packets of saffron. Write an expression for the amount of saffron sold to these customers. Then find how much saffron was sold in all.

Spice Emporium has a sale on cinnamon and nutmeg. Twenty-six customers each bought a jar of cinnamon and a jar of nutmeg. Eight customers bought only jars of cinnamon. Lena wrote an expression for the number of jars of cinnamon sold (c), and the number of jars of nutmeg sold (n).

$26(c + n) + (8 \times c)$

C. Simplify her expression.

Name ___________________________

5 Malik is mixing cayenne pepper, black pepper, and garlic powder. He puts 0.8 ounce of cayenne pepper and 0.7 ounce of black pepper in a bag. The bag can hold up to 2.2 ounces of spices.

A. Write an inequality for the amount of garlic powder (g) Malik can put in the bag. Can Malik put 0.8 ounce of garlic powder in the bag? Explain your reasoning.

Lena filled some jars with curry powder. She put 1.6 ounces of curry powder in each of the jars. She used a total of 20.8 ounces of curry powder.

B. Write and solve an equation for the number of jars Lena filled with curry powder.

Malik stocked some packages of sea salt on a shelf. Customers purchased 25 of the packages. At the end of the day, there were 8 packages still on the shelf.

C. Write and solve an equation for the number of packages of sea salt that Malik stocked on the shelf.

1 Terence and Lilly are working with a team of scientists in the Arctic. Yesterday Terence and Lilly collected water samples from the ocean. The table shows the depths of their samples.

A. Plot the depths of the water samples on the number line. Label each point. Order the samples from shallowest to deepest.

Water Sample	Depth (meters below sea level)
A	−6
B	−2
C	0
D	−3

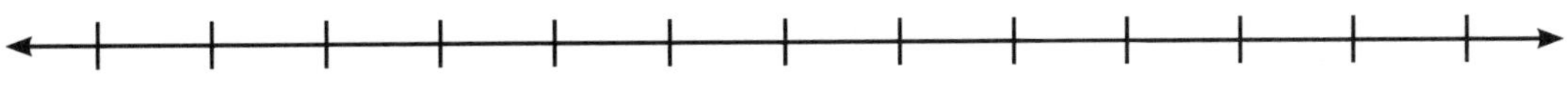

Lilly woke up at midnight and saw that the temperature was −4°C. When she got up at 7 A.M., the temperature was −6°C.

B. Which hour was colder? Explain your reasoning. Write an inequality for the temperatures.

A beluga whale swam at a depth of −38 meters. An ivory gull flew at a height of 26 meters.

C. Which animal was closer to the surface of the ocean? Write an inequality to compare the absolute values.

2 Terence is packing knapsacks with sample jars for scientists who are going to explore a rocky beach. He is given two boxes of different size jars. One box contains 14 large sample jars. A second box contains 35 small sample jars. Both sizes of sample jars should be shared equally among the scientists.

A. How many scientists can Terence pack for? How many large jars and small jars should Terence put in each daypack?

An ornithologist captured and examined some Arctic terns. She measured the lengths of the birds' bills before releasing them.

B. The table to the right shows the bill lengths of four birds.
- Rename each fraction using the LCD.
- Plot the bill lengths on the number line. Label each point.
- Order the birds from shortest to longest bill length.

Arctic Tern	Bill Length (inches)
A	$\frac{3}{4}$
B	$\frac{7}{8}$
C	$\frac{11}{12}$
D	$\frac{2}{3}$

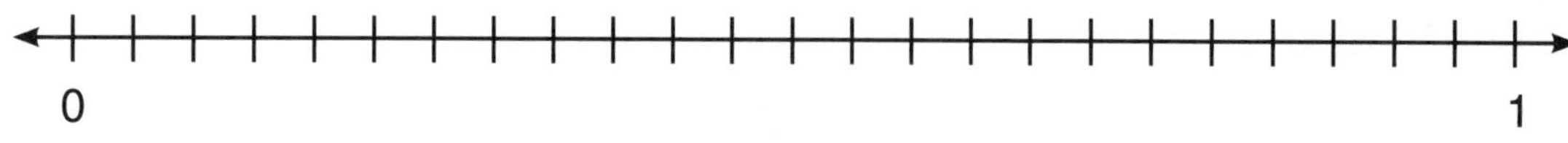

0   1

3 Lilly is cutting labels from two strips of white tape. The first strip is $\frac{4}{5}$ meter long. The second strip is $\frac{3}{10}$ meter long. Each label must be $\frac{1}{20}$ meter long.

A. How many labels can Lilly cut from the two strips?

Here are some strategies you can use.

- Draw a diagram.
- Use the relationship between multiplication and division.
- Use the reciprocal of the divisor.

A jar contains preserving liquid. Terence needs to measure equal amounts of the liquid into bottles for biological specimens. Each bottle can hold $1\frac{3}{8}$ ounces of preserving liquid.

B. Write an expression for the number of bottles Terence can fill with preserving liquid. If the jar originally had $24\frac{3}{4}$ ounces of preserving liquid, how many bottles can Terence fill?

Name ______________________

4 Lilly and Terence helped the ornithologist survey a colony of horned puffins. Horned puffins are seabirds that only come ashore to nest.

A. The box below shows Lilly and Terence's data for the eggs they measured.

Horned Puffin Egg Lengths (mm)
74, 71, 70, 72, 72, 73, 67, 73, 73, 75, 73, 74

- Make a line plot for the data.
- Identify any outliers.
- Find the mean, median, mode, and range of the data.
- Explain how the outlier affects the mean.
- Write a statistical question that could be answered by looking at your line plot.

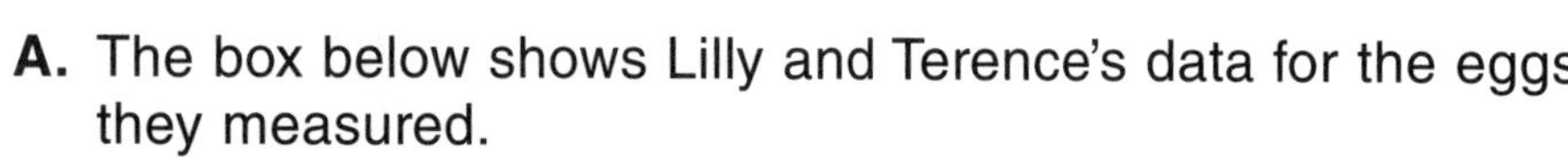

ⒸPerformance Task 2
What Is the Mass of that Horned Puffin?

5 Horned puffins need plenty of food to raise their chicks. A well-fed puffin has a greater mass than a puffin that can't find enough to eat. Lilly and Terence helped the ornithologist capture adult puffins and measure their masses. The box below shows the team's data.

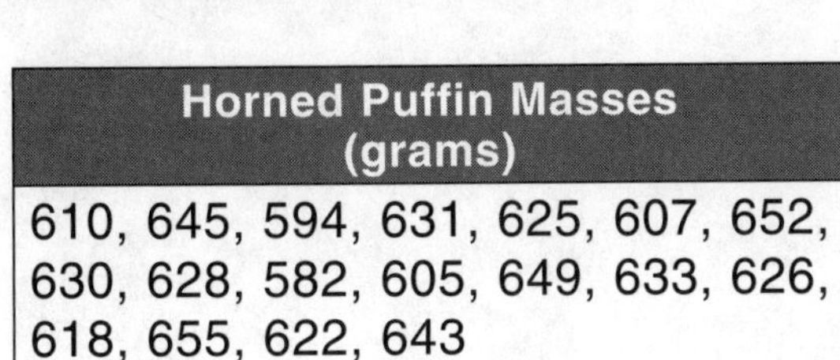

Horned Puffin Masses (grams)
610, 645, 594, 631, 625, 607, 652, 630, 628, 582, 605, 649, 633, 626, 618, 655, 622, 643

A. Complete the frequency table for the data. Then use your frequency table to complete the histogram.

Mass (g)	Tally	Frequency

B. Use the histogram to answer the questions below.

- How many puffins were measured? _______________

- Which interval of masses shows the greatest frequency? _______________

- A well-fed puffin has a mass of about 620 grams. Which birds may have trouble raising chicks this year? _______________

- Based on this data, how would you describe the overall health of the puffin colony?

____

____

Name ___________________________

1 Tremont Creek Farm has a small apple orchard. Last year, the farm's 9 Golden Delicious trees produced 7,290 pounds of apples. The farm's 7 McIntosh trees produced 5,642 pounds of apples.

A. Which trees were better producers?
Here are some strategies you can use.
- Write equivalent ratios.
- Make tables to compare ratios.
- Find the unit rates.

The farm managers want to increase the production of Golden Delicious apples to at least 30,000 pounds.

B. How many more trees do they need to plant?

Hector just packed 294 pounds of Granny Smith apples into 7 boxes. There are 672 more pounds of apples ready to be packed.

C. How many more boxes does Hector need?

2 Summer harvest has begun at the farm. Four workers are packing vegetables in the barn. Six workers are picking berries. Three workers are picking tomatoes. The last 7 workers are repairing an irrigation canal.

A. What percent of the farm's workers are packing vegetables? What percent are repairing the canal?

The next day, the farm hired 30 more workers. The farm manager sent 60% of the workers to the tomato field. She sent 22% of the workers to the berry field.

B. How many workers went to the tomato field? How many went to the berry field?

Mike, a harvest worker, is assigned to pick tomatoes. He finds wormholes in 36% of the tomatoes on one plant.

C. If Mike picked 9 tomatoes with wormholes from the plant, how many tomatoes were on the plant?

C Performance Task 3

Growing Champion Pumpkins

Name _______________________

3 Melissa is getting ready to drive a tractor that will spread organic fertilizer on the pumpkin field. The field is shaped like a trapezoid. A drawing of the pumpkin field and some of its dimensions are shown here.

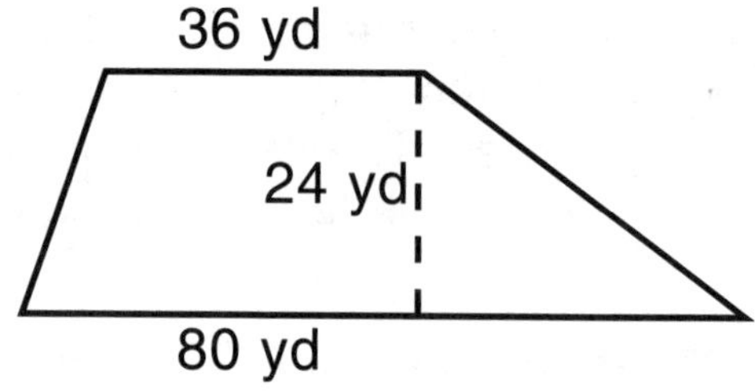

A. Melissa needs to apply 2 pounds of fertilizer for every 5 square yards. How much fertilizer should Melissa load in the tractor?

Think: Area of a trapezoid $= \frac{1}{2}(b_1 + b_2)h$.

The fertilizer is stored in a box that is shaped like a cube. It measures $3\frac{1}{2}$ feet on each edge. The box is full when Melissa starts loading the tractor.

B. How much fertilizer does the box hold? Think: Volume of a cube $= e^3$.

C. If a cubic foot of fertilizer weighs 16 pounds, what percent of the fertilizer will Melissa use to fertilize the pumpkin field?

4 Hector needs to put new fences around the goat pen
and the sheep pen. First he needs to draw both pens
on a coordinate plane. Then he needs to figure out how
much fencing to buy.

A. Help Hector complete the following.
 • Graph the points for each pen. Draw each pen.
 • Use absolute value to help you find the length and
   width of each pen.
 • If each unit on the coordinate plane measures $6\frac{1}{2}$ feet
   on all sides, how much fencing does Hector need?

Goat pen: $(-6, 2), (-2, 2), (-2, -4), (-6, -4)$

Sheep pen: $(-3, 7), (5, 7), (5, 3), (-3, 3)$

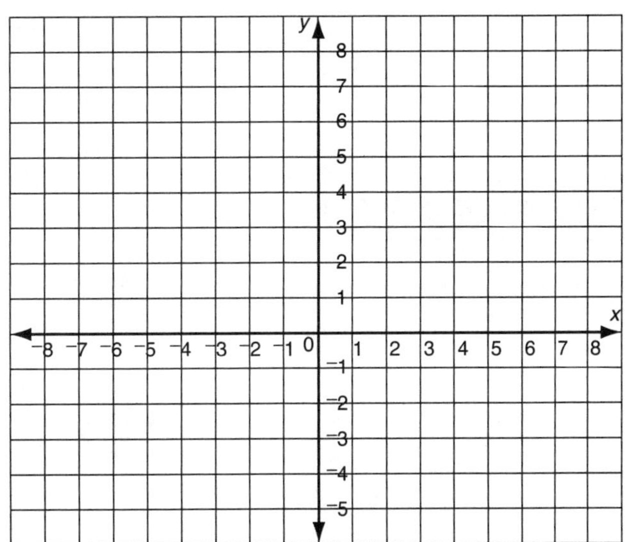

Name _______________________

5 Melissa is raising a lamb on a special diet. She hopes to show the lamb at the county fair at the end of summer. Melissa weighs the lamb each week and discovers a rule: the lamb weighs 1 pound more than double the number of weeks.

A. • Identify the independent and dependent variables. Explain your reasoning.
   • Write an equation for Melissa's rule.
   • Use the rule to complete the table below.
   • Graph the ordered pairs.

Rule: _______________________

x	y	(x,y)
1		
2		
3		
4		

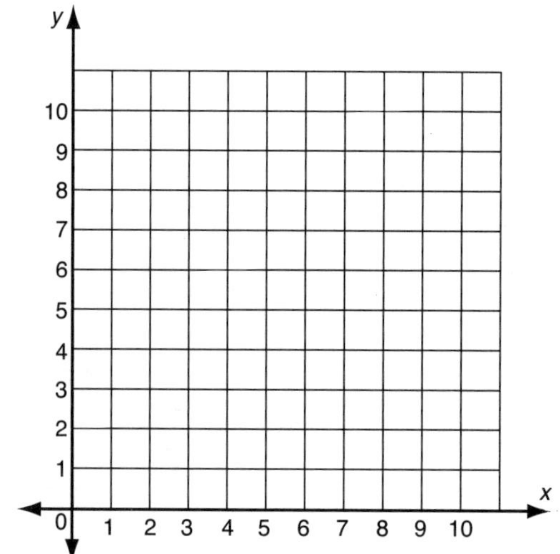

B. Assuming the lamb keeps growing at the rate given in the table, how much will it weigh in 24 weeks?